# Essential Concepts of
## BUSINESS FOR LAWYERS

# Essential Concepts of
# BUSINESS FOR LAWYERS

### ROBERT J. RHEE

*Professor of Law & Marbury Research Professor*
*Co-Director, Business Law Program*
*University of Maryland Francis King Carey School of Law*

Wolters Kluwer
Law & Business

1 2 3 4 5 6 7 8 9 0

ISBN 978-1-4548-1319-4

**Library of Congress Cataloging-in-Publication Data**

Rhee, Robert J.
    Essential concepts of business for lawyers / Robert J. Rhee.
        p. cm.
    Includes index.
    ISBN 978-1-4548-1319-4
1.  Accounting.   2.  Business law.    I. Title.
    HF5636.R48 2012
    657.024'34—dc23

                                                                    2012007608

Certified Chain of Custody
Product Line Contains At Least
20% Certified Forest Content
www.sfiprogram.org
SFI-00756

# About Wolters Kluwer Law & Business

Wolters Kluwer Law & Business is a leading global provider of intelligent information and digital solutions for legal and business professionals in key specialty areas, and respected educational resources for professors and law students. Wolters Kluwer Law & Business connects legal and business professionals as well as those in the education market with timely, specialized authoritative content and information-enabled solutions to support success through productivity, accuracy and mobility.

Serving customers worldwide, Wolters Kluwer Law & Business products include those under the Aspen Publishers, CCH, Kluwer Law International, Loislaw, Best Case, ftwilliam.com and MediRegs family of products.

**CCH** products have been a trusted resource since 1913, and are highly regarded resources for legal, securities, antitrust and trade regulation, government contracting, banking, pension, payroll, employment and labor, and healthcare reimbursement and compliance professionals.

**Aspen Publishers** products provide essential information to attorneys, business professionals and law students. Written by preeminent authorities, the product line offers analytical and practical information in a range of specialty practice areas from securities law and intellectual property to mergers and acquisitions and pension/benefits. Aspen's trusted legal education resources provide professors and students with high-quality, up-to-date and effective resources for successful instruction and study in all areas of the law.

**Kluwer Law International** products provide the global business community with reliable international legal information in English. Legal practitioners, corporate counsel and business executives around the world rely on Kluwer Law journals, looseleafs, books, and electronic products for comprehensive information in many areas of international legal practice.

**Loislaw** is a comprehensive online legal research product providing legal content to law firm practitioners of various specializations. Loislaw provides attorneys with the ability to quickly and efficiently find the necessary legal information they need, when and where they need it, by facilitating access to primary law as well as state-specific law, records, forms and treatises.

**Best Case Solutions** is the leading bankruptcy software product to the bankruptcy industry. It provides software and workflow tools to flawlessly streamline petition preparation and the electronic filing process, while timely incorporating ever-changing court requirements.

**ftwilliam.com** offers employee benefits professionals the highest quality plan documents (retirement, welfare and non-qualified) and government forms (5500/PBGC, 1099 and IRS) software at highly competitive prices.

**MediRegs** products provide integrated health care compliance content and software solutions for professionals in healthcare, higher education and life sciences, including professionals in accounting, law and consulting.

Wolters Kluwer Law & Business, a division of Wolters Kluwer, is headquartered in New York. Wolters Kluwer is a market-leading global information services company focused on professionals.

*For Nicki, Piers, and Blake*

# SUMMARY OF CONTENTS

# CONTENTS

## CHAPTER 12
# FINANCIAL INSTRUMENTS II (DERIVATIVES)   257

## CHAPTER 13
# CAPITAL MARKETS   281

# LIST OF EXAMPLES

# ACKNOWLEDGMENTS

I wish to thank Tien Pham, Brad Borden, Don Gifford, Michelle Harner, Pam Bluh, and John Lewis, who provided valuable comments. I also thank my students in the fall 2011 section of Business 101 and Corporate Finance. They were the first group of students who used a draft of this book, and their comments and corrections made it much better. This book was made possible by a generous research support from the University of Maryland Francis King Carey School of Law.

I would also like to thank the following authors and publishers for kindly granting permission to reproduce excerpts of the following material:

Bailey, Jeff, "Southwest Airlines Gains Advantage by Hedging on Long-term Oil Contracts." From the *New York Times*, November 28, 2007, copyright © 2007. *The New York Times*. All rights reserved. Used by permission and protected by the Copyright Laws of the United States. The printing, copying, redistribution, or retransmission of this Content without express written permission is prohibited.

Bajaj, Vikas and Healy, Jack, "Stocks Drop Sharply and Credit Markets Seize Up." From the New York Times, November 21, 2008, copyright © 2008. *The New York Times*. All rights reserved. Used by permission and protected by the Copyright Laws of the United States. The printing, copying, redistribution, or retransmission of this Content without express written permission is prohibited.

Bary, Andrew, "Warren Buffet Makes an Offer Goldman Sachs Can't Refuse." In *The Wall Street Journal*, September 28, 2008. Used by permission of Andrew Bary.

Berle, Adlof A., Jr., and Means, Gardiner C. *The Modern Corporation and Private Property*. Copyright © 1932 by The Macmillan Company; copyright renewed 1960 by Adelf A. Berle, Jr. and Gardiner C. Means. All rights reserved. Reprinted with permission of Scribner, a Division of Simon & Schuster, Inc.

Bernstein, Peter L., *Against the Gods: The Remarkable Story of Risk*. Copyright © 1996, 1998 by Peter L. Bernstein. Reprinted with permission of John Wiley & Sons, Inc.

Coase, R.H., "The Nature of the Firm." From *Ecomomica*, volume 4 number 16, 1937. Used by permission of John Wiley & Sons Ltd.

Cohan, William D., *House of Cards: A Tale of Hubris and Wretched Excess on Wall Street*. Copyright © 2009, 2010 by William D. Cohan. Used by permission of Doubleday, a division of Random House, Inc.

Eichenwald, Kurt, *Conspiracy of Fools: A True Story*. Copyright © 2005 by Kurt Eichenwald. Used by permission of Broadway Books, a division of Random House, Inc.

Ford Motor Company 2010 Annual Report. Used with permission from Ford Motor Company.

# PREFACE

Why this book? In the course of teaching business law classes, I have seen some students confused by the most basic concepts like "stock" or "bond" or "valuation" or "net income" or "balance sheet" or "capital markets" or "equity" or "DCF" or "present value" or "EPS" or "derivative." For most students, the first introduction to business is Business Association where students read classic cases involving complex decision-making of corporate executives and boards, such as a complex buyout transaction (*Smith v. Van Gorkom*), a corporate and accounting fraud (*Francis v. United Jersey Bank*), a spinoff of an investment involving complex accounting and finance issues (*Kamin v. American Express Co.*), the application of the efficient market hypothesis in a securities fraud action (*Basic, Inc. v. Levinson*), and valuation of the corporate entity under the discounted cash flow method (*Weinberger v. UOP, Inc.*). These cases are complicated, and the business concepts therein are significant in their own right. Bright students may read these cases and understand the legal rules, but they may be blind as to context.

As a matter of baseline knowledge, law students should have a better understanding of corporations and our complex economy. Yet we should not be surprised if they don't have such knowledge. There is no reason to expect a former philosophy or political science major to come to law school with prerequisite knowledge. This problem goes to the core of practical training of future business lawyers. Students know that they have a problem. In the past, they have asked me if there is a book they can read to learn essential business concepts. In my view, there is not an adequate book that teaches business principles with ample explanations and examples that illustrate and reinforce difficult, abstract concepts. I wrote this book because there is a need for it in legal education.

When I say "essential business concepts," the most glaring deficit is a lack of working knowledge in essential principles of accounting, financial statement analysis, essential principles of finance and valuation, the economics of the firm, financial instruments, capital markets, and corporate transactions. These concepts are interconnected. One cannot learn applied finance without some proficiency in accounting. One cannot fully understand corporate transactions and capital markets without some proficiency in finance. One cannot fully appreciate a business client's legal problems without some understanding of how markets and business transactions work. These interconnected concepts may be alien to students who may not have majored in business, finance or accounting—that is, most law students. Yet students should know them to fully appreciate concepts seen in courses such as Business Associations, Securities Regulation, Corporate Finance, Bankruptcy, Taxation, Business Planning, Mergers & Acquisitions, and any course in corporate or real estate transactions.

This book is not a substitute for formal coursework in the specific subjects covered. In the ideal world, this book would be unnecessary because law students focusing on business law would have completed formal coursework in business school in financial accounting and corporate finance, about 6 credit hours of rigorous business training. The world is not ideal, however, and such coursework in the traditional 3-year law school curriculum is rarely completed. Most law students may be constrained by time, energy, money, academic credits, or reluctance to venture across campus to the business school classroom. The purpose of this book is to give students a working knowledge of essential concepts in business.

This book is written from the business client's perspective and with an eye toward laying the foundational business knowledge for transactional practice. Having been a former investment banker and a client of business lawyers in my previous profession, I have focused on providing basic competency in business concepts that a sophisticated business client, like a public corporation, would expect from business lawyers. This book focuses on teaching useful intellectual skills associated with a working knowledge of accounting, financial statement analysis, finance, valuation, capital structure, financial instruments, capital markets, and corporate transactions.

In writing this book, I minimized tedious text. As lawyers, we are trained to be thorough in facts and information, but I have resisted this instinct. As you read this book, you will notice that there are very few footnotes, extraneous citations to various law review articles, or tangential discursions. This book teaches essential concepts of business with minimal density of facts and information that can overwhelm neophyte students. The law student is already immersed in a new, abstract discipline called "the law"; and dense text in multiple foreign and quantitatively oriented disciplines can be tedious, intimidating and a hindrance to learning. This book does not provide a comprehensive informational coverage of the subject matter, and intricacies are not explored. This may seem odd for a textbook, but students can readily look up facts and information: for example, how are generally accepted accounting principles promulgated? Such information might be nice to know and may be necessary at some point, but there are other more important priorities in teaching essential business skills. An author is always confronted with coverage choices in writing. Acquiring information is easy; learning skills is hard. I wrote this book to teach law students essential skills by emphasizing useful business concepts and their application to business and legal problems.

This book has an ambitious goal of providing the minimal information necessary for students to understand essential business concepts embedded in the analysis of many business law problems. Several factors were paramount in writing this book:

1.  students want clear, succinct explanations of difficult concepts;
2.  students don't want dense or abstract text;
3.  students don't want lengthy discussions from law review articles on intellectually fascinating but less practical topics;
4.  students want "just the basics" rather than an exhaustive "A through Z" encyclopedic treatment, which is better done in formal coursework in accounting and finance;
5.  students want business concepts to be tangibly connected to legal problems and the practice of business law and corporate advisory work.

These factors suggest a *minimalist approach*, with user-friendly explanations and concrete, engaging examples that reinforce difficult concepts. "Minimal" should not be confused with superficial. Even basic business concepts are quite difficult to grasp, and they may not come naturally to the neophyte. Some of the concepts explained in this book are the core ideas of Nobel Prize-winning works that have long been applied to the practice of business. Essential business concepts must be explained clearly. Lastly, essential concepts in business cannot be discussed in a vacuum. These subjects must be contextualized for law students.

I wrote this book with versatility in mind. It is not a casebook in the traditional sense. Concepts are generously, but succinctly, explained. This book is modeled on a university textbook in accounting, finance or economics rather than a law school casebook. However, this book has edited appellate cases at the end of every chapter. Many of the cases are classic cases in Business Associations, Corporate Finance, or Securities Regulation; others are well represented in business law casebooks; still others involve famous or notorious episodes in American business history, such as Enron, WorldCom, and Bear Stearns. The purpose of these cases is not to provide systematic coverage of legal doctrines, or to provide redundant coverage of old chestnuts from standard doctrinal courses. Rather, the purpose is to illustrate the *business principles* embedded in important or famous cases in business law. These cases augment coverage in doctrinal courses by contextualizing business concepts in the framework of legal analysis. They illustrate the connection between the familiar (appellate case law) and the unfamiliar (business concepts).

I wrote this book in a way that smart, diligent students can learn the materials independently, or use it as a continuing reference in law school and later in professional practice. This book can be used as a required text or recommended supplement to any business law course. It can also be used as a required text for an independent course that prepares law students for a sustained course of study in business law, including courses in Business Associations, Securities Regulation, Corporate Finance, Bankruptcy, Taxation, Business Planning, Mergers & Acquisitions, Entrepreneurial Law, White Collar Crime, and any courses in corporate or real estate transactions. Suggested course titles for an independent preparatory course are Business Basics, Essential Concepts in Business, Business 101, Introduction to Business & Law, or Introduction to Accounting, Finance, and Markets. From a pedagogical perspective, an introductory preparatory course in essential business concepts is a sensible addition to a law school's curriculum, perhaps offered in the tail end of spring semester for 1Ls or the first half of fall semester for 2Ls. The subject "essential concepts in business" does not fit neatly into a category of legal doctrine, but that is no reason to not offer such a course to prepare students with no prior knowledge for a rigorous study of business law. As one commentator notes,

> Yes, law students are bright and much can be learned on the job; but we are failing them when we do not provide them with the opportunity to master the essential knowledge they need for having successful careers, particularly hard-to-master knowledge that is neither easily nor quickly mastered on one's own. If you think I am over-dramatizing the situation, ask yourself, how many autodidacts in the accounting or finance profession have you met lately? While the best business lawyers do not

need to become financial economists or accountants, they need a thorough working knowledge and mastery of the concepts and the relevant literature.[1]

An introductory preparatory course fits neatly into the current trend toward greater emphasis on interdisciplinary teaching at law schools. In fact, I use this text for a standalone 1-2 credit course titled Business 101 at the University of Maryland Francis King Carey School of Law, where it is taught in the first half of the fall semester.

## AUTHOR'S NOTE ON CASE EDITING

Cases and other primary texts have been edited. The editorial process necessarily changes the style and substance of the original case opinion. As with all case editing, the most prominent editorial changes to the original text are: (1) deletions of most citations to legal sources and extraneous footnotes; (2) deletions of certain sections of opinions such as extraneous facts, procedural history, standard of review, and legal analysis. When materials were deleted, I have not indicated the deletion with ellipses ( . . . ), except that ellipses in the original text were left intact. When necessary, I have also deleted portions of sentences that may have referred to deleted materials, or other similar circumstances requiring editing. Again, these deletions were not noted with ellipses, except that capitalization of the first word of the edited sentence is noted with brackets []. There is a tradeoff between exacting accuracy and convenient reading. The editorial process strove for visual appeal and easier reading. The cases are not presented to teach legal doctrine. They are presented to illustrate business concepts in legal problems. They are a part of the narrative structure of this book. At the end of the day, multiple ellipses and editorial exactness of brief writing add little to the law student's reading experience or understanding of business concepts other than communicating the obvious fact that cases in law textbooks have been edited. The complete case opinions are readily available for students to read on their own.

Robert J. Rhee, J.D., M.B.A.
Professor of Law & Marbury Research Professor
Co-Director, Business Law Program
University of Maryland Francis King Carey School of Law
Baltimore, Maryland

March 2012

---

1. Roberta Romano, *After the Revolution in Corporate Law*, 55 J. Legal Educ. 342, 352-53 (2005).

# Essential Concepts of

## BUSINESS FOR LAWYERS

# INTRODUCTION

## IMPORTANCE OF ESSENTIAL BUSINESS CONCEPTS

Lawyers won't keep the client's books and records, or execute securities trades for them, or model the financial effects of a merger or acquisition. So why do they need to know basic concepts in accounting, finance, and capital markets? Isn't it enough to know just the law? Consider this realistic situation.

> You are a junior corporate lawyer at a big law firm. You are assisting the senior partner, Jane Law, on a client matter. The working group is meeting in a conference room on the top floor of the corporate headquarters in Midtown Manhattan. You enter and see Cathy Chiefton, the company's chief executive officer (CEO), Mike Money, chief financial officer (CFO), and Piers Blake, an investment banker. It is a small working group, for now. The executive assistant closes the conference room door behind you.
>
> After pleasant but short introductions, Chiefton starts the meeting. "I called this meeting to discuss a potential acquisition of Acme Corp. As you may recall, we took a 20 percent stake when the company was distressed several years ago. With our support, Acme has turned around quite nicely. In light of developments in the market, now is the right time to acquire the entire company. Acme has a significant presence in international markets, particularly in China and Korea, which we do not have. An acquisition makes strategic sense."
>
> Money adds, "We've done some preliminary work on a potential deal. Our models show that a deal would be accretive to earnings under specific circumstances. At current market valuations of our stock price, a stock deal wouldn't make sense because it would be too dilutive."
>
> "A cash deal then." Chiefton asserts.
>
> "Yes, we'll financing issues and we'll need to analyze our liquidity situation," Money opines. "But the problem may be mitigated somewhat by cost synergies, particularly lower combined operating expenses."
>
> "Good," Chiefton says. "We'll have to prepare the board on all the financial implications of a deal."
>
> "With respect to financing issues," Money continues, "our company has negative working capital at this moment, which poses challenges in liquidity and certainly solvency if we're going to proceed with the deal. We're funding a portion of our operations through the commercial paper market. We'll need to step up that effort. Any deal, cash or stock, would be difficult to accomplish given our tight liquidity situation. We don't have cash on hand to fund the acquisition, and so we have to tap the capital markets for long-term capital solutions. Piers and Jane can elaborate on the financing and legal limitations of this deal."
>
> Piers Blake picks up on Money's cue. "Since this is a cash deal with a payment of premium, we may need to raise capital. Mike is suggesting that debt is the only option. We'll confirm that by running our own numbers. Your company is already highly levered

*and this will affect your cost of capital and the pricing on any debt issue as well as the cost of equity. Your stock price will not be unaffected."*

*Jane Law advises on the legal issues surrounding the deal. "If debt is the acquisition funding, we'll need to check the covenants in the debt contracts and the indentures in the public bonds, and see if there are any legal issues with interest cover, leverage, or additional debt raisings. If we trigger a redemption, that'll complicate the deal, particularly since rates are going up. We may have to renegotiate interest cover covenants in a bank loans and revolvers. We'll need to check the charter to see if the terms of the preferred stock present any problems. Lastly, we'll need to assess whether we have fiduciary duty issue. There's a lot to do."*

*"Yes," Blake concurs.*

*Chiefton concludes the meeting and issues the plan of action. "Okay, Mike, Piers, and Jane will work together on the financing and legal issues. I'll schedule a meeting of the board of directors next week. We'll report on the preliminary discussions I've had with Acme, and the financial and legal issues ahead of us."*

*The meeting breaks up quickly, and the working group exits the conference room with purposeful steps. On the way to the elevator, Law turns to you and says, "We have work to do."*

Can you follow the substance of this discussion? What are the client's problems? What are the substantive issues? Conversations like this occur on a daily basis in the business world. As a junior lawyer on the deal, you want to impress your partner, but more importantly you want to participate meaningfully on the deal and add value. While each of these participants—CEO, CFO, investment banker, and lawyer—have their unique roles, it is vital for the lawyer to understand the context in full. Accounting, finance, and legal issues are interconnected in corporate transactional practice. Lawyers must create value in the transaction, and to do so they must understand the business and economic context.[1]

In law schools, the study of accounting, finance, and capital markets may not be perceived to be interesting or intellectually stimulating. These subjects seem foreign, irrelevant, boring, or perhaps intimidating, and perhaps removed from what lawyers actually do. This mindset is misguided. Make no mistake that an understanding of essential business concepts is important to a lawyer who aspires to work with sophisticated businesses such as the modern public corporation. In the world of business, accounting and finance constitute the spoken language of the profession. Clients don't speak lawyerese; they expect lawyers to help them with their business problems. Lawyers must understand business problems and propose legal solutions to business problems. If you wish to work in the business world, you must speak the language of the trade and understand the complex context of business problems.

If you are reading this book, you are studying business law. You will need to know at least a rudimentary level of essential concepts in business. Lawyers are practical people, and accounting and finance are practical tools applied every day in the business and financial marketplace. The application of these subjects in the law is broad. Their concepts can be found in corporate law, white collar criminal law, commercial

---

1. Ronald J. Gilson, *Value Creation by Business Lawyers: Legal Skills and Asset Pricing*, 94 Yale L.J. 239 (1984).

law, estate planning, tax practice, banking law, mergers and acquisitions, regulation of industries, general business advisory, just to name a few. Even a consumer lawyer should have a grasp of complex consumer finance and business practices. Since the practice of business is spoken in the language of accounting and finance, a lawyer must understand the essential concepts of these academic disciplines.

The importance of these subjects can be put in practical perspective by recent history of business and market failures in which lawyers played a key role. Accounting fraud was at the heart of the catastrophic failures of corporate governance at companies like Enron and WorldCom. These events, in 2001 and 2002, led to the enactment of the Sarbanes-Oxley Act. The enforcement lawyers at the Securities and Exchange Commission failed to catch Bernie Madoff's fraud, the world's largest Ponzi scheme, because they lacked an understanding of the most fundamental principles of finance.[2] Much of the financial crisis of 2008 is attributable to the failure of financial regulation, particularly those concerning derivatives, financial engineering, and capital structure. Accounting, finance, and capital markets are important to a sophisticated business lawyer's work, and you cannot fool yourself into thinking that you will be able to avoid such subjects in your law studies or practice. In practice, it is not enough that the lawyer can conduct legal analysis on a discrete legal issue. Increasingly, business clients are demanding more. To be business problem solvers, the business lawyer must understand more broadly the nature of the client's business problem in which the specific legal issues may be situated.

In the course of studying business law, you will read important, classic cases and complex regulations of businesses, financial transactions, and capital markets. A reading of Delaware corporation law shows that the Delaware judges display expert knowledge of accounting, financial statement analysis, finance, valuation, financial instruments, and capital markets. If you are studying partnership or corporate tax, you will need to understand how the balance sheet works and how capital accounts are constructed. The same applies for courses in bankruptcy or business planning. You cannot have a complete understanding of the legal aspects of financial instruments such as bonds, derivatives, and stock without understanding their financial logic and the workings of the capital markets.

Let's put the subject of essential business concepts in the proper light. You should not dread the study of accounting, finance, and capital markets. They are not dry and boring subjects. You will learn the interconnected logic of these academic disciplines. They help professionals solve real world problems. There is always a reward in learning an important skill or subject, and once learned you will see how relevant these subject are to not only business law and practice, but in fact to a greater understanding of our increasingly complex world. Since lawyers play such a vital role in our market economy, such understanding should be a part of every lawyer's intellectual development.

---

2. Robert J. Rhee, *The Bernie Madoff Scandal, Market Regulatory Failure, and the Business Education of Lawyers*, 35 J. Corp. L. 363 (2009).

## ORGANIZATION OF THIS BOOK

This book is organized into three main Parts covering essential concepts in (1) accounting and financial statement analysis, (2) principles of finance and valuation, and (3) financial instruments and capital markets. These subjects constitute the core foundational knowledge necessary to conduct sophisticated business and corporate transactions. For the most part, each Part and the chapters within provide a complete lesson on a discrete topic. Some interrelation of topics is inevitable. You can refer to selected chapters as needed in the future as a student or lawyer.

*Part I—Accounting and Financial Statement Analysis (Chapters 1-6).* This section covers essential concepts in accounting. It does not focus on the creation of financial statements or provide in depth discussion of accounting policies and the auditing process. For this, you should take a formal accounting course that will cover accounting more thoroughly. Instead, the focus is on comprehension and analysis of financial accounting statements. Lawyers are the end users of financial statements. Keeping with the promise of teaching only the most essential concepts with minimal density of text, this book focuses on teaching the skill of reading financial statements and understanding the vital information they provide. The focus is on understanding the three basic financial statements (income statement, balance sheet, and cash flow statement), and how these statements relate to each other.

*Part II—Principles of Finance and Valuation (Chapters 7-10).* This section covers essential concepts in finance. Finance is important because it is fundamentally about value. At the heart of most business law courses and corporate transactions is the question of value: What rules of law create the most wealth? Why are the parties doing this transaction? Most corporate managers and business professionals make decisions and form opinions grounded in the reality of financial logic and the maxim of wealth creation. Lawyers must understand the basic concepts of finance as well. Financial principles applicable to most corporate transactions are captured in simple mathematical equations. The math used is no more difficult than high school algebra and the logic necessary to understand compounding interest in one's bank checking account.

*Part III—Financial Instruments and Capital Markets (Chapters 11-14).* This section covers financial instruments and capital markets. In the real world, there are innumerable ways in which the economic return of a business entity or transaction can be packaged into financial instruments. These instruments are broadly categorized into debt, equity, and derivatives. Business transactions take place in the context of markets. An overview of capital markets is provided as well, including their informational and valuational functions. Lastly, a broad overview of major corporate transactions, which are the bases of many cases in business law, are covered, including capital raisings, mergers and acquisitions, and restructurings.

## CONCEPTUAL TOOLS

This book uses several conceptual tools to help with your learning. These tools are specially designated in boxes. They are organized into the following categories.

 This sign asks you to stop and think about the implication of a lesson you just learned.

 This sign highlights an important conceptual key point that you should appreciate.

 This sign notes an interesting fact or information that may be useful to your understanding, including important jargon.

# ACCOUNTING AND FINANCIAL STATEMENT ANALYSIS

# INTRODUCTION TO ACCOUNTING

## A. IMPORTANCE OF ACCOUNTING

The importance of accounting is succinctly stated: *One cannot understand any business beyond the proverbial lemonade stand without understanding accounting.* Accounting is the analytic tool with which the activities of businesses are recorded. Accounting is fundamentally the study of keeping track of money and things reducible to money. Many business lawyers will work with sophisticated or complex businesses, and most corporate lawyers will work with complex economic organizations whose activities are recorded and understood through an accounting prism. All businesses require an accurate accounting of revenue, expenses, cash flow, assets, and liabilities. How can one company (acquirer) purchase another company (target) without knowing the target's profits or liabilities? How can creditors lend money if they do not know how much income a business generates or the assets and liabilities of the firm? How can executives be compensated appropriately if we don't know how they performed through an accounting of results? We must have a system for accounting for the various internal economic factors that are necessary to operate a business. Serving this need is the fundamental purpose of accounting.

While it can be difficult, accounting has an internal logical structure. Some concepts are even intuitive. If we understand this logical structure and its intuitions, we will understand how business activity is recorded, and we will acquire an important analytic skill to our toolbox.

## B. FINANCIAL ACCOUNTING STATEMENTS

The accounting profession applies a set of rules and procedures called *generally accepted accounting principles*, commonly known as *GAAP*. GAAP is concerned with the measurement of economic activity, the recording of such activity, and the preparation and disclosure of such activity in the form of financial statements. Like a statute, GAAP has been codified, and the Financial Accounting Standard Board (FASB) is the principal body that articulates GAAP standards, though other bodies such as the Securities and Exchange Commission and the Public Company Accounting Oversight Board have significant influence. Accountants apply GAAP to prepare financial accounting statements (hereinafter "financial statements").

A company will produce annual financial statements. To do so, it may hire an independent accounting firm to audit and certify their financial statement. This process is called auditing, and in addition to GAAP auditors will also apply *generally accepted auditing standards*, commonly known as *GAAS*.

The auditing process provides independent verification and objective assurance of the quality of a firm's financial statements. This is important for several reason. Various interested parties may rely on these financial statements, e.g., investors, creditors, the public, and regulators. Any company with a significant business will hire auditors and produce certified financial statements because they will interact with various parties who will want to examine the company's books.

A business must account for its profit and loss, assets and liabilities, and flow of cash. This information is presented in the financial statements. Financial statements provide essential information to the businessperson, and a business lawyer must be able to read them. There are three fundamental components of financial statements:

- Balance sheet
- Income statement
- Cash flow statement

Additionally, financial statements will have a *statement of shareholders' equity*, which accounts for the status and changes in shareholders' equity. These financial statements are typically four pages (one page each for the balance sheet, income statement, cash flow statement, and statement of shareholders' equity). However, many companies provide an *annual report* to shareholders, and public companies must file financial statements with the regulatory agency, the Securities and Exchange Commission, called a Form *10-K* (annual statement) and Form *10-Q* (quarterly statements). Expanded financial statements in the form of annual reports and regulatory filings can be quite lengthy and chock-full of important information about the company.[1] They include the following important items.

- *Management discussion and analysis* (MD&A) discusses, among other things, a summary of the firm's operations, its ability to pay short-term obligations, and its ability to fund operations.
- *Notes to the financial statements* provide detailed information on accounting policies used, explanations of particular line items, and other vital information. Obviously, the notes accompanying the financial statements are important. If you want further details on a line item because you have a particular interest or because the line item is ambiguous, the notes should usually answer the question (but not always).
- *Auditor's report* is an opinion letter providing the auditor's opinion as to the fairness of the presentation of the company's financial position in accordance with GAAP. If the auditor is satisfied, it will issue an *unqualified opinion*. A qualified report indicates that the auditor has reservations about the report, and usually the specific qualification is noted.

---

1. I have often advised law students that when they become practicing attorneys, and are conducting initial client meetings, it is best to read the client's annual report or financial statements, if available, even if they are not instructed to do. They will learn much about the client.

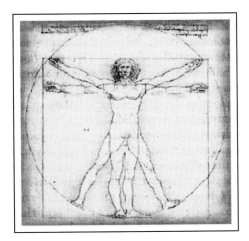

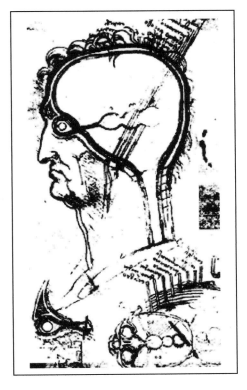

With this essential background information behind us, let's begin the analysis of how financial information is presented.

Accounting can seem arcane. Before getting to the technical details, we can think about financial statements more intuitively. Students in Business Associations, and indeed laypersons, understand that a corporation is a legal person. Let's take this concept a step further. Like the human body, this artificial person also has a body, and the various parts of this body are represented in the financial statements.

The *balance sheet* is like the skeletal system. In setting forth the assets and liabilities of the business, the balance sheet shapes the form of the firm and indicates the size of its economic parts. The *income statement* is like the digestive system. A business takes inputs and creates outputs for sale; the resulting profit, like energy from foods, is needed to support the firm's subsistence. A firm can go without profits for a while, but without sustained profits it cannot survive. The income statement records the firm's yearly revenue and expenses. Lastly, the *cash flow statement* is like the human body's circulatory system. Cash is the life blood of a firm (without it, an otherwise good firm can still go insolvent), and the cash flow statement tracks the flow of cash within the firm.

The analogy of a firm to the human body also indicates the inherent limitations of accounting. Notice what is missing from this simple analogy. The most important human organ is our brain. The collective brainpower of the firm, called *human capital*, is also the most important asset of many firms.

For example, let's consider Goldman Sachs, a leading investment bank. In 1999, it converted from a private partnership to a public corporation. A "public company" means that its stock (also called "shares") is publicly traded on a stock exchange (shares represent economic slices of ownership in the company); thus the public at large can acquire ownership of the company and trade the ownership interest with others. When a firm "goes public," it must issue a prospectus under federal securities law, which is a form of a public disclosure of important information about the company and the investment opportunity. Goldman Sachs' prospectus identified the investment bank's fourteen core business principles, the second of which states: "*Our assets are our people, capital and reputation.*" Only one of these assets—capital—is actually found in the financial statements as a line item. Reputation (the value of the "Goldman Sachs" name) is not recorded in the financial statements. The firm's employees are not an accounting asset because corporations cannot own its employees or sell them (slavery was eradicated in the nineteenth century). Does the fact that accounting does not recognize human capital and reputation mean that these factors are irrelevant? Of course not! It just means that accounting has limits.

 What are the practical consequences of accounting's limitations? Think about the reputational value of "Coca Cola" or "McDonald's" or "Disney." Consider the issue of the value of a company. These values are not recorded in the financial statements. Do financial statements measure the "true" value of the company?

Financial statements are indispensible in analyzing and assessing businesses, *but they must be taken with a grain of salt*. They are not the end of the analysis, but merely the starting point. These limitations necessarily make the financial statements materially inaccurate from the perspective of economic reality even when financial statements are prepared competently and ethically and within the bounds of GAAP. The good lawyer is a skeptical, sophisticated user of financial statements.

A few other points are worth noting. It is important to keep in mind the timeframe. Both the income statement and cash flow statement look backward in time and encompass an accounting of the full year's activities. They tell us how much profit and cash the firm generates *in the past year*. However, the balance sheet is a frozen snapshot of the firm's assets and liabilities on the last day of the fiscal year (e.g., December 31, 2010).

A balance sheet is analogous to a broken clock and only half as accurate. A broken clock is correct two times in a day. A balance sheet is only correct as of its date. In all other times, the contemporaneous assets and liabilities will be different from those recorded in the balance sheet (though most firms will have managerial accounting systems that keep contemporaneous track of various accounting measures such as the balance sheet but these figures will be unaudited, not certified by accountants). The financial statements are records of the past. If a lawyer is doing a deal, the past information is relevant only insofar as it provides information as to the present and the future.

## C. USES AND LIMITATIONS

Financial statements are not an accurate or complete reflection of the true economic condition of the firm. Why? There are several reasons. First, as discussed, financial statements cannot record certain intangible items that are clearly important to the value of a firm, e.g., human capital and goodwill in the firm's name and reputation.

Second, financial statements are recordings of the *past*. Revenue, expense, asset, liability, and cash flow arise from past transactions. Accounting principles do not permit the expectation of future profit to be recorded into the financial statements (such misuse of accounting was a core part of the Enron fraud). On the other hand, finance and economics often deal with the *future*: How much profit will this factory generate? Will Google dominate search engines for the next ten years? Will McDonald's continue to earn profit from selling Big Macs? Under the theory of finance, the value of a firm or an asset is judged on the basis of how much economic profit it will earn in the future.

However, financial statements are useful tools. They provide a picture of the firm's finances under a consistent, defined set of GAAP rules and principles applied by a professional body. That a particular tool is not perfect does not mean that it is useless. We can supplement and compensate for a rusty saw or a dull knife. Much of the missing and inaccurate information can be corrected, and the financial statements provide the essential data for a thorough analysis of the firm. They are the starting point of the analysis.

**EXAMPLE 1.1**

---

**Enron's highly controversial conference call, April 17, 2001**

The Enron Corporation represents the quintessential case of corporate fraud and ethical deviance. At one point, the company was valued at over $60 billion. Then it all came crashing down. In October 2001, it disclosed a massive accounting scandal. Shortly thereafter, the company imploded and filed for the largest corporate bankruptcy at the time. In thinking about the importance of financial statements, consider the following incident from a public conference call, several months before the company collapse. Upon the release of a periodic, quarterly earnings announcement, it is typical for companies to conduct conference calls with Wall Street analysts during which the latter can ask questions pertaining to the company's interim financial announcement. The exchange below transpired between Jeffrey Skilling, Enron's chief executive officer (CEO), and Richard Grubman, a Wall Street analyst.

> *Grubman:* "You're the only financial institution that can't produce a balance sheet or cash flow statement with their earnings [income statement]."
> *Skilling:* "You . . . you . . . you. Well, uh . . . thank you very much. We appreciate that."
> *Grubman:* "You appreciate that?"
> *Skilling:* "A\*\*hole."

This was a controversial event: What respectable CEO of a Fortune 500 company would call a stock analyst an expletive in public for daring to question the company's financial statement? Assume that this was a regrettable, unprofessional exchange concerning a matter of great importance. Grubman wanted to see a complete set of financial statements. Skilling objected. For what specific reason did Grubman want to see a balance sheet and cash flow statement along with the income statement?

Consider this assessment: "Whoever this guy Grubman was, he was asking a key question. The balance sheet—and its lesser-known cousin, the statement of cash flows—would let investors know if Enron had enough money on hand to finance growth. It might give hints about how much of Enron's earnings came from fancy accounting rather than the true generation of cash." Kurt Eichenwald, *Conspiracy of Fools* 444 (2005).

---

## D. CASE APPLICATION

The case below, *Francis v. United Jersey Bank*, is commonly found in Business Associations casebooks. It concerns Pritchard & Baird Intermediaries Corp., a family-owned reinsurance broker. Charles Jr. and William Pritchard were officers, directors, and shareholders. They looted the company by giving "shareholders' loans" to themselves without the intention of repaying. Creditors sued for the loss of their monies, which Pritchard & Baird held in trust. Among the defendants was the mother of Charles and William, Lilian Pritchard, who did not partake in the fraudulent conveyance, but who failed to properly monitor the corporation's affairs. An aspect of such monitoring is to review the company's financial books and records. The trial court entered judgment of $10,355,736 plus interest against the estate of Mrs. Pritchard. In reading the case, think about the job of a director of a company and the skills necessary to perform that job.

### *Francis v. United Jersey Bank (Part I)*
#### 432 A.2d 814 (N.J. 1981)

POLLOCK, J.

The primary issue on this appeal is whether a corporate director is personally liable in negligence for the failure to prevent the misappropriation of trust funds by other directors who were also officers and shareholders of the corporation.

Both lower courts found that [Mrs. Pritchard] was liable in negligence for the losses caused by the wrongdoing of Charles, Jr. and William. We affirm.

[The court described in detail the manner in which Charles Jr. and William looted the company.]

The corporate minute books reflect only perfunctory activities by the directors, related almost exclusively to the election of officers and adoption of banking resolutions and a retirement plan. None of the minutes for any of the meetings contain a discussion of the loans to Charles, Jr. and William or of the financial condition of the corporation. Moreover, upon instructions of Charles, Jr. that financial statements were not to be circulated to anyone else, the company's statements for the fiscal years beginning February 1, 1970, were delivered only to him.

Mrs. Pritchard was not active in the business of Pritchard & Baird and knew virtually nothing of its corporate affairs. She briefly visited the corporate offices in Morristown on only one occasion, and she never read or obtained the annual financial statements. She was unfamiliar with the rudiments of reinsurance and made no effort to assure that the policies and practices of the corporation, particularly pertaining to the withdrawal of funds, complied with industry custom or relevant law. Although her husband had warned her that Charles, Jr. would "take the shirt off my back," Mrs. Pritchard did not pay any attention to her duties as a director or to the affairs of the corporation.

As a general rule, a director should acquire at least a rudimentary understanding of the business of the corporation. Accordingly, a director should become familiar with the fundamentals of the business in which the corporation is engaged. Because directors are bound to exercise ordinary care, they cannot set up as a defense lack of the knowledge needed to exercise the requisite degree of care. If one "feels that he has not had sufficient business experience to qualify him to perform the duties of a director, he should either acquire the knowledge by inquiry, or refuse to act."

Directors are under a continuing obligation to keep informed about the activities of the corporation. Otherwise, they may not be able to participate in the overall management of corporate affairs. Directors may not shut their eyes to corporate misconduct and then claim that because they did not see the misconduct, they did not have a duty to look. The sentinel asleep at his post contributes nothing to the enterprise he is charged to protect.

While directors are not required to audit corporate books, they should maintain familiarity with the financial status of the corporation by a regular review of financial statements. In some circumstances, directors may be charged with assuring that bookkeeping methods conform to industry custom and usage. The extent of review, as well as the nature and frequency of financial statements, depends not only on the customs of the industry, but also on the nature of the corporation and the business in which it is engaged. Financial statements of some small corporations may be prepared internally and only on an annual basis; in a large publicly held corporation, the statements may be produced monthly or at some other regular interval. Adequate financial review normally would be more informal in a private corporation than in a publicly held corporation.

Of some relevance in this case is the circumstance that the financial records disclose the "shareholders' loans." Generally directors are immune from liability if, in good faith,

> they rely upon the opinion of counsel for the corporation or upon written reports setting forth financial data concerning the corporation and prepared by an independent public accountant or certified public accountant or firm of such accountants or upon financial statements, books of account or reports of the corporation represented to them to be correct by the president, the officer of the corporation having charge of its books of account, or the person presiding at a meeting of the board.

The review of financial statements, however, may give rise to a duty to inquire further into matters revealed by those statements. Upon discovery of an illegal course of action, a director has a duty to object and, if the corporation does not correct the conduct, to resign.

The most striking circumstances affecting Mrs. Pritchard's duty as a director are the character of the reinsurance industry, the nature of the misappropriated funds and the financial condition of Pritchard & Baird. The hallmark of the reinsurance industry has been the unqualified trust and confidence reposed by ceding companies and reinsurers in reinsurance brokers. Those companies entrust money to reinsurance intermediaries with the justifiable expectation that the funds will be transmitted to the appropriate parties. Consequently, the companies could have assumed rightfully that Mrs. Pritchard, as a director of a reinsurance brokerage corporation, would not sanction the comingling and the conversion of loss and premium funds for the personal use of the principals of Pritchard & Baird.

As a reinsurance broker, Pritchard & Baird received annually as a fiduciary millions of dollars of clients' money which it was under a duty to segregate. To this extent, it resembled a bank rather than a small family business. Accordingly, Mrs. Pritchard's relationship to the clientele of Pritchard & Baird was akin to that of a director of a bank to its depositors. All parties agree that Pritchard & Baird held the misappropriated funds in an implied trust. That trust relationship gave rise to a fiduciary duty to guard the funds with fidelity and good faith.

As a director of a substantial reinsurance brokerage corporation, she should have known that it received annually millions of dollars of loss and premium funds which it held in trust for ceding and reinsurance companies. Mrs. Pritchard should have obtained and read the annual statements of financial condition of Pritchard & Baird. Although she had a right to rely upon financial statements, such reliance would not excuse her conduct. The reason is that those statements disclosed on their face the misappropriation of trust funds.

From those statements, she should have realized that, as of January 31, 1970, her sons were withdrawing substantial trust funds under the guise of "Shareholders' Loans." The financial statements for each fiscal year commencing with that of January 31, 1970, disclosed that the working capital deficits and the "loans" were escalating in tandem. Detecting a misappropriation of funds would not have required special expertise or extraordinary diligence; a cursory reading of the financial statements would have revealed the pillage. Thus, if Mrs. Pritchard had read the financial statements, she would have known that her sons were converting trust funds. When financial statements demonstrate that insiders are bleeding a corporation to death, a director should notice and try to stanch the flow of blood.

In summary, Mrs. Pritchard was charged with the obligation of basic knowledge and supervision of the business of Pritchard & Baird. Under the circumstances, this obligation included reading and understanding financial statements, and making reasonable attempts at detection and prevention of the illegal conduct of other officers and directors. She had a duty to protect the clients of Pritchard & Baird against policies and practices that would result in the misappropriation of money they had entrusted to the corporation. She breached that duty.

## QUESTIONS

1. Irrespective of fraud, why is it important for a corporation like Pritchard & Baird to keep track of its monies and to report accurately its financial status?
2. With respect to financial statements, what level of knowledge and skill must a director possess?
3. With respect to financial statements, what level of knowledge and skill should a business lawyer possess?

## ESSENTIAL TERMS

Annual report

Auditing and auditors

Auditor's report

Balance sheet

Cash flow statement

Financial statements

Form 10-K and 10-Q

GAAP

GAAS

Income statement

MD&A

Notes to the financial statements

Private company

Public company

Qualified auditor opinion

Statement of shareholder's equity

Unqualified auditor opinion

## KEY CONCEPTS

1. Financial statements are prepared by accountants applying GAAP, and audits are done by applying GAAS.
2. Financial statements are important to understand the nature of the firm's business.
3. Financial statements have inherent limitations, and the lawyer must not assume that the data in financial statements are complete or fairly represent economic reality.
4. There are three essential components to financial statements: the balance sheet, the income statement, and the cash flow statement. Additionally, the statement of shareholders' equity, MD&A, notes to financial statement, and auditor's report are important.
5. The income statement and cash flow statement account for an entire year's activities. The balance sheet is a one-day snapshot of assets and liabilities.
6. Business lawyers must be minimally proficient in reading financial statements to perform their job properly.

## REVIEW QUESTIONS

1. An accounting statement provides an accurate portrait of the firm's economic condition. True or false? Explain.
2. At fiscal year ended Dec. 31, Year 1, Baltimore Corp.'s balance sheet shows that the firm had shareholder equity of $10,000,000. On June 30, Year 2, Washington Inc. offers to buy Baltimore. The offer price is stated as 1.5 times the shareholder equity. Does this mean that Washington intends to buy Baltimore for $15,000,000?

# BALANCE SHEET

## A. BALANCE SHEET EQUATION

The balance sheet provides an accounting of the firm's assets and liabilities. Assets and liabilities change every day. A day's business may bring in cash, create liabilities, and earn profit. A balance sheet is a one-day picture of the firm's assets and liabilities, and this snapshot is taken at the end of the fiscal year, which may be the end of the calendar year (December 31) or any other date marking the end of the fiscal year (e.g., the Walt Disney Company has a fiscal year ending September 30). Nevertheless, the firm may keep internal managerial accounts that track assets and liabilities contemporaneous, and some firms may produce unaudited quarterly (every three months) financial statements.

The most important point about a balance sheet is that it must balance. This means that assets must *always* equal liabilities plus equity.

$$\text{Assets} = \text{Liabilities} + \text{Equity}$$

Through simple algebraic manipulation, we can rearrange this equation to state:

$$\text{Equity} = \text{Assets} - \text{Liabilities}$$

This equation states that equity is assets net of liabilities (thus, sometimes equity is called "net assets"). We can picture the balance sheet equation as:

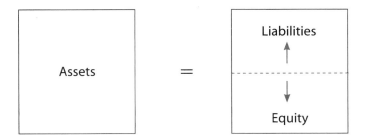

Notice that the proportion between liabilities and equity can shift up and down (see the dotted line inside the box), but liabilities plus equity must always equal assets.

> **STOP AND THINK**
>
> Not infrequently, there are times when: Assets < Liabilities.
>
> For example, when the housing bubble collapsed in 2007, American home-owners learned what it meant when liabilities (mortgage) exceeded the value of the asset (home) in their personal balance sheets. Their homes were "under water." The banks foreclosed on their homes, but could recover only a portion of their mortgage loan because the value of the home fell below the loan amounts. The financial pain was equally shared by creditors (banks) and equityholders (homeowners).

If (Assets < Liabilities), how can the fundamental balance sheet equation (Assets = Liabilities + Equity) hold true? It can and it must. The equity must be negative in an amount equal to the amount of liability in excess of assets. This is the case of *negative equity* (or *negative net worth*).

An example illustrates the principle. Assume the following: Assets have a value of $A$, and Liabilities have a value of $(A + B)$.

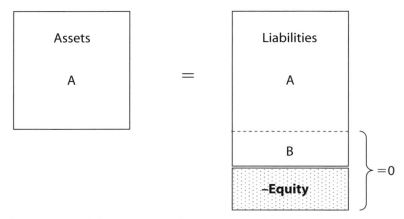

For (Assets = Liabilities + Equity), equity must be negative. The above diagram can be represented as:

$$\text{Assets} = \text{Liabilities} + \text{Equity}$$

$$A = (A + B) + (-B)$$

>   The important lesson here is that the balance sheet equation (Assets = Liabilities + Equity) must *always* hold.

## B. ASSETS AND LIABILITIES

An *asset* is defined as a probable future economic benefit obtained or controlled by a particular entity as a result of past transactions or events. Assets can be characterized by their form and duration.

An asset can be tangible or intangible. A *tangible asset* is an asset having some physical form: for example, buildings and equipment. An *intangible asset* is a non-physical, noncurrent right that gives a firm an exclusive or preferred position in the marketplace. Examples include intellectual property such as copyright, trademark, and patent, which are assets that do not have physical form.

An asset can be current (short-term) or noncurrent (long-term). A *current asset* is an asset that a firm expects to turn into cash, sell, or exchange within the normal operating cycle of the firm or one year. Examples include cash, receivables, and inventory. A *noncurrent asset* is a long-term asset. Examples include real property, physical plant, and equipment.

A *liability* is defined as a probable future sacrifice of economic benefits arising from present obligations of a particular entity to transfer assets or to provide services to another entity in the future as a result of past transactions or events. Like assets, liabilities can be characterized by duration.

A liability can be current (short-term) or noncurrent (long-term). A *current liability* is a debt or obligation that a firm expects to pay within the normal operating cycle of the firm or one year. Examples include payables such as a utility bill or monthly employee wages that have yet to be paid. A *noncurrent liability* is a long-term debt or obligation. An example is a loan with a 5-year maturity.

## C. EQUITY

*Equity* is the residual interest in assets that remains after deducting liabilities.[1] It is informally thought of as "ownership" in an asset or business: e.g., "equity" in a home means that homeowner's claim to the economic value of the home after the mortgage is paid off.

Unfortunately, there is much jargon associated with the concept of equity. Different terms are used for specific forms of equity, depending on the organizational form and valuational methods underlying the representation of equity. We must be familiar with the various terms for equity because they are commonly and often interchangeably used.

*Different terms used to denote "equity"*—Equity has several commonly used synonyms. Unfortunately, this is one set of industry jargon that you must learn because all of these synonyms are commonly used.

- *Net worth:* worth net of liabilities.
- *Net assets:* assets net of liabilities. The term "net asset" is typically used in investment vehicles such as a mutual fund or a hedge fund, which makes various investments. The accounting rules may permit the asset values to be calculated as fair market value of assets net of liabilities, which is called *net asset value* (NAV).

---

1. In law, "equity" may have different synonyms such as fairness or justice or is a reference to particular remedies, depending on the context of usage. This is not the meaning of equity in business.

Business enterprises can take various forms. They can be operated as a general partnership, a limited liability company (LLC), a corporation, just to name a few forms. Specific terms are given to the equity associated with these different business forms.

- *Partner's capital*: equity in partnerships
- *Member's interest*: equity in LLCs
- *Shareholder's equity*: equity in corporations

*Different valuations of "equity"*—The value of equity can be stated as either (1) an accounting value, or (2) a market value. These values can differ significantly. There are two terms used to denote the differences in the value of equity.

- *Book value*: equity stated in the balance sheet, which is a value assigned by accountants
- *Market capitalization ("market cap")* or *market value*: equity in corporations stated as a value assigned by the market price (in other words, the share price multiplied by the number of shares held by shareholders, also known as outstanding shares)

*Line items in equity in corporations*—In the equity account of a corporation's balance sheet, there are several line items that are commonly seen.

- *Common stock* or *capital*: many companies designate a "par value" for the stock, which is a minimum amount of consideration from the stock sale set aside to protect creditors
- *Additional paid-in-capital* (APIC): amount of capital raised by selling stock net of par value
- *Retained earnings*: net income not distributed to shareholders are recorded in the balance sheet as retained earnings under equity
- *Treasury stock*: recorded as a negative number (an offset against equity), this item records how much the firm spent to buy back its stock from shareholders

EXAMPLE 2.1

---

**Partner's capital accounts**

A partnership is defined as the co-ownership of a business for profit by two or more partners. An employee is not an owner of the business because he has a fixed contractual claim for a wage. A partner is an owner of the partnership because she is entitled to the profit of the business. Profit is the income remaining after all prior claims are paid, including the wages of employees. In a partnership, there should be a partnership agreement that, among other things, provides for the allocation of profit and loss.

Adam, Bob, Clare, and David establish a partnership. Each partner contributes $100 in capital. They also agree to split profits 25 percent each. Every partnership must maintain a capital account, which keeps track of each partner's equity (ownership interest) in the firm. At the start of this partnership, the capital account looks like this.

---

| Partner | Beginning Capital | | Profit Made | | Capital Contribution | Draw | Ending Capital | |
|---|---|---|---|---|---|---|---|---|
| | Balance | % | % | Allocation | | | Balance | % |
| Adam | 100 | 25% | 25% | -0- | | | | |
| Bob | 100 | 25% | 25% | -0- | | | | |
| Clare | 100 | 25% | 25% | -0- | | | | |
| David | 100 | 25% | 25% | -0- | | | | |
| Total | 400 | 100% | 100% | -0- | | | | |

During the year, the partnership made profit of $1,000. Additionally, the partners made these capital contributions: Adam $500, Bob $200, David $100. The partners made draws (took money out) from their separate capital accounts of these amounts, which was permitted under the partnership agreement: Adam $150, Clare $200, and David $100. At the end of these transactions, the partnership capital accounts look like this.

| Partner | Beginning Capital | | Profit Made | | Capital Contribution | Draw | Ending Capital | |
|---|---|---|---|---|---|---|---|---|
| | Balance | % | % | Allocation | | | Balance | % |
| Adam | 100 | 25% | 25% | 250 | 500 | (150) | 700 | 40% |
| Bob | 100 | 25% | 25% | 250 | 200 | 0 | 550 | 31% |
| Clare | 100 | 25% | 25% | 250 | 0 | (200) | 150 | 9% |
| David | 100 | 25% | 25% | 250 | 100 | (100) | 350 | 20% |
| Total | 400 | 100% | 100% | 1000 | 800 | (450) | 1750 | 100% |

Although each partner is an equal 25% owner of the firm in terms of profit allocation, we see that at the end of these transactions, they have different ownership claims on the capital of the firm.

Some common stock may have a *par value*, which historically was a value set to protect creditors and to set a minimum level of stock value. But this concept is a historical anachronism, and modern corporate law statutes do not require that stock set a par value. If a stock states a par value, the number is now an arbitrary number and is typically a very low figure, most commonly $0.01. The issue price in excess of par value is called *additional paid in capital*.

EXAMPLE 2.2

---

**Common stock and APIC**

Assume that Big Corporation issues 10,000,000 shares of common stock with par value of $0.01 at $10 per share. How do we account for this?

The balance sheet must balance. Cash raised augments assets in the balance sheet, and this addition must be offset ("balanced") by an increase in equity. The specific line items are calculated as:

| | | |
|---|---|---|
| Cash: | $10.00 × 10,000,000 = | $100,000,000 |
| Common stock: | $0.01 × 10,000,000 = | $100,000 |
| APIC: | $9.99 × 10,000,000 = | $ 99,900,000 |

---

EXAMPLE 2.3

---

**Market cap versus book value (Part I)**

McDonald's Corporation has 1,053 million shares outstanding (shares held by shareholders) as of December 31, 2010, the end of its fiscal year. On this day, the share price closed at $76.76 per share. What is the market value of shareholder's equity in McDonald's?

1,053 million shares × $76.76 per share = $80.8 billion market value

However, in the balance sheet, the book value of equity is stated as $14.6 billion (see McDonald's balance sheet in Part G in the line "Total shareholders' equity"). The ratio of market value ($80.8 billion) to book value ($14.6 billion) is 5.5x. This ratio is called the *price-to-book* (or P/B) ratio, and we will study these kinds of multiples later in this book.

Think about the implication of a 5.5x P/B ratio. It says that the fair market value of McDonald's is 5.5 times greater than what the accountants have recorded as the value of McDonald's equity in the balance sheet.

A significant disparity between book and market values is not so unusual. Compare the market capitalizations, book values, and P/B ratios of the companies below as of the date of their balance sheets.

| As of 12/31/2010 | No. shares outstanding (million) | | Share price | | Market cap ($ million) | | Book value ($ million) | | P/B ratio |
|---|---|---|---|---|---|---|---|---|---|
| Coca Cola | [ 2,292 | × | $65.77 | = | 150,744 ] | ÷ | 31,317 | = | 4.81x |
| McDonald's | [ 1,053 | × | $76.76 | = | 80,828 ] | ÷ | 14,634 | = | 5.52x |
| United Technologies | [ 921 | × | $78.72 | = | 72,501 ] | ÷ | 22,332 | = | 3.25x |

---

## D. HISTORICAL COST AND MARKET VALUE

Example 2.3 shows that there can be significant disparity between market value of equity and book value. The market value is economically more accurate than the book value, which is to say that market value reflects the current market prices irrespective of the value recorded in the financial statements. If market value is more accurate, what accounts for the disparity between market and book values? There are three main reasons.

1. *Historical cost.* An important accounting concept is that items in the balance sheet are generally recorded on a *historical cost* basis. This means that most items in the balance sheet are recorded at their original cost, and generally are not adjusted for their fair market value (there are exceptions under the accounting rules). This general rule reflects a conservative bias, which has served the accounting profession well but which also has limitations. The following example illustrates the point. Suppose a firm bought a nice brick factory building occupying an entire city block in Manhattan for $10 million in 1970. As far as the value of the building asset, it is generally recorded at historical cost in the financial statements. But suppose the building is really worth $100 million in today's Manhattan real estate market. The equity will vary depending on the value assigned to the building asset. The accounting statement will record the value of the building at historical cost, but others may value the asset at *fair market value* (FMV or "market value" or "fair value").

2. *Limitations of accounting.* Recall that the accounting profession has certain limitations when it comes to recording assets and liabilities. A company's good-will and human capital are not recorded in the balance sheet. Think about the true value of a law firm. The law firm's balance sheet will record the physical assets and liabilities, e.g., books, computers, and office furniture. But the equity value may not reflect the talent of its lawyers. Additionally, other aspects of the firm that cannot be recorded in the balance sheet may add to the economic value of the firm.

3. *Different valuational methods.* Accountants and "the market" value equity differently. Accountants value equity as the assets net of liabilities. These assets and liabilities are generally recorded at historical cost of past transactions. The market values equity based on how much a firm will generate income in the future. A firm may have zero book value because assets equal liabilities, but if these assets and liabilities have a combined positive future earning potential, then the market will assign a positive equity value irrespective of the fact that the net assets are zero in the books. Therefore, accountants record the value of equity based on *past transactions*, but the marketplace, such as the stock markets and private economic actors, values equity based on *future prospect*.

An exception to historical cost method of recording assets and liabilities is called *marked-to-market*. Under this method, assets and liabilities are marked to fair market value and their values are adjusted per changing market value. Accounting principles allow some assets and liabilities to be recorded under changing market values.

EXAMPLE 2.4

> ## Market cap versus book value (Part II)
>
> In its 2010 annual report, the Ford Motor Company reported the following balance sheet information (as of year ended December 31 and in $ millions).
>
> - Assets:       \$164,687
> - Liabilities:    165,329
> - Equity:          (642)
>
> Ford had 3.707 billion common shares outstanding, and the stock priced closed on December 31, 2010, at \$16.79. Thus, the market capitalization of Ford's common stock was \$62 billion. The accountants said that Ford had a negative net worth of \$642 million, but the market said that Ford's equity was worth \$62 billion.

 In many cases: Book Value ≠ Market Value.

> **F.Y.I.** In the course of your business education and career, you will often hear the term "the market." This simply means any marketplace to sell goods or services. eBay provides a marketplace for secondhand goods. There is a market for books wherein Amazon and brick-and-mortar bookstores compete. Similarly, there is a market for stocks and bonds (called securities). There is even a market for the purchase and sale of entire corporations, called the market for corporate control. In the context of corporate transactions, the market for capital (stocks, bonds, and other securities) and corporate control constitute a generic reference to "the market."

## E. HOW THE BALANCE SHEET WORKS

The balance sheet equation is deceptively simple: Assets = Liabilities + Equity. A lawyer must understand three important concepts about the balance sheet.

1. *The balance sheet is a statement of ownership.* This concept says that every asset is owned by two types of owners—creditors and equityholders.
2. *The balance sheet is a statement of risk.* This concept says that creditors and equityholders are investors in the firm, but they have chosen different forms of risk. Creditors have prior claims against the assets of the firm, and thus they have less risk.
3. *The balance sheet equation must be seen in terms of book value and market value.* This concept says that there are two balance sheet equations with potentially different values.

The simplest example of the balance sheet equation is to think about a house. Most people think in terms of a house having one owner (the homeowner). Without a mortgage, this is true. There is a single claimant of the asset—the homeowner. She "owns" the entire asset, meaning in this case two fundamental aspects: she gets the entire value of the assets upon sale, and she controls all aspects of the house. However, if the house was purchased with a mortgage, there are two economic claims on it: (1) the bank's mortgage, which is a liability; (2) the owner's equity in the home, which is the residual value remaining in the asset after liabilities are paid. Absent default, the homeowner controls the assets (thus, we can say that the homeowner "owns" the house). Upon default, the bank takes control through foreclosure. Thus, we can say that the bank now "owns" the house. This simple example illustrates the important lesson of the accounting balance sheet: *ownerships of an economic asset of the firm can be split into liabilities and equity.*

**Author's note:** In the example below, we will use the hypothetical of Kingsfield's Tavern to illustrate the balance sheet. We will continue to use the Kingsfield hypothetical throughout Part I of this book on accounting, culminating in producing a simple set of financial statements for the company in Chapter 6. In addition to Example 2.5 below, the hypothetical continues in Examples 3.1, 3.4, 4.2, 4.3, 4.4, 4.5, 5.3, 5.4, and 6.1.

EXAMPLE 2.5

---

### Professor Kingsfield starts a new business

Professor Charles W. Kingsfield Jr., an eminent professor of law, has decided that teaching Contract Law to eager 1L students is not all that it's cracked up to be. While tormenting eager 1L students certainly has personal rewards, Professor Kingsfield felt that he "needed a new gig." After consulting with his daughter Susan, he decides to open up a bar: Kingsfield's Tavern. "I'd rather drink a pint of brew with my 1Ls than terrify them with my intellectual prowess," he said with a wry smirk.

The first order of business is to buy a building that would house Kingsfield's Tavern. Having also taught Business Associations, Professor Kingsfield creates a corporation, Kingsfield Inc. He invests $20,000 of his personal money and buys 100 shares of common stock, constituting 100 percent of the stock at an issue price of $200 per share. He now has a corporation, which is a separate and distinct legal entity. The corporation's balance sheet looks like this.

| ASSETS | | LIABILITIES | |
|---|---|---|---|
| Cash | $20,000 | | $0 |
| | | EQUITY | |
| | | Common stock | $20,000 |
| | | (100 shares issued) | |
| Total assets | $20,000 | Total liab. & equity | $20,000 |

This means that Kingsfield Inc. has $20,000 of assets, in the form of cash. Since the company has no liabilities (debt), the money is claimed by the equityholder (Professor Kingsfield), who has 100 percent of the equity (which is represented in 100 shares in the common stock, constituting the entire issued shares of the company).

Luckily, Kingsfield Inc. buys a foreclosed old building, at the low price of $100,000. He arranges to take out a corporate loan of $80,000 from Big Bank. With the $100,000 cash in hand, Kingsfield Inc. buys the property, which is proudly dubbed "𝕂𝕚𝕟𝕘𝕤𝕗𝕚𝕖𝕝𝕕 𝕳𝖔𝖚𝖘𝖊." It is now the corporation's sole asset. Additionally, he purchases $50,000 of equipment from Bob's Equipment with 100 percent financing and secured interested in the equipment. These transactions are completed by December 31, Year 0. The corporation's balance sheet looks like this.

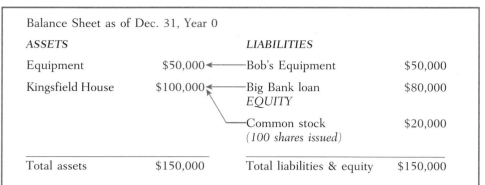

Balance Sheet as of Dec. 31, Year 0

| ASSETS | | LIABILITIES | |
|---|---|---|---|
| Equipment | $50,000 | Bob's Equipment | $50,000 |
| Kingsfield House | $100,000 | Big Bank loan | $80,000 |
| | | EQUITY | |
| | | Common stock (100 shares issued) | $20,000 |
| Total assets | $150,000 | Total liabilities & equity | $150,000 |

The acquisition of assets must always be funded. The assets of Kingsfield Inc. have three economic owners: Bob's Equipment, Big Bank, and Professor Kingsfield. Bob's Equipment and Big Bank are creditors and have a prior fixed claim against the company's assets. Their financial claims must be satisfied first. If their claims are not satisfied, they have legal options to take possession of the assets through the commercial laws of secured transactions and bankruptcy. Professor Kingsfield is the stockholder and has the equity claim, which is in the nature of a residual claim. A residual claim means that the equityholder has a claim on net profit, which is the residual income after everyone else is paid, and the equity in the balance sheet, which constitutes the residual assets after creditors are paid in the event of insolvency or dissolution.

Example 2.5 illustrates the importance of the rule of *limited liability*, which is the most important rule in organizational law. Corporations and other business organizations, such as limited liability companies (LLC), have limited liability as to the equityholders. Without limited liability, Big Bank can seek recourse for its unpaid loan from the equityholder personally (Professor Charles Kingsfield) if Kingsfield Inc. does not have sufficient assets to cover the liability. With limited liability, however, the creditor can only claim against the assets of Kingsfield Inc. This does not mean that the equityholder "wins" when the company fails to do well because Professor Kingsfield would lose the value of his initial equity investment, which is $20,000.

The balance sheet equation is not an arbitrary construct. The balance sheet says: *All assets are subject to an ownership claim from two categories of people—creditors and equityholders*. This statement has an intuitive logic. Throughout this book, we will use the metaphor of a line (a queue).

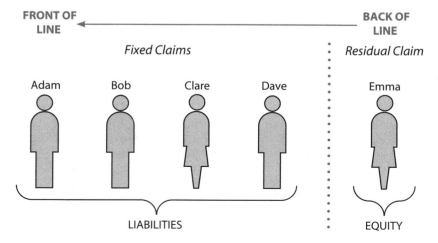

Imagine that Adam, Bob, Clare, Dave, and Emma collectively "own" 100 percent of the assets of the firm (each person has a specific claim on the assets). The fixed claims of Adam, Bob, Clare, and Dave are liabilities; their claims are "fixed" in that the amounts of the liability are a sum certain, e.g., the principal and interest of a loan or the wages of a salary. These claims on the economics assets of the firm may be made by employees, vendors, suppliers, or creditors. The residual claim is held by the equityholder Emma, e.g., shareholders in a corporation and partners in a partnership. The equityholder gets whatever remains after all liabilities are paid.

Equity is a theoretical concept. It is a form of an economic interest in a business or asset whose return is variable because it stands subordinate to prior fixed claims. A good way to think about this is a buffet line: the last person in line takes the greatest risk for the possibility of getting whatever remains, which could be nothing or quite a lot of food.

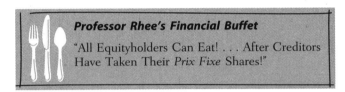

**Professor Rhee's Financial Buffet**

"All Equityholders Can Eat! . . . After Creditors Have Taken Their *Prix Fixe* Shares!"

 There is a *priority* of legal and economic claims against the assets and income of the firm. Creditors always have priority over equityholders in their claims against the assets. Among creditors as well, there may be an order of priority per security interest and collateral on assets.

## F. WORKING CAPITAL AND CAPITAL ASSETS

Thus far, we have divided the balance sheet vertically, as between assets on the left side, and liabilities and equity on the right side.

We can also conceptually divide the balance sheet horizontally, as between (1) current (or short-term) assets and liabilities, and (2) noncurrent (or long-term) assets and liabilities and equity. This is the division between working capital and capital assets. Equity is always long-term capital because it has no maturity, i.e., the corporation has no fixed date obligation to repurchase the stock unlike any debt instrument (e.g., student loans and mortgages have a definite maturity on principal).

**BALANCE SHEETS**

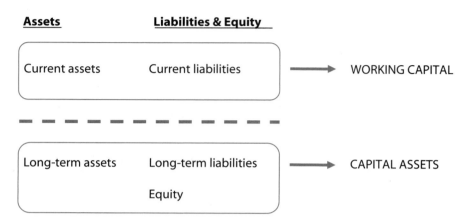

We glean two aspects of the firm's operations by horizontally splitting the balance sheet into working capital and capital assets. Working capital concerns the capital (funds) needed to operate the business on a current basis. Capital assets concern the assets used to generate income on a long-term basis.

*Working capital* measures the funds available to operate the firm's daily business. In operating a business, a firm has to be able to pay its current liabilities, such as utility bills and payroll. Otherwise, it faces a liquidity crisis wherein it cannot pay its bills. Expenses are paid with cash or assets that can be quickly converted to cash. Working capital is a measure of a firm's liquidity, and it is defined as:

$$\text{Working Capital} = \text{Current Assets} - \text{Current Liabilities}$$

*Current assets* are cash and other assets that the company reasonably expects to convert to cash or use up within one year. *Current liabilities* are obligations that a company reasonably expects to pay within one year. For most companies, cash and receivables constitute the bulk of current assets, and payables constitute the bulk of current liabilities. If the company's current liabilities cannot be satisfied through payment, creditors can throw it into insolvency. Note that even good companies can occasionally run into a cash crunch. Thus, working capital is important.

*Capital assets* are long-term assets used to generate income. Capital assets include *property, plant, and equipment* (PP&E), which are long-term tangible assets. Think about an automobile manufacturer such as Toyota or Hyundai. It needs a factory to manufacture cars. Such factories can cost in excess of over a billion dollars. Consider a restaurant operator such as McDonald's, which needs heavy kitchen equipment. Each restaurant may have hundreds of thousands of dollars of equipment. These are long-term assets that are used to generate income on a long-term basis.

Capital assets must be financed by long-term capital: either long-term debt or equity or a combination of both. Long-term debt is debt that matures in the long-term future.

**Capital assets ...... are ...... financed by**

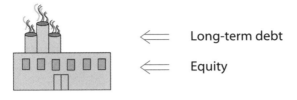

$\Longleftarrow$    Long-term debt

$\Longleftarrow$    Equity

## G. MCDONALD'S BALANCE SHEET

| In millions except per share data | December 31, 2010 | 2009 |
|---|---|---|
| **ASSETS** | | |
| **Current assets** | | |
| Cash and equivalents | $2,387.0 | $1,796.0 |
| Accounts and notes receivable | 1,179.1 | 1,060.4 |
| Inventories, at cost, not in excess of market | 109.9 | 106.2 |
| Prepaid expenses and other current assets | 692.5 | 453.7 |
| **Total current assets** | 4,368.5 | 3,416.3 |
| **Other assets** | | |
| Investments in and advances to affiliates | 1,335.3 | 1,212.73 |
| Goodwill | 2,586.1 | 2,425.2 |
| Miscellaneous | 1,624.7 | 1,639.2 |
| **Total other assets** | 5,546.1 | 5,277.1 |
| **Property and equipment** | | |
| Property and equipment, at cost | 34,482.4 | 33,440.5 |
| Accumulated depreciation and amortization | (12,421.8) | (11,909.0) |
| **Net property and equipment** | 22,060.6 | 21,531.5 |
| **Total assets** | **$31,975.2** | **$30,224.9** |
| **LIABILITIES AND SHAREHOLDERS' EQUITY** | | |
| **Current liabilities** | | |
| Accounts payable | 943.9 | 636.0 |
| Income taxes | 111.3 | 202.4 |
| Other taxes | 275.6 | 277.4 |
| Accrued interest | 200.7 | 195.8 |
| Accrued payroll and other liabilities | 1,384.9 | 1,659.0 |
| Current maturities of long-term debt | 8.3 | 18.1 |
| **Total current liabilities** | 2,924.7 | 2,988.7 |
| **Long-term liabilities** | | |
| Long-term debt | 11,497.0 | 10,560.3 |
| Other long-term liabilities | 1,586.9 | 1,363.1 |
| Deferred income taxes | 1,332.4 | 1,278.9 |
| **Total long-term liabilities** | 14,416.3 | 13,202.3 |
| **Total liabilities** | 17,341.0 | 16,191.09 |
| **Shareholders' equity** | | |
| Common stock, $0.01 par value, authorized | | |
| 3.5 billion shares, issued 1,660.6 million shares | 16.6 | 16.6 |
| Additional paid-in-capital | 5,196.4 | 4,853.9 |
| Retained earnings | 33,811.7 | 31,270.8 |
| Accumulated other comprehensive income | 752.9 | 747.4 |
| Common stock in treasury, at cost; 607.0 and | | |
| 583.9 million shares | (25,143.4) | (22,854.8) |
| **Total shareholders' equity** | 14,634.2 | 14,033.9 |
| **Total liabilities and shareholders' equity** | **$31,975.2** | **$30,224.9** |

**ASSETS**
**Current assets**
    Cash and equivalents
    Accounts receivable and other current
      assets

**Total current assets**

**Other assets**
    Investments in and advances to affiliates
    Goodwill

**Total other assets**

**Property and equipment**
    Property and equipment, at cost
    Accumulated depreciation and amortization

**Net property and equipment**
**Total Assets**

**LIABILITIES AND SHAREHOLDERS' EQUITY**
**Current liabilities**
    Accounts payable and other current
      liabilities

**Total current liabilities**

**Long-term liabilities**
    Long-term liabilities
    Deferred income taxes

**Total long-term liabilities**

**Total liabilities**

**Shareholders' equity**
    Common stock, $0.01 par value,
      authorized 3.5 billion shares, issued
      1,660.6 million shares

    Additional paid-in-capital

    Retained earnings

    Common stock in treasury, at cost; 607.0
      and 545.3 million shares

**Total shareholders' equity**

---

Goodwill—In Chapter 1 we said that goodwill is not recorded in the financial statements. There is a caveat. The firm's goodwill is not recorded: for example, Coca-Cola cannot record the goodwill associated with "Coke" or "Coca-Cola." But if Coca-Cola purchases another company, a certain amount of the purchase price can be said to have been the purchase of the acquired firm's goodwill, which *is* recorded as an intangible asset on the acquirer's balance sheet.

Accumulated depreciation and amortization—Tangible and intangible assets can decline in value, and this line item records the diminution in value, which deducts from the historical cost of the asset.

Deferred income taxes—Some tax liabilities can be deferred in payment under tax laws. Thus, they are a liability, payable at some point in the future.

Authorized and issued shares—Corporate charters must specify the total number of shares the corporation is authorized (legally empowered) to issue. The corporate charter sets this number, and it is usually a large number for practical reasons (the corporation does not want to run out of authorized shares to issue). Corporation will issue to shareholders from the authorized number. Shares that have been issued are called issued shares.

Common stock—Some stock have a par value, which is an arbitrary value, typically very low amount such as $0.01. When shares are issued, the number of issued shares multiplied by the par value is the "common stock." For example, McDonald's issued 1,660 million shares at a $0.01 par value. Therefore, common stock is $16.6 million.

Additional paid-in-capital (APIC)—When shares are issued, the amount in excess of the par value is APIC, thus: Stock Issue Price = Par Value + APIC.

Retained earnings—Net income that is not distributed to shareholders as dividend goes to the retained earning account as shareholder equity.

Treasury stock—Sometimes a company will buy back its stock from shareholders. Treasury stock is the account that notes the number of shares the company bought back and the amount paid. Treasury stock are issued stock, but not outstanding.

## H. CASE APPLICATION

In *Francis v. United Jersey Bank* (Chapter 1), we saw that Lilian Pritchard, a director of the reinsurance broker Pritchard & Baird, was held liable for failing to monitor the company. Below is another edited portion of *Francis v. United Jersey Bank* in which the court described how her two sons, Charles Jr. and William, systematically looted the company under her nose. If Mrs. Pritchard had read the financial statements and understood them, she could have prevented the fraud. In reading the case, think about the true nature of her sons' transactions in light of how the balance sheet works.

*Francis v. United Jersey Bank (Part II)*

432 A.2d 814 (N.J. 1981)

POLLOCK, J.

Contrary to the industry custom of segregating funds, Pritchard & Baird commingled the funds of reinsurers and ceding companies with its own funds. All monies (including commissions, premiums and loss monies) were deposited in a single account. Charles, Sr. began the practice of withdrawing funds from the commingled account in transactions identified on the corporate books as "loans." As long as Charles, Sr. controlled the corporation, the "loans" correlated with corporate profits and were repaid at the end of each year. Starting in 1970, however, Charles, Jr. and William begin to siphon ever-increasing sums from the corporation under the guise of loans. As of January 31, 1970, the "loans" to Charles, Jr. were $230,932 and to William were $207,329. At least by January 31, 1973, the annual increase in the loans exceeded annual corporate revenues. By October 1975, the year of bankruptcy, the "shareholders' loans" had metastasized to a total of $12,333,514.47.

The trial court rejected the characterization of the payments as "loans." No corporate resolution authorized the "loans," and no note or other instrument evidenced the debt. Charles, Jr. and William paid no interest on the amounts received. The "loans" were not repaid or reduced from one year to the next; rather, they increased annually.

The designation of "shareholders' loans" on the balance sheet was an entry to account for the distribution of the premium and loss money to Charles, Sr., Charles, Jr. and William. As the trial court found, the entry was part of a "woefully inadequate and highly dangerous bookkeeping system."

The "loans" to Charles, Jr. and William far exceeded their salaries and financial resources. If the payments to Charles, Jr. and William had been treated as dividends or compensation, then the balance sheets would have shown an excess of liabilities over assets. If the "loans" had been eliminated, the balance sheets would have depicted a corporation not only with a working capital deficit, but also with assets having a fair market value less than its liabilities. The balance sheets for 1970-1975, however, showed an excess of assets over liabilities. This result was achieved by designating the misappropriated funds as "shareholders' loans" and listing them as assets offsetting the deficits. Although the withdrawal of the funds resulted in an obligation of repayment to Pritchard & Baird, the more significant consideration is that the "loans" represented a massive misappropriation of money belonging to the clients of the corporation.

The "loans" were reflected on financial statements that were prepared annually as of January 31, the end of the corporate fiscal year. Although an outside certified public accountant prepared the 1970 financial statement, the corporation prepared only internal financial statements from 1971-1975. In all instances, the statements were simple documents, consisting of three or four $8\frac{1}{2} \times 11$ inch sheets.

The statements of financial condition from 1970 forward demonstrated:

| Year | Working Capital Deficit | Shareholders Loan | Net Brokerage Income |
|---|---|---|---|
| 1970 | $389,022 | $509,941 | $807,229 |
| 1971 | not available | not available | not available |
| 1972 | $1,684,289 | $1,825,911 | $1,546,263 |
| 1973 | $3,506,460 | $3,700,542 | $1,736,349 |
| 1974 | $6,939,007 | $7,080,629 | $876,182 |
| 1975 | $10,176,419 | $10,298,039 | $551,598 |

Those financial statements showed working capital deficits increasing annually in tandem with the amounts that Charles, Jr. and William withdrew as "shareholders' loans." In the last complete year of business (January 31, 1974, to January 31, 1975), "shareholders' loans" and the correlative working capital deficit increased by approximately $3,200,000.

The funding of the "loans" left the corporation with insufficient money to operate. Pritchard & Baird could defer payment on accounts payable because its clients allowed a grace period, generally 30 to 90 days, before the payment was due. During this period, Pritchard & Baird used the funds entrusted to it as a "float" to pay current accounts payable. By recourse to the funds of its clients, Pritchard & Baird not only paid its trade debts, but also funded the payments to Charles, Jr. and William. Thus, Pritchard & Baird was able to meet its obligations as they came due only through the use of clients' funds.

The pattern that emerges from these figures is the substantial increase in the monies appropriated by Charles Pritchard, Jr. and William Pritchard after their father's withdrawal from the business and the sharp decline in the profitability of the operation after his death. This led ultimately to the filing in December, 1975, of an involuntary petition in bankruptcy and the appointments of the plaintiffs as trustees in bankruptcy of Pritchard & Baird.

## QUESTIONS

1. How did Charles Jr. and William loot the company?
2. Assume that in 1970, prior to any shareholders loan being made, the company has total assets of $2,000,000 in cash, liabilities of $1,700,000, and equity of $300,000. What is the effect on the balance sheet after Charles Jr. and William executed a "shareholders loan" of $509,941 (assume that this transactions was legitimate, meaning that Charles Jr. and William were honest officers

having the intent to repay the loans)? What would the new balance sheet look like?

3. Of course, the $509,941 "loan" was not a true loan because Charles Jr. and William never intended to pay the money back. What is the effect of the balance sheet when the fraud is taken into account?

4. Section 402 of the Sarbanes-Oxley Act prohibits public companies governed by the statute to make personal loans to officers and directors. Such loans can result in outright fraud, as in *Francis v. United Jersey Bank*. Outside of theft, are there other problems with such loans? What are the policy implications of corporate loans to officers and directors?

---

Accurate representation of financial information is important to the company, its creditors, and its shareholders. More broadly, it is important to the broader economic system. A sophisticated market economy depends on a certain level of trust, honesty, and integrity in transactions and representations. Thus, accountants play an important gatekeeping function. Accuracy in representation is the hallmark of professional work. Below is a case in which accountants failed in that obligation. The facts speak for themselves. In reading the case, pay particular attention to the representations made in the notes to the financial statements and think about them in the context of the underlying facts.

### United States v. Simon
#### 425 F.2d 796 (2d Cir. 1969)

FRIENDLY, Circuit Judge:

Defendant Carl Simon was a senior partner, Robert Kaiser a junior partner, and Melvin Fishman a senior associate in the internationally known accounting firm of Lybrand, Ross Bros. & Montgomery. They stand convicted after trial by Judge Mansfield and a jury in the District Court for the Southern District of New York under three counts of an indictment charging them with drawing up and certifying a false or misleading financial statement of Continental Vending Machine Corporation (hereafter Continental) for the year ending September 30, 1962. After denying motions for acquittal or a new trial, the judge fined Simon $7,000 and Kaiser and Fishman $5,000 each.

Count One of the indictment was for conspiracy to violate 18 U.S.C. 1001 and 1341 and 32 of the Securities Exchange Act of 1934, 15 U.S.C. 78ff. Section 1001 [which prohibits "makes or uses any false writing or document knowing the same to contain any false, fictitious or fraudulent statement or entry"]. Section 1341 makes criminal the use of the mails in aid of "any scheme or artifice to defraud." Section 32 of the Securities Exchange Act renders criminal the willful and knowing making of a statement in any required report which is false or misleading with respect to any material fact.

### I.

The trial hinged on transactions between Continental and an affiliate, Valley Commercial Corporation (hereafter "Valley"). The dominant figure in both was

Harold Roth, who was president of Continental, supervised the day-to-day operations of Valley, and owned about 25% of the stock of each company.

Valley, which was run by Roth out of a single office on Continental's premises, was engaged in lending money at interest to Continental and others in the vending machine business. Continental would issue negotiable notes to Valley, which would endorse these in blank and use them as collateral for drawing on two lines of credit, of $1 million each, at Franklin National Bank ("Franklin") and Meadowbrook National Bank ("Meadowbrook"), and would then transfer to Continental the discounted amount of the notes. These transactions, beginning as early as 1956, gave rise to what is called "the Valley payable." By the end of fiscal 1962, the amount of this was $1,029,475, of which $543,345 was due within the year.

In addition to the Valley payable, there was what is known as the "Valley receivable," which resulted from Continental loans to Valley. Most of these stemmed from Roth's custom, dating from mid-1957, of using Continental and Valley as sources of cash to finance his transactions in the stock market.[3] At the end of fiscal 1962, the amount of the Valley receivable was $3.5 million, and by February 15, 1963, the date of certification, it has risen to $3.9 million. The Valley payable could not be offset, or "netted," against the Valley receivable since, as stated, Continental's obligations to Valley were in the form of negotiable notes which Valley had endorsed in blank to the two banks and used as collateral to obtain the cash which it then lent to Continental.

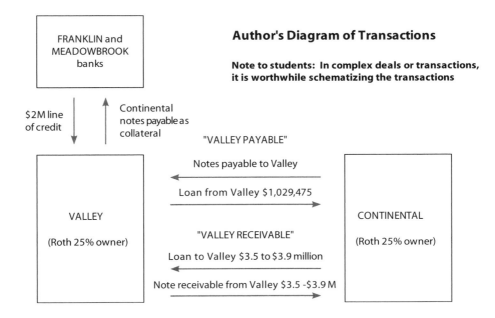

Harold

In complex deals or transactions, it is worthwhile schematizing the transactions

---

3. From mid-1957 until January 1963 Continental thus advanced more than $16 million to Valley and Valley advanced more than $13 million to Roth. Of the latter sum the payment of approximately $6.5 million would have resulted in an overdraft in Valley's account but for the deposit of a Continental check on the same day.

By the certification date, the auditors had learned that Valley was not in a position to repay its debt, and it was accordingly arranged that collateral would be posted. Roth and members of his family transferred their equity in certain securities to Arthur Field, Continental's counsel, as trustee to secure Roth's debt to Valley and Valley's debt to Continental. Some 80% of these securities consisted of Continental stock and convertible debentures.

The 1962 financial statements of Continental, which were dismal by any standard,[4] reported the status of the Valley transactions as follows:

**ASSETS**

| | |
|---|---|
| Current assets | |
| Accounts and notes receivable: | |
| Valley Commercial Corp., affiliate (Note 2) | $2,143,335 |
| Noncurrent accounts and notes receivables: | |
| Valley Commercial Corp., affiliate (Note 2) | 1,400,000 |

**LIABILITIES**

| | |
|---|---|
| Current liabilities | |
| Long-term debt, portion due within one year | $8,203,788 |
| Long-term debt (Note 7) | |
| Valley Commercial Corp., affiliate (Note 2) | 486,130 |

**NOTES TO CONSOLIDATED FINANCIAL STATEMENTS**

2. The amount receivable from Valley Commercial Corp. (an affiliated company of which Mr. Harold Roth is an officer, director and stockholder) bears interest at 12% a year. Such amount, less the balance of the notes payable to that company, is secured by the assignment to the Company of Valley's equity in certain marketable securities. As of February 15, 1963, the amount of such equity at current market quotations exceeded the net amount receivable.

7. . . . The amounts of long-term debt, including the portion due within one year, on which interest is payable currently or has been discounted in advance, are as follows:

| | |
|---|---|
| Valley Commercial Corp., affiliate | $1,029,475 |

The case against the defendants can be best encapsulated by comparing what Note 2 stated and what the Government claims it would have stated if defendants had included what they knew:

2. The amount receivable from Valley Commercial Corp. (an affiliated company of which Mr. Harold Roth is an officer, director and stockholder), which bears interest at 12% a year, was uncollectible at September 30, 1962, since Valley had loaned approximately the same amount to Mr. Roth who was unable to pay. Since that date Mr. Roth and others have pledged as security for the repayment of his obligation to Valley and its obligation to Continental (now $3,900,000, against which Continental's liability to Valley cannot be offset) securities which, as of February 15, 1963, had a market value of $2,978,000. Approximately 80% of such securities are stock and convertible debentures of the Company.

---

4. The Company reported an operating loss of $867,000 and write-offs of some $3 million as compared with after-tax profits of $1,249,000 in the preceding year. Even with the inclusion of $2,143,335 of the total Valley receivable of $3,543,335, current assets, $20,102,504, barely exceeded current liabilities, $19,043,262.

II.

In 1961 and 1962, the cash payments giving rise to the Valley receivable continued to be frequent, in round amounts, and without written explanation. Moreover, the balance in the Valley receivable account characteristically was parabolic, rising after the end of one fiscal year and falling prior to the end of the next. The payments and repayments and the year-end balances for 1958-1962 are shown by the following table:

| Year | Advances to Valley | Repayment by Valley | Receivable at Year-End |
|------|--------------------|--------------------|------------------------|
| 1958 | $3,356,239 | $2,583,172 | $-0- |
| 1959 | 4,586,000 | 3,510,451 | 384,402 |
| 1960 | 2,511,000 | 2,670,500 | 397,996 |
| 1961 | 2,390,674 | 1,520,000 | 848,006 |
| 1962 | 4,708,000 | 1,986,500 | 3,543,335 |

[A]ccording to Roth, he had contacted Simon in December and said that although Valley had a net worth of $2 million, it was not in a position to repay its $3.5 million debt to Continental as it had lent him approximately the same amount which he was unable to repay. He suggested that he secure the indebtedness with his equity in stocks, bonds and other securities of Continental and Hoffman International if this would be acceptable. Roth called Simon some ten days later and received the latter's assent. On December 31 Roth placed Arthur Field, counsel for Continental, in charge of preparing the assignments.

Late in January 1963 Fishman visited Roth and showed him a draft of Note 2 substantially identical with the final form; he told Roth that Simon wanted to see him. They met in the Lybrand office on February 6. Defendants concede that at this meeting Roth informed Simon that Valley could not repay Continental and offered to post securities for the Valley receivable, and also to post as collateral a mortgage on his house and furnishings. Simon agreed that if adequate collateral were posted, a satisfactory legal opinion were obtained, and Continental's board approved the transactions, Lybrand could certify Continental's statements without reviewing Valley's, which still were not available.

On February 12 Roth told Simon that Field had the collateral ready for verification. [T]he bulk of the collateral would consist of an equity in Continental stock and debentures. Kaiser made a number of calls having reference to this information and prepared notes of them which he later showed Simon. At Kaiser's request Field prepared a letter stating that $3.5 million in collateral was being posted and outlining the mechanics of the collateralization. On the following business day, Simon called to request that Field amend the letter to include an opinion that the collateral adequately secured the Valley receivable; the amended letter was sent on February 15 or 18. Meanwhile Field had informed Simon and Kaiser on February 13 that Continental's board of directors had disapproved of the loans to Valley.

The financial statements were mailed as part of Continental's annual report on February 20. By that time the market value of the collateral had declined some $270,000 from its February 15 value. The value of the collateral fell an additional

$640,000 on February 21. When the market reopened on February 25 after the long Washington's birthday recess, it fell another $2 million and was worth only $395,000. The same day a Continental check to the Internal Revenue Service bounced. Two days later the Government padlocked the plant and the American Stock Exchange suspended trading in Continental stock. Investigations by the SEC and bankruptcy rapidly ensued.

## III.

The defendants called eight expert independent accountants, an impressive array of leaders of the profession. They testified generally that, except for the error with respect to netting, the treatment of the Valley receivable in Note 2 was in no way inconsistent with generally accepted accounting principles or generally accepted auditing standards, since it made all the informative disclosures reasonably necessary for fair presentation of the financial position of Continental as of the close of the 1962 fiscal year. Specifically, they testified that neither generally accepted accounting principles nor generally accepted auditing standards required disclosure of the make-up of the collateral or of the increase of the receivable after the closing date of the balance sheet, although three of the eight stated that in light of hindsight they would have preferred that the make-up of the collateral be disclosed. The witnesses likewise testified that disclosure of the Roth borrowings from Valley was not required, and seven of the eight were of the opinion that such disclosure would be inappropriate. The principal reason given for this last view was that the balance sheet was concerned solely with presenting the financial position of the company under audit; since the Valley receivable was adequately secured in the opinion of the auditors and was broken out and shown separately as a loan to an affiliate with the nature of the affiliation disclosed, this was all that the auditors were required to do. To go further and reveal what Valley had done with the money would be to put into the balance sheet things that did not properly belong there; moreover, it would create a precedent which would imply that it was the duty of an auditor to investigate each loan to an affiliate to determine whether the money had found its way into the pockets of an officer of the company under audit, an investigation that would ordinarily be unduly wasteful of time and money.

Defendants asked for two instructions which, in substance, would have told the jury that a defendant could be found guilty only if, according to generally accepted accounting principles, the financial statements as a whole did not fairly present the financial condition of Continental at September 30, 1962, and then only if his departure from accepted standards was due to willful disregard of those standards with knowledge of the falsity of the statements and an intent to deceive. The judge declined to give these instructions.

Defendants contend that the charge and refusal to charge constituted error. We think the judge was right in refusing to make the accountants' testimony so nearly a complete defense. The critical test according to the charge was the same as that which the accountants testified was critical. We do not think the jury was also required to accept the accountants' evaluation whether a given fact was material to overall fair presentation. Such evidence may be highly persuasive, but it is not conclusive, and so the trial judge correctly charged.

Defendants next contend that, particularly in light of the expert testimony, the evidence was insufficient to allow the jury to consider the failure to disclose Roth's borrowings from Valley, the make-up of the collateral, or the post-balance sheet increase in the Valley receivable. [I]t simply cannot be true that an accountant is under no duty to disclose what he knows when he has reason to believe that, to a material extent, a corporation is being operated not to carry out its business in the interest of all the stockholders but for the private benefit of its president. For a court to say that all this is immaterial as a matter of law if only such loans are thought to be collectible would be to say that independent accountants have no responsibility to reveal known dishonesty by a high corporate officer. If certification does not at least imply that the corporation has not been looted by insiders so far as the accountants know, or, if it has been, that the diversion has been made good beyond peradventure (or adequately reserved against) and effective steps taken to prevent a recurrence, it would mean nothing, and the reliance placed on it by the public would be a snare and a delusion. Generally accepted accounting principles instruct an accountant what to do in the usual case where he has no reason to doubt that the affairs of the corporation are being honestly conducted. Once he has reason to believe that this basic assumption is false, an entirely different situation confronts him. At least this must be true when the dishonesty he has discovered is not some minor peccadillo but a diversion so large as to imperil if not destroy the very solvency of the enterprise.

Turning to the failure to describe the collateral, defendants concede that they could not properly have certified statements showing the Valley receivable as an asset when they knew it was uncollectible. That was why Roth proposed collateralization and they accepted it. As men experienced in financial matters, they must have known that the one kind of property ideally unsuitable to collateralize a receivable whose collectibility was essential to avoiding an excess of current liabilities over current assets and a two-thirds reduction in capital already reduced would be securities of the very corporation whose solvency was at issue—particularly when the 1962 report revealed a serious operating loss. Failure to disclose that 80% of the "marketable securities" by which the Valley receivable was said to be "secured" were securities of Continental was thus altogether unlike a failure to state how much collateral were bonds or stocks of General Motors and how much of U.S. Steel. Indeed one of the defense experts testified that disclosure would be essential if Continental stock constituted more than 50% of the collateral.

Finding that the evidence was sufficient for submission to the jury and that no legal errors were committed, we must let the verdict stand.

Affirmed.

## QUESTIONS

1. Continental was experiencing a cash flow problem. Why? What specific figures in the opinion highlight the problem?
2. What is the role of the notes to the financial statement in this case?
3. What crucial information did the accountants fail to disclose?
4. On what legal and factual grounds did the court reject the testimonies of the defendant's expert witnesses? Why do you think that such "an impressive array of leaders of the profession" would testify in defense of the accountant here?
5. What is the fundamental economic problem of securing Valley's debt to Continental with Roth's securities of Continental?

The case below illustrates the difference between market value and book value of equity. This is a crucial distinction to understand because a lawyer must understand that financial statements do not necessarily reflect economic reality. The facts of the case and concepts therein are complicated, but the case is well worth working through. In reading the case, think about the relationship among financial statements, market valuation, and the law of mergers and acquisitions.

**Author's Summary of Facts:** The following Delaware case, *Klang v. Smith's Food & Drug Centers, Inc.*, involved a transaction to purchase Smith's Food & Drug Centers, Inc. ("SFD") by The Yucaipa Companies ("Yucaipa"). Such transactions can be complex. Under this merger agreement, the transaction had three steps: (1) SFD would issue to Yucaipa over 3 million shares of SFD in exchange for Yucaipa stock; (2) SFD would borrow money from creditors; (3) with this money, SFD would repurchase from outside shareholders up to 50 percent of its shares at $36 per share (not including shares it just issued to Yucaipa), as well as 3 million shares of preferred stock held by the company's founding family. The transaction is schematized below.

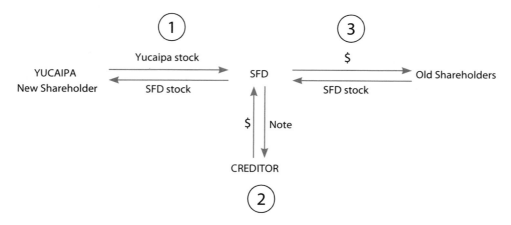

In this way, SFD buys out many "old shareholders" with borrowed money, and Yucaipa would become the majority controlling "new shareholder."

The business problem concerned whether SFD was sufficiently solvent to repurchase its stock with borrowed money—see steps (2) and (3). The legality of such repurchases is governed by corporate law. Delaware General Corporation Law (DGCL) §160(a) provides:

> (a) Every corporation may purchase . . . its own shares; provided, however, that *no corporation shall*:
> (1) *Purchase or redeem its own shares . . . when the capital of the corporation is impaired or when such purchase or redemption would cause any impairment of the capital of the corporation. . . .*

A repurchase impairs capital if the funds used in the repurchase exceed the amount of the corporation's "surplus." DGCL §154 provides:

> Any corporation may . . . determine that only a part of the consideration . . . received by the corporation for . . . its capital stock . . . shall be capital. . . . The excess . . . of the net assets of the corporation over the amount so determined to be capital shall be surplus. Net assets means the amount by which total assets exceed total liabilities.

Surplus means net assets minus the par value of the corporation's issued stock. A corporation may determine that only a part of the consideration received from the sale of its stock shall be capital. Typically, capital is a small amount. For example, if a company issues stock at $10.00 per share, it may designate only $0.01 as capital and the remaining $9.99 in additional paid in capital (note that McDonald's has "common stock," the label to designate capital, of only $16.6 million, at par value of $0.01 per share, and compare this amount to the book equity of $14 billion).

We can summarize these legal requirements into these equations:

DGCL §154:        Net Assets = Assets − Liabilities

DGCL §154:        Net Assets = Surplus + Capital

DGCL §154:        Surplus = Net Assets − Capital

DGCL §160(a):     Surplus ≥ Repurchase Price

The issue in the case is easily stated. SFD had a negative net worth (negative book value) in its balance sheet, which necessarily means that SFD's surplus (the largest component of equity) is negative as well, at least on its books. The implication is that liability is greater than assets in the books since equity is negative. With an apparent negative surplus, SFD could not repurchase its stock; the crucial step in the transaction could not be legally executed. However, the court took a different view, and its reasoning relied on the difference between book value and market value, the difference between the accountant's view of equity value and the market's view. The legal question depends on the meaning of "surplus."

SFD hired an investment bank, Houlihan Lokey Howard & Zukin ("Houlihan"), to provide a solvency opinion. Houlihan opined that, despite SFD's negative book value, the company was solvent, meaning that the market value of equity was actually positive. If equity is actually positive, then there *is* a surplus from which to repurchase stock. Based on this opinion, the board proceeded to execute the stock repurchase. Dissenting shareholders sued. When reading this case, you should pay attention to the underlying accounting issue concerning the equity of the balance sheet.

### *Klang v. Smith's Food & Drug Centers*
702 A.2d 150 (Del. 1997)

VEASEY, Chief Justice:

Plaintiff asked the Court of Chancery to rescind the transactions in question as violative of Section 160. As we understand it, plaintiff's position breaks down into two analytically distinct arguments. First, he contends that SFD's balance sheets constitute conclusive evidence of capital impairment. He argues that the negative net worth that appeared on SFD's books following the repurchase compels us to find a violation of Section 160. Second, he suggests that even allowing the Board to "go behind the balance sheet" to calculate surplus does not save the transactions from violating Section 160. In connection with this claim, he attacks the SFD Board's off-balance-sheet method of calculating surplus on the theory that it does not adequately take into account all of SFD's assets and liabilities.

*SFD's balance sheets do not establish a violation of 8 Del. C. §160*

In an April 25, 1996 proxy statement, the SFD Board released a pro forma balance sheet showing that the merger and self-tender offer would result in a deficit to surplus on SFD's books of more than $100 million. A balance sheet the SFD Board issued shortly after the transactions confirmed this result. Plaintiff asks us to adopt an interpretation of 8 Del. C. §160 whereby balance-sheet net worth is controlling for purposes of determining compliance with the statute. Defendants do not dispute that SFD's books showed a negative net worth in the wake of its transactions with Yucaipa, but argue that corporations should have the presumptive right to revalue assets and liabilities to comply with Section 160.

Plaintiff advances an erroneous interpretation of Section 160. We understand that the books of a corporation do not necessarily reflect the current values of its assets and liabilities. Among other factors, unrealized appreciation or depreciation can render book numbers inaccurate. It is unrealistic to hold that a corporation is bound by its balance sheets for purposes of determining compliance with Section 160. Accordingly, we adhere to the principles allowing corporations to revalue properly its assets and liabilities to show a surplus and thus conform to the statute.

It is helpful to recall the purpose behind Section 160. The General Assembly enacted the statute to prevent boards from draining corporations of assets to the detriment of creditors and the long-term health of the corporation. That a corporation has not yet realized or reflected on its balance sheet the appreciation of assets is irrelevant to this concern. Regardless of what a balance sheet that has not been updated may show, an actual, though unrealized, appreciation reflects real economic value that the corporation may borrow against or that creditors may claim or levy upon. Allowing corporations to revalue assets and liabilities to reflect current realities complies with the statute and serves well the policies behind this statute.

*The SFD Board appropriately revalued corporate assets to comply with 8 Del. C. §160*

Plaintiff contends that SFD's repurchase of shares violated Section 160 even without regard to the corporation's balance sheets. Plaintiff claims that the SFD Board was not entitled to rely on the solvency opinion of Houlihan, which showed that the transactions would not impair SFD's capital given a revaluation of corporate assets. The argument is that the methods that underlay the solvency opinion were inappropriate as a matter of law because they failed to take into account all of SFD's assets and liabilities. In addition, plaintiff suggests that the SFD Board's resolution of May 17, 1996 itself shows that the transactions impaired SFD's capital, and that therefore we must find a violation of 8 Del. C. §160. We disagree, and hold that the SFD Board revalued the corporate assets under appropriate methods. Therefore the self-tender offer complied with Section 160, notwithstanding errors that took place in the drafting of the resolution.

On May 17, 1996, Houlihan released its solvency opinion to the SFD Board, expressing its judgment that the merger and self-tender offer would not impair SFD's capital. Houlihan reached this conclusion by comparing SFD's "Total Invested Capital" of $1.8 billion—a figure Houlihan arrived at by valuing SFD's assets under the "market multiple" approach—with SFD's long-term debt of $1.46 billion. This comparison yielded an approximation of SFD's "concluded equity value" equal to $346 million, a figure clearly in excess of the outstanding par value of SFD's stock. Thus, Houlihan concluded, the transactions would not violate 8 Del. C. §160.

Plaintiff contends that Houlihan's analysis relied on inappropriate methods to mask a violation of Section 160. Noting that 8 Del. C. §154 defines "net assets" as "the amount by which total assets exceeds total liabilities," plaintiff argues that Houlihan's analysis is erroneous as a matter of law because of its failure to calculate "total assets" and "total liabilities" as separate variables. In a related argument, plaintiff claims that the analysis failed to take into account all of SFD's liabilities, i.e., that Houlihan neglected to consider current liabilities in its comparison of SFD's "Total Invested Capital" and long-term debt. Plaintiff contends that the SFD Board's resolution proves that adding current liabilities into the mix shows a violation of Section 160. The resolution declared the value of SFD's assets to be $1.8 billion, and stated that its "total liabilities" would not exceed $1.46 billion after the transactions with Yucaipa. As noted, the $1.46 billion figure described only the value of SFD's long-term debt. Adding in SFD's $372 million in current liabilities, plaintiff argues, shows that the transactions impaired SFD's capital.

We believe that plaintiff reads too much into Section 154. The statute simply defines "net assets" in the course of defining "surplus." It does not mandate a "facts and figures balancing of assets and liabilities" to determine by what amount, if any, total assets exceeds total liabilities. The statute is merely definitional. It does not require any particular method of calculating surplus, but simply prescribes factors that any such calculation must include. Although courts may not determine compliance with Section 160 except by methods that fully take into account the assets and liabilities of the corporation, Houlihan's methods were not erroneous as a matter of law simply because they used Total Invested Capital and long-term debt as analytical categories rather than "total assets" and "total liabilities."

The record contains, in the form of the Houlihan opinion, substantial evidence that the transactions complied with Section 160. Therefore, we defer to the board's determination of surplus, and hold that SFD's self-tender offer did not violate 8 Del. C. §160.

## QUESTIONS

1. The court states that "the books of a corporation do not necessarily reflect the current values of its assets and liabilities." Why?
2. The court identifies different ways to calculate net assets, which may produce different answers. What are two ways?
3. What role did the investment bank, Houlihan, play in the transaction and the litigation?

## ESSENTIAL TERMS

Additional paid in capital (APIC)
Asset
Balance sheet formula
Book value
Capital assets
Common stock
Creditor
Current (short-term) assets
Current (short-term) liabilities
Equity
Equityholder
Fair market value ("market value")
Historical cost
Intangible asset
Liabilities
Long-term debt
Marked-to-market
Market capitalization ("market cap")

Member's interest
Negative equity (negative net worth)
Net assets
Net asset value (NAV)
Net worth
Noncurrent (long-term) assets
Noncurrent (long-term) liabilities
Partner's capital
Partner's capital account
Price-to-book ratio (P/B)
Property, plant and equipment (PP&E)
Residual claim
Retained earnings
Shareholder's equity
Tangible asset
Treasury stock
Working capital

## KEY CONCEPTS

1. The balance sheet equation must always hold: Assets = Liabilities + Equity.
2. The balance sheet equation encapsulates the idea that all assets of the firm are claimed by creditors and equityholders.
3. An asset is a probable future economic benefit obtained or controlled by an entity as a result of past transactions or events.
4. A liability is a probable future sacrifice of economic benefit arising from present obligations of a particular entity to transfer assets or to provide services to another entity in the future as a result of past transactions or events.
5. Equity is the residual interest in assets that remains after deducting liabilities.
6. There are many different terminologies used for equity, depending on the context.
7. As a matter of general accounting principle, the balance sheet records values at historical cost and does not adjust assets and liabilities to fair market values. However, accounting rules may permit periodic adjustments to the values of assets and liabilities. These rules are beyond the scope of this book, but the attorney should be aware that they exist.
8. The balance sheet can be conceptualized as having two parts: working capital and capital assets. Capital assets are typically financed by long-term debt and/or equity. Working capital is current assets and current liabilities.
9. Working capital is a measure of liquidity, and it is calculated as current assets minus current liabilities.

## REVIEW QUESTIONS

1. In what way can reviewing a balance sheet at any given time be misleading as to providing an accurate picture of the firm?
2. Is it possible to have a negative book value and a positive market value of equity? If so, what factors could account for this discrepancy?
3. What does it mean that an equityholder is a residual claimant?

*Questions on McDonald's balance sheet*

4. What are McDonald's capital assets? How are they financed?
5. Calculate McDonald's working capital.
6. Assess McDonald's liquidity as measured by working capital.
7. In 2010, the statement of shareholder's equity shows that McDonald's issued 14.7 million shares from Treasury stock due to exercise of options as a part of its stock option compensation plan, and it received $359.9 million as a result of the exercise in options. If so, how many shares did McDonald's buy back from shareholders? What is the average price at which McDonald's bought shares back?

# INCOME STATEMENT

## A. INCOME STATEMENT EQUATION

What is the fundamental activity of any business enterprise? A business entity sells goods or services. It takes inputs and makes outputs. For instance, a beverage company like The Coca Cola Company purchases various ingredients and labor (inputs) and manufactures Coke (output). If it sells the soda for more than the price of the inputs, it earns a profit. In our continuing hypothetical on Kingsfield Inc., Professor Kingsfield buys beer from a distributor (input) and sells it in a nice tavern environment to patrons in Cambridge (output). These activities are tracked by the income statement.

$$\text{Revenue} - \text{Expenses} = \text{Net Income}$$

Revenue is also sometimes called *sales*. Revenue is defined as the increase in the equity (in the balance sheet) caused by services rendered or the sale of goods. In other words, after deducting expenses, the remaining revenue (which is called net profit) adds to the equity in the balance sheet.

> **F.Y.I.** *Earnings* and *profit* and *net profit* are synonymous with net income. When these terms are modified, however, they do not refer to net income. For example, *earnings before interest and tax* (EBIT) and *operating profit* are not the same as net income even though they reference "earnings" and "profit." This loose use of these terms can be confusing, but these jargon-driven distinctions are important because knowledgeable professionals understand these differences and assume others do as well.

## B. ACCRUAL ACCOUNTING

Financial statements are prepared under the principle of *accrual accounting*, which is consistent with the matching principle. The *matching principle* means that revenue and expenses are matched and recognized at the time of the transaction, and not when cash is received or disbursed. Under accrual accounting, then, the flow of cash into or out of the firm may not be perfectly correlated to revenue, expense, and profit. Counting cash makes accounting simpler (the payment or receipt of cash leaves little ambiguity and exercise of discretion), but cash accounting would also be more misleading as to the nature of the revenue, expense, and profit of the firm because transactions are not matched in a way that reflects economic reality. The following example illustrates the point.

EXAMPLE 3.1

### Benefits of accrual accounting and the matching principle

On New Year's Eve, James Hart, an earnest 1L student, went to Kingsfield's Tavern to celebrate. Hart said, "Professor Kingsfield, I want a pint of Guinness, but I don't have any money. My student loan will be disbursed two weeks from now, when spring semester starts. Can I get a drink and put my bill on the tab?" Professor Kingsfield gazed upon Hart with steely eyes and said, "I agree to sell you a drink for $5.00. By accepting this pint of beer, we now have a binding contract. Your 'bar tab' will be recorded by my accountant as an account receivable—an I.O.U. so to speak in plebeian parlance. Enjoy your Guinness at your leisure for you shall not have the luxury of leisure when I have you for Contracts II in the spring semester."

Two weeks later in the New Year, Hart went to Kingsfield's Tavern to pay his $5 bar tab from the previous year. He just learned that he got an "A" in Professor Kingsfield's Contract I class, and so he celebrated by consuming another pint. This time, he paid $5.00 in cash. The pint of Guinness served to Hart cost Kingsfield Inc. $3.00.

The transactions took place in these time periods.

|  | Old Year | New Year |
|---|---|---|
| Hart's consumption of beer (sale) | + One beer | + One beer |
| Kingsfield's loss of beer through sale (expense) | − One beer | − One beer |
| Hart's cash payment for beer sale | None | Two payments |

Let's see the results from cash and accrual accounting (assume that there are no taxes).

|  |  |  | Old Year | New Year |
|---|---|---|---|---|
| Cash accounting: | ⟶ | Revenue | $ 0.00 | $ 10.00 |
|  |  | Expenses | 3.00 | 3.00 |
|  |  | *Net loss/profit* | −3.00 | 7.00 |
|  |  |  |  |  |
| Accrual accounting: | ⟶ | Revenue | $5.00 | $5.00 |
|  |  | Expenses | 3.00 | 3.00 |
|  |  | *Net profit* | 2.00 | 2.00 |

Which system of accounting is better? Why?

Cash accounting produces misleading results that do not reflect the actual economic reality. In the above example, it ignores the fact that there were two discrete economic transactions: a consummated contract for the sale of beer in Old Year, and another in New Year. While cash accounting is simpler in that it keeps track of the receipt of cash, it is often misleading because the receipt of cash may have no relationship to the underlying economics of the transaction. Accurate representation of the economics of the transaction is important. Accrual accounting better matches revenue, expenses, and profit or loss.

Yet, accrual accounting is not perfect either. It requires assumptions about future payments, which can turn out to be wrong. Also, accrual accounting may allow certain discretion in terms of recognizing transactions, and such discretion can lead to uncertainty or abuse.

---

 **STOP AND THINK** What are some of the ways in which revenue and expense recognition can be abused? Is timing of revenue and expense recognition important? Why is matching revenue and expense important?

---

## C. HOW THE INCOME STATEMENT WORKS

Let's break down the income statement further. The income statement generally identifies the following line items. Because a firm's earnings are such an important measure of firm value, some of these items are heavily used in financial analysis. The items in the income statement can be categorized into the following items, though the labeling of these items in individual income statements may vary significantly.

| | |
|---|---|
| Revenue ................................. | sales of goods and services |
| – Cost of goods sold ............................ | called "COGS," including the direct cost of the production of the goods or services, including supplies and payroll attributable to the direct production of the goods or services |
| Gross profit ......................................... | revenue minus COGS |
| – Sales, general & administrative .......... | called "SG&A," operating expenses not connected to the direct production of specific goods and services, including overhead and administrative expenses (sometimes also called "G&A") |
| Operating profit (income) .................... | operating income is revenue minus operating expenses (COGS + SG&A) |
| – Interest expense ............................... | expense from the payment of interest to creditors (lenders) |
| Pretax profit ......................................... | taxable income |
| – Tax expense ....................................... | money paid to the government in tax (Uncle Sam gets its slice of the economic pie!) |
| Net profit (or loss) ............................... | residual income after deduction of all expenses from revenue |

The items Revenue through Operating profit (income) are grouped under **Operation**; Interest expense and Pretax profit are grouped under **Debt**; Net profit (or loss) is grouped under **Equity**.

*Earnings before interest and tax (EBIT)* is synonymous with operating profit, except that EBIT may include special or one-off (nonrecurring) revenue or expense items not associated with core operations.

*Operating profit* is profit from operations and would not include special or nonrecurring revenue or expenses. If there are none, then operating profit and EBIT are the same.

*Earnings before interest, tax, depreciation, and amortization (EBITDA)* is EBIT plus depreciation and amortization, which are noncash expense items. EBITDA is a rough approximation of the amount of cash flow generated by the company's operations.

The income statement is organized in a way that the claims on the operating side (COGS and SG&A) are deducted first. This gives us gross profit and operating profit, which are measures of profitability before the claims of the government (taxes) and the company's financiers (creditors and shareholders) are deducted.

There is an intuitive logic to the income statement. Like the balance sheet, there is a line of people who have economic claims on the economic benefit from the sale of goods and services. This line is formed in a specific priority. Let's see what that line looks like.

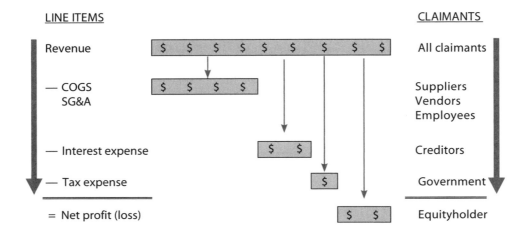

Net profit is the residual income claimed by the equityholders after all expenses are paid to other claimants including employees, vendors, creditors, and the government.

Net income can be distributed to shareholders in the form of a *dividend*, which is a cash payment to shareholders. If it is not distributed to shareholders but is instead retained by the company, it is recorded in the balance sheet as *retained earnings* under equity. Since the balance sheet must always balance, an increase in retained earnings must also correspond to an increase in assets. In this case, cash or account receivables increases since the company now has more cash representing the profit made. Note that the residual need not be a profit. No firm is guaranteed a profit. If revenue is smaller than the claims on it, there is a net loss. Of course, the equity-holder must assume this net loss.

**EXAMPLE 3.2**

---

### Relationship between income statement and balance sheet

At the start of the year, ABC Corp. has assets of $100,000 (property), liabilities of $80,000, and equity capital of $20,000. During the year, it sells $90,000 of goods, which cost the company $60,000 in expenses. All revenue and expenses are *in cash*. There are no other expenses associated with this revenue. Tax on pretax profit is 33 percent. What is the net income? How is the balance sheet adjusted after accounting for these sales?

| Income Statement | | | Balance Sheet (Start of Year) | | | |
|---|---|---|---|---|---|---|
| Revenue | 90,000 | | Assets | | Liabilities | 80,000 |
| Expense | 60,000 | | *Property* | 100,000 | Equity | |
| Pretax profit | 30,000 | | | | *Capital* | 20,000 |
| Taxes | 10,000 | | Assets | 100,000 | L&E | 100,000 |

| | | | Balance Sheet (End of Year) | | | |
|---|---|---|---|---|---|---|
| Net income | 20,000 | | Assets | | Liabilities | 80,000 |
| | | | *Property* | 100,000 | Equity | |
| | | | Cash | 20,000 | *Capital* | 20,000 |
| | | | | | *Retained earnings* | 20,000 |
| | | | Assets | 120,000 | L&E | 120,000 |

If there is an addition to assets, there must be a corresponding addition to either liabilities or equity. In other words, someone in the firm must own the additional $20,000 in cash. The claimant is either a creditor or an equityholder. In this case, it is the equityholder since the $20,000 represents net income. Creditors only have their fixed contractual claims against the firm.

## D. DEPRECIATION AND AMORTIZATION

It is natural to think about revenue and expenses (a firm's economic inflow and outflow) in cash. As seen in Example 3.1, the inflow or outflow of cash can be delayed for a number of reasons such as when a customer purchases a good or service but has yet to pay (account receivable); when the firm owes money for the receipt of a good or service (account payable); or when a tax liability does not need to be paid at the time. Ultimately, the firm expects to convert its receivables or payables into cash. However, sometimes expenses are simply noncash items.

Many assets do not hold their value in a constant manner. Some assets may increase in value due to various economic factors, e.g., securities such as stocks and bonds. Other assets may decrease in value due to various economic factors, e.g., the diminishment of value of money due to inflation. Still other assets may decrease in value due to use, e.g., cars, computers, equipment, software, patents, and factories. Hyundai's and Honda's factories depreciate in value. McDonald's heavy restaurant equipment depreciates in value. General Electric's enterprise software slowly becomes obsolete. These are real expenses (costs) of running a business, and they must be recognized, even though the company is not paying for the expense in the form of cash payments akin to wages, utility bills, and insurance premiums.

*Depreciation* is the diminishment of value of *tangible assets* such as physical plant, property, or equipment. *Amortization* is the diminishment of value of *intangible assets* such as patents and goodwill. Depreciation and amortization (D&A) connote a common idea of a gradual loss of value in an asset.

D&A are costs that are recognized as expenses in the income statement. Importantly, accounting principles allow various methods to depreciate or amortize assets. With respect to depreciation policy, they may allow a firm and its accountant to choose the best or most appropriate methods. Let's see how some common depreciation methods work.

*Straight Line Method.* The asset is depreciated by a fixed amount over its life. For example, assume that a railway boxcar was bought for $50,000 and has a useful life of 10 years with no residual value. Under a straight-line method, the firm's depreciation expense is $5,000 per year for the next 10 years.

*Accelerated Depreciation.* There are several ways to accelerate depreciation. Let's consider just one such method—the declining balance method. The asset is depreciated by a constant percentage of the purchase cost of the asset adjusted each subsequent year for depreciation. For example, the above railway boxcar can be depreciated by 40 percent of the adjusted book value each year.

| Year | Starting asset value net of depreciation | | Depreciation rate | | Depreciation expense | Ending asset value (net of depreciation) |
|---|---|---|---|---|---|---|
| | A | × | B | = | C | (A − C) |
| 1 | 50,000 | × | 40% | = | 20,000 | 30,000 |
| 2 | 30,000 | × | 40% | = | 12,000 | 18,000 |
| 3 | 18,000 | × | 40% | = | 7,200 | 10,800 |

In the declining balance method, depreciation is accelerated. Compare Year 1 depreciation of $20,000 with Year 2 depreciation of $12,000.

EXAMPLE 3.3

---

**Effect of depreciation policy on income statement**

Obviously, since depreciation is an expense item, the method of depreciation affects the income statement. Suppose the above railway company has revenue of $100,000, non-depreciation expense of $75,000, and tax rate of 30 percent. Assume that under current tax law, accelerated depreciation can reduce taxable income.

| Straight Line Method | | Accelerated Method | |
|---|---|---|---|
| Revenue | 100,000 | Revenue | 100,000 |
| Non-depreciation expense | 75,000 | Non-depreciation expense | 75,000 |
| Depreciation expense | 5,000 | Depreciation expense | 20,000 |
| Pretax profit | 20,000 | Pretax profit | 5,000 |
| Tax expense | 6,000 | Tax expense | 1,500 |
| Net income | 14,000 | Net income | 3,500 |

   Notice that the same firm, applying different accounting policies, can produce different pretax and net income figures. What could be the effect of depreciation policy on current tax liability?

---

Depreciation is a non-cash expense, meaning that the company does not "pay" in cash the expense as it pays, for example, employee wages. Depreciation is simply recognized as an expense. On the other hand, tax expense is paid in cash (Uncle Sam wants your money). Can accounting policy affect a company's value by reducing or delaying tax liability?

   Delayed tax liability is liability incurred but not obligated to be paid at the moment. It is called "deferred incomes taxes" or "deferred tax liability" on the balance sheet. Why is a delayed payment of taxes a good thing?

   There are different ways that an asset can be depreciated or amortized (the above examples illustrating just two methods). At this point in one's career, a law student need not be familiar with the technical details of these various methods. Instead, you must understand that (1) there *are* different methods to calculate depreciation and amortization under GAAP, allowing discretion in these matters, and (2) the choice of method will affect the financial statements as well as potential tax liabilities. The implications are significant for business and tax planning. Remember that a good lawyer is a critical user of financial statements.

Depreciation and amortization are accumulated in the balance sheet, and deduct from the book value of the assets. Let's continue with the above railway car example. Under a straight line method, the railway car depreciates by $5,000 per year. The balance sheet of the company will include these items.

| YEAR 1 | | YEAR 2 | |
|---|---|---|---|
| ASSETS | | ASSETS | |
| Railway car | $50,000 | Railway car | $50,000 |
| Accumulated depreciation | (5,000) | Accumulated depreciation | (10,000) |

Thus, depreciation is also recognized in the balance sheet as a reduction in the value of the asset.

Like a tangible asset, goodwill is an asset that can diminish in value. If goodwill is impaired, the impairment is a noncash cost. In Chapter 2, we said that a company cannot recognize the goodwill value of its name and reputation: for example, McDonald's cannot put in its balance sheet the value of the "McDonald's" name, though obviously this name and brand are very valuable. However, when the company purchases another company, a part of the purchase price may be allocated to the acquired company's goodwill, which is an intangible asset.

> **F.Y.I.** The following is the McDonald's Corporation's statement on goodwill in its 2010 annual report.
>
> *Goodwill represents the excess of cost over the net tangible assets and identifiable intangible assets of acquired restaurant businesses. The Company's goodwill primarily results from purchases of McDonald's restaurants from franchisees and ownership increases in international subsidiaries or affiliates, and it is generally assigned to the reporting unit expected to benefit from the synergies of the combination.*

In the acquisition of another company, certain accounting criteria may require that the acquirer revalues the assets and liabilities on the target's balance sheet to fair market values (thus, historical costs on the target's balance sheet are readjusted to market values when those assets and liabilities are brought onto the acquirer's balance sheet). *Goodwill* is the amount of the purchase price that exceeds the fair market values of the target's assets and liabilities. It is recognized on the balance sheet of the acquirer because it is considered a purchased asset, very much like a purchased building.

EXAMPLE 3.4

> ## Kingsfield Inc. earns a profit
>
> Recall that at the end of Year 0, Kingsfield Inc. bought $50,000 in equipment, 100 percent financed at 10 percent, bought a building for $100,000, borrowed $80,000 at 12%. The annual interest expense will be $14,600. Assume that the building and equipment will be depreciated using the straight line method for the period of 40 and 10 years, respectively: thus, the annual depreciation expense will be $2,500 and $5,000, respectively.
>
> Year 1 is the first year of operation. At the end of the year, Kingsfield Inc. had revenue of $600,000, and its operating expenses were: beer and food costs $300,000, employee wages $215,000, and SG&A 30,900. All employee wages are attributable to operations. Assume a tax rate of 25 percent. The income statement for Year 1 is the following.
>
> **Income statement**
>
> | | |
> |---|---:|
> | Revenue | $ 600,000 |
> | COGS | 522,500 |
> | Gross profit | 77,500 |
> | SG&A | 30,900 |
> | Operating profit | 46,600 |
> | Interest expense | 14,600 |
> | Pretax profit | 32,000 |
> | Tax expense | 8,000 |
> | Net profit | 24,000 |
>
> Not only is Professor Kingsfield a brilliant law professor, but apparently he is a good business manager.

## E. CAPITALIZED COSTS

A firm will spend $100 on some aspect of a firm's business. This expenditure is normally expensed, meaning simply that $100 will be recognized in the income statement as an expense, which reduces profit. However, GAAP rules allow certain expenditures to be recognized as a *capitalized cost*. This means that the expenditure will not be immediately recognized as an expense in the income statement upon expenditure, but instead can be recognized as an asset. Thus, profit increases as compared to when the expenditure is recognized immediately in the income statement.

Why not recognize the expense if it is money spent? When permitted under GAAP, the expenditure can be classified as an asset. If so, the expenditure can be thought of as a transformation of one form of an asset to another form, from cash to a capital asset.

Transforms into

The theory is that the cost goes toward developing or improving an asset, and so it is really a transformation of an asset instead of an incurred expense. Think about additions and improvement to building structure or the development of a new drug. The costs are expenditures in the sense that cash is spent, but they are not an expense in the income statement. Instead, the cash really goes toward the "purchase" of additional assets.

> **F.Y.I.** At one time, Northwest Airlines spent $120 million to renovate and improve 40 DC9-30 jets. The jets were on average 24 years old. Northwest capitalized this cost. This capital improvement extended the life of the jets by 10 to 15 years, and saved about $560 million compared to the cost of buying new planes. Expensing the cost would have reduced revenue by $120 million. Capitalizing the cost adds $120 million in PP&E (planes), and the cost is then depreciated over the life of the jets.[1]

How do we account for capitalized cost? There is little to no *immediate* income statement effect, meaning that capitalized cost of $100 spent will have minimal effect, if any, on the income statement of the current period. Because the capitalized cost is an asset, it affects the balance sheet. Cash will be reduced by $100, and there will be a corresponding increase in some other assets such as PP&E.

> **STOP AND THINK** Ultimately, capitalized cost finds its way into the income statement just as a cost of purchasing a building finds its way into the income statement. How?
>
> Capitalized cost reduces expense and increase profit in the short term. Instead of recognizing the cost in its entirety at once, a firm can spread out the cost over a period of time through depreciation. Can this accounting rule be abused? How?

---

1. Paul D. Kimmel et al., Accounting: Tools for Business Decision Making 445 (3d ed. 2009).

## F. MCDONALD'S INCOME STATEMENT

| In millions except per share data | December 31, 2010 | 2009 |
|---|---|---|
| REVENUES | | |
| Sales by Company-operated restaurants | $16,233.3 | $15,458.5 |
| Revenues from franchise restaurants | 7,841.3 | 7,286.2 |
| **Total revenue** | 24,074.6 | 22,744.7 |
| OPERATING COSTS AND EXPENSES | | |
| Company-operated restaurant expenses | | |
| Food & paper | 5,300.1 | 5,178.0 |
| Payroll & employee benefits | 4,121.4 | 3,965.6 |
| Occupancy & other operating expenses | 3,638.0 | 3,507.6 |
| Franchise restaurants-occupancy expenses | 1,377.8 | 1,301.7 |
| Selling, general & administrative expense | 2,333.3 | 2,234.2 |
| Impairment and other charges, net | 29.1 | (61.1) |
| Other operating (income) expense, net | (198.2) | (222.3) |
| **Total operating cost and expense** | 16,601.5 | 15,903.7 |
| **Operating income** | 7,473.1 | 6,841.0 |
| Interest expense-net of capitalized interest of $12.0 and $11.7 | 450.9 | 473.2 |
| Nonoperating (income) expense, net | 21.9 | (24.3) |
| Gain on sale of investment | | (94.9) |
| **Income from continuing operations before tax** | 7,000.3 | 6,487.0 |
| Provision for income taxes | 2,054.0 | 1,936.0 |
| **Net income** | $4,946.3 | $4,551.0 |
| **Earnings per share—basic** | $4.64 | $4.17 |
| **Earnings per share—diluted** | $4.58 | $4.11 |
| **Dividends declared per common stock** | $2.26 | $2.05 |
| **Weighted-average shares outstanding (basic)** | 1,066.0 | 1,092.2 |
| **Weighted-average shares outstanding (diluted)** | 1,080.3 | 1,107.4 |

REVENUES
Sales by Company-operated restaurants
Revenues from franchise restaurants

**Total revenue**

OPERATING COSTS AND EXPENSES
Company-operated restaurant expenses
  Food & paper
  Payroll & employee benefits
  Occupancy & other operating expenses
Franchise restaurants-occupancy expenses
Selling, general, & administrative expense

Impairment and other charges, net

Other operating (income) expense, net

**Total operating cost and expense**

**Operating income**

Interest expense-net of capitalized interest

Nonoperating (income) expense, net

Gain on sale of investment

**Income from continuing operations
  before tax**

Provision for income taxes

**Net income**

Earnings per share—basic

Earnings per share—diluted

Dividends declared per common stock

Weighted-average shares outstanding (basic)

Weighted-average shares outstanding (diluted)

What are these items? We don't know specific information based on just the line item descriptions. We will most likely find a more detailed description of these times in the notes to the financial statements or the MD&A.

*Earnings per share* (EPS)—EPS is calculated as:

$$EPS = \frac{\text{Net Income for Common Stock}}{\text{Average Shares Outstanding}}$$

EPS is the earnings attributable to each outstanding share of stock.

*Basic and diluted*—Shares outstanding can be calculated as basic or diluted figures. Basic means the shares of common stock outstanding. Diluted shares outstanding include the number of options and other securities that can convert into common stock.

*Dividends*—A corporation may distribute to shareholders dividends, which are cash payments from equity. Dividends declared is the total amount of dividends declared by the board divided by the shares outstanding.

*Weighted-average shares outstanding*—The average shares outstanding, basic and diluted, on a weighted basis for the entire fiscal year.

## G. CASE APPLICATION

Along with Enron, WorldCom is an iconic case of accounting fraud. Arthur Andersen was the accounting firm for both companies. In July 2002, WorldCom filed the largest bankruptcy in U.S. history at the time. Enron and WorldCom show how unethical or illegal accounting can destroy companies and the lives of their employees. The collapse of these companies precipitated the enactment of the Sarbanes-Oxley Act. In reading the case, think about how the earnings were manipulated.

### In re WorldCom, Inc. Securities Litigation
294 F. Supp. 2d 392 (S.D.N.Y. 2003)

COTE, District Judge.

WorldCom, Inc. ("WorldCom"), once a giant of the telecommunications industry, is now the subject of colossal litigation. On July 21, 2002, WorldCom filed the largest bankruptcy in United States history. WorldCom executives have pleaded guilty to violating the securities laws; WorldCom's stock and bondholders, including numerous state and private pension funds, have lost hundreds of millions of dollars in investments; state and federal governments have conducted investigations into WorldCom's ascent and collapse; and those associated with the company have been sued in venues across the country.

Plaintiffs contend that WorldCom officers, directors, auditors, underwriting syndicates, and its most influential outside analyst disseminated materially false and misleading information. The false information appeared in analyst reports, press releases, public statements, and filings with the Securities and Exchange Commission ("SEC") from April 1999 through May 2002, including registration statements issued in conjunction with WorldCom's May 2000 note offering ("2000 Offering") and May 2001 note offering ("2001 Offering," together the "Offerings"). Plaintiffs allege that as WorldCom faced growing pressure to satisfy increasingly unrealistic earnings expectations, the company engaged in a series of illegitimate accounting strategies in order to hide losses and inflate reported earnings. By concealing losses to exaggerate reported earnings, plaintiffs argue, WorldCom affected the price of its securities and misled investors regarding the true value of the company.

### B. Defendants

#### WorldCom Executives

Four of WorldCom's former executive officers are named as defendants. Bernard J. Ebbers ("Ebbers") was the President, Chief Executive Officer and a WorldCom Director during the class period. He resigned from the company under pressure on April 29, 2002. Ebbers has not been indicted on criminal charges relating to WorldCom.

Scott D. Sullivan ("Sullivan") was WorldCom's Chief Financial Officer and a Director during the class period. After Ebbers's resignation, Sullivan served as Executive Vice President from April 30, 2002 until June 25, 2002, when WorldCom terminated his employment. In a criminal complaint dated July 31, 2002, Sullivan was charged with felonies in connection with his activities at WorldCom, including securities fraud, conspiracy to commit securities fraud and making false filings with the SEC. He was arrested on August 1, and indicted on August 28, 2002.

## II. The Fraud

For many years, WorldCom grew by acquisitions. By 1998, it had acquired more than sixty companies in transactions valued at over $70 billion. Its largest acquisition was of MCI on September 14, 1998, a transaction valued at $40 billion. In early 2000, however, its attempt to acquire Sprint collapsed. During this period of acquisition-driven expansion, WorldCom had used accounting devices to inflate its reported earnings. Senior WorldCom management instructed personnel in the company's controller's office on a quarterly basis to falsify WorldCom's books to reduce WorldCom's reported costs and thereby to increase its reported earnings. When the pace of acquisitions slowed, it added new strategies to disguise a decline in its revenues. In 2002, however, the scheme collapsed.

On June 25, 2002, WorldCom announced that it had improperly treated more than $3.8 billion in ordinary costs as capital expenditures in violation of generally accepted accounting principles ("GAAP") and would have to restate its publicly-reported financial results for 2001 and the first quarter of 2002. WorldCom later announced that its reported earnings for 1999 through the first quarter of 2002 had been affected by manipulation of various reserves and had overstated earnings by $3.3 billion. WorldCom also announced that it would likely write off goodwill of $50 billion. The impact of those disclosures on the price of WorldCom shares and the value of its notes was catastrophic. Its common stock dropped from a high of $65 per share to pennies.

### A. Accounting Irregularities

WorldCom manipulated its books in two main areas: (1) its charges to income and classification of assets in connection with acquisitions, and (2) its accounting for "line" costs. In each of these areas, WorldCom failed to follow GAAP, and instead freely reworked its numbers in order to meet marketplace earnings projections.

### 1. Acquisitions

Part of the acquisition process involves identifying costs incurred in connection with each merger and taking corresponding charges to income. WorldCom improperly recorded expenses at the time of the acquisition that should not have been included. The effect was to inflate earnings in later periods when the expenses were actually incurred and should have been recorded.

In addition, at the time of acquisitions, WorldCom took overly large and unjustified charges to income, creating inflated merger reserves that it would later tap into when it needed to do so to boost reported earnings. Enormous charges were typical of the mergers and acquisitions in the 1990s and "WorldCom and its senior officers knew that Wall Street would not be concerned with the size of the charges."

WorldCom used the acquisition of MCI in particular to manipulate its earnings statements by improperly classifying the assets it obtained. WorldCom understated the book value of MCI's property, plant and equipment assets and overstated the value of the goodwill acquired. By classifying MCI's value in terms of a slowly depreciating asset like goodwill rather than hard assets, which depreciate in one-tenth of the time, WorldCom improperly inflated its earnings during the years immediately following the MCI acquisition.

### 2. Line Costs

With a decline in its revenue, and further prompted by the failure of its attempt to acquire Sprint, WorldCom began a new accounting fraud, no later than 2000, in connection with its single largest operating expense: line costs. WorldCom had entered into long-term lease agreements with other telecommunications companies for the use of their networks. Pursuant to these leases, WorldCom was obligated to make fixed monthly payments for the use of the networks, or lines, regardless of whether WorldCom or its customers in fact used the leased lines. When demand did not grow as WorldCom had hoped, the company found itself with substantial fixed line costs for networks that were not generating any income.

Under GAAP, line costs must be reported as an expense.

In 2001, WorldCom changed its method for disguising the impact of line costs on its revenues. Sullivan directed that line costs simply be reclassified as capital expenditures that could be depreciated over time. The effect of the reclassification was to inflate WorldCom's reported earnings.

## QUESTIONS

1. With respect to time, how are tangible (hard) assets and goodwill depreciated? How did WorldCom abuse the policy on goodwill to manipulate its earnings?
2. As to acquisitions, WorldCom took large inflated merger charges against earnings at the time of acquisition. This is a single charge in a single period, and thus only one year's worth of earnings was adversely affected. In what way did this policy manipulate WorldCom's earnings?
3. In what way did WorldCom abuse the policy on line costs?

## ESSENTIAL TERMS

Accelerated depreciation

Accrual accounting

Amortization

Capitalized cost

Cash accounting

COGS

D&A

Depreciation

Dividend

Earnings

EBIT

EBITDA

EPS (basic and diluted)

Expense

Goodwill

Gross profit

Income statement equation

Matching principle

Net income (or profit)

Operating profit

Overhead expense

Pretax profit

Profit

Revenue

Sales

SG&A (or G&A)

Shares outstanding (basic and diluted)

Straight line method of depreciation

## KEY CONCEPTS

1. The income statement equation is: Revenue − Expense = Net Income.
2. Like the balance sheet, the income statement lists a priority of claims against the revenue of the firm.
3. The equityholder owns the residual claim in an income statement, which is net income.
4. Accrual accounting more accurately reflects economic reality, even though there may be timing differences between transactions and receipt/payment of cash.
5. Non-cash expenses such as depreciation and amortization are important.

## REVIEW QUESTIONS

1. What is the internal logic behind an income statement?
2. In what way can a company's earnings be reduced legally and ethically?
3. When net income is not distributed to shareholders, how is it accounted for?

*Questions on McDonald's income statement*

4. What are the two primary sources of revenue for McDonald's?
5. What are McDonald's gross profit and operating profit?
6. What is McDonald's single largest component of the cost of goods sold?
7. Calculate McDonald's EPS for basic and diluted shares outstanding.

# CHAPTER 4

# CASH FLOW STATEMENT

## A. "CASH IS KING"

> *"Cash is king."*
> —Quotation origin unknown.

Cash is important. Cash is the blood flow within a business. As we learned earlier in Chapter 3, accrual accounting may result in real profit but not cash. Think of Mr. Hart's bar tab with Professor Kingsfield. The bar tab is an economic benefit from a prior transaction that must be recorded as an asset of the firm. However, it is not cash, and this fact may have implications on how Kingsfield Inc. can operate. Ultimately, all transactions must be reducible to cash. Employees, creditors, utilities, and other vendors, like attorneys, are paid in cash.

Without cash, a firm—even a good one from the perspective of management and business model—can be in danger of insolvency. Many companies become insolvent because they are bad businesses. But not all insolvent companies are bad businesses. Some great businesses can become insolvent because they run out of cash.

EXAMPLE 4.1

---

**Enron's accounting problem (one of many)**

At the height of its fame and reputation, Enron was heralded as one of the most innovative companies, but in truth Enron couldn't even do the basic things competently, like keeping track of cash. Consider this account of a conversation among Enron finance executives.

\* \* \*

Kurt Eichenwald, *Conspiracy of Fools: A True Story* 559-60 (2005)

Ten minutes later came another slap in the face.

"We don't have any method for tracking our *cash*?" McMahon sputtered. "That's *impossible*! We're a Fortune 50 company! We *have* to be tracking our cash!"

Bowen looked shaken. "Come on, guys. I mean, how can we manage our finances if we don't track our cash?"

Despain looked at his new bosses with a stricken expression. "Ray, I've never . . . nobody's ever asked us before to focus on it," he stuttered. "Nobody ever said this was something they wanted us to do."

McMahon sat back in his seat, lifting his eyes to the ceiling. *Oh. My. God*. This was Finance 101. Companies needed to track their cash to know when they were experiencing shortfalls, to know when they could pay their bills. It was the same reason that people *balanced their checkbooks*! If Enron didn't know how much cash it had, it couldn't know how much to draw down on the revolvers!

---

Cash balance and cash flow are important to a firm's ability to function and solvency.

The cash flow statement keeps track of all cash that is circulating throughout the firm during the fiscal year. Cash flow can be categorized into three activities:

- Cash flow from operations
- Cash flow from investing
- Cash flow from financing

These categories recognize the three main activities of a firm that raise or consume cash. Let's examine each of these separately.

## B. CASH FLOW FROM OPERATIONS

*Cash flow from operations* is all cash flow attributable to the operational aspect of the business. The firm's operations are the activities associated directly with the provision of products or services that the firm sells. If the firm is Nike, the operations consist of the factory production, distribution, sales of shoes, and G&A functions.

Cash flow from operations is simply calculated. Start with net income. We assume that net income is all cash, but of course this assumption is wrong because of accrual accounting and non-cash expenses. Net income is not always perfectly correlated to the cash receipts and disbursements. Customers could have been served on credit with the expectation that they will later pay their obligations. The firm could have incurred liabilities that it has not yet paid. Also, depreciation is an expense, but there is no cash outlay.

Since not all transactions are executed in cash, adjustments will need to be made. There can be many adjustments, but there are three primary adjustments that are commonly seen:

1. *D&A:* add back depreciation and amortization because they are expenses reducing net income, but they are noncash expenses
2. *Receivables:* adjust for the difference in receivables from the prior year because they are a part of revenue (think of Mr. Hart's bar tab in Chapter 3) and thus flow down to net income, but customers have yet to pay.
   - Lower receivable amount than the previous year means that, absent default, customers have paid down their I.O.U.s, and thus cash increased (and vice versa). See Example 4.2.
3. *Payables:* adjust for the difference in payables from the prior year because they are a part of expenses and thus flow down to net income, but the firm has yet to pay.
   - Lower payables amount than the previous year means that the firm paid its obligations, and thus cash decreased (and vice versa). See Example 4.2.

Cash flow from operations can be calculated as the following adjustments to net income.

*CASH FLOW FROM OPERATIONS*

Net Income
+ Depreciation and amortization expense
+/− Change in receivables
+/− Change in payables

Cash Flow from Operations

A change (as noted by the symbol $\Delta$) in receivables or payables is calculated as the difference between the current year's receivable or payable and the prior year's receivable or payable:

$$\Delta = \text{Current Year} - \text{Prior Year}$$

The direction of change (positive or negative value) and its effect on the current year's cash flow from operations is the following:

| | Direction of Change $\Delta$ | Effect on Cash Flow |
|---|---|---|
| Receivables | $\Delta$ + | ↓ |
| | $\Delta$ − | ↑ |
| Payables | $\Delta$ + | ↑ |
| | $\Delta$ − | ↓ |

If receivables increase from the prior year, why does cash decrease? If payables decrease from the prior year, why does cash decrease?

 **STOP AND THINK** What is the relationship among profit, depreciation, working capital, and cash flow?

Is it possible to have significant quantity of cash flow and yet have little or no profit?

EXAMPLE 4.2

---

### Kingsfield Inc.'s cash flow from operations

In the second year (Year 2) of operation, assume that Kingsfield Inc. had net income of $50,000 and depreciation expense of $7,500. Also, the relevant balance sheet items are reported as:

|  | YEAR 2 | YEAR 1 | Δ |
|---|---|---|---|
| Receivable | $5,000 | $15,000 | ($10,000) |
| Payable | $2,000 | $ 5,000 | ($ 3,000) |

We calculate cash flow from operations as follows.

#### CASH FLOW FROM OPERATIONS

| | |
|---|---|
| Net income | $50,000 |
| + Depreciation | 7,500 |
| + Receivable | 10,000 |
| − Payable | (3,000) |
| Cash flow from operations | $64,500 |

Although Kingsfield Inc. made only $50,000 in net profit, its operation produced $64,500 in cash. There are several reasons.

- Depreciation expense was $7,500. Since this was a noncash expense, which reduced net income, the amount must be added to net income to reflect actual cash transactions.
- Receivables declined from $15,000 to $5,000 from Year 1 to Year 2 (a negative change in the receivables). This means that a net of $10,000 in receivables were paid to Kingsfield Inc., which represents positive cash flow. Professor Kingsfield's customers are no deadbeats!
- Payables declined from $5,000 to $2,000 from Year 1 to Year 2 (a negative change in payables). This means that Kingsfield Inc. paid off a net of $3,000 in payables, which represents negative cash outflow. Professor Kingsfield is no deadbeat either!

## C. CASH FLOW FROM INVESTING

*Cash flow from investing* is all cash flow attributable to investing activities. A firm must invest to make profit. Nike may invest in a new factory in China. Walmart may invest in a new superstore in Kansas. Goldman Sachs may invest in a new head-quarters building on Wall Street. McDonald's may invest in new restaurants.

Cash flow from investing is simply calculated. Investments made are recorded as negative cash flow. Divestitures of investment are recorded as positive cash flow. Typically, investments are in the form of property, plant, or equipment (PP&E) and investments in securities or other companies.

Cash flow from investing can be calculated as the following.

$$\left(\begin{array}{l} \textit{CASH FLOW FROM INVESTING} \\[4pt] + \text{ Sale of investments} \\ - \text{ Payment of investments} \\ \hline \text{Case Flow from Investing} \end{array}\right)$$

EXAMPLE 4.3

---

**Kingsfield Inc.'s cash flow from investing**

In Year 2 of operation, Kingsfield Inc. bought $40,000 of bar and restaurant equipment. What is the cash flow from investing?

| CASH FLOW FROM INVESTING | |
|---|---|
| − Purchase of PP&E | ($40,000) |
| Cash flow from investing | ($40,000) |

---

## D. CASH FLOW FROM FINANCING

*Cash flow from financing* is all cash flow attributable to financing activities. A firm must be financed. This means that it must raise funds necessary to engage in business activities. Pfizer must have funds to do research on promising new drugs. FedEx must have funds to buy new airplanes. Recall that all assets must have a claim against them. As discussed, capital assets such as factories and airplanes generate profit. These assets must be financed, either by creditors or equityholders.

Cash flow from financing is simple to calculate. Funds raised by the issuance of stocks or bonds are recorded as cash inflow. Funds used to pay off bonds or purchase the company's own stock in the open market are recorded as cash outflow. Also, funds used to pay dividends are recorded as cash outflow.

Cash flow from financing can be calculated as the following.

$$\left(\begin{array}{l} \textit{CASH FLOW FROM FINANCING} \\[4pt] + \text{ Issuance of stocks or bonds} \\ - \text{ Repayment of bonds} \\ - \text{ Stock buyback} \\ - \text{ Payment of dividends} \\ \hline \text{Cash Flow from Financing} \end{array}\right)$$

EXAMPLE 4.4

---

### Kingsfield Inc.'s cash flow from financing

At the law school, the word got out that Kingsfield Tavern is a great success. When he's contracting to sell beer, Professor Kingsfield can be a fairly nice guy and is a keen business person. In Year 2 of operation, Kingsfield Inc. raises $50,000 of equity from fellow law professors. It issues 100 shares of stock at $500 per share. With this new money, Kingsfield Inc. pays down the $50,000 of debt to Bob's Equipment. It also issued $10,000 in dividends to the common stockholders.

*CASH FLOW FROM FINANCING*

| | |
|---|---:|
| + Issuance of stock | $ 50,000 |
| − Repayment of debt | (50,000) |
| − Payment of dividends | (10,000) |
| Cash flow from financing | ($10,000) |

---

## E. PUTTING THE CASH FLOWS TOGETHER

The three cash flow statements are added together to determine whether the firm generated net cash inflow or outflow for the year. They also indicate how the company has managed its cash and the cash activities of the fiscal year. The net cash amount is then added to the previous year's cash balance to calculate the current year's cash balance.

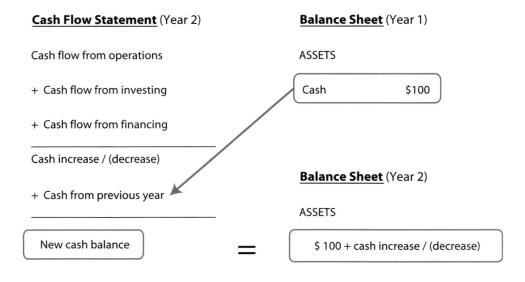

**Cash Flow Statement** (Year 2)

Cash flow from operations

+ Cash flow from investing

+ Cash flow from financing

Cash increase / (decrease)

+ Cash from previous year

New cash balance

**Balance Sheet** (Year 1)

ASSETS

Cash                    $100

**Balance Sheet** (Year 2)

ASSETS

$ 100 + cash increase / (decrease)

=

EXAMPLE 4.5

---

### Kingsfield Inc.'s cash flow statement

Assume that at end of Year 1, Kingsfield Inc. had $21,500 cash on its balance sheet. What is the new cash balance at the end of Year 2?

*CASH FLOW STATEMENT*

| | |
|---|---:|
| + Cash from operations | $64,500 |
| + Cash from investing | (40,000) |
| + Cash from financing | (10,000) |
| Net cash inflow/(outflow) | $14,500 |
| + Cash from beginning of the year | 21,500 |
| New cash balance | $36,000 |

---

## F. MCDONALD'S CASH FLOW STATEMENT

| In millions | December 31, 2010 | 2009 |
|---|---|---|
| **OPERATING ACTIVITIES** | | |
| Net income | $4,946.3 | $4,551.0 |
| Adjustments to reconcile to cash provided by operations | | |
| Charges and credits: | | |
| Depreciation and amortization | 1,276.2 | 1,216.2 |
| Deferred income taxes | (75.7) | 203.0 |
| Impairment and other charges (credits), net | 29.1 | (61.1) |
| Gain on sale of investments | | (94.9) |
| Share-based compensation | 83.1 | 112.9 |
| Other | 211.6 | (347.1) |
| Changes in working capital items: | | |
| Accounts receivable | (50.1) | (42.0) |
| Inventory, prepaid expenses, and other current assets | (50.8) | 1.0 |
| Account payable | (39.8) | (2.2) |
| Income taxes | 54.9 | 212.1 |
| Other accrued liabilities | (43.2) | 2.1 |
| **Cash provided by operations** | 6,341.6 | 5,751.0 |
| **INVESTING ACTIVITIES** | | |
| Property and equipment expenditures | (2,135.5) | (1,952.1) |
| Purchases of restaurant businesses | (183.4) | (145.7) |
| Sales of restaurant businesses and property | 377.9 | 406.0 |
| Proceeds on sale of investments | | 144.9 |
| Other | (115.0) | (108.4) |
| **Cash used for investing activities** | (2,056.0) | (1,655.3) |
| **FINANCING ACTIVITIES** | | |
| Net short-term borrowings | 3.1 | (285.4) |
| Long-term financing issuances | 1,931.8 | 1,169.3 |
| Long-term financing repayments | (1,147.5) | (664.6) |
| Treasury stock purchases | (2,698.5) | (2,797.4) |
| Common stock dividends | (2,408.1) | (2,235.5) |
| Proceeds from stock option exercises | 463.1 | 332.1 |
| Excess tax benefit on share-based compensation | 128.7 | 73.6 |
| Other | (1.3) | (13.1) |
| **Cash used for financing activities** | (3,728.7) | (4,421.0) |
| **Effects of exchange rates on cash and equivalents** | 34.1 | 57.9 |
| **Cash and equivalents increase (decrease)** | 591.0 | (267.4) |
| Cash and equivalents at beginning of year | 1,796.0 | 2,063.4 |
| **Cash and equivalent at end of year** | $ 2,387.0 | $ 1,796.0 |

| | |
|---|---|
| **OPERATING ACTIVITIES**<br>Net income<br>Adjustments to reconcile to cash<br>    Charges and credits:<br>    Depreciation and amortization<br>    Deferred income taxes | D&A are noncash expenses. Deferred income tax is a tax liability recognized in the income statement, thus affecting net income, but not yet paid. |
| Impairment and other charges (credits) | Impairment is a decline in the market value of an asset. The recognition of impairment does not affect cash because loss of value in an asset does not affect cash. |
| Gain on sale of investments<br><br>Share-based compensation | Wages to employees usually take the form of cash. However, employees can be paid in shares of stock. When stock is issued, it results in an expense (because the firm is paying the employees), but cash is not affected. Therefore, share-based compensation must be added back to net income. |
| Changes in working capital items:<br>    Accounts receivable Inventory, prepaid<br>    expenses, and other current assets<br>    Account payable<br>    Income taxes<br>    Other accrued liabilities<br>**Cash provided by operations** | These are adjustments to changes in working capital. An increase in receivables means that customers have increased the amount of their deferred payments. An increase in payables means that the firm has accrued liabilities for which it has yet to pay. |
| **INVESTING ACTIVITIES**<br>Property and equipment expenditures<br>Purchases of restaurant businesses<br>Sales of restaurant businesses and property<br>Proceeds on sale of investments<br>**Cash used for investing activities** | These activities record the purchase and sale of PP&E and investments. A purchase is a cash outflow, and a sale is a cash inflow. |
| **FINANCING ACTIVITIES**<br>Net short-term borrowings<br>Long-term financing issuances<br>Long-term financing repayments | These activities record capital raisings and debt repayments. Raising capital is a cash inflow, and repayment of debt is a cash outflow. |
| Treasury stock purchases<br><br>Common stock dividends<br>Proceeds from stock option exercises<br>Excess tax benefit on share-based<br>compensation<br>**Cash used for financing activities** | Treasury stock purchase means that the company bought back issued shares from shareholders. Bought-back shares are called treasury stock. The purchase of stock is a cash outflow. Dividends are cash payments to shareholders. Option holders may exercise their option to become shareholders, and thus pay money to purchase shares. |
| Effects of exchange rates on cash<br>and equivalents | International businesses receive and pay money in different currencies. When foreign currencies are converted to the home currency such as the US dollar, a firm may end up with less cash than reported in the financial statements. This line makes the adjustment. |

## G. CASE APPLICATION

The case below, *Smith v. Van Gorkom*, is a classic Delaware corporate law case concerning the fiduciary duty of care. It is found in most corporate law casebooks. The case arises from an acquisition of Trans Union. The CEO of the company, Jerome Van Gorkom, sought to sell his company to Jay Pritzker. The central issue is whether the board of directors properly exercised its duty of care when it approved the sale of the company. The court held that it did not, much to the shock of the Delaware bar and legal scholars. Not only was the decision controversial, but the court's legal analysis was also complex and nuanced—all reasons why it is a terrific law school case. The case is richer still when one understands the context of the business decision and the concerns of the CEO, and this requires an understanding of the basic accounting and tax issues. The core accounting issue explains why Van Gorkom sought to sell Trans Union, a decision that led to the announcement of this seminal case. In reading the case, think about the relationship among depreciation, cash flow, and tax consequences.

### *Smith v. Van Gorkom (Part I)*
488 A.2d 858 (Del. 1985)

Horsey, Justice:

Trans Union was a publicly-traded, diversified holding company, the principal earnings of which were generated by its railcar leasing business. During the period here involved, the Company had a cash flow of hundreds of millions of dollars annually. However, the Company had difficulty in generating sufficient taxable income to offset increasingly large investment tax credits (ITCs). Accelerated depreciation deductions had decreased available taxable income against which to offset accumulating ITCs. The Company took these deductions, despite their effect on usable ITCs, because the rental price in the railcar leasing market had already impounded the purported tax savings.

In the late 1970's, together with other capital-intensive firms, Trans Union lobbied in Congress to have ITCs refundable in cash to firms which could not fully utilize the credit. During the summer of 1980, defendant Jerome W. Van Gorkom, Trans Union's Chairman and Chief Executive Officer, testified and lobbied in Congress for refundability of ITCs and against further accelerated depreciation. By the end of August, Van Gorkom was convinced that Congress would neither accept the refundability concept nor curtail further accelerated depreciation.

Beginning in the late 1960's, and continuing through the 1970's, Trans Union pursued a program of acquiring small companies in order to increase available taxable income. In July 1980, Trans Union Management prepared the annual revision of the Company's Five Year Forecast. This report was presented to the Board of Directors at its July, 1980 meeting. The report projected an annual income growth of about 20%. The report also concluded that Trans Union would have about $195 million in spare cash between 1980 and 1985, "with the surplus growing rapidly from 1982 onward." The report referred to the ITC situation as a "nagging problem" and, given that problem, the leasing company "would still appear to be constrained to a tax breakeven." The report then listed four alternative uses of the projected 1982-1985 equity surplus: (1) stock repurchase; (2) dividend increases; (3) a major acquisition program; and

(4) combinations of the above. The sale of Trans Union was not among the alternatives. The report emphasized that, despite the overall surplus, the operation of the Company would consume all available equity for the next several years, and concluded: "As a result, we have sufficient time to fully develop our course of action."

On August 27, 1980, Van Gorkom met with Senior Management of Trans Union. Van Gorkom reported on his lobbying efforts in Washington and his desire to find a solution to the tax credit problem more permanent than a continued program of acquisitions. Various alternatives were suggested and discussed preliminarily, including the sale of Trans Union to a company with a large amount of taxable income.

Donald Romans, Chief Financial Officer of Trans Union, stated that his department had done a "very brief bit of work on the possibility of a leveraged buy-out." This work had been prompted by a media article which Romans had seen regarding a leveraged buy-out by management. The work consisted of a "preliminary study" of the cash which could be generated by the Company if it participated in a leveraged buy-out. As Romans stated, this analysis "was very first and rough cut at seeing whether a cash flow would support what might be considered a high price for this type of transaction."

On September 5, at another Senior Management meeting which Van Gorkom attended, Romans again brought up the idea of a leveraged buy-out as a "possible strategic alternative" to the Company's acquisition program. Romans and Bruce S. Chelberg, President and Chief Operating Officer of Trans Union, had been working on the matter in preparation for the meeting. According to Romans: They did not "come up" with a price for the Company. They merely "ran the numbers" at $50 a share and at $60 a share with the "rough form" of their cash figures at the time. Their "figures indicated that $50 would be very easy to do but $60 would be very difficult to do under those figures." This work did not purport to establish a fair price for either the Company or 100% of the stock. It was intended to determine the cash flow needed to service the debt that would "probably" be incurred in a leveraged buy-out, based on "rough calculations" without "any benefit of experts to identify what the limits were to that, and so forth." These computations were not considered extensive and no conclusion was reached.

At this meeting, Van Gorkom stated that he would be willing to take $55 per share for his own 75,000 shares. He vetoed the suggestion of a leveraged buy-out by Management, however, as involving a potential conflict of interest for Management. Van Gorkom, a certified public accountant and lawyer, had been an officer of Trans Union for 24 years, its Chief Executive Officer for more than 17 years, and Chairman of its Board for 2 years. It is noteworthy in this connection that he was then approaching 65 years of age and mandatory retirement.

Van Gorkom decided to meet with Jay A. Pritzker, a well-known corporate takeover specialist and a social acquaintance.

## QUESTIONS

1. In what way could Trans Union have significant cash flow, but little taxable income to show for it? In what way would an accelerated depreciation policy aggravate the problem?
2. Why couldn't Trans Union make use of the investment tax credits?
3. How would Jay Pritzker's acquisition of Trans Union create value?

Enron Corporation is well known today as an icon of corporate fraud and deviance. It engaged in a massive accounting fraud. The financial statements were replete with misrepresentations. The company's managers and its accountant, the accounting firm of Arthur Andersen, inflated earnings, mischaracterized the amount of debt, and distorted the true picture of how Enron was generating cash. Enron engaged in innumerable fraudulent transactions. Excerpted below is a discussion of one such deal. In reading the case, think about the true nature of Enron's transaction with Barclays.

### *In re Enron Corp. Securities, Derivative & "ERISA" Litigation*
#### 439 F. Supp. 2d 692 (S.D. Tex. 2006)

HARMON, District Judge.

Lead Plaintiff also references two metals transactions between Enron and Barclays [an investment bank], one involving metal warrants and warehouse receipts and closing in September 2000 for $750 million [the warrant described here is a certificate for the delivery of a specific sum of metals], and the other involving a sale of physical metal and closing in December 2000 for $1 billion, that allowed Enron to conceal up to $1,750 million of debt and improperly report the same amount as cash flow from operations. Lead Plaintiff describes the scheme as follows. Enron sold the metal warrants or physical metal to Barclays at a discounted price in exchange for lump sum payments, while Barclays contemporaneously granted Enron an option with the right to purchase the same amount of warrants or metals at the same price. The discount was a strong incentive for Enron to purchase the metal from Barclays.

### QUESTIONS

1. Presumably, Enron's metal assets, valued at approximately $1.75 billion, were almost entirely financed with debt. How do we know this?
2. What is the true nature of these two metal transactions?
3. In what way did Enron misrepresent the nature of its cash flow? In what way did Enron misrepresent the nature of its balance sheet?
4. How did Enron distort its creditworthiness?
5. Multiply this one series of transactions with Barclays by many such transactions. How did Enron collapse?

---

## ESSENTIAL TERMS

Cash flow from financing
Cash flow from investing

Cash flow from operation
Net cash inflow/outflow

## KEY CONCEPTS

1. Cash flow is important to the solvency of a firm. The cash flow statement measures the flow of cash associated with the activities of operation, investing, and financing.
2. Cash flow from operations is the cash flow generated by operations. It starts from the premise that net income is cash and then makes adjustments for noncash expenses such as depreciation and amortization, and changes in working capital.
3. Cash flow from investing is the cash flow generated by investment activities, which primarily constitute the purchase and sale of PP&E and other investments.
4. Cash flow from financing is the cash flow generated by financing. It includes capital raising, debt repayment, stock buybacks, and dividends.
5. Cash flow statements record the change in cash on the balance sheet.

## REVIEW QUESTIONS

1. How is the new cash balance on the balance sheet calculated?
2. What is the effect of foreign currency on the cash flow statement?

*Questions on McDonald's cash flow statement*

3. In 2010, did total cash increase or decrease from the previous year? By how much?
4. In which year (2009 or 2010) did McDonald's pay its employees more in stock?
5. In 2009, how much cash did McDonald's use to pay back long-term debt?
6. In 2010, McDonald's used $2.056 billion in investing and $3.728 billion in financing activities. Where did it get the cash for these cash outlays?

# FINANCIAL STATEMENT ANALYSIS

Financial statements are tools. The income statement, balance sheet, cash flow statement, and the accompanying notes convey much information about the company. Additionally, we can take that information and conduct some simple analyses to acquire more information. Let's see how.

## A. PROFITABILITY ANALYSES

Much of accounting and financial analyses employ simple ratio analysis. Assume that a firm made a net profit of $100 million. Is this good or bad? Of course, we can't answer this question in the abstract. A $100 million profit from revenue of $100 billion may not be considered very profitable, a puny margin compared to revenues. A $100 million profit for General Electric may be very disappointing (in fiscal year 2010, it generated $150.2 billion in revenue, and earned $12.1 billion in net income), but it may be a stunning return for an Internet startup whose business plan was put together on the back of a pizza box. To answer the question "how profitable is the firm?" we need more information.

## 1. MARGIN ANALYSES

Profitability can be measured against revenue as the benchmark. These are margin analyses.

$$\text{Gross Profit Margin} = \frac{\text{Gross Profit}}{\text{Revenue}}$$

$$\text{Operating Profit Margin} = \frac{\text{Operating Profit}}{\text{Revenue}}$$

$$\text{Net Income Margin} = \frac{\text{Net Income}}{\text{Revenue}}$$

These measures are useful for forecasting purposes. They are also useful to compare the company with its peers.

**EXAMPLE 5.1**

## Big Mac vs. Whopper (Part I)

McDonald's and Burger King are competitors. The following are their fiscal year 2010 profitability measures (year ended December 31 for McDonald's and June 30 for Burger King).

| ($ million) | McDonald's | Burger King |
|---|---|---|
| Revenue | $24,074 | $2,502 |
| Gross profit | 9,637 | 887 |
| *Gross profit margin* | *40%* | *35%* |
| Operating profit | 7,473 | 332 |
| *Operating profit margin* | *31%* | *13%* |
| Net profit | 4,946 | 186 |
| *Net profit margin* | *21%* | *7%* |

Based on these profitability measures, which company performs better?

## 2. RETURN ON ASSETS AND EQUITY (ROA AND ROE)

Profitability can be measured against assets and equity. These measures answer the questions: How much assets are required to generate a quantum of profit? How much equity is required?

$$\text{Return on Assets (ROA)} = \frac{\text{Net Income}}{\text{Average Total Assets}}$$

$$\text{Return on Equity (ROE)} = \frac{\text{Net Income}}{\text{Average Total Equity}}$$

Average total assets and average total equity can be calculated by averaging last year's assets and equity with this year's figures.

**EXAMPLE 5.2**

## Big Mac vs. Whopper (Part II)

The following are ROA and ROE measures for fiscal year 2010.

| ($ million) | McDonald's | Burger King |
|---|---|---|
| Net income | $ 4,946 | $ 186 |
| Assets (2009) | 30,224 | 2,707 |
| Assets (2010) | 31,975 | 2,747 |
| Average assets | 31,100 | 2,727 |
| *ROA* | *16%* | *7%* |
| Equity (2009) | 14,033 | 974 |
| Equity (2010) | 14,634 | 1,128 |
| Average equity | 14,334 | 1,051 |
| *ROE* | *35%* | *18%* |

Burger King's Whopper may be tastier, but it seems that McDonald's operates a more profitable company as measured by ROA and ROE.

ROA and ROE are measures of efficiency.

A firm wants to generate more profit with less assets. Why?

A firm wants to generate more profit with less equity. Why?

## 3. EARNINGS PER SHARE (EPS)

Profit is attributable to shareholders. A shareholder would want to know how much profit is attributable to each share.

$$\text{Earnings per Share (EPS)} = \frac{\text{Net Income Attributable to Common Stock}}{\text{Average Common Shares Outstanding}}$$

*Net income attributable to common stockholders* is net income after payment of dividends to preferred stockholders. Preferred stock is a form of stock wherein the stockholder is entitled to a fixed dividend. Preferred stock is a form of equity for reasons discussed in Chapter 11, but they stand in priority to common stockholders. Dividends to preferred stockholders must be paid before common stockholders can claim against the remaining profit.

EPS is an important measure of a firm's profitability. It tells a shareholder how much profit can be ascribed to each share she purchases. In one sense, EPS is an arbitrary number because it depends on the number of shares outstanding.

EXAMPLE 5.3

> ### Kingsfield Inc.'s EPS
>
> In Examples 4.2 and 4.4, we saw that Kingsfield Inc. earned $50,000 in net income in Year 2, and that it issued another 100 shares to other law professors. With Professor Kingsfield's 100 shares, the shares outstanding are 200. Assume that in Year 2, the average shares outstanding are 200 shares.
>
> $$\text{EPS} = \frac{\$50,000}{200 \text{ shares}} = \frac{\$250}{\text{Share}}$$
>
> If Kingsfield Inc. decided to split its stock two-for-one, such that Professor Kingsfield would have 200 shares and other professors would have 200 shares, the EPS would be $125 per share (= $50,000/400 shares).

EXAMPLE 5.4

### EPS and valuation—McDonald's vs. Kingsfield Inc.

Because EPS is a measure of earnings, it is also an important factor in the value of a company. The value of a company is frequently expressed as multiples of its various financial outputs, e.g., net income, EBIT, EBITDA, and book value.

In the fiscal year ended December 31, 2010, McDonald's earned $4.946 billion in profit. It had average shares outstanding (basic) of 1.066 billion (see its income statement in Chapter 3). This produced an EPS (basic) of $4.64 per share. Example 2.3 shows that its share price and market cap on that day were $76.76/share and $80.828 billion based on the year end shares outstanding, 1.053 billion shares outstanding shares at year end (or $81.826 billion based on the 1.066 billion average shares outstanding). Share price and market capitalization can be expressed as multiples of earnings, called *price-to-earnings* (P/E) multiple.

$$P/E = \frac{\text{Share Price}}{\text{EPS}} = \frac{\$76.76}{\$4.64} = 16.5x$$

Note that the P/E multiple can be expressed as a multiple of market cap to net income. The ratios are the same. Why?

$$P/E = \frac{\text{Market Cap}}{\text{Net Income}} = \frac{\$81.828 \text{ B}}{\$4.946 \text{ B}} = 16.5x$$

These multiples can be used as valuation metrics. McDonald's sells the Filet-o-Fish with fries and soda, and Kingsfield Inc. sells Charles' Fish-n-Chips with Guinness. A plausible argument could be made that McDonald's and Kingsfield Inc. are similar enough businesses that they can be compared. If true, the market value of McDonald's serves as a reference point for Kingsfield Inc.'s value.

If we apply a 16.5x multiple to Kingsfield Inc.'s earnings, this implies that the company would be worth $825,000 (= 16.5 × $50,000). Since there are 200 shares outstanding, this means that each share is worth $4,125.

Recall that Professor Kingsfield invested at a price of $200 per share (Example 2.4), and his fellow professors invested at $500 per share (Example 4.4). If McDonald's is a fair comparable, their shares are valued at $4,125 per share. Professor Kingsfield, other shareholders, creditors, employees, and law student customers—collectively, the constituents of Kingsfield Inc.—have created wealth by partaking in a successful entrepreneurial enterprise.

## B. LIQUIDITY

Liquidity ratios measure the short-term, operational ability of the firm to pay its current obligations. Obviously, a firm's ability to pay its short-term obligations is important. Recall back to the lesson in Chapter 2 where we distinguished current (short-term) assets and liabilities, and capital assets and long-term financing.

$$\text{Working Capital} = \text{Current Assets} - \text{Current Liabilities}$$

$$\text{Current Ratio} = \frac{\text{Current Assets}}{\text{Current Liabilities}}$$

Negative working capital and a current ratio less than 1.0 mean that current liabilities are greater than current assets. This could be a problem.

Many businesses use a bank line of credit or a market for short-term credit, such as the commercial paper market, to manage day-to-day cash needs. As long as this market is available, firms can smoothly operate even when there is a cash need in the short-term.

**EXAMPLE 5.5**

> ### Enron's liquidity crisis
>
> The death of Enron is a complicated corporate murder story with a chain of causal acts and events contributing to the death of a public corporation. The final event in this chain was a liquidity crisis—Enron ran out of cash because no one lent it money to operate. Credit is important to consumers and corporations alike. If cash is akin to blood in a human body, Enron bled to death. Consider this account from Kurt Eichenwald's *Conspiracy of Fools: A True Story* 554-55 (2005).
>
> * * *
>
> It couldn't be seen. It couldn't be heard. But on that day, October 23 [2001], the financial underpinnings of Enron were snapped apart. The first person to catch wind of the problem was an executive named Tim Despain. Enron's short-term loans in the commercial-paper market weren't rolling over. Institutions were taking the cash from maturing loans and not buying new paper [short-term debt]. This was what had happened weeks before, after [the terrorist attack of] September 11 [2001]. But that had been a market problem. This was more serious; it was an Enron problem.

## C. SOLVENCY

Solvency measures the ability of a firm to remain solvent over a long-term period. It concerns the capital structure of the firm and the ability of the firm to pay long-term creditors. At issue is the firm's ability to service its debt obligations. Creditors must be paid; otherwise they can throw the firm into bankruptcy. We focus on two questions: (1) Can the firm pay its debt obligations? (2) How are the firm's assets funded?

*Income statement analysis*—The first question concerns the ability to pay interest on debt (known as "debt service" or "service of debt"), and thus it is answered by an analysis of the income statement.

$$\text{Interest Cover Ratio} = \frac{\text{Net Income} + \text{Interest Expense} + \text{Tax Expense}}{\text{Interest Expense}}$$

The interest cover ratio measures the amount of funds available to pay interest payments due to creditors. The funds from operations are net income plus interest expense paid, and tax expense. Tax expense is added back because interest expense is paid before taxes. The sum of net income, interest expense, and tax expense constitute the funds available to pay the interest expense. The higher the interest cover ratio, the more the firm has the ability to pay interest on its debts.

*Balance sheet analysis*—The funding of assets is answered by an analysis of the balance sheet.

$$\text{Leverage Ratio} = \frac{\text{Assets}}{\text{Equity}}$$

The leverage ratio measures how much of assets are funded by equity. This ratio is particularly important to financial institutions.

$$\text{Debt to Equity Ratio} = \frac{\text{Long-term Debt}}{\text{Equity}}$$

The long-term debt-to-equity ratio measures the ratio of long-term financing. It answers the questions: How are the firm's long-term capital requirements funded? What is the mix of debt and equity?

**EXAMPLE 5.6**

---

### Solvency of investment banks during the financial crisis

During the historic financial crisis of 2008-2009, many financial institutions became distressed. At the center of the maelstrom were investment banks. At the time, there were only five large independent investment banks left after a long period of industry consolidation. During the financial crisis, three of these investment banks collapsed. Lehman Brothers filed for bankruptcy in September 2008. Staring in the face of bankruptcy, Bear Stearns was acquired by JPMorgan Chase in March 2008, and a financially distressed Merrill Lynch was acquired by Bank of America in September 2008. The collapse of these financial institutions, among others, precipitated the financial crisis. Let's see what their balance sheets looked like as the financial crisis was unfolding.

| ($ million) | Bear Stearns as of 2/28/08 | Lehman Brothers as of 5/31/08 | Merrill Lynch as of 6/27/08 |
|---|---|---|---|
| Assets | $ 398,995 | $ 639,432 | $ 966,210 |
| Liabilities | 387,099 | 613,156 | 931,432 |
| Equity | 11,896 | 26,276 | 34,778 |

As you look at these balance sheets, what is the fundamental problem with how these investment banks operated?

What would happen if the market value of assets on their balance sheets fell because the market believed that a collapsing housing market would reduce the value of the housing-tied securities on their balance sheets?

---

A *commercial bank* is a depository institution, and most of us deposit our cash with these banks and write checks therefrom. An investment bank is not a "bank" in the sense of a depository institution that serves the banking needs of most people. An *investment bank* is a financial institution whose core activities are providing financial advisory services to corporations, underwriting securities, and trading securities. The role of investment banks is discussed in greater detail in Chapter 12.

*Leverage* means debt. For example, a *leverage buyout* is a purchase of a company that is financed by debt. "To lever" a firm, means to increase its debt load. Consider this statement: "These days, the personal balance sheets of law students are heavily levered."

## D. CASE APPLICATION

The case below illustrates the use of financial statement analyses, including working capital and solvency analyses, in the context of bidding for a government contract. The ability to analyze a company's finances is an important general business skill. In reading the case, think about the accounting-based reasons why the company in question was determined to be too risky.

*Author's Summary of Facts*: Ryder Move Management, a subsidiary of its parent company Budget Group, submitted a proposal for a Department of Defense contract for moving services. The government contract was subject to competitive bidding. The solicitation provided the factors that would be evaluated, and the basis upon which the award would be made. One factor was "the best overall (i.e., best value) proposal that is determined to be the most beneficial to the Government, with appropriate consideration given to the four evaluation factors: Overall Performance Risk, Technical, Statements of Requirements, and Price." The "overall performance risk" factor, deemed the most significant factor, consisted of two subfactors of equal weight: "past performance risk" and "financial risk." The financial risk subfactor was defined to include an assessment of the offerors' "profitability, liquidity, and solvency." These criteria are the focus of this litigation. The government used Dun & Bradstreet ("D & B"), a private advisory firm, to provide financial analysis. Ultimately, the government rejected Ryder and Budget's proposal based on its assessment of financial risk.

### *Ryder Move Management, Inc. v. United States*
48 Fed. Cl. 380 (Fed. Cl. 2001)

FIRESTONE, Judge.

### I. Facts

Based on its review of Budget Group's financial statements, D & B concluded that the offeror, Ryder, presented a "moderate" financial risk. Specifically, D & B's report stated that the consolidated financial statement submitted by the parent company, Budget Group, reflected "a moderate solvency position highlighted by a satisfactory liquidity position and a fair leverage ratio." The report demonstrated that

Budget Group sustained a net loss for the year ending December 31, 1998: Budget Group's financial statement revealed that it had sustained a net operating loss after taxes of $48,927,000 based on gross revenues of $2,616,199,000, resulting in a loss of 1.8%. The D & B report further stated that this "1.8% net margin loss ... compared unfavorably to the industry norm" of +2.4%. The D & B report also noted that "the parent company's total debt to equity ratio was 644%," which D & B considered "fair" compared to the industry norm of 103.1%. D & B derived this information from Budget Group's financial statements showing a ratio of total liabilities of $4,192,321,000 versus stockholder equity of $650,590,000.

DoD evaluated Ryder's proposal, including the associated financial risk, in three stages: initial (July 2, 2000), interim, and final. At each stage, DoD evaluated both Ryder's financial risk and overall performance risk as "moderate." In reaching this conclusion, the DoD contracting officer concurred with D & B's determination that Ryder presented a "moderate solvency position, highlighted by a satisfactory liquidity position and an unfavorable leverage ratio." The contracting officer noted that the information Ryder submitted reflected a debt to equity ratio of 644%, which she considered "fair" when compared to an industry norm of 103.1%. She found that Budget Group sustained a net loss for the year ending December 31, 1998, although she noted an upward trend, and she determined that Budget Group's 1.8% net loss margin compared unfavorably to an industry norm of +2.4%. The 1.8% net loss and the debt to equity ratio of 644% were consequently listed as specific disadvantages against Ryder in the contracting officer's "Narrative Rationale for the Rating Assigned." Ryder was therefore given an overall "moderate" rating for the most important category, the overall performance risk factor. The "Source Selection Decision Document" explains that "moderate risk" means "some doubt exists based on the Offeror's performance and/or financial record that the Offeror can perform the proposed effort." Outside of the financial evaluation, Ryder received favorable ratings in the other three factors: technical, SORs, and price.

[Ultimately, the contracting officer determined that those with "moderate" overall performance risk should be eliminated from further consideration.]

## II. Discussion

The heart of Ryder's complaint is its contention that D & B's, and hence the contracting officer's, conclusion that Ryder presented a "moderate" financial risk was irrational. Ryder argues that the contracting officer's conclusion was irrational because it was based on a "flawed" analysis of Budget Group's financial statements by D & B. Ryder contends that D & B erred by: 1) failing to compare Budget Group's financial ratio to the proper peer group; and, 2) failing to give Ryder credit for certain positive aspects of Budget Group's financial statement. In its brief, Ryder states that it was simply "irrational" for the contracting officer to conclude that Ryder, which was "backed with evaluation-year assets of $5.1 billion, revenues of $3 billion, and cash on hand of over $550 million," deserved a "moderate" financial risk rating.

As noted at the outset, the court has a very limited role in reviewing the contracting officer's decision. The court may not itself re-weigh the evidence presented to the contracting officer. Rather, the court's role is limited to determining whether, taking the record as a whole, the contracting officer's conclusion that Ryder presented a "moderate" financial risk was rational and supported.

Despite the errors Ryder attributes to the D & B analysis, the court concludes the contracting officer was not "irrational" in relying on D & B's evaluation in reaching her decision that Ryder presented a "moderate" financial risk rating. First, the court is persuaded that D & B did not err by comparing Budget Group's financial data to that of companies in Ryder's SIC category. The offerors were told that D & B would be comparing their financial information to that of others in the *offerors'* primary SIC category. Ryder was undisputably the "offeror," and D & B reasonably believed, based on Ryder's submission of Budget Group's data, that this data reflected Ryder's financial position. Because Ryder did not have separate financial data, the Budget Group data was the best indication of Ryder's financial risk.

Second, D & B's comparison of Budget Group's unfavorable financial data to that of Ryder's peer companies is not the dispositive factor in this case, even if the comparison of Budget Group's data to the data of companies in Ryder's SIC category was inappropriate. Rather, the dispositive factor here is that Budget Group's financial data is itself unfavorable. As described in the solicitation, each offeror was evaluated for liquidity, solvency, and profitability. Budget Group's 1.8% net margin loss and 644% debt to equity ratio are patently problematic. A loss of 1.8% is a loss, no matter how small the profit margin enjoyed by other companies in the same category. Similarly, a high debt to equity ratio is a key factor in determining financial risk, regardless of whether others in a company's peer group are also highly leveraged.

For this reason as well, D & B's analysis is not irrational simply because D & B failed to perform a "more sophisticated" analysis of Budget Group's financial picture, as Ryder alleges. Given that profit margin and debt to equity ratio are two of the most common measurements of a company's financial health, Ryder's assertion that its 1.8% net loss and 644% debt to equity ratio are somehow misleading is simply untenable. D & B's own guidance documents explain these two key measures of financial strength as follows:

> Return on Sales (Profit Margin)—Ratio measures the profits after taxes on the year's sales. The higher this ratio, the better prepared the business is to handle downtrends brought on by adverse conditions; Measures the efficiency of the operation.

> Total Liabilities to Net Worth—Compares the company's total indebtedness to the venture capital invested by the owners. High debt levels can indicate greater risk; The higher this ratio, the less protection there is for creditors of the business.

Similarly, Ryder's argument that Budget Group's size entitled it to special treatment under D & B's analysis is without merit. The fact that Budget Group may be larger than other companies and therefore may possess certain beneficial financial attributes does not mean that D & B arbitrarily concluded that Ryder presented a "moderate" versus a "low" financial risk, based on Budget Group's net loss and high debt to equity ratio. Even Fortune 500 companies are susceptible to market forces and, if they are too highly leveraged, can face financial risks.

In this connection, the court also recognizes that D & B is a recognized leader in the field of evaluating the financial strength of companies, and is known as an independent reporting service that is frequently used by government contracting officials. A.R. 184-85 (D & B has had "over 150 years of experience making these types of [credit evaluation] decisions. . . . It's a standardized, comprehensive evaluation process.").

[Based on the foregoing, the court held that the contracting officer's decision was not irrational.]

## QUESTIONS

1. Why do you think one of the bases for selection in the government contract bidding was financial risk? Why would the government be concerned about its contractor's financial condition?
2. What factors led the contracting officer to her conclusion that Ryder was "moderate risk"?
3. The opinion does not reproduce a balance sheet, but we can take some educated guesses about what we would expect to see on the balance sheet. What are the principal assets of the Budget Group? What would the liabilities and equity side of the balance sheet look like?
4. What was the Budget Group's leverage ratio?
5. Budget Group argued that it was bigger than its competitors. This argument did not sway the court. Why not?

———————

## ESSENTIAL TERMS

Common stock
Current ratio
Debt-to-equity ratio
Earnings per share (EPS)
Gross profit margin
Interest cover ratio
Leverage ratio
Net income attributable to common
  stock

Net income margin
Operating profit margin
Preferred stock
Return on assets (ROA)
Return on equity (ROE)
Working capital

## KEY CONCEPTS

1. Simple ratio analyses can provide essential information about a firm's profitability, liquidity, and solvency.
2. Profitability analyses measure several things: (1) gross, operating, or net profit as a ratio of revenue, (2) net profit as a ratio of assets or equity, and (3) net profit as a ratio of shares outstanding.
3. Liquidity concerns the firm's short-term ability to pay for its operations, which is determined by the firm's working capital.
4. Solvency concerns the firm's longer term ability to fund its business.

## REVIEW QUESTIONS

1. Calculate the leverage ratios of the investment banks in Example 5.6. Compare these figures with the leverage ratios of commercial banks (e.g., look up Wells Fargo and calculate its leverage ratio). What do these differences say about the financial risks undertaken by investment banks?
2. The SEC, a government agency operated mostly by lawyers, was the principal regulator of the investments banks. Should the SEC have permitted investment banks to conduct their businesses in this manner?
3. During the financial crisis, mortgage bonds tied to the housing market collapsed in value. These bonds were held by these investment banks as assets on the balance sheet. What happens to the equity of these investment banks when these bonds substantially declined in economic value as the house market collapsed?

*Questions on McDonald's financial statements*

4. Calculate McDonald's ROA and ROE for 2010.
5. Assess McDonald's liquidity and solvency.
6. Assess McDonald's ability to service its debt.

# CREATING FINANCIAL STATEMENTS

## A. INTERCONNECTIONS OF FINANCIAL STATEMENTS

It is important to understand that the income statement, cash flow statement, and balance sheet are interconnected. This understanding gives us a sense of the financial statements as a whole, and thus the operations and activities as a whole. Recall Enron's highly controversial conference call from Example 1.1. Wall Street analysts wanted to see the cash flow statement and balance sheet along with Enron's income statement. The reason is that these financial statements are interconnected. Seeing them together reveals the financial condition of the firm as a whole.

To illustrate this interconnectivity in greater detail, we continue the Kingsfield Inc. hypothetical. Let's consolidate and summarize the facts as disclosed throughout the previous chapters.

*Kingsfield Inc.: Year 0 Activities and Results*

Example 2.5 provided that Professor Kingsfield created a corporation and capitalizes it with $20,000, for which he received 100 shares of stock, constituting 100 percent ownership of equity and an initial value of $200 per share. Professor Kingsfield found a building that would house the business, which was priced at $100,000. To fund this purchase, the corporation borrowed $80,000 from Big Bank at a 12 percent rate. With the $100,000 in cash at hand, the company bought the property. Additionally, the company purchased $50,000 of equipment from Bob's Equipment with 100 percent financing at a 10 percent rate and collateralized by a security interest in the equipment.

The above transactions were completed at December 31, Year 0. At this time, the balance sheet looks like this.

| Assets | | Liabilities | |
|---|---|---|---|
| Equipment | $50,000 | Secured loan | $50,000 |
| Building | 100,000 | Bank loan | 80,000 |
| | | **Equity** | |
| | | *Common stock* | $20,000 |
| | | (100 shares issued) | |
| Assets | $150,000 | Liabilities and equity | $150,000 |

*Kingsfield Inc.: Year 1 Activities and Results*

Let's now introduce the following additional facts. The accountant depreciated the building and equipment on the straight line method using 40 years for the building and 10 years for the equipment: thus annual depreciation expense of $2,500 and $5,000 respectively.

In Year 1, Kingsfield Inc. had revenue of $600,000 (apparently 𝕶𝖎𝖓𝖌𝖘𝖋𝖎𝖊𝖑𝖉 𝕳𝖔𝖚𝖘𝖊 is popular with law students). Its operating expenses were as follows:

| | |
|---|---|
| Beer and food costs | $ 300,000 |
| Employees | 215,000 |
| Depreciation expense | 7,500 |
| SG&A | 30,900 |

The company's financing expenses were as follows:

| | |
|---|---|
| $80,000 Big Bank loan at 12% | $ 9,600 |
| $50,000 Bob's Equipment loan at 10% | 5,000 |

The tax rate is 25 percent. Of the sales, $15,000 were receivables, because many students did not get their student loans in December when they celebrated the end of the Fall semester. Also, as of the end of the Year 1, Kingsfield Inc. did not pay $5,000 to trade creditors (beer suppliers). There were no distributions to shareholders. Instead, Kingsfield Inc. plowed its profits back into the company.

How do we put together the financial statement for Year 1?

## KINGSFIELD INC. FINANCIAL STATEMENTS (YEAR 1)

### Income Statement

| | |
|---|---|
| Revenue | 600,000 |
| Beer and food cost | (300,000) |
| Wages | (215,000) |
| Depreciation | (7,500) |
| SG&A | (30,900) |
| Operating profit | 46,600 |
| Interest expense | (14,600) |
| Pretax profit | 32,000 |
| Tax expense @ 25% | (8,000) |
| **Net income** | **24,000** |

### Balance Sheet

| Assets | | Liability | |
|---|---|---|---|
| Cash | 21,500 | Payable | 5,000 |
| Receivable | 15,000 | Secured loan | 50,000 |
| | | Bank loan | 80,000 |
| Equipment | 50,000 | Equity | |
| (Accum. depr.) | (2,500) | | |
| Building | 100,000 | Common stock | 20,000 |
| (Accum. depr.) | (5,000) | Retained earning | 24,000 |
| **Total assets** | **179,000** | **Total L&E** | **179,000** |

### Cash Flow Statement

| | |
|---|---|
| Cash from operations | |
| Net income | 24,000 |
| +/– Receivable | (15,000) |
| +/– Payable | 5,000 |
| Depreciation | 7,500 |
| Cash from financing | |
| No activities | |
| Cash from investing | |
| No activities | |
| **Net cash flow** | **21,500** |

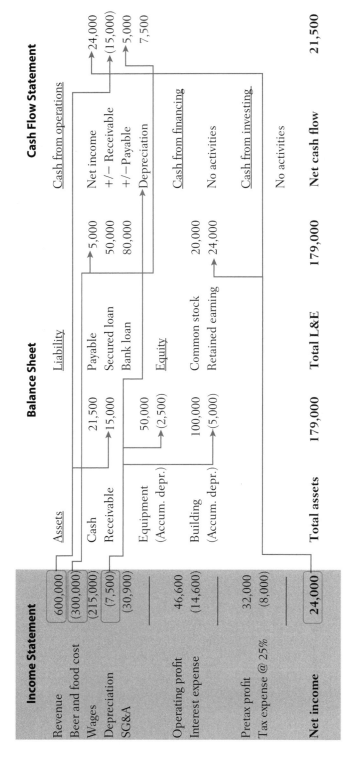

INTERCONNECTIONS OF THE FINANCIAL STATEMENTS

Flow of Income Statement Line Items

INTERCONNECTIONS OF THE FINANCIAL STATEMENTS

Flow of Cash Flow Line Items

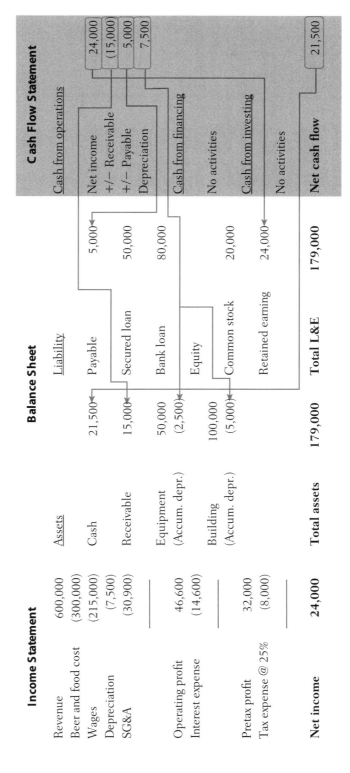

**STOP AND THINK** Notice that many line items from the income statement and the cash flow statement feed into the balance sheet. This is one reason why the balance sheet is so important.

*Kingsfield Inc.: Year 2 Activities and Results*

In Year 2, Kingsfield Inc. had revenue of $1,100,000 (the business is a huge success!). Its operating expenses were as follows:

| | |
|---|---|
| Beer and food costs | $ 600,000 |
| Employees | 370,000 |
| Depreciation expense | 7,500 |
| SG&A | 41,233 |

Customers paid off old receivables from Year 1, and the company paid off its old payables from Year 1. Example 4.2 provides the receivables and payables. The information is summarized as follows. Of the new sales, $5,000 were paid in receivables (student loans were issued timely this year). As of the end of Year 2, Kingsfield Inc. did not pay $2,000 to trade creditors. To summarize, receivables and payables for the two years are:

| | Year 2 | Year 1 |
|---|---|---|
| Receivable | 5,000 | 15,000 |
| Payable | 2,000 | 5,000 |

The word got out that Kingsfield Tavern is a great success. Examples 4.3 and 4.4 provided the company's investing and financing activities. The information is summarized as follows. Anticipating future growth, Kingsfield Inc. raised $50,000 of equity from fellow law professors: 100 shares were issued to these new investors at a stock price of $500 per share. The company used this new money to pay down the $50,000 of debt to Bob's Equipment at the end of Year 2 (thus interest for the year was paid). It also bought $40,000 of bar and restaurant equipment at the end of Year 2 (thus no depreciation expense for the year on these assets). Lastly, given its success, the company returned some money to shareholders by declaring and paying $10,000 in dividends to common stockholders.

How do we put together the financial statement for Year 2?

KINGSFIELD INC. FINANCIAL STATEMENTS (YEAR 2)

## Income Statement

| | |
|---|---:|
| Revenue | 1,100,000 |
| Beer and food cost | (600,000) |
| Wages | (370,000) |
| Depreciation | (7,500) |
| SG&A | (41,233) |
| Operating profit | 81,267 |
| Interest expense | (14,600) |
| Pretax profit | 66,667 |
| Tax expense @ 25% | (16,667) |
| Net income | 50,000 |
| Dividend payment | (10,000) |
| **Net income after dividends** | **40,000** |

## Balance Sheet

| Assets | | Liability | |
|---|---:|---|---:|
| Cash | 36,000 | Payable | 2,000 |
| Receivable | 5,000 | Secured loan | 0 |
| Equipment | 90,000 | Bank loan | 80,000 |
| (Accum. depr.) | (5,000) | Equity | |
| Building | 100,000 | Common stock | 70,000 |
| (Accum. depr.) | (10,000) | Retained earning | 64,000 |
| **Total assets** | **216,000** | **Total L&E** | **216,000** |

## Cash Flow Statement

| | |
|---|---:|
| Cash from operations | |
| Net income | 50,000 |
| +/– Receivable net | 10,000 |
| +/– Payable net | (3,000) |
| Depreciation | 7,500 |
| Cash from financing | |
| New common stock | 50,000 |
| Loan repayment | (50,000) |
| Dividend payment | (10,000) |
| Cash from investing | |
| Equipment purchase | (40,000) |
| **Net cash flow** | **14,500** |

## KINGSFIELD INC. FINANCIAL STATEMENTS (YEAR 2)

For the purpose of illustrating the differences between the balance sheets and cash flow statements in Year 1 and Year 2, balance sheet and cash flow line items below are broken up into "old" and "new." Old denotes carryover items from the prior Year 1 and are *italicized*. For example, "Old cash" is the cash balance at the end of Year 1 and "New cash" is the cash generated by the activities in Year 2. The typical financial statements do not make these distinctions, and lines items are consolidated, e.g., "cash" or "receivables" or "PP&E."

### Income Statement

| | |
|---|---:|
| Revenue | 1,100,000 |
| Beer and food cost | (600,000) |
| Wages | (370,000) |
| Depreciation | (7,500) |
| SG&A | (41,233) |
| Operating profit | 81,267 |
| Interest expense | (14,600) |
| Pretax profit | 66,667 |
| Tax expense @ 25% | (16,667) |
| Net income | 50,000 |
| Dividend payment | (10,000) |
| **Net income after dividends** | **40,000** |

### Balance Sheet

| Assets | | | Liability | |
|---|---:|---:|---|---:|
| *Old cash* | 21,500 | | *Old payable* | 0 |
| New cash | 14,500 | | New payable | 2,000 |
| *Old receivables* | 0 | | *Secured loan* | 0 |
| New receivables | 5,000 | | Bank loan | 80,000 |
| *Old equipment* | 50,000 | | Equity | |
| *(Accum. depr.)* | (5,000) | | *Old common stock* | 20,000 |
| New equipment | 40,000 | | New common stock | 50,000 |
| (Accum. depr.) | 0 | | *Old retained earning* | 24,000 |
| *Building* | 100,000 | | New retained | |
| *(Accum. depr.)* | (10,000) | | earning | 40,000 |
| **Total assets** | **216,000** | | **Total L&E** | **216,000** |

### Cash Flow Statement

| | |
|---|---:|
| Cash from operations | |
| Net income | 50,000 |
| + *Old receivables paid* | 15,000 |
| − New receivables | (5,000) |
| − *Old payable paid* | (5,000) |
| + New payables | 2,000 |
| Depreciation | 7,500 |
| Cash from financing | |
| New common stock | 50,000 |
| Loan repayment | (50,000) |
| Dividend payment | (10,000) |
| Cash from investing | |
| Equipment purchase | (40,000) |
| **Net cash flow** | **14,500** |

The income statement, balance sheet, and cash flow statement are interconnected, and they must be viewed together to view the company as a whole.

## B. T-ACCOUNTS, DEBITS AND CREDITS

As the Kingsfield Inc. hypothetical shows, even a simple business can become quite complicated to keep track of its transactions. Every beer that the firm buys or sells is a separate transaction. How do accountants keep the books straight at the end of the day?

A key principle in accounting is the *double entry bookkeeping* system. This system requires that each transaction is recorded in two separate sides of a *T-account*, which separates the left side called a *debit* entry (noted as "Dr.") and the right side called a *credit* entry (noted as "Cr."). Every transaction has two entries: a debt entry and a credit entry.

|  | DEBIT | CREDIT |  |
|---|---|---|---|
| LEFT |  |  | RIGHT |

 You should not confuse a debit with something bad (perhaps on the wrong intuition that "debit" is somehow related to "debt"), or credit with something good (perhaps on the wrong intuition that "getting credit" for something is a good thing). Below is a recollection of an amusing event from the author's past.

*When thinking about accounting, I am always reminded of a personal experience as a summer associate in the summer of 1990 at the New York office of a large Los Angeles-based national law firm. As a part of the training, summer associates as well as lawyers from the firm were given lessons on basic accounting from PriceWaterhouse (now Pricewaterhouse-Coopers). During the lecture on debits and credits, a litigation partner at the firm interrupted to ask, "So, let me get this straight, credit is good and debit is bad, right?" I knew nothing about accounting then, but I had the sneaking suspicion that this question was off. The look on the accountant's face confirmed my suspicion.*[1]

Don't think too much about the deeper meaning of debit or credit (there isn't any) . . . debit is left and credit is right.

---

1. Robert J. Rhee, *The Madoff Scandal, Market Regulatory Failure and the Business Education of Lawyers,* 35 J. Corp. L. 363, 384 (2009).

For every transaction, there must be a debit entry that equals a corresponding credit entry—like the balance sheet, debit and credit must balance. Any given transaction can affect the income statement and the balance sheet. Let's first consider the entries affecting the balance sheet. Recall that the balance sheet is separated by the left side (assets) and the right side (liabilities and equity). Consistent with this division, a debit to a balance sheet item increases assets and decreases liabilities and equity. Conversely, a credit decreases assets and increases liabilities and equity.

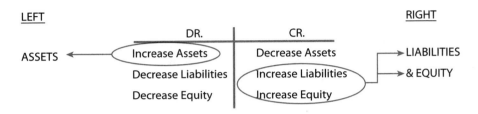

Next consider the entries affecting the income statement. An increase in revenue increases retained earnings, and thus equity. Accordingly, revenue is recognized as a credit entry. Why assign revenue to the right side (a credit)? Because revenue increases equity (sales increases the value of the firm's equity), and an increase in equity is recorded as a matter of accounting convention as a credit. Revenue is paid by customers in the form of cash or receivable. Thus, the corresponding debit entry would be an equivalent amount of cash or receivables (which increases assets).

 There is an internal logic to the double-entry bookkeeping system. In the above, revenue increases equity (which is recorded as a credit to equity), and revenue increases cash or receivables (which is recorded as a debit to assets). The T-accounts balance as to debits and credits, just the way that the balance sheet balances among assets, liabilities, and equity.

Expenses are recognized as a debit entry (because they decrease equity), and the corresponding credit entry would be cash or payable that the firm use to pay expenses, or assets that are consumed in the process of producing goods or services.

Keeping track of these accounts seems complicated, but they are not in principle if we understand that debits and credits must balance because they tie into the balance sheet. Recall that the fundamental balance sheet equation is: Assets = Liabilities + Equity. The specific T-account categories can be represented as the following.

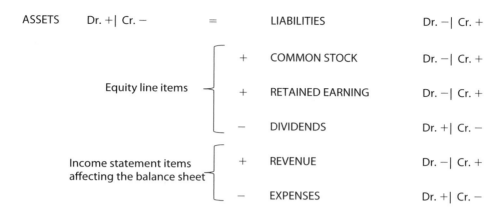

The above categories are tied to the balance sheet. Clearly, assets, liabilities, and equity (common stock and retained earnings) are the major categories in the balance sheet, and we see the effects of debit and credit entries for these categories. Revenue increases equity and expenses decrease equity. Revenue is an addition to the right side of the balance sheet, which means that a credit increases revenue and it must be offset by a debit (increase) in assets. Expense decreases equity, which means that a debit decreases equity and it must be offset by a credit (decrease) to assets or a credit (increase) to liabilities.

All T-account entries are kept in a *general ledger*, which contains all the assets, liabilities, equity, revenue, and expense accounts. Accountants will then conduct a trial balance, track down errors or omission, and ultimately finalize the financial statements.

Lawyers are not accountants and they will not do the work of accountants. Most business lawyers will not be working through the details of book entries, but they should know generally how books and records are kept, including the broad concept of double-entry bookkeeping and the terminology of debits and credits.

**EXAMPLE 6.1**

---

**Keeping track of Kingsfield Inc.'s books**

Let's work through some examples so that we can get a feel for how these entries work. Kingsfield Inc. engaged in several transactions. It raised capital and invested in PP&E.

(1) Kingsfield Inc. raises $20,000 in cash through the sale of common stock to Professor Kingsfield.
(2) Kingsfield Inc. borrows $80,000 from Big Bank.
(3) Kingsfield Inc. buys a building for $100,000.
(4) Kingsfield Inc. purchases $50,000 in equipment from Bob's Equipment, which provides financing for the purchase.
(5) Kingsfield Inc. declares and pays $10,000 dividend from earnings.
(6) Kingsfield Inc. generates revenue of $600,000, of which $585,000 is cash and $15,000 are receivables.
(7) Kingsfield Inc. incurs beer and food costs of $300,000, of which $295,000 is paid in cash and $5,000 are payables.

---

These transactions are recorded in the T-accounts under familiar line items. Follow along each numbered transaction. Remember that debiting an asset records an increase in the asset, and crediting decreases the asset; conversely, debiting a liability or equity records a decrease, whereas crediting records an increase.

| CASH | | | PP&E | | |
|------|------|------|------|------|------|
| Debit | | Credit | Debit | | Credit |
| (1) 20,000 | (3) | 100,000 | (3) 100,000 | | |
| (2) 80,000 | (5) | 10,000 | (4) 50,000 | | |
| (6) 585,000 | (7) | 295,000 | | | |

| RECEIVABLES | | | PAYABLES | | |
|------|------|------|------|------|------|
| Debit | | Credit | Debit | | Credit |
| (6) 15,000 | | | | | (7) 5,000 |

| EQUITY | | | DEBT | | |
|------|------|------|------|------|------|
| Debit | | Credit | Debit | | Credit |
| (5) 10,000 | (1) | 20,000 | | | (2) 80,000 |
| | | | | | (4) 50,000 |

| REVENUE | | | EXPENSES | | |
|------|------|------|------|------|------|
| Debit | | Credit | Debit | | Credit |
| | (6) | 600,000 | (7) 300,000 | | |

## EXAMPLE 6.2

### Arthur Andersen's catastrophic accounting error in Enron[2]

Let's see the application of debits and credits in a complex financial transaction involving the Enron Corporation. Arthur Andersen was Enron's auditor and played a key role in Enron's collapse. Among other things, it mischaracterized certain transactions

---

2. This example is based on the descriptions in Malcolm S. Salter, Innovation Corrupted: The Origins and Legacy of Enron's Collapse at 146-49, 163-65, 339-49 (2008); Malcolm S. Salter, Innovation Corrupted: The Rise and Fall of Enron (B), at 5-6 (Harvard Business School, October 11, 2005).

designed to manipulate Enron's earnings and balance sheet. When these accounting errors were disclosed and corrected in October 2001, Enron's house of cards came crashing down. Let's see how Arthur Andersen erred.

Enron had lots of investments on its balance sheet, and the values of these investments were volatile, meaning that it could negatively affect earnings. Enron needed to hedge this risk (seek insurance for downside risk). It couldn't find a counterparty to sell it insurance. So, being the "innovative" company that it was, it created its own counterparty. With Enron's consent, Andy Fastow, Enron's CFO, established a partnership with Wall Street investors called LJM2, which established subsidiary entities called Raptors. The end goal was for the Raptors to provide Enron with the hedges it sought.

Of course, the Raptors needed funds to provide the hedges. Enron "lent" $2 billion of its own stock, and LJM2 provided a small amount of "independent" equity (3% of the total capitalization) sufficient to satisfy the Raptors' independence from Enron for accounting purposes (otherwise, the Raptors would be considered a part of Enron and thus would defeat the purpose of the hedge). The Enron stock in the Raptors served as the assets from which Enron would be paid if Enron needed to call on the insurance.

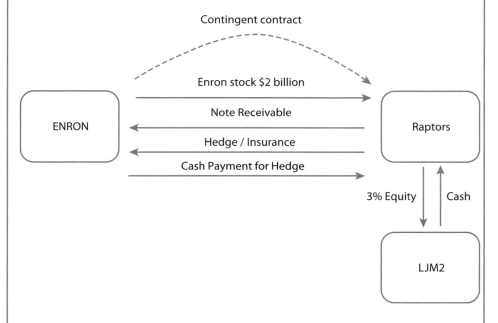

The transaction between Enron and the Raptors was a simple accounting entry. Enron issued $2 billion in its stock and got a note receivable (an IOU). Thus, equity increases (credit) with new issue of $2 billion of stock, and assets increases (debit) with the addition of a note receivable for $2 billion. The entries were as follows:

| Assets | | Equity | |
|--------|--------|--------|--------|
| **Receivables** | | **Common Stock** | |
| Debit | Credit | Debit | Credit |
| $2 billion | | | $2 billion |

However, Enron had a contingent contract to deliver to the Raptors more Enron stock if the stock price of Enron fell (which could result in the Raptors not having enough assets to cover the insurance policies it wrote to Enron . . . so Enron's solution to this problem was to promise to deliver more stock to the Raptors so that they can pay Enron on the insurance policies from the stock it delivered to the Raptors . . . Enron was, after all, an "innovative" company). However, as Enron stock price fell, the entire structure ultimately collapsed. The Raptors had assets of $2.5 billion, but liabilities of $3.2 billion. There was a $710 million hole ($544 million after taxes) in the Raptors' balance sheet. This loss ultimately flowed to Enron because it was owed $3.2 billion from the Raptors, but they only had $2.5 billion in assets to cover the claims.

In September 2001, Arthur Andersen determined that some of the notes receivable should have been a reduction in shareholder's equity given the increase in liability under the contingent contract. In addition to the problem of the contingent contract, "under GAAP, a note received in exchange for a company's own stock offsets shareholder equity until the note is paid."[3] Accordingly, the following correction was made.

| Liabilities | | Equity | |
|--------|--------|--------|--------|
| Debit | Credit | Debit | Credit |
| | $1.2 billion | $1.2 billion | |

This adjustment increased (credit) liabilities by $1.2 billion, and decreased (debit) equity by $1.2 billion. Note what just happened: Enron had originally recorded the transaction as an increase in assets and equity; then it corrected this entry and recorded an increase in liabilities and a decrease in equity. Overnight, $1.2 billion of liabilities appears on Enron's balance sheet, and $1.2 billion of equity disappeared in the accounting correction.

In October 2001, Enron disclosed the prior accounting error and the correction, along with other disclosures of accounting errors. It also decided to wind up the Raptors, and disclosed a $544 million after tax charge (loss) against earnings related to the wind up. Enron's creditor and shareholders had a right to be very upset and alarmed by these changes. Shortly thereafter, Enron collapsed and filed for the largest corporate bankruptcy at the time.

---

3. Salter at 349 (2008).

## C. AUDITING AND CERTIFIED FINANCIAL STATEMENTS

Irrespective of whether a firm is required to produce audited financial statements, companies with significant businesses hire an independent accounting firm to audit their financial statements and accounting processes. They may do this as a part of their own internal control process, but importantly as well they may engage an independent audit because third-parties such as creditors and investors expect to see audited financial statements giving them confidence that the firm's financial results have been independently scrutinized. Indeed, publicly traded companies are required to have audited financial statements under federal securities laws.

Independent accounting firms conduct their audits consistent with GAAP and GAAS. At the end of the audit, the accounting firm produces an *auditor's report*. If the accounting firm is satisfied that the company's books and records are consistent with the applicable accounting standard, it will issue an *unqualified opinion* stating that the financial statements "present fairly, in all material respects" the financial position of the company (see the auditor's opinion for the McDonald's Corporation's financial statements). If the company's financial statements do not meet this standard, the auditor will issue a *qualified opinion*, which will highlight a material deficiency in the financial statements.

Public companies are also required to maintain adequate internal controls under various federal laws. Internal controls are a firm's internal processes and procedures that provide reasonable assurance that the firm is complying with laws and has an adequate financial reporting process. The financial statements of public companies contain reports on the internal controls of the company by the independent accounting firm and the management of the company.

These reports—the auditor's report and the internal control reports—provide essential representations concerning the company's financial data. These reports confirm three things: first, an independent accounting firm certified the financial statement; second, the standards used to report that data were consistent with GAAP and GAAS; and third, internal controls necessary to produce financial data were accurate, and both the accounting firm and the management of the company have certified as such. These representations give the confidence to the investment community and the public at large that they may rely on the financial statements.

 Anything but an unqualified opinion as to the financial statements and internal controls raises a red flag. The accounting problems may not necessarily be fatal, but the lawyer must be aware that there is a serious problem at hand.

## D. MCDONALD'S AUDITOR OPINION AND REPORTS ON INTERNAL CONTROLS

---

### Report of Independent Registered Public Accounting Firm

**The Board of Directors and Shareholders of McDonald's Corporation**

We have audited the accompanying consolidated balance sheets of McDonald's Corporation as of December 31, 2010 and 2009, and the related consolidated statements of income, shareholders' equity, and cash flows for each of the three years in the period ended December 31, 2010. These financial statements are the responsibility of the Company's management. Our responsibility is to express an opinion on these financial statements based on our audits.

We conducted our audits in accordance with the standards of the Public Company Accounting Oversight Board (United States). Those standards require that we plan and perform the audit to obtain reasonable assurance about whether the financial statements are free of material misstatement. An audit includes examining, on a test basis, evidence supporting the amounts and disclosures in the financial statements. An audit also includes assessing the accounting principles used and significant estimates made by management, as well as evaluating the overall financial statement presentation. We believe that our audits provide a reasonable basis for our opinion.

*In our opinion, the financial statements referred to above **present fairly, in all material respects, the consolidated financial position** of McDonald's Corporation at December 31, 2010 and 2009, and the consolidated results of its operations and its cash flows for each of the three years in the period ended December 31, 2010, in conformity with U.S. generally accepted accounting principles.* [Emphases added.]

We also have audited, in accordance with the standards of the Public Company Accounting Oversight Board (United States), McDonald's Corporation's internal control over financial reporting as of December 31, 2010, based on criteria established in Internal Control-Integrated Framework issued by the Committee of Sponsoring Organizations of the Treadway Commission, and our report dated February 25, 2011 expressed an unqualified opinion thereon.

ERNST & YOUNG LLP
February 25, 2011

---

## Management's Assessment of Internal Control over Financial Reporting

The financial statements were prepared by management, which is responsible for their integrity and objectivity and for establishing and maintaining adequate internal controls over financial reporting.

The Company's internal control over financial reporting is designed to provide reasonable assurance regarding the reliability of financial reporting and the preparation of financial statements for external purposes in accordance with generally accepted accounting principles.

The Company's internal control over financial reporting includes those policies and procedures that:

I. pertain to the maintenance of records that, in reasonable detail, accurately and fairly reflect the transactions and dispositions of the assets of the Company;

II. provide reasonable assurance that transactions are recorded as necessary to permit preparation of financial statements in accordance with generally accepted accounting principles, and that receipts and expenditures of the Company are being made only in accordance with authorizations of management and directors of the Company; and

III. provide reasonable assurance regarding prevention or timely detection of unauthorized acquisition, use or disposition of the Company's assets that could have a material effect on the financial statements.

There are inherent limitations in the effectiveness of any internal control, including the possibility of human error and the circumvention or overriding of controls. Accordingly, even effective internal controls can provide only reasonable assurances with respect to financial statement preparation. Further, because of changes in conditions, the effectiveness of internal controls may vary over time.

Management assessed the design and effectiveness of the Company's internal control over financial reporting as of December 31, 2010. In making this assessment, management used the criteria set forth by the Committee of Sponsoring Organizations of the Treadway Commission ("COSO") in Internal Control—Integrated Framework.

*Based on management's assessment using those criteria, as of December 31, 2010, management believes that the Company's **internal control over financial reporting is effective**.* [Emphases added.]

Ernst & Young, LLP, independent registered public accounting firm, has audited the financial statements of the Company for the fiscal years ended December 31, 2010, 2009 and 2008 and the Company's internal control over financial reporting as of December 31, 2010. Their reports are presented on the following pages. The independent registered public accountants and internal auditors advise management of the results of their audits, and make recommendations to improve the system of internal controls. Management evaluates the audit recommendations and takes appropriate action.

McDONALD'S CORPORATION
February 25, 2011

## Report of Independent Registered Public Accounting Firm on Internal Control over Financial Reporting

### The Board of Directors and Shareholders of McDonald's Corporation

We have audited McDonald's Corporation's internal control over financial reporting as of December 31, 2010, based on criteria established in Internal Control—Integrated Framework issued by the Committee of Sponsoring Organizations of the Treadway Commission (the COSO criteria). McDonald's Corporation's management is responsible for maintaining effective internal control over financial reporting, and for its assessment of the effectiveness of internal control over financial reporting included in the accompanying report on Management's Assessment of Internal Control over Financial Reporting. Our responsibility is to express an opinion on the Company's internal control over financial reporting based on our audit.

We conducted our audit in accordance with the standards of the Public Company Accounting Oversight Board (United States). Those standards require that we plan and perform the audit to obtain reasonable assurance about whether effective internal control over financial reporting was maintained in all material respects. Our audit included obtaining an understanding of internal control over financial reporting, assessing the risk that a material weakness exists, testing and evaluating the design and operating effectiveness of internal control based on the assessed risk, and performing such other procedures as we considered necessary in the circumstances. We believe that our audit provides a reasonable basis for our opinion.

A company's internal control over financial reporting is a process designed to provide reasonable assurance regarding the reliability of financial reporting and the preparation of financial statements for external purposes in accordance with generally accepted accounting principles. A company's internal control over financial reporting includes those policies and procedures that (1) pertain to the maintenance of records that, in reasonable detail, accurately and fairly reflect the transactions and dispositions of the assets of the company; (2) provide reasonable assurance that transactions are recorded as necessary to permit preparation of financial statements in accordance with generally accepted accounting principles, and that receipts and expenditures of the company are being made only in accordance with authorizations of management and directors of the company; and (3) provide reasonable assurance regarding prevention or timely detection of unauthorized acquisition, use, or disposition of the company's assets that could have a material effect on the financial statements.

Because of its inherent limitations, internal control over financial reporting may not prevent or detect misstatements. Also, projections of any evaluation of effectiveness to future periods are subject to the risk that controls may become inadequate because of changes in conditions, or that the degree of compliance with the policies or procedures may deteriorate.

*In our opinion, McDonald's Corporation **maintained, in all material respects, effective internal control** over financial reporting as of December 31, 2010, based on the COSO criteria.* [Emphases added.]

We also have audited, in accordance with the standards of the Public Company Accounting Oversight Board (United States), the consolidated financial statements of McDonald's Corporation as of December 31, 2010 and 2009 and for each of the three years in the period ended December 31, 2010, and our report dated February 25, 2011 expressed an unqualified opinion thereon.

ERNST & YOUNG LLP
February 25, 2011

# E. CASE APPLICATION

The case below illustrates the circumstances under which an auditor will disclaim an opinion because a company's internal controls were found woefully inadequate. In reading the case, think about the lawyer's role in maintaining accurate accounting of the client's books and records, and the potential legal liability arising from deficient accounting and internal control processes.

## SEC v. World-Wide Coin Investments, Ltd.
### 567 F. Supp. 724 (N.D. Ga. 1983)

VINING, District Judge.

This is a securities fraud action in which the Securities and Exchange Commission (SEC) seeks a permanent injunction against World-Wide Coin Investments, Ltd. (World-Wide) and the individual defendants as well as an order for a full accounting and disclosure of wrongfully received benefits. In an order entered March 29, 1983, this court directed the clerk to enter judgment for the SEC on all counts of the complaint.

### Factual Background

World-Wide Coin Investments, Ltd., is a Delaware corporation with its principal offices in Atlanta, Georgia, and is engaged primarily in the wholesale and retail sale of rare coins, precious metals, gold and silver coins, bullion, and, until 1979, in the retail sale of camera equipment. Its operations also include the sale of Coca-Cola collector items and certain commemorative items. Its inventory of rare coins comes from its purchases of collections from estates and private individuals, purchases from dealers, purchases on domestic commodities exchanges, and purchases at coin shows.

World-Wide's common stock is registered with the SEC pursuant to the Securities Exchange Act of 1934, 15 U.S.C. §78 l(b), and until late 1981 was listed on the Boston Stock Exchange. Prior to July 1979, the company's assets totaled over $2,000,000, and it had over 40 employees. In August 1981, the time of the filing of this lawsuit, the company's assets amounted to less than $500,000, and it had only three employees.

Defendant Joseph H. Hale took over the management and control of World-Wide on July 24, 1979, as the controlling shareholder, chairman of the board, chief executive officer, and president. He was formerly a national bank examiner with the United States Treasury Department and was employed as an accountant and auditor for General Motors and the Glidden Company, where he obtained an understanding of the importance of internal controls and the concept of "GAAP" (generally accepted accounting principles). Following these experiences, he became a broker-dealer and is registered with the National Association of Securities Dealers (NASD) and the New York Stock Exchange.

Defendant Floyd Seibert is an employee of Health-Care International, Inc., a member of the board of directors of Florafax, Inc., and in September 1979 became a member of World-Wide's board of directors; he also constitutes World-Wide's one-man audit committee.

III. Events Following Hale's Takeover

A. 1979 10K Report and Related Events

Soon after Hale acquired control of World-Wide, he terminated the chief financial officer of the company, and for the next month or so, the company's accounting books were virtually ignored. General ledgers and general journals were not kept, and the checks written on World-Wide's five checking accounts were not reconciled.

In early October 1979, Hale hired Patricia Allen as a bookkeeper to set up the books and to take full responsibility for maintaining the books and records of World-Wide. Another part of her responsibilities included preparing the 10Q reports to be filed with the SEC. Ms. Allen was not a high school graduate; her only experience for this position consisted of five months of vocational school training and seven years of bookkeeping for a privately held lumber company.

The only other person in the company's accounting department was Seibert, the one-man audit committee, who was also Ms. Allen's theoretical supervisor. Seibert had no experience with a publicly held company such as World-Wide and in fact was not a paid employee of the company, since he was a full-time employee of Health Care, one of World-Wide's subsidiaries. As a result, he was rarely available to advise Ms. Allen on any bookkeeping matters.

On November 5, 1979, Kanes, Benator [the company's accountant] wrote a letter to Hale following a routine, required evaluation of World-Wide's system of internal controls, expressing grave concern over certain accounting procedures and lack of internal controls that Kanes, Benator considered to be detrimental to the company. In this letter, Kanes, Benator noted the following material weaknesses and conditions: (1) An evaluation of the company's internal controls during the period subsequent to the fiscal year ending July 31, 1979, disclosed that an adequate segregation of duties between employees was not properly maintained. One employee was posting the cash receipts journal, the disbursements journal, the general ledger, and the accounts receivable subsidiary ledger, filing all sales invoices, making bank deposits, reconciling bank statements, and issuing disbursement checks. (2) Numerous transactions recorded on the company books by general entries were not properly explained nor accompanied by readily available documentation. (3) The accounting records in general were not properly filed nor available for proper inspection. (4) The accounting and other staff familiar with the company's procedures were not available to assist the auditors at the requested or even at a prearranged time.

This letter from Kanes, Benator officially notified World-Wide of its deficiencies in its internal accounting controls and further stated that these deficiencies would be considered by Kanes, Benator in its examinations of the company's financial statements in the future. Even with this official notice that improvements were needed, Hale and Seibert did nothing to remedy the situation, and the criticisms of Kanes, Benator were virtually ignored. Kanes, Benator was dismissed as the company's auditor following this 1979 audit, and May, Zima & Co. was selected as the replacement on May 6, 1980. A form 8K disclosing this change was filed with the SEC on August 13, 1980, over two and a half months after it was due.

## B.  1980 10K Report and Related Events

The company's problems increased in 1980, mostly resulting from its chaotic book-keeping practices and total disregard for an adequate internal control system. World-Wide's problems in this regard will be emphasized in the following subsection of this order; the focus of this subsection will be the misrepresentations and omissions contained in the 1980 10K report. May, Zima & Co., World-Wide's independent auditor for its 1980 10K report, declined to give an opinion with respect to the company's 1980 financial statements[21] stating:

> [T]he company was advised of an uncertainty relating to a possible violation of the provisions of the Foreign Corrupt Practices Act of 1977. The ultimate outcome of the implications of the violations of the federal act cannot be determined and no provision or any liability that may result has been made in the 1980 financial statements.
>
> The company had significant deficiencies in internal controls including the lack of detailed records and certain supporting data which were not available for our examination. Therefore, we were not able to obtain sufficient evidence in order to form an opinion on the accompanying financial statements including whether the inventory at July 31, 1980 ($450,750) was stated at the lower of the cost or market or whether the detailed subscription revenue ($60,878) is an adequate estimate for the applicable liability. . . .
>
> Because of the significance of the matters discussed in the preceding paragraphs, the scope of our work was not sufficient to enable us to express, and we do not express, an opinion on the accompanying financial statements and related schedules.

This 1980 10K report, also prepared by Hale and Seibert without assistance of counsel, indicated that the company was in the process of correcting the deficiencies in its internal accounting controls because of May, Zima's disclaimer opinion. It soon became apparent, however, that no substantive improvements were ever made.

## C.  Problems with Internal Controls and Accounting Procedures

On November 5, 1979, Kanes, Benator, as World-Wide's independent auditor, warned Hale and World-Wide that a good and sound internal accounting control system was necessary to ensure the safeguarding of assets against losses from unauthorized use of dispositions and of financial records for preparing financial statements and maintaining accountability for assets. Although the company was notified of the importance of a good system of internal controls, this warning was

---

21. Plaintiff's Exhibit Number 59 (p. F-1) is May, Zima's report of its 1980 audit of World-Wide, which states that an opinion of the auditor is disclaimed. Robert Johnson, a certified public accountant and a securities partner at May, Zima, testified that there were four types of opinions that an auditor can render following a detailed examination of the company's internal controls systems and books and records: (1) an unqualified opinion, expressing no reservations about the company's financial operation, (2) a qualified opinion, stating that the auditor's opinion contains significant contingencies about the company's well-being, (3) an adverse opinion, stating that the company's financial statements do not represent a fair and accurate picture of the company, and (4) a disclaimer, stating that because of certain circumstances, including limited work opportunities, the auditor could not reach an opinion. The reasons for the disclaimer of World-Wide, according to Johnson, were that the company's internal controls and accounting methods had too many internal weaknesses, supporting documents and records were non-existent, inventory control was totally non-existent, there was a lack of qualified personnel running the business operations, and there was a failure to properly amortize receipts from subscriptions to The Coin Wholesaler.

ignored, and any control system that had existed at World-Wide ceased to exist. The problems that occurred at the company with respect to internal controls and accounting procedures can be divided into three areas: (1) inventory problems, (2) problems with separation of duties and the lack of documentation of transactions, and (3) problems with the books, records, and accounting procedures of the company.

## (1) Inventory Problems

The safeguarding of World-Wide's physical inventory was one of its most severe problems; there was considerable testimony at trial to the effect that the company's vault, where most of the rare coins were kept, was unguarded and left open all day to all employees. Furthermore, no one employee was responsible for the issuance of coins from the vault, according to the accountants from May, Zima, who performed the 1980 audit. Scrap silver and bags of silver coins were left unattended in the hallways and in several cluttered, unlocked rooms at World-Wide's offices. During the trial, Hale admitted that he was worried about thefts due both to faulty record-keeping and the system of safeguarding the assets.

Hale also failed to initiate an adequate system of itemizing World-Wide's physical inventory. Rather than maintaining a perpetual inventory system, the company relied on a manual quarterly system, which, in light of the company's inadequate securities measures, was not effective in safeguarding the assets or in keeping an accurate account of the inventory. World-Wide's system made it relatively simple for an employee to improperly value and/or misappropriate large items of inventory undetected. Furthermore, employees were allowed to take large amounts of inventory off the premises of World-Wide for purposes of effecting a sale without giving a receipt.

An accurate valuation of World-Wide's inventory was never accomplished, and Clifford Haygood, the accountant from May, Zima who performed the field work for the 1980 audit, testified that a major reason for the disclaimed opinion in 1980 was the inability to determine the valuation of the cost of inventory.

## (2) Separation of Duties

The lack of qualified personnel working in World-Wide's offices and the company's policy of allowing one individual to accomplish numerous transactions was another primary reason for May, Zima's disclaimed opinion, and was a major concern of Kanes, Benator in its letter of November 5, 1979. This court has previously noted the lack of supervision over the accounting department, managed by Patricia Allen, and her lack of expertise in the area. World-Wide maintains no separation of duties in the area of purchase and sales transactions, and valuation procedures for ending inventory.

Employees, none of whom was bonded, were also allowed to take large amounts of inventory off the company's premises for purposes of effecting a sale without giving a receipt, as well as being given cash to purchase the precious metals and coins at various locations, also without giving a receipt. Nor were employees required to write source documents relating to the purchase and sale of coins, bullion, and other inventory, making it impossible, as Haygood testified, to ascertain whether a particular inventory item had been sold at a profit or loss, or whether it had even been sold. Although pre-numbered invoices could have been used to help alleviate this problem, they were not; there was a complete lack of control over any retail countersales, and Haygood testified that he could not match cash coming in or out with the merchandise going out.

### (3) Books and Records

During his inspection of World-Wide's offices, Haygood stated that the records of operations for Hale's subsidiaries, such as World-Wide Camera Fair, were scattered throughout the office and were not in any order. Although Haygood was aware of the existence of World-Wide Camera Fair following a review of Kanes, Benator's work papers from 1979, he stated that he was unsure about the documentation and the sale of other companies such as World-Wide Rare Metals and Chattanooga Coin and Stamp. With respect to this latter subsidiary, Haygood was unable to identify it as a separate and existing corporation since it had been merged into World-Wide's balance sheet, making it impossible to differentiate between the good will of World-Wide and that of Chattanooga Coin and Stamp. Furthermore, this failure to consolidate the subsidiaries into the form and financial statements rendered the 10Q reports incorrect for fiscal year 1980.

Haygood also testified the company's books were chaotic with respect to the deferred revenue received from subscriptions to the company newspaper, The Coin Wholesaler. There were no accurate records setting out the dates of subscriptions; therefore, the amount of deferred revenue simply had to be estimated on the company's books.

During May, Zima's inspection at the premises, on July 31, 1980, Haygood and other representatives from May, Zima met with Jones and Seibert to express their concern about the state of World-Wide's control procedures and accounting methods. Seibert and Jones acknowledged the problems noted and agreed that a totally separate inventory would be prepared by Nofal and later compared to the inventory prepared by the company's employee with appropriate reconciliation of differences in order to establish an acceptable, reasonable valuation of inventory. Robert Johnson, a partner at May, Zima, suggested that the company immediately obtain and consult with a securities attorney relative to the necessary action that should be taken as a result of the information May, Zima provided concerning its evaluation of the company's internal accounting control system and the effect on May, Zima's opinion. Johnson further indicated that there was a possible violation of the Foreign Corrupt Practices Act and that World-Wide should seek advice concerning that possibility.

World-Wide eventually agreed to retain the law firm of Jones, Bird & Howell and met with Frank Bird of that firm on August 18, 1980. At that meeting, there was a discussion of how World-Wide should communicate to the SEC. Bird agreed that the disclosure should be made immediately and that a Form 8K should be filed on the report received from the company's auditors advising it of a possible problem with the provisions of the Foreign Corrupt Practices Act, a possible disclaimer of opinion on the company's financial statements and the effects on the company's estimated net income resulting from the write-off of investments and subsidiaries. Seibert agreed to draft a Form 8K to disclose these items and to make a press release on the revised estimated income.

Application of Law

I. Foreign Corrupt Practices Act

The Foreign Corrupt Practices Act, 15 U.S.C. §78m(b)(2) (Amend.1977) ("FCPA") was enacted by Congress as an amendment to the 1934 Securities Exchange Act and was the legislative response to numerous questionable and illegal foreign payments by United States corporations in the 1970's. Although one of the major substantive provisions of the FCPA is to require corporate disclosure of assets as a deterrent to foreign bribes, the more significant addition of the FCPA is the accounting controls or "books and records" provision, which gives the SEC authority over the entire financial management and reporting requirements of publicly held United States corporations.

The FCPA was enacted on the principle that accurate recordkeeping is an essential ingredient in promoting management responsibility and is an affirmative requirement for publicly held American corporations to strengthen the accuracy of corporate books and records, which are "the bedrock elements of our system of corporate disclosure and accountability." A motivating factor in the enactment of the FCPA was a desire to protect the investor, as was the purpose behind the enactment of the Securities Acts. It is apparent that investors are entitled to rely on the implicit representations that corporations will account for their funds properly and will not channel funds out of the corporation or omit to include such funds in the accounting system so that there are no checks possible on how much of the corporation's funds are being expended in the manner management later claims.

Like the anti-fraud provisions of the 1934 Securities Exchange Act, the FCPA's provisions on accounting controls are short and deceptively straightforward. Section 13(b)(2) of the FCPA provides that every issuer having a class of securities registered pursuant to section 12 of the Exchange Act shall:

   (a) Make and keep books, records, and accounts which, in reasonable detail, accurately and fairly reflect the transactions and dispositions of the assets of the issuer; and

   (b) Devise and maintain a system of internal accounting controls sufficient to provide reasonable assurances that

      (i) transactions are executed in accordance with management's general or specific authorization;

     (ii) transactions are recorded as necessary (I) to permit preparation of financial statements in conformity with generally accepted accounting principles or any other criteria applicable to such statements, and (II) to maintain accountability for assets;

    (iii) access to assets is permitted only in accordance with management's general or specific authorization; and

    (iv) the recorded accountability for assets is compared with the existing assets at reasonable intervals and appropriate action is taken with respect to any differences.

The accounting provisions of the FCPA will undoubtedly affect the governance and accountability mechanisms of most major and minor corporations, the work of their independent auditors, and the role of the Securities and Exchange Commission. The maintenance of financial records and internal accounting controls are major every-day activities of every registered and/or reporting company. The

FCPA also has important implications for the SEC, since the incorporation of the accounting provisions into the federal securities laws confers on the SEC new rule-making and enforcement authority over the control and record-keeping mechanisms of its registrants. The FCPA reflects a congressional determination that the scope of the federal securities laws and the SEC's authority should be expanded beyond the traditional ambit of disclosure requirements. The consequence of adding these substantive requirements governing accounting control to the federal securities laws will significantly augment the degree of federal involvement in the internal management of public corporations.

Section 13(b)(2) contains two separate requirements for issuers in complying with the FCPA's accounting provisions: (1) a company must keep accurate books and records reflecting the transactions and dispositions of the assets of the issuer, and (2) a company must maintain a reliable and adequate system of internal accounting controls. In applying these two separate requirements to the instant case, the court will examine the requirements of each provision and the problems inherent in their interpretation.

Internal accounting control is, generally speaking, only one aspect of a company's total control system; in order to maintain accountability for the disposition of its assets, a business must attempt to make it difficult for its assets to be misappropriated. The internal accounting controls element of a company's control system is that which is specifically designed to provide reasonable, cost-effective safeguards against the unauthorized use or disposition of company assets and reasonable assurances that financial records and accounts are sufficiently reliable for purposes of external reporting. "Internal accounting controls" must be distinguished from the accounting system typically found in a company. Accounting systems process transactions and recognize, calculate, classify, post, summarize, and report transactions. Internal controls safeguard assets and assure the reliability of financial records, one of their main jobs being to prevent and detect errors and irregularities that arise in the accounting systems of the company. Internal accounting controls are basic indicators of the reliability of the financial statements and the accounting system and records from which financial statements are prepared.

Although not specifically delineated in the Act itself, the following directives can be inferred from the internal controls provisions: (1) Every company should have reliable personnel, which may require that some be bonded, and all should be supervised. (2) Account functions should be segregated and procedures designed to prevent errors or irregularities. The major functions of recordkeeping, custodianship, authorization, and operation should be performed by different people to avoid the temptation for abuse of these incompatible functions. (3) Reasonable assurances should be maintained that transactions are executed as authorized. (4) Transactions should be properly recorded in the firm's accounting records to facilitate control, which would also require standardized procedures for making accounting entries. Exceptional entries should be investigated regularly. (5) Access to assets of the company should be limited to authorized personnel. (6) At reasonable intervals, there should be a comparison of the accounting records with the actual inventory of assets, which would usually involve the physical taking of inventory, the counting of cash, and the reconciliation of accounting records with the actual physical assets. Frequency of these comparisons will usually depend on the cost of the process and upon the materiality of the assets involved.

The definition of accounting controls does comprehend reasonable, but not absolute, assurances that the objectives expressed in it will be accomplished by the system. The concept of "reasonable assurances" contained in section 13(b)(2)(B) recognizes that the costs of internal controls should not exceed the benefits expected to be derived. It does not appear that either the SEC or Congress, which adopted the SEC's recommendations, intended that the statute should require that each affected issuer install a fail-safe accounting control system at all costs. It appears that Congress was fully cognizant of the cost-effective considerations which confront companies as they consider the institution of accounting controls and of the subjective elements which may lead reasonable individuals to arrive at different conclusions. Congress has demanded only that judgment be exercised in applying the standard of reasonableness. The size of the business, diversity of operations, degree of centralization of financial and operating management, amount of contact by top management with day-to-day operations, and numerous other circumstances are factors which management must consider in establishing and maintaining an internal accounting controls system. However, an issuer would probably not be successful in arguing a cost-benefit defense in circumstances where the management, despite warnings by its auditors or significant weaknesses of its accounting control system, had decided, after a cost benefit analysis, not to strengthen them, and then the internal accounting controls proved to be so inadequate that the company was virtually destroyed. It is also true that the internal accounting controls provisions contemplate the financial principle or proportionality—what is material to a small company is not necessarily material to a large company.

No organization, no matter how small, should ignore the provisions of the FCPA completely, as World-Wide did. Furthermore, common sense dictates the need for such internal controls and procedures in a business with an inventory as liquid as coins, medals, and bullion.

## QUESTIONS

1. This case illustrates the importance of proper accounting. Knowing these facts, would you feel comfortable lending money to World-Wide Coin Investments?
2. Suppose the auditors did not do their job properly and gave an unqualified opinion to World-Wide Coin Investments. What are the broader economic consequences of their failure?
3. What were the accounting problems at World-Wide Coin Investments?
4. Imagine that you are a corporate lawyer with expertise in securities laws and compliance with the Foreign Corrupt Practices Act. In concrete terms, what will be the daily activities of your practice? What skill sets will you need?
5. The court writes: "The definition of accounting controls does comprehend reasonable, but not absolute, assurances that the objectives expressed in it will be accomplished by the system." Assume that this was a part of legislative design. If so, why do you think that the legislature did not provide specific legislative definition of reasonable and unreasonable internal controls?
6. What is the distinction between a firm's accounting systems and its internal control system?

## ESSENTIAL TERMS

Audit
Auditor's opinion letter
Credit
Debit

Double entry bookkeeping
General ledger
Internal control reports
T-accounts

## KEY CONCEPTS

1. Financial statements are interconnected.
2. Accountants record transactions, keep books, and construct financial statements using the double-entry bookkeeping system.
3. A double-entry bookkeeping system means that every transaction will have offsetting debit and credit entries.
4. An auditor's report is important to provide an independent verification of the firm's financial results.
5. An unqualified report states that "the financial statements present fairly, in all material respects" the financial position of the company. This is good.
6. A qualified report must be inspected closely and it presents a serious issue concerning some aspect of the company's finances and accounting process.
7. In addition to the auditor's report, the independent accounting firm and the company's management report on the state of the company's internal controls.

## REVIEW QUESTIONS

1. What were the opinions given on the state of McDonald's internal control?
2. Kingsfield Inc.'s receivables were: $15,000 in Year 1, and $5,000 in Year 2. Construct the T-accounts to record these transactions.
3. Suppose that Kingsfield Inc. did not raise $50,000 in new equity from Professor Kingsfield's colleagues. Assume that all other transactions were executed. What effect does this have on the balance sheet for Year 2? How would the loan repayment to Bob's Equipment have been funded?
4. Conduct a financial analysis of Kingsfield Inc.'s Year 1 and Year 2 results, including profit margin, ROA, ROE, liquidity, and solvency analyses.

# PART TWO

# PRINCIPLES OF FINANCE AND VALUATION

## CHAPTER 7

# TIME VALUE OF MONEY

---

## A. WHAT IS FINANCE?

Finance is a subfield of economics that fundamentally concerns the valuation of uncertain cash flows in the future. It is the economic discipline that has the most direct application to business and corporate transactions. Business lawyers who routinely advise corporations can work effectively without knowing the academic foundations of other economics disciplines such as microeconomics or macroeconomics, or even economic analysis of law (apologies to economists and law & economics professors). The same cannot be said for their ignorance in basic principles of finance. One must have a basic grasp of finance to understand what business clients are thinking, why corporate deals get done, and how they are structured. Without it, the business lawyer is merely a form document caretaker and a cut-and-paste functionary.

Before we undertake the study of basic concepts, we briefly ponder the philosophy of risk and uncertainty. We live in a risky world. Our lives and endeavors are subject to uncertain outcomes, for example: Will it rain tomorrow? Will a magnitude 9.0 earthquake strike California in the next ten years? Will next week's lottery hit 8656? Will the jury find the defendant liable at the end of trial? Will next year's earnings of Google increase? In the practical sense, certainty means there is only one possible future outcome, for example: Will the sun rise from the east tomorrow? Or will a six-sided die with the number "1" on each side roll a "1" on the next turn? Few things in life are so certain. Life is full of surprises, pleasant and unpleasant. Unpleasant uncertainty is the reason why we have a robust insurance market—we want to protect the economic value of our lives, health, and properties from risk.

Uncertainty is the governing condition of our lives. It is also the governing condition of most business propositions. How many surefire ways are there to make a profit? Such opportunities are few and far between, and most business enterprises are subject to great uncertainty of future prospect. If economic fortune could be controlled, we would all be billionaires. Fortunes are made and lost in a market economy. The engagement of business is risky. If so, how do we value a business or a corporate transaction? Finance provides the principles to value the economic return expected in the *future*. This is important because all economic assets and business enterprises—such as corporations—are valued based on their *expected future* economic returns.

EXAMPLE 7.1

---

### When Harry met Sally . . . and started a business

In the bliss of romance, Harry and Sally wanted to do something "wild and crazy." Tired of always being rational, Sally said, "Let's create a corporation that will do absolutely nothing. We'll drop one dollar into its bank account and let it sit there." Harry replied, "I always wanted to be the CEO of a company." Sally demanded to be the chairwoman of the board. "Deal!" Harry declared. They giggled like children. Continuing their silliness, they incorporated One Dollar Corp. by filing the necessary charter papers with the state of Delaware. They capitalized the company with one dollar, which is deposited into the company's bank account. The corporation has no other assets or liabilities. It has no corporate purpose yet and is not expected to engage in any enterprise.

*Assuming no transaction cost, if someone wants to buy 100 percent of the shares in One Dollar Corp. held by Harry and Sally, how much is it worth? Why?*

Having grown tired of their frivolity, Harry and Sally sought to take their relationship to a more serious level. Rather than liquidating their purposeless company, Sally saw a business opportunity. She proposed, "Our romance is a great story. It's an asset. We can sell our story. One Dollar Corporation can produce a film called *When Harry Met Sally*, based on our romance." Harry replied, "I like it! The idea has commercial potential. Let's commit to pursing this enterprise seriously." The company still has only one dollar in its bank account, but it now has a serious purpose, a commercially viable enterprise to pursue, and a management team (Harry and Sally) devoted to turning a profit. Of course, we don't know if the venture will ultimately make a profit.

*If someone wants to invest in One Dollar Corp. now, how much is the company worth?*

We don't know the exact value because we lack critical financial information. But a company with a commercially viable enterprise is probably worth more than the one dollar that is in its bank account as reflected in the firm's balance sheet. Why? Because some value must be attributed to the expectation that this company can make a profit in the future from a promising movie called *When Harry Met Sally*.

---

The primary function of a business lawyer is to advise clients on various transactions. Corporate transactions are done to create value (wealth), and accordingly valuation and finance are often critical issues. The law plays important roles in creating and distributing value. To properly advise clients, the lawyer must have a basic understanding of finance and valuation. The study of finance always begins with an understanding of the time value of money.

A fair warning: sections B and C involve some mathematical concepts. The math is not difficult, but the concepts are abstract and require some reflection on your part. The math performed in sections B and C is done in some variation thereof by business clients and their financial advisers in most large or complex corporate transactions. *All sophisticated clients* understand as basic knowledge the concepts in sections B and C. Shouldn't you?

## B. TIME VALUE OF MONEY

Money has a time value. To illustrate, imagine that you are a time traveler. When you travel, you take all of your money with you, which is a single $100 bill. As you travel through Einstein's space-time continuum, you are subject to a number of weird and exotic phenomena. In addition to the strange visual sensation of traveling almost at the speed of light, you also notice that even the $100 bill in your pocket displays magical properties: although its physical form (a $100 paper note) remains the same, the money changes in value as you travel through time. When you go back in time, you discover that it has greater value (you are richer than you were in the present); and when you travel into the future, you find that the same note has less value (you are poorer). Time travel is weird in physics, and it is weird in finance as well.

Consider another more earthly example. The U.S. government wants to borrow $1,000 from you, and it will return this principal in ten years. Assume that the U.S. government's promise is risk-free (there is no credit risk). Would you lend the government your hard-earned $1,000 at no interest since you will certainly get it back ten years later? Of course not!

 **Money has a time value:** *a dollar today is always worth more than a dollar tomorrow.*

Several factors contribute to the time value of money. First, money depreciates in value. This is called *inflation*, which is the economic phenomenon where the price of goods and services increase relative to the same dollar.

EXAMPLE 7.2

### Inflation and the price of movie tickets

The author remembers a time in the 1970s when movie tickets were about $2.00. Below is historic data for the average cost of a movie ticket.

| Year | Price | Year | Price |
|------|-------|------|-------|
| 2010 | 7.89 | 1975 | 2.03 |
| 2005 | 6.41 | 1971 | 1.65 |
| 2000 | 5.39 | 1967 | 1.22 |
| 1995 | 4.35 | 1963 | 0.86 |
| 1990 | 4.22 | 1958 | 0.68 |
| 1985 | 3.55 | 1954 | 0.49 |
| 1980 | 2.69 | 1948 | 0.36 |

Source: National Association of Theatre Owners

The nominal price of movie tickets increased almost 300 percent from the 1970s (from $2.03 in 1975 to $7.89 in 2010). This is primarily attributable to the fact that inflation decreases the value of money. The true value of the film experience did not increase three-fold for the average moviegoer (meaning that moviegoers probably enjoyed the movie experience in the 1970s about the same as they do now and pay accordingly . . . was *Avatar* so much more enjoyable than *Star Wars* at their respective releases?). The increase in the nominal price is mostly attributable to inflation. Inflation has increased the nominal price of a movie ticket, but concomitantly the wages of the average worker have also increased.

Thus, dollar values from different periods of time must be adjusted from "nominal" values (the unadjusted numeric values of price and money) to "real" values, which account for inflation and the time value of money.

Second, money also has time value because by not spending the money today, one is delaying consumption until the future. Since consumption is a benefit, its delay is a detriment and the investor (who lends his capital) must be awarded with a financial return. As the old adage goes, "Good things come to those who wait."

 **STOP AND THINK**  If money depreciates with time due to inflation, does it make sense to put all of your investment money in a zero-interest checking bank account because it will be "safe" in a bank?

## 1. FUTURE VALUE

If money has a time value, we must be able to calculate the future value. *Future value* means the value of money in some future time.

EXAMPLE 7.3

### The power of compounding

1. *You deposit $100 in an interest-bearing account that earns 5 percent. At the end of one year, how much will you have in your account?*

$$\$100.00 \times (1 + 5\%) = \$105.00$$

2. *You are thrifty, and you leave the money in the account for another year. At the end of the second year, how much will you have in your account?*

$$\$105.00 \times (1 + 5\%) = \$110.25$$

At an interest rate of 5 percent, the depositor earned $10.25 on a deposit of $100 at the end of two years. This is a 10.25 percent total return.

3. *Why isn't the return simply 10% (= 2 x 5%), or $10.00 instead of $10.25?*

The additional $0.25 is the additional 5 percent return on the $5 earned in the first year ($5.00 x 5% = $0.25). Therefore, at the end of the second year, the total return is: $5 first year interest, $0.25 interest on $5 interest, and $5 second year interest. This is the power of *compounding*.

We can generalize the above example to calculate future value. Future value is expressed as:

$$FV = PV \times (1 + R)^T$$

where PV = present value, R = rate of return, and T = time. Future value calculates a sum that an investor would have at some future point in time $T$ given an initial investment $PV$ and an investment rate $R$. The term $(1 + R)^T$ captures the compounding effect of time. For example, in the above bank account hypothetical, we can write:

$$\$110.25 = \$100 \times (1 + 5\%)^2$$

EXAMPLE 7.4

---

**The relationship between time and discount rate**

1. *You deposit $100 in an interest-bearing account that earns 98 percent. At the end of one year, how much is in your account?*

$$\$100 \times (1 + 98\%) = \$198$$

2. *You deposit $100 in an interest-bearing account that earns 5 percent. At the end of 14 years, how much is in your account?*

$$\$100 \times (1 + 5\%)^{14} = \$198$$

At a return rate of 98 percent, it only took one year for an investment of $100 to have a future value of $198. But at a rate of 5 percent, it took 14 years to grow the $100 into the same future value of $198.

---

## 2. PRESENT VALUE

*Present value* is the value of a future sum of money expressed as a present dollar equivalent. Because a dollar today is always worth more than a dollar tomorrow, a future value (or a past value) cannot be compared to the present dollar value unless it is a converted to a present value equivalent.

EXAMPLE 7.5

---

**Discounting future value to present value**

1. *You lend the U.S. government $100 interest-free for five years. Immediately thereafter, you want to sell your right to the return of the principal ($100) five years from now. How should a buyer value this contract?*

2. *Suppose the borrower is not the U.S. government but it is your old college friend Eric, who is sometimes irresponsible with money. The U.S. government will certainly pay back the principal, but Eric is not as creditworthy as the U.S. government. You want to sell your right to the return of the principal ($100) from Eric five years from now. How should a buyer value this contract?*

We intuit several propositions. (1) A buyer would pay less than $100 irrespective of the debtor's creditworthiness. A dollar tomorrow is always worth less than a dollar today. (2) A buyer would not be able to get the contract for nothing. The contracts are not worthless. Therefore, the present value of the contracts are worth somewhere in the

---

---

range between $0 to $100. (3) The U.S. government's promise to repay the $100 is worth more than irresponsible Eric's promise.

Therefore, the present value of the U.S. government debt should be worth more than the present value of Eric's debt (which would you rather own, the promise of payment from the U.S. government or from Eric?).

---

In the above example, the essential problem is converting a future value ($100) to an equivalent present value such that an investor can pay money now (present value) for the right to receive a sum of money in the future. The formula for future value states that there is a mathematical relationship between future value and present value. By simple algebraic rearrangement of the future value formula, we can also calculate the present value if we are given *FV*, *R* and *T*.

The following are the algebraic steps toward deriving the formula for present value.

Step 1:     Start with the formula for future value:

$$PV \times (1 + R)^T = FV$$

Step 2:     Multiply each side of the future value equation by the term $\frac{1}{(1+R)^T}$ so that we can algebraically isolate PV on left side of the equation.[1]

$$PV \times (1 + R)^T \times \frac{1}{(1 + R)^T} = FV \times \frac{1}{(1 + R)^T}$$

$$PV \times \cancel{(1 + R)^T} \times \frac{1}{\cancel{(1 + R)^T}} = FV \times \frac{1}{(1 + R)^T}$$

This equation simplifies to the expression:

$$PV = \frac{FV}{(1 + R)^T}$$

Thus, the *present value* is defined as the future value discounted by an appropriate discount rate and time.

---

**F.Y.I.** *Discount rate* is the term *R* used to perform a present value calculation. It is the rate at which the future value is discounted to derive the present value. Notice that as the discount rate increases, the present value decreases, and vice versa.

---

1. For those of you who are rusty in algebra, multiplying each side of an equation by the same number or term keeps the equation true. For example, if A = A, then multiplying each side by 3 keeps the equation true: 3A = 3A.

EXAMPLE 7.6

> ## More applications and examples of discounting
>
> 1. *Recall in the bank account Problem 7.3, you deposited $100 in an interest-bearing account that earns 5 percent. At the end of one year, your account will have a future value of $105. At the end of two years, it will have a future value of $110.25. Calculate the present value of these future values.*
>
> $$PV = \frac{\$105}{(1 + 5\% )^1} = \$100$$
>
> $$PV = \frac{\$110.25}{(1 + 5\% )^2} = \$100$$
>
> 2. *Your rich uncle Charles leaves you $100,000 in a trust fund that matures in 10 years. Assume that the discount rate is 10 percent. What is the present value of this future value?*
>
> $$PV = \frac{\$100,000}{(1 + 10\% )^{10}} = \frac{\$100,000}{2.5937} = \$38,554$$
>
> We see that $100,000 ten years in the future at a discount rate of 10 percent is not as much money as you initially thought. Still, don't look a gift horse in the mouth (Uncle Charles could have given the gift to someone else).
>
> 3. *A plaintiff suffered injury fairly valued at $100,000. The defendant offers a structured settlement. The defendant offers to pay $20,000 now, and will pay $120,000 five years from now. Assume that the appropriate discount rate is 10 percent (later in this book, in Chapter 9, we will discuss how discount rates are calculated). Should the plaintiff accept this settlement offer?*
>
> $$PV = \frac{\$120,000}{(1 + 10\% )^5} = \frac{\$120,000}{1.6105} = \$74,511$$
>
> The present value of $120,000 is $74,511. The plaintiff also receives $20,000 now. Therefore, the present value of the total settlement offer if $94,511. Since the value of the injury is $100,000, this structured settlement offer is less than the injury value. The plaintiff should reject this offer.

Why do we need to discount future value to present value? Because a dollar today is worth more than a dollar in the future, we cannot compare future values with present values on a like-for-like basis. What does this have to do with business? The value of an asset or a business entity is the economic returns it is expected to generate in the future. These expected cash flows in the future have a present value, which is the value of the asset or business entity. The purchase of a security instrument such as stocks or bonds is paid with cash today, which is a present value. Thus, the business entity or asset must be valued to present value.

## 3. ANNUITY

An annuity is a fixed payment made over a fixed period of time. The formula for calculating an annuity is:

$$PV = \frac{A}{(1+R)^1} + \cdots \cdots + \frac{A}{(1+R)^N}$$

where $A$ is the fixed annuity amount, and the time period is the years $(1 \ldots N)$. An annuity is a series of present value calculations made on a fixed future value and discount rate, but over a defined period of time.

## 4. PERPETUITY FORMULA

Assume that you can live in perpetuity (this is not an unrealistic assumption for a corporation). You are given the right to receive $1 each year in perpetuity. How much is this annuity worth? It is clearly worth more than 0. Is it worth an infinite amount since you are getting an infinite stream of $1? The answer is "no." Somewhere in between zero and infinity $(0, \infty)$ is the correct answer.

The formula to calculate the value is the following, where $A$ is the annuity amount.

$$PV = \frac{A}{R}$$

Note that if $R = 0$, then $PV = \infty$ (any positive value divided by zero is an infinite value). This is intuitively apparent. If $R = 0$, a dollar in the future is worth the same as a dollar today; you are entitled to receive a dollar for every year in perpetuity; thus the stream of cash must be worth an infinite amount. However, if $R > 0$, then $PV \neq \infty$. It must be some finite value.

If the annuity is expected to grow at a constant rate in perpetuity, an unrealistic assumption in many cases (what earnings grow in perpetuity?), the *growth perpetuity formula* calculates the present value.

$$PV = \frac{A}{R - g} \quad \text{where } g \text{ is growth rate}$$

We know that the discount rate $R$ cannot be zero because a fundamental principle of finance is that a dollar tomorrow is *always* worth less than a dollar today. If so, the present value of the infinite stream of $1 cannot be an infinite sum. Assume that the discount rate is 10 percent. What is the value of a perpetual stream of $10?

$$PV = \frac{\$10}{10\%} = \$100$$

Therefore, if a corporation is expected to generate $10 in cash flow in perpetuity and its discount rate is 10%, the value of that corporation must be $100.

Note that growth assumptions can dramatically affect the present value. An aggressive growth assumption can result in high present value. For example, if the $10 annuity is expected to grow at a 5 percent rate with the same discount rate, the present value is $200 (= $10 / (10% − 5%)). If the growth rate is assumed to be 9 percent, the present value is $1,000.

*Capitalization* (or *"cap"*) *rate*: the term *R* when an economic return is assumed to be perpetual. It is the rate at which a perpetual return is "capitalized" to derive the perpetuity value.

## EXAMPLE 7.7

### Valuing corporate earnings

1. *A corporation is expected to receive $10 per year for the reminder of its perpetual life. Assume that the discount rate is 10 percent. What is the present value of this perpetual annuity?*

$$PV = \frac{\$10}{10\%} = \$100$$

2. *A corporation is expected to receive $10 per year for the next 50 years, and then per its charter it will terminate its business and dissolve. Assume that the discount rate is 10 percent. What is the present value of this 50-year annuity? We can discount all 50 cash flows individually.*

$$PV = \frac{\$10}{(1 + 10\%)^1} + \frac{\$10}{(1 + 10\%)^2} + \cdots\cdots + \frac{\$10}{(1 + 10\%)^{49}} + \frac{\$10}{(1 + 10\%)^{50}} = \$99.15$$

Notice that the value attributable to the time period (51 years → infinity) accounts for only $0.85 of value. The further out an expected return is in time, the greater it will be discounted. Therefore, its present value contribution to the total value is minimal.

3. *A corporation is expected to receive $10 next year, and this sum is expected to grow at a constant 2 percent rate. Assume that the discount rate is 10 percent. What is the present value of this perpetual growth annuity?*

$$PV = \frac{\$10}{10\% - 2\%} = \$125$$

## EXAMPLE 7.8

### Valuing real estate

A commercial building is expected to have a rentable life of 100 years. It is expected to generate operating profit of $100 for each year of rentable life. Assume that the building cost $1,000 to buy. Approximately what cap rate does this imply?

$$PV = \frac{A}{R} \text{ can be rearranged to } R = \frac{A}{PV}$$

$$10\% = \frac{\$100}{\$1,000}$$

This means that an investment of $1,000 in a building is expected to earn an approximate return of 10 percent during the rentable life of the building.

Very few things involving economic transactions have perpetual existence, including people and corporations. However, since most of the present value is captured within a specific duration (see question #2 of Example 7.7), we use the capitalization rate to calculate the value of a regular stream of income as a reasonable approximation.

## 5. USING TIME VALUE TABLES

In calculating future value, we take a present value and multiple it by the term $(1 + R)^T$. For example, consider the following series of calculations:

$$
\begin{array}{lll}
6 \text{ years at } 10\% & \Rightarrow (1 + 10\%)^6 & = 1.772 \\
7 \text{ years at } 10\% & \Rightarrow (1 + 10\%)^7 & = 1.949 \\
10 \text{ years at } 6\% & \Rightarrow (1 + 6\%)^{10} & = 1.791 \\
10 \text{ years at } 5\% & \Rightarrow (1 + 5\%)^{10} & = 1.629
\end{array}
$$

Since there are two variables, $R$ and $T$, these calculations can be presented in convenient tabular format.

**FUTURE VALUES TABLE**

|  | | | | | TIME | | | | | |
|---|---|---|---|---|---|---|---|---|---|---|
| | 1 | 2 | 3 | 4 | 5 | 6 | 7 | 8 | 9 | 10 |
| 20% | 1.200 | 1.440 | 1.728 | 2.074 | 2.488 | 2.986 | 3.583 | 4.300 | 5.160 | 6.192 |
| 19% | 1.190 | 1.416 | 1.685 | 2.005 | 2.386 | 2.840 | 3.379 | 4.021 | 4.785 | 5.695 |
| 18% | 1.180 | 1.392 | 1.643 | 1.939 | 2.288 | 2.700 | 3.185 | 3.759 | 4.435 | 5.234 |
| 17% | 1.170 | 1.369 | 1.602 | 1.874 | 2.192 | 2.565 | 3.001 | 3.511 | 4.108 | 4.807 |
| 16% | 1.160 | 1.346 | 1.561 | 1.811 | 2.100 | 2.436 | 2.826 | 3.278 | 3.803 | 4.411 |
| 15% | 1.150 | 1.323 | 1.521 | 1.749 | 2.011 | 2.313 | 2.660 | 3.059 | 3.518 | 4.046 |
| 14% | 1.140 | 1.300 | 1.482 | 1.689 | 1.925 | 2.195 | 2.502 | 2.853 | 3.252 | 3.707 |
| 13% | 1.130 | 1.277 | 1.443 | 1.630 | 1.842 | 2.082 | 2.353 | 2.658 | 3.004 | 3.395 |
| 12% | 1.120 | 1.254 | 1.405 | 1.574 | 1.762 | 1.974 | 2.211 | 2.476 | 2.773 | 3.106 |
| 11% | 1.110 | 1.232 | 1.368 | 1.518 | 1.685 | 1.870 | 2.076 | 2.305 | 2.558 | 2.839 |
| 10% | 1.100 | 1.210 | 1.331 | 1.464 | 1.611 | 1.772 | 1.949 | 2.144 | 2.358 | 2.594 |
| 9% | 1.090 | 1.188 | 1.295 | 1.412 | 1.539 | 1.677 | 1.828 | 1.993 | 2.172 | 2.367 |
| 8% | 1.080 | 1.166 | 1.260 | 1.360 | 1.469 | 1.587 | 1.714 | 1.851 | 1.999 | 2.159 |
| 7% | 1.070 | 1.145 | 1.225 | 1.311 | 1.403 | 1.501 | 1.606 | 1.718 | 1.838 | 1.967 |
| 6% | 1.060 | 1.124 | 1.191 | 1.262 | 1.338 | 1.419 | 1.504 | 1.594 | 1.689 | 1.791 |
| 5% | 1.050 | 1.103 | 1.158 | 1.216 | 1.276 | 1.340 | 1.407 | 1.477 | 1.551 | 1.629 |
| 4% | 1.040 | 1.082 | 1.125 | 1.170 | 1.217 | 1.265 | 1.316 | 1.369 | 1.423 | 1.480 |
| 3% | 1.030 | 1.061 | 1.093 | 1.126 | 1.159 | 1.194 | 1.230 | 1.267 | 1.305 | 1.344 |
| 2% | 1.020 | 1.040 | 1.061 | 1.082 | 1.104 | 1.126 | 1.149 | 1.172 | 1.195 | 1.219 |
| 1% | 1.010 | 1.020 | 1.030 | 1.041 | 1.051 | 1.062 | 1.072 | 1.083 | 1.094 | 1.105 |

DISCOUNT RATE

EXAMPLE 7.9

> ## Using future values table
>
> 1. *What is the future value of $1,000 earning a rate of 7 percent for 7 years? Use the future values table to find the multiple.*
>
> $$\$1,000 \times 1.606 = \$1,606$$
>
> 2. *What is the future value of $1500 earning a rate of 9 percent for 5 years? Use the future values table to find the multiple.*
>
> $$\$1,500 \times 1.539 = \$2,308$$

In calculating present value, we take a future value and discount it by multiplying it with the mathematical term $\dfrac{1}{(1 + R)^T}$.

 *Discount factor* is the term $\dfrac{1}{(1 + R)^T}$ which discounts the future value to present value as determined by the discount rate $R$ and time $T$.

For instance, consider the following series of calculations:

| | | |
|---|---|---|
| 6 years at 10%: | $\Rightarrow \quad \dfrac{1}{(1 + 10\%)^6}$ | $= \quad 0.564$ |
| 7 years at 10%: | $\Rightarrow \quad \dfrac{1}{(1 + 10\%)^7}$ | $= \quad 0.513$ |
| 10 years at 6%: | $\Rightarrow \quad \dfrac{1}{(1 + 6\%)^{10}}$ | $= \quad 0.558$ |
| 10 years at 5%: | $\Rightarrow \quad \dfrac{1}{(1 + 5\%)^{10}}$ | $= \quad 0.614$ |

Since there are two variables, $R$ and $T$, the discount factors can be presented in convenient tabular format.

**PRESENT VALUES TABLE**

| | | | | | TIME | | | | | |
|---|---|---|---|---|---|---|---|---|---|---|
| | 1 | 2 | 3 | 4 | 5 | 6 | 7 | 8 | 9 | 10 |
| 20% | 0.833 | 0.694 | 0.579 | 0.482 | 0.402 | 0.335 | 0.279 | 0.233 | 0.194 | 0.162 |
| 19% | 0.840 | 0.706 | 0.593 | 0.499 | 0.419 | 0.352 | 0.296 | 0.249 | 0.209 | 0.176 |
| 18% | 0.847 | 0.718 | 0.609 | 0.516 | 0.437 | 0.370 | 0.314 | 0.266 | 0.225 | 0.191 |
| 17% | 0.855 | 0.731 | 0.624 | 0.534 | 0.456 | 0.390 | 0.333 | 0.285 | 0.243 | 0.208 |
| 16% | 0.862 | 0.743 | 0.641 | 0.552 | 0.476 | 0.410 | 0.354 | 0.305 | 0.263 | 0.227 |
| 15% | 0.870 | 0.756 | 0.658 | 0.572 | 0.497 | 0.432 | 0.376 | 0.327 | 0.284 | 0.247 |
| 14% | 0.877 | 0.769 | 0.675 | 0.592 | 0.519 | 0.456 | 0.400 | 0.351 | 0.308 | 0.270 |
| 13% | 0.885 | 0.783 | 0.693 | 0.613 | 0.543 | 0.480 | 0.425 | 0.376 | 0.333 | 0.295 |
| 12% | 0.893 | 0.797 | 0.712 | 0.636 | 0.567 | 0.507 | 0.452 | 0.404 | 0.361 | 0.322 |
| 11% | 0.901 | 0.812 | 0.731 | 0.659 | 0.593 | 0.535 | 0.482 | 0.434 | 0.391 | 0.352 |
| 10% | 0.909 | 0.826 | 0.751 | 0.683 | 0.621 | 0.564 | 0.513 | 0.467 | 0.424 | 0.386 |
| 9% | 0.917 | 0.842 | 0.772 | 0.708 | 0.650 | 0.596 | 0.547 | 0.502 | 0.460 | 0.422 |
| 8% | 0.926 | 0.857 | 0.794 | 0.735 | 0.681 | 0.630 | 0.583 | 0.540 | 0.500 | 0.463 |
| 7% | 0.935 | 0.873 | 0.816 | 0.763 | 0.713 | 0.666 | 0.623 | 0.582 | 0.544 | 0.508 |
| 6% | 0.943 | 0.890 | 0.840 | 0.792 | 0.747 | 0.705 | 0.665 | 0.627 | 0.592 | 0.558 |
| 5% | 0.952 | 0.907 | 0.864 | 0.823 | 0.784 | 0.746 | 0.711 | 0.677 | 0.645 | 0.614 |
| 4% | 0.962 | 0.925 | 0.889 | 0.855 | 0.822 | 0.790 | 0.760 | 0.731 | 0.703 | 0.676 |
| 3% | 0.971 | 0.943 | 0.915 | 0.888 | 0.863 | 0.837 | 0.813 | 0.789 | 0.766 | 0.744 |
| 2% | 0.980 | 0.961 | 0.942 | 0.924 | 0.906 | 0.888 | 0.871 | 0.853 | 0.837 | 0.820 |
| 1% | 0.990 | 0.980 | 0.971 | 0.961 | 0.951 | 0.942 | 0.933 | 0.923 | 0.914 | 0.905 |

*DISCOUNT RATE* (label on left side of table)

EXAMPLE 7.10

> **Using present values table**
>
> 1. *What is the present value of $1,000 at a discount rate of 8 percent in 10 years? Use the present values table to find the discount factor.*
>
>    $$\$1,000 \times 0.463 = \$463$$
>
> 2. *What is the present value of $1500 at a discount rate of 3 percent in 7 years? Use the present values table to find the discount factor.*
>
>    $$\$1,500 \times 0.813 = \$1,220$$

In calculating the present value of an annuity, we discount the annuity stream by the term $(1 + R)^T$. For example, consider the following series of calculations:

$$6 \text{ years at } 10\% \Rightarrow \frac{A}{(1 + 10\%)^1} + \frac{A}{(1 + 10\%)^2} + \frac{A}{(1 + 10\%)^3}$$
$$+ \frac{A}{(1 + 10\%)^4} + \frac{A}{(1 + 10\%)^5} + \frac{A}{(1 + 10\%)^6}$$

This calculation produces a multiple (in this case 4.355) that we apply to the value $A$ to get the present value of sum of the annuity steam ($A_1 \ldots A_6$).

Since there are two variables, $R$ and $T$, these calculations can be presented in convenient tabular format.

**ANNUITY TABLE**

| DISCOUNT RATE | TIME | | | | | | | | | |
|---|---|---|---|---|---|---|---|---|---|---|
| | 5 | 6 | 7 | 8 | 9 | 10 | 15 | 20 | 25 | 30 |
| 20% | 2.991 | 3.326 | 3.605 | 3.837 | 4.031 | 4.192 | 4.675 | 4.870 | 4.948 | 4.979 |
| 19% | 3.058 | 3.410 | 3.706 | 3.954 | 4.163 | 4.339 | 4.876 | 5.101 | 5.195 | 5.235 |
| 18% | 3.127 | 3.498 | 3.812 | 4.078 | 4.303 | 4.494 | 5.092 | 5.353 | 5.467 | 5.517 |
| 17% | 3.199 | 3.589 | 3.922 | 4.207 | 4.451 | 4.659 | 5.324 | 5.628 | 5.766 | 5.829 |
| 16% | 3.274 | 3.685 | 4.039 | 4.344 | 4.607 | 4.833 | 5.575 | 5.929 | 6.097 | 6.177 |
| 15% | 3.352 | 3.784 | 4.160 | 4.487 | 4.772 | 5.019 | 5.847 | 6.259 | 6.464 | 6.566 |
| 14% | 3.433 | 3.889 | 4.288 | 4.639 | 4.946 | 5.216 | 6.142 | 6.623 | 6.873 | 7.003 |
| 13% | 3.517 | 3.998 | 4.423 | 4.799 | 5.132 | 5.426 | 6.462 | 7.025 | 7.330 | 7.496 |
| 12% | 3.605 | 4.111 | 4.564 | 4.968 | 5.328 | 5.650 | 6.811 | 7.469 | 7.843 | 8.055 |
| 11% | 3.696 | 4.231 | 4.712 | 5.146 | 5.537 | 5.889 | 7.191 | 7.963 | 8.422 | 8.694 |
| 10% | 3.791 | 4.355 | 4.868 | 5.335 | 5.759 | 6.145 | 7.606 | 8.514 | 9.077 | 9.427 |
| 9% | 3.890 | 4.486 | 5.033 | 5.535 | 5.995 | 6.418 | 8.061 | 9.129 | 9.823 | 10.274 |
| 8% | 3.993 | 4.623 | 5.206 | 5.747 | 6.247 | 6.710 | 8.559 | 9.818 | 10.675 | 11.258 |
| 7% | 4.100 | 4.767 | 5.389 | 5.971 | 6.515 | 7.024 | 9.108 | 10.594 | 11.654 | 12.409 |
| 6% | 4.212 | 4.917 | 5.582 | 6.210 | 6.802 | 7.360 | 9.712 | 11.470 | 12.783 | 13.765 |
| 5% | 4.329 | 5.076 | 5.786 | 6.463 | 7.108 | 7.722 | 10.380 | 12.462 | 14.094 | 15.372 |
| 4% | 4.452 | 5.242 | 6.002 | 6.733 | 7.435 | 8.111 | 11.118 | 13.590 | 15.622 | 17.292 |
| 3% | 4.580 | 5.417 | 6.230 | 7.020 | 7.786 | 8.530 | 11.938 | 14.877 | 17.413 | 19.600 |
| 2% | 4.713 | 5.601 | 6.472 | 7.325 | 8.162 | 8.983 | 12.849 | 16.351 | 19.523 | 22.396 |
| 1% | 4.853 | 5.795 | 6.728 | 7.652 | 8.566 | 9.471 | 13.865 | 18.046 | 22.023 | 25.808 |

EXAMPLE 7.11

**Using annuity tables**

1. *What is the present value of 10-year $1,000 annuity discount rate of 8 percent? Use the annuity table to find the multiple.*

$$\$1,000 \times 6.710 = \$6,710$$

2. *What is the present value of 20-year $1,000 annuity discount rate of 14 percent? Use the annuity table to find the multiple.*

$$\$1,000 \times 6.623 = \$6,623$$

In the first question, the person received $10,000 in future payments; and in the second question, the person receives $20,000 in future payments. Yet on a present value basis, the 10-year annuity is more valuable. The difference is the discount rate used, 8 percent versus 14 percent, over different time periods.

## C. INTERNAL RATE OF RETURN

In many financial or corporate transactions, an investment is made today (resulting in cash outflow) and the payback is received in the future. We need to calculate the rate of return R. Why? Suppose the investor has a *"benchmark"* or *"hurdle"* rate that must be met. We must be able to calculate the return rate R so that we can determine whether this business opportunity meets the investment requirement.

The *internal rate of return* (IRR) is the implied rate of return given an investment today and a future payout—in other words, it is the discount rate that equates a present value cash outflow and expected future values given a specific time horizon. The formula below captures this concept (IRR is the discount rate $R$ that satisfies the equation).

$$0 = -PV + \frac{FV}{(1 + R)^T}$$

EXAMPLE 7.12

**How venture capital firms evaluate investment opportunities**

Venture Capital LP ("VC") must consider whether to invest $1,000 in Legal Documents Inc., a company that sells efficient document review services. The financial models indicate that after 7 years, the company can do an IPO or sell itself to a larger company, and VC can exit (monetize) the investment at a value of $3,000. The investors of VC have a hurdle rate of 20 percent, which is their expectation of a return based on the riskiness of venture capital investments (many venture capital investments never pan out and so investors demand a high rate of return). Should VC invest in Legal Documents?

This is a simple time value problem. We are told that we make an investment of $1,000 in present value, and we anticipate a return of $3,000 in future value. We are also given a time horizon, 7 years. We are only missing the rate of return $R$.

$$1,000 = \frac{3,000}{(1 + R)^7}$$

Although formulating the problem is simple, calculating $R$ manually cannot be done because of the complex polynomial term $(1 + R)^7$. Typically, these calculations are done through iterative trial and error, or with a calculator or spreadsheet. When calculated, the IRR is 17 percent. This means that $1,000 growing at a 17 percent rate on a compounded basis will yield $3,000 in 7 years. Do the math yourself and check.

The investment is expected to produce $3,000 in profit after 7 years. But this investment is not profitable enough. The IRR does not meet the hurdle rate of 20 percent, which is the expectation that investors have given the risks they are taking. This means that VC should pass on the opportunity, even though the opportunity is projected to make $3,000 in profit in seven years. The opportunity is simply *not profitable enough* based on the VC's benchmark to invest.

We can visualize the concept of investment and IRR with this schematic.

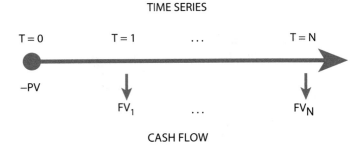

At $T = 0$ (denoting the present time), an investment of PV is made. An investment is a cash outflow, thus $-PV$. At various time, $T = (1 \ldots N)$, there are corresponding future values ($FV_1 \ldots FV_N$). The IRR is the discount rate that must be used to discount all future cash flows ($FV_1 \ldots FV_N$) such that they equal PV.

EXAMPLE 7.13

---

### Calculating IRR using Excel (Part I)

The spreadsheet Excel easily calculates IRR. The function is "=IRR()". For example, Venture Capital LP's investment in Legal Document Inc.'s business is calculated as:

| ROW | | A | B | C | D | E | F | G | H | I |
|---|---|---|---|---|---|---|---|---|---|---|
| | | | | | | COLUMN | | | | |
| | 1 | Year 0 | Year 1 | Year 2 | Year 3 | Year 4 | Year 5 | Year 6 | Year 7 | |
| | 2 | | | | | | | | | |
| | 3 | (1,000) | 0 | 0 | 0 | 0 | 0 | 0 | 3,000 | =IRR(A3:H3) |

The cash flows are laid out as $(-1,000 \ldots +3,000)$ in cells A3 to H3, for years Year 0 (now) to Year 7. Excel has a formula "IRR." To use it properly, we type in "=IRR(A3:H3)" which captures the cash flows from Years 0 to Year 7. Excel goes through an iterative process of trial and error until it finds the correct solution, which in this case is 17%, *i.e.*, $\$1,000 \times (1 + 17\%)^7 = \$3,000$.

---

EXAMPLE 7.14

---

### Calculating IRR using Excel (Part II)

Recall the above example concerning Venture Capital LP ("VC"). When calculated that a $1,000 investment with a $3,000 exit in seven years produces an IRR of 17 percent, which does not meet our hurdle rate of 20 percent.

Further due diligence and financial modeling shows that in addition to the $3,000 exit in year 7, Legal Documents Inc. can pay a dividend of $75 for the years 1 through 7.

| ROW | | A | B | C | D | E | F | G | H | I |
|---|---|---|---|---|---|---|---|---|---|---|
| | | | | | | COLUMN | | | | |
| | 1 | Year 0 | Year 1 | Year 2 | Year 3 | Year 4 | Year 5 | Year 6 | Year 7 | IRR |
| | 2 | | | | | | | | | |
| | 3 | (1,000) | 75 | 75 | 75 | 75 | 75 | 75 | 3,075 | 22.0% |

What is the IRR of the investment now? Does the investment meet VC's benchmark rate?

---

## D. WHAT'S THE POINT?

You went to law school thinking that you'll never see another math formula. What's the point of this math? Why do lawyers need to understand this?

The above mathematical exercises seem abstract and dry (and perhaps tedious), but the math is rich in meaning. Time value of money is the critical concept in the value of assets, such as corporations (or even lost earnings calculations to remedy a tort victim). In economics and business, the value of an asset, such as a corporation or the economic value of a person, is the amount of cash flow it is expected to generate *in the future*. Remember that the future is always uncertain, and that money in the future is always worth less than today's money. Therefore, the value of a thing is the expected future return discounted by *time* and *risk*.

Time value of money is not simply rote math calculations. The mathematical process and its underlying concept have deep significance in understanding the value of corporations and business transactions. Clients always think in terms of value and wealth creation. If business lawyers do not understand the concept of value—an issue that is always on the minds of business clients—they cannot function on a high level.

 The economic value of an asset, such as a corporation, is measured by the amount of the free cash available to the capital providers of the firm (creditors and equityholders) after operating expenses are paid. The free cash flow is expected in the future, which means that these future values must be discounted to present value.

Economic Value = Future Cash Flow Discounted by Time and Risk

## E. CASE APPLICATION

In Chapters 8 and 9, we will build up to a rigorous analysis of valuation in business transactions. In the meantime, below is a case on remedying a tort victim. An essential component of compensation is lost earnings, lost *future* earnings. What does time value of money have to do with tort law? Quite a lot, as Judge Richard Posner notes. In reading this case, think about the tort victim as an economic asset, which is the premise of the remedy structure: How is the asset valued?

### *O'Shea v. Riverway Towing Co.*
677 F.2d 1194 (7th Cir. 1982)

POSNER, Circuit Judge.

This is a tort case under the federal admiralty jurisdiction. We are called upon to decide questions of contributory negligence and damage assessment, in particular the question—one of first impression in this circuit—whether, and if so how, to account for inflation in computing lost future wages.

On the day of the accident, Margaret O'Shea was coming off duty as a cook on a towboat plying the Mississippi River. A harbor boat operated by the defendant, Riverway Towing Company, carried Mrs. O'Shea to shore and while getting off the boat she fell and sustained the injury complained of. The district judge found Riverway negligent and Mrs. O'Shea free from contributory negligence, and assessed damages in excess of $150,000.

The accident happened in the following way. When the harbor boat reached shore it tied up to a seawall the top of which was several feet above the boat's deck. There was no ladder. The other passengers, who were seamen, clambered up the seawall without difficulty, but Mrs. O'Shea, a 57-year-old woman who weighs 200 pounds (she is five foot seven), balked. According to Mrs. O'Shea's testimony, which the district court believed, a deckhand instructed her to climb the stairs to a catwalk above the deck and disembark from there. But the catwalk was three feet above the top of the seawall, and again there was no ladder. The deckhand told her that she should jump and that the men who had already disembarked would help her land safely. She did as told, but fell in landing, carrying the assisting seamen down with her, and broke her leg.

The more substantial issues in this appeal relate to the computation of lost wages. Mrs. O'Shea's job as a cook paid her $40 a day, and since the custom was to work 30 days consecutively and then have the next 30 days off, this comes to $7200 a year although, as we shall see, she never had earned that much in a single year. She testified that when the accident occurred she had been about to get another cook's job on a Mississippi towboat that would have paid her $60 a day ($10,800 a year). She also testified that she had been intending to work as a boat's cook until she was 70—longer if she was able. An economist who testified on Mrs. O'Shea's behalf used the foregoing testimony as the basis for estimating the wages that she lost because of the accident. He first subtracted federal income tax from yearly wage estimates based on alternative assumptions about her wage rate (that it would be either $40 or $60 a day); assumed that this wage would have grown by between six and eight percent a year; assumed that she would have worked either to age 65 or to age 70; and then discounted the resulting lost-wage estimates to present value, using a discount rate of 8.5 percent a year. These calculations, being based on alternative assumptions concerning starting wage rate, annual wage increases, and length of employment, yielded a range of values rather than a single value. The bottom of the range was $50,000. This is the present value, computed at an 8.5 percent discount rate, of Mrs. O'Shea's lost future wages on the assumption that her starting wage was $40 a day and that it would have grown by six percent a year until she retired at the age of 65. The top of the range was $114,000, which is the present value (again discounted at 8.5 percent) of her lost future wages assuming she would have worked till she was 70 at a wage that would have started at $60 a day and increased by eight percent a year. The judge awarded a figure—$86,033—near the midpoint of this range. He did not explain in his written opinion how he had arrived at this figure, but in a preceding oral opinion he stated that he was "not certain that she would work until age 70 at this type of work," although "she certainly was entitled to" do so and "could have earned something"; and that he had not "felt bound by (the economist's) figure of eight per cent increase in wages" and had "not found the wages based on necessarily a 60 dollar a day job." If this can be taken to mean that he thought Mrs. O'Shea would probably have worked till she was 70, starting at $40 a day but moving up from there at six rather than eight percent a year, the economist's estimate of the present value of her lost future wages would be $75,000.

We come at last to the most important issue in the case, which is the proper treatment of inflation in calculating lost future wages. Mrs. O'Shea's economist based the six to eight percent range which he used to estimate future increases in the wages of a boat's cook on the general pattern of wage increases in service occupations over the past 25 years. During the second half of this period the rate of inflation has been substantial and has accounted for much of the increase in nominal wages in this period; and to use that increase to project future wage increases is therefore to assume that inflation will continue, and continue to push up wages. Riverway argues that it is improper as a matter of law to take inflation into account in projecting lost future wages. Yet Riverway itself wants to take inflation into account-one-sidedly, to reduce the amount of the damages computed. For Riverway does not object to the economist's choice of an 8.5 percent discount rate for reducing Mrs. O'Shea's lost future wages to present value, although the rate includes an allowance—a very large allowance—for inflation.

To explain, the object of discounting lost future wages to present value is to give the plaintiff an amount of money which, invested safely, will grow to a sum equal to those wages. So if we thought that but for the accident Mrs. O'Shea would have earned $7200 in 1990, and we were computing in 1980 (when this case was tried) her damages based on those lost earnings, we would need to determine the sum of money that, invested safely for a period of 10 years, would grow to $7200. Suppose that in 1980 the rate of interest on ultra-safe (i.e., federal government) bonds or notes maturing in 10 years was 12 percent. Then we would consult a table of present values to see what sum of money invested at 12 percent for 10 years would at the end of that time have grown to $7200. The answer is $2318. But a moment's reflection will show that to give Mrs. O'Shea $2318 to compensate her for lost wages in 1990 would grossly undercompensate her. People demand 12 percent to lend money risklessly for 10 years because they expect their principal to have much less purchasing power when they get it back at the end of the time. In other words, when long-term interest rates are high, they are high in order to compensate lenders for the fact that they will be repaid in cheaper dollars. In periods when no inflation is anticipated, the risk-free interest rate is between one and three percent. Additional percentage points above that level reflect inflation anticipated over the life of the loan. But if there is inflation it will affect wages as well as prices. Therefore to give Mrs. O'Shea $2318 today because that is the present value of $7200 10 years hence, computed at a discount rate—12 percent—that consists mainly of an allowance for anticipated inflation, is in fact to give her less than she would have been earning then if she was earning $7200 on the date of the accident, even if the only wage increases she would have received would have been those necessary to keep pace with inflation.

There are (at least) two ways to deal with inflation in computing the present value of lost future wages. One is to take it out of both the wages and the discount rate—to say to Mrs. O'Shea, "we are going to calculate your probable wage in 1990 on the assumption, unrealistic as it is, that there will be zero inflation between now and then; and, to be consistent, we are going to discount the amount thus calculated by the interest rate that would be charged under the same assumption of zero inflation." Thus, if we thought Mrs. O'Shea's real (i.e., inflation-free) wage rate would not rise in the future, we would fix her lost earnings in 1990 as $7200 and, to be consistent, we would discount that to present (1980) value using an estimate of the real interest rate. At two percent, this procedure would yield a present value of $5906. Of course, she would not invest this money at a mere two percent. She would invest it at the much higher prevailing interest rate. But that would not give her a windfall; it would just enable her to replace her lost 1990 earnings with an amount equal to what she would in fact have earned in that year if inflation continues, as most people expect it to do. (If people did not expect continued inflation, long-term interest rates would be much lower; those rates impound investors' inflationary expectations.)

An alternative approach, which yields the same result, is to use a (higher) discount rate based on the current risk-free 10-year interest rate, but apply that rate to an estimate of lost future wages that includes expected inflation. Contrary to Riverway's argument, this projection would not require gazing into a crystal ball. The expected rate of inflation can, as just suggested, be read off from the current long-term interest rate. If that rate is 12 percent, and if as suggested earlier the real or inflation-free interest rate is only one to three percent, this implies that the market is anticipating 9-11 percent inflation over the next 10 years, for a long-term interest rate is simply the sum of the real interest rate and the anticipated rate of inflation during the term.

Either approach to dealing with inflation is acceptable (they are, in fact, equivalent) and we by no means rule out others; but it is illogical and indefensible to build inflation into the discount rate yet ignore it in calculating the lost future wages that are to be discounted. That results in systematic undercompensation, just as building inflation into the estimate of future lost earnings and then discounting using the real rate of interest would systematically overcompensate.

Applying our analysis to the present case, we cannot pronounce the approach taken by the plaintiff's economist unreasonable. He chose a discount rate—8.5 percent—well above the real rate of interest, and therefore containing an allowance for inflation. Consistency required him to inflate Mrs. O'Shea's starting wage as a boat's cook in calculating her lost future wages, and he did so at a rate of six to eight percent a year. If this rate had been intended as a forecast of purely inflationary wage changes, his approach would be open to question, especially at the upper end of his range. For if the estimated rate of inflation were eight percent, the use of a discount rate of 8.5 percent would imply that the real rate of interest was only .5 percent, which is lower than most economists believe it to be for any substantial period of time. But wages do not rise just because of inflation. Mrs. O'Shea could expect her real wages as a boat's cook to rise as she became more experienced and as average real wage rates throughout the economy rose, as they usually do over a decade or more. It would not be outlandish to assume that even if there were no inflation, Mrs. O'Shea's wages would have risen by three percent a year. If we subtract that from the economist's six to eight percent range, the inflation allowance built into his estimated future wage increases is only three to five percent; and when we subtract these figures from 8.5 percent we see that his implicit estimate of the real rate of interest was very high (3.5-5.5 percent). This means he was conservative, because the higher the discount rate used the lower the damages calculated.

If conservative in one sense, the economist was most liberal in another. He made no allowance for the fact that Mrs. O'Shea, whose health history quite apart from the accident is not outstanding, might very well not have survived—let alone survived and been working as a boat's cook or in an equivalent job-until the age of 70. The damage award is a sum certain, but the lost future wages to which that award is equated by means of the discount rate are mere probabilities. If the probability of her being employed as a boat's cook full time in 1990 was only 75 percent, for example, then her estimated wages in that year should have been multiplied by .75 to determine the value of the expectation that she lost as a result of the accident; and so with each of the other future years. The economist did not do this, and by failing to do this he overstated the loss due to the accident.

Although we are not entirely satisfied with the economic analysis on which the judge, in the absence of any other evidence of the present value of Mrs. O'Shea's lost future wages, must have relied heavily, we recognize that the exactness which economic analysis rigorously pursued appears to offer is, at least in the litigation setting, somewhat delusive. Therefore, we will not reverse an award of damages for lost wages because of questionable assumptions unless it yields an unreasonable result. We cannot say the result here was unreasonable. If the economist's method of estimating damages was too generous to Mrs. O'Shea in one important respect it was, as we have seen, niggardly in another.

JUDGMENT AFFIRMED.

## QUESTIONS

1. How important is an understanding of the process of discounting to a tort lawyer's work?
2. In what way did the economist err in calculating lost earnings?
3. Why was this error harmless in that it did not constitute reversible error?
4. The court mentions two ways to deal with the problem of inflation. What are these two methods? Why are they equivalent?

## ESSENTIAL TERMS

Annuity
Capitalization rate
Discount factor
Discount rate
Future value
Growth perpetuity formula
Hurdle (benchmark) rate

Inflation
Internal rate of return (IRR)
Nominal price
Perpetuity formula
Present value
Real price
Time value of money

## KEY CONCEPTS

1. Money has a time value.
2. Future value is money expected to be received at some specific point in the future. Unless the expected return is risk-free, the expectation is subject to risk of some form. Future value must be discounted to present value to compare it with money in hand today.
3. Receiving an infinite flow of money in the future does not equal an infinite sum of money, counterintuitive as this may seem. The present value equivalent is determined by the discount rate at which the infinite future cash flow is discounted.
4. Given a series of future cash flows and a present value investment (cash outflow today), the internal rate of return is the discount rate that would make the future cash flows equivalent to the present value.

## REVIEW QUESTIONS

1. A lottery winner is typically given a choice of a lump sum payout or an annuity. For example, suppose you won a $1 million lottery. You are given the choice of an annuity of $100,000 per year for 10 years, or a lump sum of $375,000. Assume that the discount rate is 10 percent, there are no taxes, and the ticketholder wants to maximize the economic gain. Which option is best?
2. Which would you rather have: (1) $1,000 today, (2) $1,500 four years from now, or (3) $2,100 eight years from now. Why is this question an impossible question to answer? What additional information do you need?
3. A zero coupon bond is a debt instrument that pays no interest. The interest is actually incorporated into a higher bond principal that must be paid upon maturity. Suppose that a bond is issued for $1,000 today. There is no interest payment to the bondholder. At the end of five years, the firm pays back $1,500 to the bondholder. What is the effective interest rate on this debt?
4. In a tort case, the defendant offers two settlement options: (1) $10,000 cash now, (2) a structured settlement in which $5,000 is paid now, and the plaintiff received a 6-year annuity for $1,000. Assume that the applicable discount rate is 10 percent. Which settlement offer should you advise your client to take?

# RISK AND RETURN

*We next consider the rule that the investor does (or should) consider expected return a desirable thing* and *variance of return an undesirable thing. This rule has many sound points, both as a maxim for, and hypothesis about, investment behavior.*
— Harry Markowitz, *Portfolio Selection*, 7 J. Fin. 77 (1952)

## A. RISK AVERSION

Answer this question: Which describes your attitude more—"I like risk" or "I dislike risk." Many people will answer correctly that they dislike risk. Some people will answer incorrectly that they like risk or risk-taking. "Incorrectly" because their stated risk preference does not match their actual preference. Some people answer mistakenly because, perhaps, they ascribe a normative value to risk preference. Perhaps risk-taking is seen as a positive trait—something exciting, interesting, or sexy even. Risk-averse people may be considered boring, afraid, or uninteresting. These viewpoints are misguided. Risk preference is simply a preference, in the same vein as whether a person likes apples better than oranges, or prefers the color blue to red.

The plain fact is that most people are risk averse. People don't like risk. One is exposed to risk when one faces the possibility of two or more different outcomes. The possibility of two different outcomes in the future creates uncertainty, and people don't like uncertainty when a potential outcome in the future can be negative.

EXAMPLE 8.1

---

**People will choose the sum certain**

We can illustrate this principle through a simple experiment. Imagine that you may select Option 1 or Option 2. Which do you prefer?

Option 1:    $1,000 in cash, no strings attached
Option 2:    50/50 chance of $2,000 or $0 based on a coin flip

From an ex ante expected value perspective (probability multiplied by the outcome), the two choices are the same. However, if you are like most people, you would prefer Option 1. Why?

---

Most people don't like uncertain outcomes and prefer certain outcomes. This is the reason why people buy insurance: They would rather part with a fixed, small sum of money each year than risk the possibility of having to part with a large sum of money in an accident, even though the chance of an accident in any given year may be fairly small.

EXAMPLE 8.2

**People will pay to eliminate risk, or require payment to bear it**

In the above example, most people would sacrifice some expected value in favor of the risk-free option. Suppose the options change to these:

Option 1:  $1,000 in cash
Option 2:  50/50 chance of $2,400 or $0 (where the expected value is now $1,200)

For an additional $200 in ex ante value, would you now forego the certain result? If you are like most people, you would still select Option 1. For many people, the risk of walking away with $0 would not be worth the additional $200 in ex ante compensation. But the choice is much closer now because there is additional compensation for taking Option 2. Some risk-averse people will now take a chance.

---

**STOP AND THINK**

In *Steinman v. Hicks*, 352 F.3d 1101, 1104 (7th Cir. 2003), Judge Posner wrote:

"Risk-averse people will pay to avoid risk, as they do when they buy insurance knowing that an insurance premium includes a loading charge (that is, a fee to compensate the insurance company for its administrative expenses) on top of the estimate of the loss to the insured discounted by the probability that the loss will occur. That discounted loss would be the actuarial value of the policy, and a risk-neutral person would pay no more. In fact he would never buy insurance, because there is always a loading charge."

The typical loading charge for an insurance company is between 10 percent to 50 percent. This suggests that policyholders are willing to pay quite a hefty amount in excess of the actuarial value of their future loss to the insurance company to eliminate their risk. The purchase of insurance makes sense to a person only if she is risk averse.

---

People (or companies) must be compensated to take risk. If someone needs money for a business enterprise, and that money is subject to risk, an investor who provides capital will want to be compensated for putting that money at risk. The greater the risk, the more that the investor will want in compensation.

## B. RISK

We can formalize the above intuitions about risk. In finance and business, the concept of *risk* means an uncertainty as to future economic outcome. An investment of X, such as the purchase of stock, is made today, and we do not know how this investment may turn out. On an ex ante perspective, the future has multiple paths.

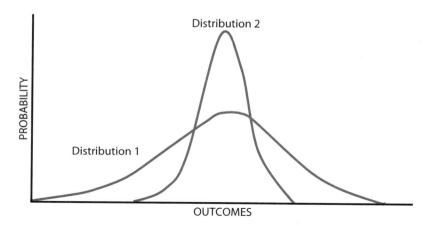

In the above graph, the *x*-axis represents the number of potential different outcomes, ranging from terrible result (a loss of the entire investment) to fabulous result (a tremendous rise in the stock price), and everything in between. The *y*-axis represents a probability for a particular outcome. (For students unfamiliar with statistical concepts, think of a grading curve in which there are a few A's and C's, and a big clump of students in the middle of the pack with B's.) Notice that the outcomes under Distribution 1 are more spread out than the outcomes for Distribution 2, which are much more tightly clustered. Risk is the measure of this dispersion.

 In statistical parlance, *variance* measures how far a set of numbers or outcomes are spread out from each other. In finance, variance is the measure of risk.

When we say that people are risk averse, it means that people don't like uncertain futures, several paths of which can be terrible results. Imagine a student's grade of an A or C depending on the outcomes of a coin flip: Would a student prefer to just take a B rather than subject himself to a variable outcome?

 Investments in businesses are risky, and investors need to be compensated for taking this risk. This is the fundamental principle behind the valuation of assets and firms.

## C. RETURN

If people don't like risk, then they must be compensated to take risk. People are compensated for taking risk in many different ways. The greater the risk taken, the greater the potential return must be. The credit risks associated with lending money to the U.S. government and to your next door neighbor are qualitatively different. You may charge 5 percent to the U.S. government, but perhaps 10 percent to your neighbor. There is a tradeoff between risk and return.

The compensation for risk can be graphically represented. The chart below shows that as risk increases, the expected return must increase as well.

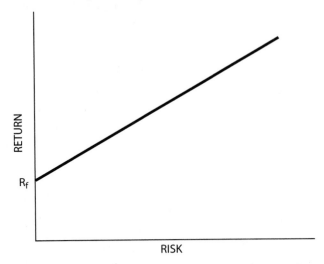

The point $R_f$ on the y-axis represents the risk-free rate, which is the rate of return on an investment that carries no risk. There is only one financial investment that carries no risk, and it is an investment in United States government debt, typically called Treasury securities or Treasuries. By purchasing Treasuries, an investor is lending the U.S. government money for the rate of return $R_f$. The assumption of the risk-free rate is that the U.S. government carries no credit risk; an investment is free of risk as to principal and interest. Therefore, the expected return on the investment is low compared to investments in other securities such as corporate bonds.

On a basic level, we order the various instruments along the risk-return horizon. From the least risky to the most, the instruments are corporate bonds, preferred stock, and common stock.

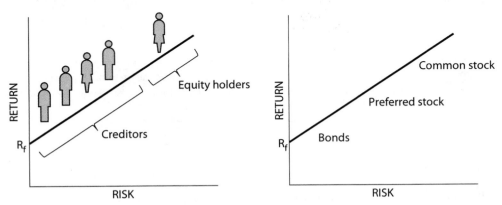

As we saw in Chapter 2, which explained the difference between creditors and equityholders, the line along the risk-return continuum represents a queue of investors who have contractually agreed to undertake different risks. Creditors take less risk and get less return; equityholders take greater risk for greater return. Remember that equity is a concept. It connotes the residual economic claim. Because equityholders stand last in the financial queue for distribution from the income statement and the balance sheet, they bear the greatest economic risk. If so, they must be compensated the most. Accordingly, equityholders should earn greater returns than $R_f$ or creditors.

Risk and return are conjoined twins. As risk increases, investors demand more return and thus the investment must yield a greater return, and vice versa. There is a direct relationship between risk and return.

There is always a tradeoff between risk and return. Because people are risk averse, a more risky investment opportunity must incentivize an investor by providing greater prospect of return. Investors will not take financial risks for free. However, greater risk means that an investor is exposed to increased potential for bad things to happen—that is the definition of risk.

**F.Y.I.** The tradeoff between risk and return is fairly intuitive to most people. Popular colloquialism embodies this principle: "nothing ventured, nothing gained"—"no pain, no gain"—"there's no free lunch." These comments go to the principle that sacrifice must be made for gains. In the case of investments, sacrifice means the assumption of risk.

### EXAMPLE 8.3

**Analysis of Bernie Madoff's Ponzi scheme (Part I, the implication of riskless profit)**

In 2008, Bernie Madoff was arrested for operating the world's largest Ponzi scheme. He pled guilty to the charges. Before his arrest, he marketed his investment advisory services to wealthy clients and hedge funds that invested their funds with him. Below are the purported returns of one such hedge fund as indexed and compared to the S&P 100 market index. The hedge fund's marketing document shows that the fund averaged 12 percent yearly return, net of large hedge fund fees, for many years, and there were no losses in any year dating back to 1990.

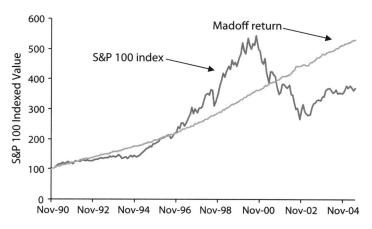

What strikes you as odd about the hedge fund's returns compared to the broader market index? Is it plausible that someone can make consistently profit (long-term average of 12%) year-in, year-out? Should we expect to see some variance in the return? Indeed, in the 174 months in the time period 1990 to 2005, there were only 7 months of negative returns, and the largest loss was -0.55 percent, which means that a fund balance of $100,000 would have suffered a loss of $550 for the month. This was the allure of an investment with Bernie Madoff: you can get 12 percent on your investment, which consistently beats the long-term market return on stocks (about 10%) with no risk. Guaranteed riskless profit that beats the risk-free rate is like the power to print money, isn't it? The enforcement lawyers at the SEC had the above information, but they failed to realize its import because they did not have a basic working knowledge of finance.

## D. DIVERSIFICATION OF RISK

> *"My ventures are not in one bottom trusted, Nor to one place; nor is my whole estate*
> *Upon the fortune of this present year: Therefore, my merchandise makes me not sad."*
> —William Shakespeare, *The Merchant of Venice*, act 1, scene 1

If risk is bad, it can be eliminated or reduced through various financial means. One method is through diversification. To illustrate the principle of diversification, we continue the example in section A, where we analyzed two financial choices: a sum certain of $1,000 or a 50/50 chance for $2,000. Most people would select the sum certain. Let's change the facts slightly.

EXAMPLE 8.4

### Effect of diversification

We are again given two choices.

Option 1:     $1,000 in cash
Option 2:     aggregate of 100 coin flips (50/50 chance on each flip), where for each "tails" the person would receive $24 or for each "heads" $0

Expected value of this option is $1,200 (= 100 flips × 50% × $24)

Which option do you prefer? In what way is Option 2 different from that of Example 8.2?

If you think hard about the above choice, you will probably select Option 2 even if you are risk averse. Most people will take a risk here because the 100 coin flips diversifies the risk inherent in each coin flip. Thus, much of the risk is eliminated. Perhaps in flipping 100 coins, "heads" will be the result all 100 times thus resulting in $0 earned, but this is highly unlikely. Nor is 100 "tails" with earnings of $2,400 very likely. Due to the high number of coin flips, most people would expect "tails" to be somewhere in the range of 50 (this is the law of large numbers at work). Perhaps a reasonable range of expectation is 40 to 60 times in the course of 100 flips. The expected amounts can range: 40 tails = $960, 50 tails = $1,200, 60 tails = $1,440.

Option 2 can still fare worse than Option 1: $960 versus $1,000 if only 40 tails are flipped. But look at the upside: an additional $200 if tails are flipped exactly 50 percent of the time, or additional $440 if you get lucky and tails are flipped 60 times. To many people, the risk is now worth it because the extremes in outcomes (all or nothing) have been reduced to "some possible loss with significant possible gain."

 Diversification reduces the risk of investment by spreading risk to various investments such that no single investment can create large variance in outcomes.

## E. CASE APPLICATION

The business judgment rule is a foundational rule of law in corporation law. The rule is a presumption that in making a decision or exercising judgment, directors acted on an informed basis, in good faith and in the honest belief that the action taken was in the best interests of the company. Once applied, the business judgment rule shields directors from personal liability for bad outcomes. This is an unusual rule. In the tort context, for example, a negligent doctor will be found liable for his errors. In the corporation context, however, a negligent director will be excused from liability through the operation of the business judgment rule, which effectively says that the decision was informed and in good faith, and thus courts will not impose liability. In the case below, Judge Ralph Winter explains the theoretical basis for the business judgment rule. In reading the case, pay particular attention to footnote 6 of the opinion.

### *Joy v. North*
692 F.2d 880 (2d Cir. 1982)

RALPH K. WINTER, Circuit Judge:

While it is often stated that corporate directors and officers will be liable for negligence in carrying out their corporate duties, all seem agreed that such a statement is misleading. Whereas an automobile driver who makes a mistake in judgment as to speed or distance injuring a pedestrian will likely be called upon to respond in damages, a corporate officer who makes a mistake in judgment as to economic conditions, consumer tastes or production line efficiency will rarely, if ever, be found liable for damages suffered by the corporation. Whatever the terminology, the fact is that liability is rarely imposed upon corporate directors or officers simply for bad judgment and this reluctance to impose liability for unsuccessful business decisions has been doctrinally labelled the business judgment rule. Although the rule has suffered under academic criticism, it is not without rational basis.

First, shareholders to a very real degree voluntarily undertake the risk of bad business judgment. Investors need not buy stock, for investment markets offer an array of opportunities less vulnerable to mistakes in judgment by corporate officers. Nor need investors buy stock in particular corporations. In the exercise of what is genuinely a free choice, the quality of a firm's management is often decisive and information is available from professional advisors. Since shareholders can and do select among investments partly on the basis of management, the business judgment rule merely recognizes a certain voluntariness in undertaking the risk of bad business decisions.

Second, courts recognize that after-the-fact litigation is a most imperfect device to evaluate corporate business decisions. The circumstances surrounding a corporate decision are not easily reconstructed in a courtroom years later, since business imperatives often call for quick decisions, inevitably based on less than perfect information. The entrepreneur's function is to encounter risks and to confront uncertainty, and a reasoned decision at the time made may seem a wild hunch viewed years later against a background of perfect knowledge.

Third, because potential profit often corresponds to the potential risk, it is very much in the interest of shareholders that the law not create incentives for overly cautious corporate decisions. Some opportunities offer great profits at the risk of very substantial losses, while the alternatives offer less risk of loss but also less potential profit. Shareholders can reduce the volatility of risk by diversifying their holdings. In the case of the diversified shareholder, the seemingly more risky alternatives may well be the best choice since great losses in some stocks will over time be offset by even greater gains in others.[6] Given mutual funds and similar forms of diversified investment, courts need not bend over backwards to give special protection to shareholders who refuse to reduce the volatility of risk by not diversifying. A rule which penalizes the choice of seemingly riskier alternatives thus may not be in the interest of shareholders generally.

[Footnote 6 is reproduced below.]

Consider the choice between two investments in an example adapted from Klein, *Business Organization and Finance* 147-49 (1980):

INVESTMENT A

| Estimated Probability of Outcome | Outcome Profit or Loss | Value |
|---|---|---|
| .4 | +15 | 6.0 |
| .4 | +1 | .4 |
| .2 | −13 | −2.6 |
| 1.0 | | 3.8 |

INVESTMENT B

| Estimated Probability of Outcome | Outcome Profit or Loss | Value |
|---|---|---|
| .4 | +6 | 2.4 |
| .4 | +2 | .8 |
| .2 | +1 | .2 |
| 1.0 | | 3.4 |

Although A is clearly "worth" more than B, it is riskier because it is more volatile. Diversification lessens the volatility by allowing investors to invest in 20 or 200 A's which will tend to guarantee a total result near the value. Shareholders are thus better off with the various firms selecting A over B, although after the fact they will complain in each case of the 2.6 loss. If the courts did not abide by the business judgment rule, they might well penalize the choice of A in each such case and thereby unknowingly injure shareholders generally by creating incentives for management always to choose B.

## QUESTIONS

1. What is the relationship among the business judgment rule, risk-taking, and profit?
2. Given this relationship, why does corporate law shield directors from bad mistakes in judgment?
3. What would happen to the value of corporations if managers and directors acted in a risk-averse manner?
4. What can shareholders do to protect themselves from the bad mistakes of managers and directors of any given corporation?
5. With respect to footnote 6, assume that you represent a creditor bank and the firm owes $6 in interest per year. As between Investment A and B, which investment would you prefer the corporation to make? Does your answer suggest that there is an inherent tension between the interests of creditors and equityholders?

---

Officers and directors owe fiduciary duty to the corporation. Because shareholders hold the residual claim, fiduciary duty is also owed to shareholders. In most ordinary cases, what is good for shareholders is good for the corporation and its constituents. However, in circumstances where the corporation is insolvent or nearly insolvent, the incentives between shareholders and creditors conflict significantly. The case below stands for the proposition that fiduciary duty is conditional, and under certain circumstances it may shift from shareholders to creditors. In reading the case, pay particular attention to footnote 55 explaining the reason why this should be good policy.

### Credit Lyonnais Bank Nederland, N.V. v. Pathe Comm'n Corp.
#### 1991 WL 277613 (Del. Ch. 1981)

ALLEN:

At least where a corporation is operating in the vicinity of insolvency, a board of directors is not merely the agent of the residu[al] risk bearers, but owes its duty to the corporate enterprise.[55]

[Footnote 55 is reproduced below.]

The possibility of insolvency can do curious things to incentives, exposing creditors to risks of opportunistic behavior and creating complexities for directors. Consider, for example, a solvent corporation having a single asset, a judgment for $51 million against a solvent debtor. The judgment is on appeal and thus subject to modification or reversal. Assume that the only liabilities of the company are to bondholders in the amount of $12 million. Assume that the array of probable outcomes of the appeal is as follows:

| | Expected Value |
|---|---|
| 25% chance of affirmative ($51 million) | $12.75 |
| 70% chance of modification ($4 million) | 2.8 |
| 5% chance of reversal ($0) | 0 |
| Expected value of judgment on appeal | $15.55 |

Thus, the best evaluation is that the current value of the equity is $3.55 million. ($15.55 million expected value of judgment on appeal-$12 million liability to bondholders). Now assume an offer to settle at $12.5 million (also consider one at $17.5 million). By what standard do the directors of the company evaluate the fairness of these offers? The creditors of this solvent company would be in favor of accepting either a $12.5 million offer or a $17.5 million offer. In either event they will avoid the 75% risk of insolvency and default. The stockholders, however, will plainly be opposed to acceptance of a $12.5 million settlement (under which they get practically nothing). More importantly, they very well may be opposed to acceptance of the $17.5 million offer under which the residual value of the corporation would increase from $3.5 to $5.5 million. This is so because the litigation alternative, with its 25% probability of a $39 million outcome to them ($51 million - $12 million = $39 million) has an expected value to the residual risk bearer of $9.75 million ($39 million x 25% chance of affirmance), substantially greater than the $5.5 million available to them in the settlement. While in fact the stockholders' preference would reflect their appetite for risk, it is possible (and with diversified shareholders likely) that shareholders would prefer rejection of both settlement offers.

But if we consider the community of interests that the corporation represents it seems apparent that one should in this hypothetical accept the best settlement offer available providing it is greater than $15.55 million, and one below that amount should be rejected. But that result will not be reached by a director who thinks he owes duties directly to shareholders only. It will be reached by directors who are capable of conceiving of the corporation as a legal and economic entity. Such directors will recognize that in managing the business affairs of a solvent corporation in the vicinity of insolvency, circumstances may arise when the right (both the efficient and the fair) course to follow for the corporation may diverge from the choice that the stockholders (or the creditors, or the employees, or any single group interested in the corporation) would make if given the opportunity to act.

## QUESTIONS

1. In insolvency or the vicinity of insolvency, the shareholder may no longer have a residual claim because much of the equity value has been destroyed. In that case, if shareholders have control of firm, they would be playing with other people's (creditors) money. What perverse incentives may this create?
2. Why should a director's fiduciary duty shift to creditors when the firm is in the vicinity of insolvency?
3. In thinking about the implication of *Credit Lyonnais Bank Nederland, N.V. v. Pathe Comm'n Corp.*, consider the following account of the conversations inside the Bear

Stearns boardroom. Bear Stearns was collapsing due to toxic assets on its balance sheet, which essentially wiped out the equity in the firm. The firm was essentially insolvent. The Bear Stearns board was considering a $2 per share offer from JPMorgan Chase to rescue the company. Obviously, Bear Stearns shareholders, including Jimmy Cayne, the former CEO and prominent shareholder, wanted more money, and the negotiation leverage was the "nuclear" option of filing for bankruptcy, which would harm the value of creditors' claims and also cause systemic disturbances in the greater financial system.

> For his part, Cayne was livid. At breakfast with Tese earlier that day, he had come to realize that blowing up the firm wouldn't do anyone any good. But now, upon hearing that JPMorgan deal was at $2 per share—meaning that his six million or so shares, which at their height had been worth more than $1 billion, would now be worth around $12 million—he was incensed. His finger moved back over the red ["nuclear"] button. He wondered if the firm's bondholders, who together held $70 billion of debt and who in a merger with JPMorgan would be made whole but in bankruptcy would be severely impaired, should be asked to make a contribution to the shrinking pie for shareholders. . . . As Cayne knew, the bondholders had by far the most to gain from a deal with JPMorgan. Whereas all through the week, the cost of insuring against a default in Bear Stearns debt had been increasing rapidly—the so-called credit default swaps—a deal with JPMorgan would transfer these obligations to JPMorgan's balance sheet and immediately make them worth 100 cents on the dollar.
>
> . . .
>
> The moment had come to seal the fate of Bear Stearns, the fifth-largest Wall Street securities firm. The lawyers walked the board through its fiduciary duties under Delaware law, which required them to consider their duty to creditors if they turned down the JPMorgan deal and opted for bankruptcy. Given that the choice was between nominal consideration for shareholders and 100 cents on the dollar for creditors or nothing for shareholders and pennies for creditors, Sullivan & Cromwell's advice for the board was that its fiduciary duties had shifted from shareholders to all the other stakeholders of Bear Stearns, among them creditors, employees, and retirees. . . .

William D. Cohan, *House of Cards: A Tale of Hubris and Wretched Excess on Wall Street* 103-04, 108-09 (2010).

---

## ESSENTIAL TERMS

Diversification                          Risk-free rate
Risk                                     Variance
Risk aversion

## KEY CONCEPTS

1. Risk is the measure of dispersion in expected outcomes.
2. People are generally risk averse.
3. To incentize people to take risk, they must be offered compensation.
4. In the context of business investments, an investor must be compensated to provide capital to firms, and the level of compensation must be commensurate with the level of risk taken.

## REVIEW QUESTIONS

1. Should creditors or equityholders generally get paid more? Why?
2. What is one way to reduce risk in equity investments?

## CHAPTER 9

# VALUATION

Lawyers will not be asked to conduct valuations of companies. Investment bankers typically do this work. However, lawyers should know the foundational concepts of valuation because value is a key factor in many corporate transactions:

- Mergers and acquisitions, including legal documentation
- Capital raisings, including legal documentation
- Bankruptcies and restructurings, including legal documentation
- Legal disputes concerning a board of directors' fiduciary duty
- Legal disputes concerning the price at which dissenting shares are purchased in a merger or acquisition of a target company
- Issues arising out of securities laws on fraud and insider trading
- Structure and terms of executive compensation contracts

How much should the acquirer pay for the target company? At what price should shares of common stock in an initial public offering be offered? What is the value of assets available to creditors in bankruptcy? What are the damages in a securities fraud or a breach of a board's fiduciary duty? What is the remedy for dissenting shareholders in a merger or acquisition? In all business transactions, the participants believe that the transaction creates value, and disputes may arise out of how value is allocated among parties who have economic claims.

Valuation is not just relevant to the corporate lawyer. Lawyers in the twenty-first century may perform various functions. It is not uncommon for lawyers to become members of a board of directors or business managers rising as high as the CEO level. Lawyers are also entrepreneurs who start their own businesses, and they frequently advise entrepreneurial firms on general business issues. A business lawyer must understand the foundational concepts in valuation not because they will be asked to do it, but because valuation is always on the client's mind. Shouldn't you have some understanding of it to serve the client properly?

Chapter 8 set forth the foundational principle of risk and return. The principle is fairly intuitive in qualitative form. In this chapter, we will make the leap toward a theoretical framework for understanding valuation. A fair warning: This chapter is difficult to grasp, but the principles herein are important and understanding them will open up a valuable new perspective on business and corporate transactions.

## A. CONCEPTUALIZING THE VALUE OF A FIRM

Value can be thought of in a number of ways. There is not a single concept or number associated with value. When we ask "what's the value?", a fair response is "which value?" In Chapter 2, we saw that the accountant's view of value does not always reflect economic reality because historical cost and fair market value frequently diverge, thus producing a disparity between book value and market value. In this chapter, we focus on economic value. The concept of economic value can be thought of in different ways.

### 1. LIQUIDATION VALUE

When a firm is dissolved and wound up, its assets are sold. After liabilities are paid off to creditors, whatever remains belongs to the equityholder. The sale value of assets net of liabilities is called the liquidation value. Liquidation value only applies when a firm is no longer a going concern; thus its assets are sold off and liabilities are paid off therefrom. Clearly, liquidation valuation may be an inappropriate measure of value for a going concern because the value of a going concern will be the expectation of the future returns, and not the current sale value of assets and liabilities.

Think about the Harry and Sally's One Dollar Corporation from Example 7.1 in Chapter 7. The liquidation value of a corporation with one dollar in assets and no debt must be one dollar. However, if we assume that turning their love story into a hit movie is a commercially feasible idea (e.g., a film script could eventually be written giving the corporation copyrights, a management team could be hired giving the company operating expertise, etc.), the going concern value of the One Dollar Corporation must be more than the liquidation value.

*Going concern* means a firm that is expected to operate without the immediate threat of liquidation in the future.

### 2. MARKET VALUE

*The actual price at which any commodity is commonly sold is called its market price. It may either be above, or below, or exactly the same with its natural price.*
—Adam Smith, *An Inquiry into the Nature and Causes of the Wealth of Nations*, book I, chapter 7 (1776)

A firm may be valued by the market as a going concern. Market value means the prevailing market price of assets, liabilities, and equity of the firm. The market value of a firm can be stated as (1) equity value which is market cap, or as (2) firm value which is market cap plus debt. We saw in Chapter 2 that in many cases market value may be significantly more than the accountant's book value or the liquidation value.

 In most cases, the market value exceeds the book value for reasons discussed in Chapter 2. In some unusual circumstances, the market value of equity may be less than the book value. This means that the capital market, through its pricing, is signaling that the true value of assets net of liabilities is less than the stated value in the books. There are several reasons why this phenomenon can occur. What might be some reasons why?

How does the capital market value a firm or its securities? In other words, on April 29, 2011, the following were the closing share prices on the New York Stock Exchange for these companies: McDonald's $78.31, Goldman Sachs $151.01, General Electric $20.45, and United Technologies $89.58. How did these prices come to be? The short answer is that the capital markets serve as an information aggregator. The market price is determined by countless number of buyers and sellers in the capital market, ranging from multibillion dollar investment funds to the proverbial moms and pops. Their collective transactions with each other set the market clearing price of any given security, just as there is a clearing price on an eBay auction for a used golf set and a used law school casebook. Still, how do these investors determine when to buy and when to sell? And at what price? A thorough answer to this question is beyond the scope of this book. However, a simple answer is that the markets are composed of two fundamentally different types of investors: those who do valuation well, and those who do not. While everyone is looking for good investment opportunities, savvy market participants who do valuations engage in a process of arbitrage, a process in which they sell overpriced securities and buy underpriced securities. The process of arbitrage maintains prices in a relationship to the intrinsic value of the securities.

The existence of a market price does not mean that the price is perfect in the sense of reflecting some intrinsic (inherent or theoretical) value of the thing (see the above quotation from Adam Smith). The market is not perfect. Stock market bubbles and crashes, and periods of "irrational exuberance," have shown that markets err, and sometimes very badly. The recent housing and credit bubbles that precipitated the financial crisis of 2008-2009 are just the latest example. Were housing prices rational in 2006 at the height of the real estate bubble? Just as any given eBay auction may not yield a "true" price, the market price should not be mistaken for the intrinsic value. Moreover, a fundamental paradox of the market is that a degree of uncertainty about the intrinsic value is necessary for an active trading market to exist. For example, an investor buys a share of McDonald's because he thinks that it will appreciate in value; on the other side of that transaction is an investor who sells McDonald's because she thinks the opposite. If a share of McDonald's was always set at the "true" price, there would be no rationale for trading, and thus no market to speak of.

In the history of the stock market, there have been a number of stock market crashes. During these times, the market value of stocks fell by more than 20 percent within a short time period, which led to panic and severe economic downturns, called recessions and depressions. These were the front page headlines of the *New York Times* chronicling the most famous stock market crashes in 1929, 1987, and most recently 2008.

- Tuesday, October 29, 1929: *Stock Prices Slump $14,000,000,000 in Nationwide Stampede to Unload; Bankers to Support Market Today*
- Tuesday, October 20, 1987: *Stocks Plunge 508 Points, A Drop of 22.6%; 604 Million Volume Nearly Doubles Record*
- Wednesday, September 17, 2008: *Bailout Fails to Stem Global Stock Slump; Dow Falls by More than 440 Points in Jittery Trading*

## 3. MARKET CAP VERSUS FIRM VALUE

When thinking about the value of a firm, we make a distinction between (1) market capitalization for public companies, and market value of equity for private companies, and (2) *firm value* (or sometimes called *enterprise value*), which is the combined market value of equity and debt. Market cap is the value of shareholders' equity only. In Chapter 2, we saw that equity is one form of capital. Capital assets are funded by debt, equity or a combination of both. Firm value is total invested capital, the sum of long-term debt and equity that finances the firm's capital assets. Thus, firm value (or enterprise value) is:

$$\text{Firm Value} = \text{Market Value of Equity} + \text{Market Value of Debt}$$

In *Credit Lyonnais Bank Nederland, N.V. v. Pathe Comm'n Corp.* (Chapter 8), the court held that fiduciary duty may shift from shareholders to creditors when the firm operates in the zone of insolvency. Can this rule be explained by a desire to increase firm value vis-à-vis equity value?

Consider this assertion from an economist whose work we will study in Chapter 10: "Briefly put, value maximization states that managers should make all decisions so as to increase the total long-run market value of the firm. Total value is the sum of the values of all financial claims on the firm—including equity, debt, preferred stock, and warrants." Michael C. Jensen, *Value Maximization, Stakeholder Theory, and the Corporate Objective Function*, 12 Bus. Ethics Q. 235 (2002).

## 4. THEORETICAL VALUE

At any given moment, market value may deviate from theoretical or intrinsic value. A theory-based, intrinsic value is separate and apart from whatever the market trading value may be, given the relevant information at the time. Intrinsic value is not calculated as a product of deductive logic in the way that $(2 + 2 = 4)$. While there is a generally accepted quantitative technique for calculating the theoretical value of a corporation, there is no scientific method producing a precise, single value with logical certainty, and no credible investment banker or financial adviser would make such an assertion. In conducting a proper valuation, an analyst will engage in a very detailed and complex quantitative analysis and financial modeling to assess theoretical intrinsic value, but the appearance of quantitative rigor and scientific method should not mask the fact that there is much judgment and discretion that go into an expert opinion concerning the intrinsic value of a thing. Intrinsic value is an elusive target. Experienced lawyers will tell you that reasonable experts in whatever field may differ substantially, particularly in an adversarial environment or situations where there are conflicting interests.

Let's begin to conceptualize theoretical value by building on the lessons from the previous chapters. In Chapter 7, we learned that money has a time value, and that the process of discounting can convert future value into present value. Two variables affect the discounting process: time $T$ and discount rate $R$. The further out in time in the future, the greater is the discounting, and vice versa. The greater the discount rate, the greater is the discounting and value decreases, and vice versa. In Chapter 8, we learned that risk and return are conjoined twins: as risk increases, an investor will demand greater return; greater return is achieved if the share price is priced at levels that the same dollar can buy more shares to achieve the appropriate return. These concepts must be incorporated into a rational valuational framework.

- How should we conceptualize the theoretical value of a corporation?
- How should the corporation's future returns and risks be calculated and incorporated into a valuational framework?

The theoretical value of a firm is *the present value of its future stream of free cash flow, discounted by the riskiness of that cash flow.*

> The value of any economic asset is the future cash it will generate as discounted by the riskiness of that cash flow. If so, a critical inquiry is this: What is the discount rate $R$ used to discount the future cash flows? The discount rate applicable for discounting the streams of income a corporation is expected to generate is called the *cost of capital.*

## B. COST OF CAPITAL (OR WHAT IS *R*?)

When you work in corporate transactions, you will hear the term "cost of capital." *The cost of capital is the discount rate used to value a firm.* It answers the question "What is $R$ used to discount the free cash flows?"

A firm needs capital to engage in business activities. It rents capital from investors, who seek a return. They will expect a certain rate of return for the risk they take. If the investment is risk-free, the expectation of return would be low. The U.S. government has historically had a very low cost of borrowing because its credit rating was perfect (risk-free). If the investment is high risk, investors would not rent out their capital unless the expected return is high. Note that the return is an expectation, and not a guarantee. The investor's return is always subject to market fluctuations on the value of their investment.

The *cost of capital* is the cost associated with the rent of capital. Capital has a cost. The cost of capital is the firm's cost of renting its capital from various capital providers. There are generally two forms of capital—debt and equity. Accordingly, the cost of capital can be segregated into the cost of debt and cost of equity.

## 1. COST OF DEBT

The *cost of debt* is the rate of return required by creditors to provide debt financing, which is a cost to the firm. This is intuitive enough. What is the interest rate charged by the creditor? However, there is an important nuance. The government subsidizes the use of debt capital by allowing interest expense to be deductible from taxable income. In Chapter 3, we saw that the line item "interest expense" is above the tax line. This tax policy effectuates an *interest tax shield*: The interest deduction reduces the effective cost of debt by shielding some of the firm's profit from tax liability.

EXAMPLE 9.1

### Effect of tax shield

Let's see how the interest tax shield works by comparing two income statements. Assume common financial inputs: (1) revenue $1,000 and operating expense $400, (2) interest expense of $200 representing a rate of 8 percent on debt of $2,500, and (3) tax rate of 25 percent.

| *With Tax Shield* | | *Without Tax Shield* | |
|---|---|---|---|
| Revenue | 1,000 | Revenue | 1,000 |
| Operating expense | (400) | Operating expense | (400) |
| *Interest expense* | (200) | | |
| | | Pretax profit | 600 |
| | | Taxes at 25% | (150) |
| Pretax profit | 400 | | |
| Taxes at 25% | (100) | After-tax profit | 450 |
| | | *Interest expense* | (200) |
| Net income | 300 | Net income | 250 |

By deducting the interest expense from taxable (pretax) income, there is less tax liability. Less money going to the government means more profit. Thus, the interest tax shield is a government subsidy that promotes the use of debt.

The cost of debt must take into account the benefit of the tax shield. In the above example, the firm must pay an interest expense of $200. The tax rate is 25 percent. The net benefit of the tax shield is $50, which is a deduction of 25 percent (the tax rate) of the interest payment. There is a mathematical relationship defined as:

$$\text{Cost of debt} = R\ (1-T)$$

where $R$ is the interest rate and $T$ is the tax rate. The above equation precisely calculates the effective cost of borrowing. It says that *the cost of debt is the interest rate on debt, net of tax benefit* which is captured in the term $(1-T)$. Therefore, in the above example the effective cost of debt is 6% ($= 8\% \times (1-25\%)$).

 Businesses are not the only recipients of a government subsidy on the use of debt. Homeowners have a mortgage interest deduction, which allows the deduction of mortgage interest payments from a taxpayer's income, thus lowering taxable income from which tax liability is assessed. What incentives does the home mortgage interest deduction create?

## 2. COST OF EQUITY AND CAPM

Most people intuitively understand the concept of the cost of debt because we are familiar with paying interest payments on loans, whether they are home mortgages, credit cards, or student loans. We pay interest in cash, and we notice cash inflows and outflows out of our wallets. However, the cost of equity is not intuitive. It is a very difficult concept to grasp at first because it does not involve cash transfers akin to interest payments. Neither corporate law nor the typical corporate charter requires any cash payment or other direct compensation to common shareholders. In fact, many companies do not pay dividends (though many other firms pay them). Irrespective of any given company's dividend policy, dividends are paid at the rational discretion of the board of directors. Unlike the creditors, shareholders cannot throw the company into default for failure to pay dividends and the disappointed shareholder's sole remedy, in the vast majority of cases, is to exercise the "Wall Street rule" (i.e., sell the shares of stocks that disappoint expectations).

Think about this: A corporation can issue stock to shareholders, take their money in exchange for giving them paper that says they own stock, and never have a legal obligation to pay dividends or repurchase the shares. Because of the separation of ownership and control, the typical shareholder will also have little say in the matter. A corporation can take shareholders' money and run. Therefore, equity capital must be free. Right? Our intuition says this is wrong. Equity capital cannot be "free" even if shareholders are not legally entitled to dividends or any other form of direct compensation from the company. In fact, equity capital must be expensive since shareholders are the residual claimants, standing last in the queue and taking greater risk than creditors.

So what does it mean when we say that equity has a capital cost just the way debt has a cost of debt? To rent equity capital from shareholders, the firm must compensate them. The cost of capital must reflect the shareholder's expectation of return. Thus, the short answer to the question is that *the cost of equity is the shareholder's expected return commensurate with the specific risk associated with the firm, and shareholders are compensated in the process of valuation of the stock, which can be monetized through the capital markets.* Let's unpack this difficult concept step-by-step.

We start the analysis by noting the range of an investor's opportunities. What can an investor do with his money from his savings? He can stuff it under his pillow and leave it there, but this would be irrational. Aside from the risk of fire and theft, he would earn no return on his money. He can invest the money in various ways: for example, buy gold, invest in real estate, or invest in his friend's pizza shop, etc. These may be fine investments. He can also invest in the capital markets—lend money to institutional borrowers such as governments and corporations, and to invest in the equity of corporations through the purchase of stock. If he invests his money this way, he is a seller of capital in the capital markets. In this marketplace, he has a number of investment options: (1) risk-free government bonds, (2) stock in individual companies, and (3) a diversified portfolio of stocks that mirror market returns. On the safest end of the spectrum are risk-free investments, which are federal government debt instruments. Since there is no risk, the return on the risk-free rate is comparatively low.

Federal government debt instruments, called *Treasury bills, notes,* and *bonds* (the terms denote differences in the length of maturity and collectively called *Treasury securities* or *Treasuries*), are considered risk-free investments. When the government cannot meet its expenses (such as providing for Social Security, Medicare, and the national defense), it borrows money by issuing government debt. Many people invest in these securities, including moms and pops, pension funds, insurance companies, and the government of China. These people are lenders to the U.S. government. Treasury securities are considered risk-free because the assumption is the United States government will not default on its loans.

However, it is only an assumption, based on historical performance and past assumptions. At the time of writing this book, the U.S. national debt is over $14 trillion and future obligations, including interest payment service on the national debt and entitlements, continue to grow. There will be ongoing political dialogue on the debt limit and fiscal policies. Credit rating agencies will continue to monitor the U.S. government's credit worthiness. In spring and summer of 2011, the two major credit rating agencies made these announcements: "Whether the outlook on the [U.S. government's credit] rating would be stable or negative would depend upon whether [there is] meaningful progress toward substantial and credible long-term deficit reduction," *Moody's Updates on Rating Implication of US Debt Limit, Long-Term Budget Negotiations*, Moody's Investors Services (June 2, 2011); "Because the U.S. has, relative to its 'AAA' peers, what we consider to be very large budget deficits and rising government indebtedness and the path to addressing these is not clear to us, we have revised our outlook on the long-term rating to negative from stable," *'AAA/A-1+' Rating On United States of America Affirmed; Outlook Revised To Negative*, Standard & Poor's (April 18, 2011).

Following S&P's warning in spring 2011, it downgraded the U.S. debt from AAA to AA+, which was the first time that the creditworthiness of the U.S. government has been less than a perfect AAA. *United States of America Long-Term Rating Lowered to 'AA+' on Political Risks and Rising Debt Burden; Outlook Negative*, Standard & Poor's (August 5, 2011). Whether S&P was correct to downgrade or not is debatable. As of October 14, 2011, the yield on 10-year Treasury notes was 2.23 percent, which is the U.S. government's borrowing rate. It seems that, despite S&P's downgrade, the market believes that U.S. Treasuries are a safe bet. However, this does not detract from the fact that in the future U.S. government debt could be considered more risky.

For now, the capital markets operate under the assumption that there is a risk-free rate. If a risk-free rate is undesirable because it pays so little, the other option is to invest in the stock of any given company. There is a qualitative difference in the riskiness of a loan to the United States government and a stock investment in any given company, even seemingly safe companies. If investors choose to invest in equity, they undertake the firm specific or unique risk associated with that company. Firm specific risk is any risk that is unique to the firm, and it may include risks associated with management competence, business strategy, and competitive position. A number of bad things can happen to any given firm. For example, if the investment is the Walt Disney Co., perhaps tomorrow Mickey Mouse will cease to be popular with children. If McDonald's Corp., perhaps more people will prefer the Whopper over the Big Mac. If Eastman Kodak Co., perhaps one day the firm's leading technology in paper-and-pulp film processing will be made obsolete by digital cameras and computer imaging technology. If the Enron Corp., perhaps one day the senior executives of the company will orchestrate one of the largest accounting frauds in business history and destroy the company. An investment of stock in a specific company is always subject to the *unique risk* (sometimes called firm-specific or unsystematic risk) associated with that company.

EXAMPLE 9.2

---

**Enron's unique risk**

Before its collapse in late 2001, Enron was one of the lauded companies in Corporate America. Among other plaudits, *Fortune* magazine named Enron "The Most Innovative Company in America," and *CFO* magazine named Andrew Fastow, the architect of the massive accounting fraud, "CFO of the Year."

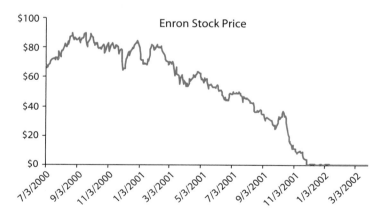

Many investors, including thousands of Enron employees, had much of their investment tied up in Enron stock. You can see that an investment in any given stock is very risky.

---

Individual investments in stock are risky. Imagine that you have come across an inheritance of $1,000,000—a princely sum. Would you feel comfortable investing the entire sum in shares of General Electric? To be sure, GE is the company that "brings good things to life" (the company's slogan); it is a world-class company and an admirable enterprise. But many people would be uneasy with putting all one million eggs in one basket, particularly if this represents the only investment of one's assets. As Antonio, the merchant of Venice, advised, "My ventures are not in one bottom trusted, Nor to one place; nor is my whole estate Upon the fortune of this present year." Antonio was well diversified, and thus he was not sad when misfortune fell upon one investment.

If an all-in investment in one firm is undesirable, an investor can diversify away firm specific risk by investing in a diversified portfolio of stocks. If Enron was in the basket, the firm's implosion would certainly affect the return on the portfolio. But a diversified portfolio of stock would always have some laggards (and scoundrels), but for every laggard there may be a star. If Enron was in the basket of stocks, perhaps a company like Google would have been in the basket as well. A diversified portfolio would smooth out the ups and downs of individual stock movements, and thus eliminate the unique risks associated with any individual company in the basket. If well diversified, a portfolio will mirror the return on the broader market.

One should not confuse diversification with the elimination of all risk (only risk-free investments are risk-free). Diversification only eliminates exposure to firm specific risk of investing in a particular company, i.e., the risk of bad things happening to a specific investment in Disney, McDonald's, Eastman Kodak, or Enron. An investment in the market is still risky. The market moves. It can go up, and it can go down (think of a rollercoaster ride). Diversification cannot eliminate the risk inherent in an investment in a market portfolio. This risk is called *market risk* (sometimes called systematic risk).

EXAMPLE 9.3

**Market risk**

In thinking about the risks of investing in the stock market, consider the stock market crash of 1929, which precipitated the Great Depression, and the crash of 2008, which precipitated what is dubbed the Great Recession.

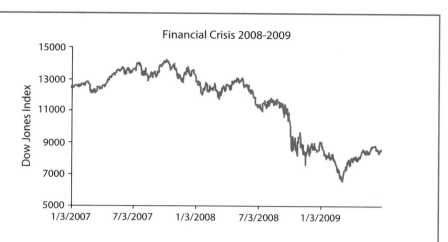

Only investors of risk-free instruments bear no risk. Investors in the market must bear the market risk because this risk cannot be eliminated without relinquishing the expected return on the market. This simply means that there is no way to have your financial cake and eat it too!

With this background, we can embark on a rigorous analysis of how investors set the expectation of return in a specific stock (remember the expected return on the stock is the firm's cost of equity). The conventional and generally accepted way of calculating the cost of equity is the Capital Asset Pricing Model, which was developed by among others William Sharpe, a Nobel Prize winning financial economist.[1] CAPM states:

$$\text{Cost of equity} = \text{\ss} \ (R_m - R_f) + R_f$$

where $\text{\ss} = \text{beta}$, $R_m = \text{market return}$, and $R_f = \text{risk-free rate}$.

CAPM is a part of the discount rate used to discount the corporation's future cash flows, which is the process of valuing the corporation's equity (it is the $R$ in the time value of money calculation). CAPM has an elegant logic, which goes like this.

1. An investor always has the opportunity to invest in risk-free instruments and get $R_f$, and she would bear no risk.
2. An investor also has the opportunity to invest in a diversified market portfolio and get $R_m$, and she would bear the market risk.
3. If an investor chooses to invest in the market portfolio and forego the opportunity to invest in a risk-free rate, she must be compensated additionally for bearing the market risk: thus, $R_m > R_f$.
4. The difference is measured as $(R_m - R_f)$, called the *equity risk premium*, which is the additional compensation that an investor requires to forego the opportunity to earn a risk-free return and bear the market risk.

1. John Lintner, *The Valuation of Risk Assets and the Selection of Risky Investments in Stock Portfolios and Capital Budgets*, 47 Rev. Econ. & Stat. 13 (1965); William F. Sharpe, *Capital Asset Prices: A Theory of Market Equilibrium Under Conditions of Risk*, 19 J. Fin. 425 (1964).

5. Thus far, we have focused on the difference between the market rate and the risk-free rate. The investor also has the option to forego a market return and invest in the stock of an individual company. This risk must be measured so that the investor can be appropriately compensated.

This last step (5) is where beta $\beta$ comes into the picture. *Beta* is the measure of covariance between the market return and the return on the company's stock. In plain English, this means that beta is the sensitivity of a company's stock return to the movement of the market return. A beta of 1.0 means that the stock return is correlated one-for-one with the market return. Assume a market return of 11 percent. The return on the company's stock would be: +22 percent for a beta of 2.0; +11 percent for a beta of 1.0; +5.5 percent for a beta of 0.5; −11 percent for a beta of −1.0.

EXAMPLE 9.4

## Applying beta

Think about what a beta of 2.0 means. If the market return is $+R_m$, the particular stock return would be $+2R_m$; and if the market return is $-R_m$, the stock return would be $-2R_m$. It is correlated with the market movement at twice the sensitivity.

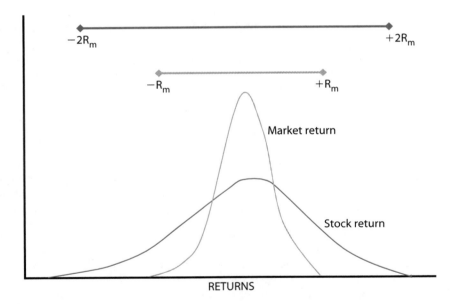

At a beta of 2.0, notice that the stock return is more variable than the market return. This means that an investment in the stock is more risky than an investment in a well diversified portfolio. Thus, an investor in the stock must be compensated more than the rate of the market return.

Beta is the measure of the stock's risk *relative to the market risk*. Why a comparison to market risk? Answer: Because market risk cannot be eliminated. An investor in a diversified market portfolio must always bear the market risk. Accordingly, the measure of a stock return is compared to the market return.

The concept of beta—that stocks can be empirically measured in their sensitivity to the market return—leads to a very simple idea: all stocks rest on a sloping line called the *security market line*. The security market line says that as risk increases, the expected return must also increase in a precise mathematical relationship such that stocks literally "line up" on the security market line. In the graph below, the security market line starts from the risk-free rate and slopes upward along the risk—return continuum.

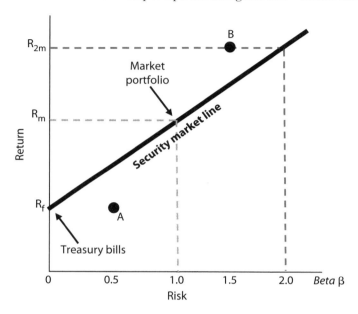

A diversified portfolio has a beta of 1.0, which means that the portfolio's return mimics the market's movements and earns the average return on the market of $R_m$.

Can a stock lie below the security market line such as Stock A? No. For a beta of 0.5, the investor in Stock A gets a return of $R_f$. For this rate, she can simply buy Treasuries and assume no risk. If she seeks to assume the risk of a beta 0.5, she can get greater returns through an alternative investment. With the same amount of money, she can invest in a 50/50 mix of Treasury bills and a market portfolio that creates a return resting on the security market line with a beta of 0.5. The return would be $(R_m + R_f)/2$, which is more than simply $R_f$. Thus, if Stock A really sits below the security market line, its share price would drop until the return to the shareholder increase to $(R_m + R_f)/2$.

A drop in the share price increases the return to prospective *new* shareholders who would get more stock for the same money, thus increasing returns. Obviously, *old* shareholders who bought at a higher price pay the penalty for making a bad stock selection.

Can a stock lie above the security market line such as Stock B? No. If such opportunity exists, other investors would soon see an arbitrage opportunity (a chance to make *abnormal* profit). Remember the market is full of bad *and* good investors. The "smart money" would buy Stock B, increasing its price until the return on the stock declines, in accordance to the risk—return continuum of the security market line.

Since beta measures the riskiness of a stock relative to the market risk, we now have a way to ascertain the compensation needed to incentivize an investment in the stock given the investor's opportunity to invest in the market or a risk-free rate. Keep in mind that risk is defined as the variance of return. A return that is more variable is considered more risky. The golden rule is this: *The more variance in an investment, the more the investor must be compensated.*

Bearing more risk means more compensation must be given, and vice versa. Therefore, the market risk premium $(R_m - R_f)$ is multiplied by beta to calculate the premium above the risk-free rate required to incentivize an investment in the specific company. Once this equity premium is calculated, we add back the risk-free rate since it is the baseline return from which different investment opportunities are measured.

Through these logical steps, we have a way to calculate the cost of equity as the discount rate used to value the firm's equity.

1. The greater the risk, the greater the beta.
2. The greater the beta, the greater the discount rate.
3. The greater the discount rate, the less the equity value.
4. The less the equity value, the more that the investor's dollar can purchase equity ownership of the firm, *and thus* earn an increased rate of return.

In this way, the investor is compensated through the process of equity valuation vis-à-vis cash payments akin to interest payments on debt.

---

It is useful to know certain market benchmarks. For the long-term period 1900-2008, the following are important market benchmarks.[2]

*Market return*: the average return on common stocks is about 11%

*Risk-free return*: the average return on Treasury bills is about 4%

*Market risk premium*: $R_m - R_f = 7\%$

*Inflation*: the average inflation is about 3%

It is important to note that these are *long-term averages*, and in any given year the market return and the risk-free rates can vary. For instance, on December 31, 2007, the S&P 500 index closed at 1,411.63, and on December 29, 2008, it closed at 903.25, which is a decline of 36 percent. Any investment in the stock market is a risky proposition.

---

2. Richard A. Brealey et al., Principles of Corporate Finance 158 (concise 2d ed., 2011).

EXAMPLE 9.5

## How shareholders are compensated, and why equity is not "free"

Assume two corporations, Acme and Zulu. Corporations are valued based on (1) how much free cash flow they generate in the future (2) discounted by the riskiness of that cash flow (we will study the Discounted Cash Flow method of valuation in the next section). If Acme and Zulu are assumed to exist in perpetuity, we can use the perpetuity formula to discount the free cash flow.

Acme and Zulu have no debt such that their cost of equity is the appropriate discount rate (the cap rate). Both firms have 100 outstanding shares of common stock. Both are expected to generate $1,200 in free cash flow in perpetuity. Assume the following:

$$R_m = 11\% \quad R_f = 4\% \quad \beta_{Acme} = 0.86 \quad \beta_{Zulu} = 1.57$$

Zulu is almost twice as risky as Acme as measured by beta. Under CAPM, the cost of equity for each firm is:

Acme    $0.86 \times (11\% - 4\%) + 4\% = 10\%$

Zulu    $1.57 \times (11\% - 4\%) + 4\% = 15\%$

Using the perpetuity formula and the cost of equity as the capitalization rate, we calculate the present value of all free cash flow as:

$$Acme = \frac{1,200}{10\%} = 12,000$$

$$Zulu = \frac{1,200}{15\%} = 8,000$$

Each firm has 100 outstanding shares, and thus the share prices are: Acme $120 per share, and Zulu $80 per share. Why is Zulu share price lower?

Assume that an investor, Robert, has $720 to invest in either Acme or Zulu. The $720 buys the following choices:

Acme  ⇒  6 shares at $120 per share, which is 6% of the total equity

Zulu  ⇒  9 shares at $80 per share, which is 9% of the total equity

It is important to reiterate that both Acme and Zulu are expected to generate *the same level of free cash flow of $1,200 per year in perpetuity*. Yet with the same $720, Robert can buy more Zulu shares than Acme shares. Why? Because Zulu is more risky, as measured by *beta*. Robert must be compensated more for choosing Zulu over Acme. If the investor holds the stock in perpetuity, the investor will get, per the valuation method, the following *gross* economic claims (i.e., not discounted):

Acme  ⇒  $72 per year in perpetuity (which is 6% of $1,200 per year)

Zulu  ⇒  $108 per year in perpetuity (which is 9% of $1,200 per year)

Thus, Robert is additionally compensated through the valuation process by investing in the more risky Zulu stock. This is what we mean when we say that *the cost of equity is embedded in the company's stock valuation*. The investor is not compensated in cash like an interest payment (because neither corporate law nor the typical corporate charter requires cash payment to shareholders), but instead the shareholder is compensated in the form of valuation allowing him to purchase more or less of the company for the same dollar depending on the riskiness of that company. Of course, the investment can be converted to cash by selling shares in the market.

 Assume that the share price of a company falls on a sustained basis: i.e., day-to-day market prices may be volatile, but over a sustained period the share price is falling. Should the company's management be worried? What can an investor do? She can obviously exercise the Wall Street rule and sell the shares, which may decrease the share price more.

Alternatively, if she has significant purchasing power, she can acquire more shares. Why might a rational, wealth maximizing investor want to purchase more shares in a stock that is underperforming? If an investor gains control of the corporation, what can she do?

## 3. WEIGHTED AVERAGE COST OF CAPITAL

To finance its enterprise, a firm can use a combination of debt, preferred stock, and common stock. Debt and equity are simply means of financing, and an enterprise can use any proportional mix. Each form of capital has its own cost as determined by the risk undertaken by the capital provider. This implies that the firm has an average cost of capital that must be weighted for the different forms of capital it deploys, which is the *weighted average cost of capital* (WACC). WACC is the average cost of capital given a firm's capital structure.

$$\text{WACC} = \frac{D}{V}C_d(1 - T) + \frac{P}{V}C_p + \frac{E}{V}C_e$$

Where  $V$ = firm value (total debt, preferred and common stock)
 $D$ = value of debt
 $P$ = value of preferred stock
 $E$ = value of common stock (market cap)
 $C_d$ = cost of debt (which must be adjusted for the tax shield)
 $C_p$ = cost of preferred stock
 $C_e$ = cost of equity (as calculated by CAPM)

EXAMPLE 9.6

### Calculating WAAC

Acme Inc. has a firm value of 1,000, which is composed of: 250 debt, 300 preferred stock, and 450 common stock. The interest rate on the debt is 9 percent. The annual cumulative dividend rate on preferred stock is 8 percent, which is the cost of the preferred stock. Based on the application of CAPM, the cost of equity is 12 percent. The tax rate is 33 percent. What is Acme's WACC?

$$\text{WACC} = \frac{250}{1,000}9\%(1-33\%) + \frac{300}{1,000}8\% + \frac{450}{1,000}12\%$$

$$\text{WACC} = 1.5\% + 2.4\% + 5.4\% \quad \Rightarrow \quad 9.3\%$$

Based on Acme's capital structure, its weighted average cost of capital is 9.3 percent. This is the discount rate that would be used to discount the future free cash flow Acme is expecting. And, the sum of the discounted free cash flow is the theoretical value of the company.

Note that the cost of debt is 6 percent because interest expense is tax deductible, and thus the cost of debt is net of the interest tax shield. However, the cost of the preferred stock is 8 percent because dividends are paid from net profit and they do not create a tax benefit for the issuing company.

WACC is the cost of capital given a firm's capital structure. It is the discount rate R used to discount the future free cash flow of the firm, which is the value of the firm.

## C. THEORETICAL VALUATION BASED ON DISCOUNTED CASH FLOW (DCF)

At this point, a big picture perspective is needed. We learned the meaning of cost of capital and the method to calculate it. The cost of capital is an important concept. It tells a manager how much the firm must earn to meet the expectations of its capital providers given that they have other investment opportunities. In the long-term, the share price will adjust to meet the expectations of shareholders: i.e., the value of bad companies will decline, and that of good companies will rise. That's the business side of financial management.

What relevance does cost of capital have for a lawyer? It is relevant in several ways. First, the client's concerns must be the lawyer's. Business clients are always seeking ways to enhance value and create wealth, and lawyers help to do this. Second, cost of capital may be central to many corporate transactions for which lawyers will be hired as advisers. Third, valuation is always a critical issue in both capital raisings and mergers and acquisitions. This is true on the transactional side and, for mergers and acquisitions specifically, on the litigation side as well because dissenting shareholders are legally entitled under corporate law to an appraisal of their shares if they don't like the consideration offered in a merger or acquisition.

The cost of capital is not just an abstract number derived from finance theory. It is a practical tool in the exercise of valuation. Under the *discounted cash flow (DCF) method*, the theoretical value of a corporation is the sum of the future stream of free cash flow it is expected to generate, discounted by its cost of capital. A properly conducted DCF analysis is a very complex study requiring expert hands; a mastery of the nuances requires formal coursework in finance and significant practice experience. Lawyers will not be asked to conduct such analysis, but they must understand the basic concept and framework of the financial analysis to know, minimally at least, what is going on in the transaction. Conceptually, a DCF analysis is simply a present value calculation (once again we return to the concept of time value of money!). Any present value problem has two large variables: What is the expected future return? What is the discount rate $R$? In a DCF valuation, these variables are: (1) What is the future stream of free cash flow? (2) What is the cost of capital?

## 1. FREE CASH FLOW

What is free cash flow? How is it different from the accounting cash flow statements? "Free cash flow is the after-tax cash flow available to *all* investors: debt holders and equity holders. Unlike 'cash flow from operations' reported in a company's financial statement, free cash flow is independent of financing and nonoperating items."[3] Free cash flow (FCF) is defined as:

$$FCF = \left( \begin{array}{l} + \text{ NOPLAT} \\ + \text{ Noncash Operating Expenses} \\ - \text{ Investments in Invested Capital} \end{array} \right)$$

Noncash operating expenses are depreciation and amortization. Investments in invested capital are capital expenditures and investments in working capital (as a going concern, a company must continuously purchase capital assets and manage its working capital).

NOPLAT is net operating profit less adjusted taxes. It is the after-tax operating income that is available to all capital providers of the firm. It differs from the accountant's income statement in these ways. First, it is operating profit only. It does not include any non-operating income or expense (income or expense not related to core operation). Also, operating profit is *before* the interest expense deduction; thus it is income available to creditors and equityholders. Second, "adjusted taxes" are calculated on the basis of operating income, and not pretax profit based on the income statement. We start from the reported tax liability in the income statements, add back the tax shield on interest expense, and remove taxes paid for non-operating income.

3. Tim Koller, Marc Goedhart & David Wessels, Valuation: Measuring and Managing the Value of Companies 164 (4th ed., Wiley 2005) (emphasis in original).

EXAMPLE 9.7

---

### Income Statement vs. NOPLAT

This example illustrates the difference between the income statement, which provides the inputs to a projection of free cash flow, and NOPLAT.

| Income statement | | NOPLAT | |
|---|---|---|---|
| Revenue | 1,000 | Revenue | 1,000 |
| Operating expense | (700) | Operating expense | (700) |
| Depreciation | (100) | Depreciation | (100) |
| | | | |
| Operating profit | 200 | Operating profit | 200 |
| Interest expense | (50) | Operating taxes at 25% | (50) |
| Non-operating income | 10 | | |
| Pretax profit | 160 | NOPLAT | 150 |
| Taxes at 25% | (40) | | |
| | | | |
| Net income | 120 | | |

---

Conceptually, free cash flow is cash that is available to all capital providers from core operations of the firm after payment of all operating expenses, taxes on operations, and continuing investments in capital assets and working capital. For a going concern, it is the cash that remains (cash that is free) to all capital providers.

 What is the value of a corporation? It has no aesthetic value like art. Owning stock does not give us inherent pleasure like a hug from a loved one. There is only one measure of value: How much cash will the corporation generate after payment to everyone else?

## 2. DISCOUNTING FREE CASH FLOW

An investor pays dollars today (a cash outflow) in a financial instrument for the promise of dollars tomorrow. The value of a corporation is the sum of the future stream of free cash flow discounted by the firm's cost of capital measuring the riskiness of that free cash flow. After projecting out the future free cash flow, a DCF analysis must now discount that cash flow with the firm's cost of capital.

A going concern is a firm that operates indefinitely into the future, resulting in free cash flow in perpetuity. The typical DCF model is broken into two time periods: (1) forecast period constituting the first several years of projections; (2) perpetuity period constituting the remaining time in perpetuity. The typical forecast period of modeling is anywhere from 7 to 20 years (practices by professionals can vary). The value attributable to the perpetuity period, called the terminal (or continuing) value, constitutes the perpetuity stream of cash flow after the final year of the forecast period. How is a perpetual stream of money calculated? Recall from Chapter 7 section B the perpetuity formula. The terminal value is typically calculated under the perpetuity formula or its cousin the growth perpetuity formula, using WACC as the capitalization rate. We capitalize the final projected year's free cash flow by the WACC.

$$\text{Terminal Value} = \frac{\text{FCF(final year)}}{\text{WACC} - \text{g}}$$

Once the forecast of the free cash flow is made, the last step in the DCF analysis is to discount the free cash flow using the firm's WACC. The illustration below summarizes the DCF analysis. The period ($\text{FCF}_1 \ldots \text{FCF}_N$) is the forecast period, and the period ($\text{FCF}_{(N+1)} \ldots \text{FCF}_\infty$) is the perpetuity period. Together, these cash flows constitute the entire stream of free cash that the firm is expected to generate and that is available to all capital providers. This stream of cash must be discounted in a way that reflects its riskiness, which is the firm's WACC.

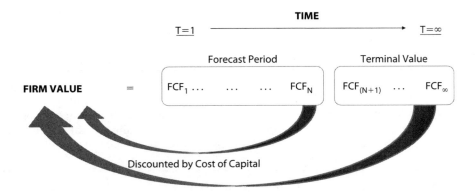

Thus, we see that the DCF analysis, while complex in execution, is conceptually nothing more than a time value of money problem. The variables affecting firm value are (1) the amount of free cash flow in the future (the measure of expected return), and (2) the discount rate (the measure of risk). Obviously, the more free cash flow in the future, the greater would be the value, and vice versa. Obviously as well, the greater the discount rate used, the less would be the value, and vice versa. These two variables ultimately determine firm value. The table below summarizes these effects.

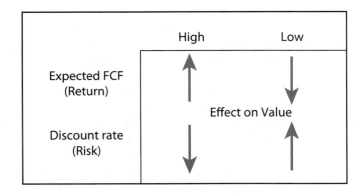

# D. MARKET-BASED VALUATION AND MULTIPLES ANALYSIS

How is the concept of market value implemented in a market valuation? The primary method to calculate the value of a firm based on market metrics is a comparable companies analysis. This analysis uses market values of other companies to calculate the implied value of the company in question. The companies being compared to must be comparable. Proverbially speaking, it makes no sense to compare apples to oranges.

---

Assume that you are working with Nike, Inc. Its value is at issue. Nike is a maker of sports shoes and sportswear. Which of the following are appropriate comparable companies?

- Adidas Group
- American Airlines
- Pfizer, Inc.
- Walmart

- McDonald's Corp.
- Under Armour, Inc.
- JPMorgan Chase
- Verizon

---

EXAMPLE 9.8

---

**Valuing residential homes**

Most of us will buy a home at some point, and it may be the single most significant investment for many people. Thus, this example may be of personal significance. Depending on the location, the average home price can range from mid-five to high-six figure sums ($50,000 to $900,000). How are homes priced? How much should one pay? Are home values pulled out of thin air?

- Suppose homes in the area sell on average at $100 per square foot. The home you are considering is 2,000 square feet. It is priced at $300,000. Based on just this information, is it fairly priced?
- Does it make sense to value this home with the price per square foot data from an entirely different geographic region?

The above is a comparable homes analysis. The metric for valuation is the ratio of price per square foot ($/s.f.). Homes come in different sizes (e.g., 1,500 versus 3,000 square feet), but there is a common valuational metric to compare prices.

- Suppose the home has been substantially remodeled. Among other things, it has an upgraded kitchen and bathrooms. Most homes in the area are older homes and have not been renovated. Does this information change your assessment of value?
- Suppose big homes and small homes in the same geographic area differ in valuations. Big homes (> 3,000 square feet) go for $120 per square foot, and smaller homes (<2,000 square feet) go for $80 per square foot. What factors could account for these differences?

---

In making value judgments about real estate assets, you are implicitly engaging in comparable analysis. Indeed, most competent real estate agents will provide a comparable analysis as a part of the home purchase or sale transaction.

Just the way that similar homes are compared in price, similar companies are compared based on various measures of profitability and equity.

## 1. MARKET CAP MULTIPLES

In Chapter 2, we saw that one measure of market value is the ratio of market price of stock to book value.

$$\text{Price/Book ratio} = \frac{\text{Market cap}}{\text{Book value}}$$

The P/B ratio measures the ratio of market value of stock to the book value. By getting the average and range of comparable companies, we can infer the range of market value of equity given a firm's book value.

The price-to-earnings ratio is the ratio of market price of stock to net income.

$$\text{Price/Earnings ratio} = \frac{\text{Market cap}}{\text{Earnings}} = \frac{\text{Stock Price}}{\text{EPS}}$$

The P/E multiple says that the value of the company is the multiple of its earnings.

The P/E multiple resembles the multiple derived from a perpetuity formula. For example, perpetual future earnings of $100 capitalized at a 10 percent rate results in a present value equivalent of $1,000, or a multiple of 10.0x earnings.

Why are net income and book value compared to market cap? Market cap is the market value of *equity*. Net income is the claim of equityholders (shareholders) after creditors are paid. Book value is the equity in the financial statements. Thus, P/E and P/B are multiples measured against like-for-like metrics.

## 2. FIRM VALUE MULTIPLES

In addition to earnings (net income), EBIT and EBITDA can be used as metrics. However, these financial metrics must be measured against firm (enterprise) value vis-à-vis market cap. *Enterprise value (EV), also called firm value, is the market value of all securities issued by the company: i.e., debt, preferred stock, and common stock.*

$$\text{EBIT ratio} = \frac{\text{Enterprise Value}}{\text{EBIT}}$$

$$\text{EBITDA ratio} = \frac{\text{Enterprise Value}}{\text{EBITDA}}$$

Why a multiple of firm value? EBIT and EBITDA are *above* the tax line, and thus are claims on the earnings made by creditors *and* equityholders. Since the money belongs to both creditors and equityholders, it makes no sense to take a ratio of just market cap (which is equity) to the earnings attributable to both creditors and equityholders.

However, these multiples can still give an implied value of the equity. Suppose that an analysis of the EV/EBIT multiple for comparable companies results in an average multiple of 12.0x EBIT. The company we are valuing has an EBIT of $10 million and debt of $40 million. This implies a firm value of $120 million. Since firm value is market cap plus debt, the implied equity value of the firm under this analysis is $80 million (firm value minus debt).

EXAMPLE 9.9

<hr>

### AOL and Time Warner merger

In 2000, AOL and Time Warner announced a merger with an anticipated combined company value of $350 billion. By most accounts, the merger was a colossal failure. In a 2005 Washington Post article, the CEO of AOL at the time of the merger conceded: "How this widely heralded 'merger of the century' quickly became widely derided as the 'worst merger in history' has been the subject of considerable commentary. I have my own views, but now is not the time for that debate. Instead, it is time for everyone with a stake in Time Warner to focus on putting this company on a better path." Steve Case, *It's Time to Take It Apart: My Case for Dividing the Media Giant*, Washington Post (Dec. 11, 2005). Below are relevant excerpted portions of Time Warner's merger proxy statement filed with the SEC, providing the investment banker's comparable companies analysis for Time Warner, Inc. The analysis was a part of the investment banker's fairness opinion. Note that the multiple is based on "equity value adjusted for capital structure," a concept similar to enterprise value.

\*\*\*

The market value of shares of common stock generally reflects a "multiple" of selected measures of financial performance, such as operating profits or earnings per share.

*Comparable Companies Analysis.* Morgan Stanley calculated aggregate value, i.e., equity value adjusted for capital structure, to EBITDA multiples for Time Warner for fiscal years 1999 through 2001 based on publicly available Morgan Stanley research estimates. Morgan Stanley then compared the EBITDA multiples obtained for Time Warner with multiples obtained for a group of selected media and entertainment companies.

. . .

The group of selected media and entertainment companies included Cablevision Systems Corporation, The Walt Disney Company, Fox Corporation, News Corp. Ltd., The Seagram Company Ltd. and the combined Viacom/CBS Corporation entity. Morgan Stanley selected these companies because they are publicly traded companies with media and entertainment operations that for purposes of this analysis may be considered similar to those of Time Warner.

. . .

The analysis showed the following multiples:

| | Estimated Aggregate Value/EBITDA | | |
|---|---|---|---|
| | *1999* | *2000* | *2001* |
| Time Warner | 19.4x | 17.5x | 15.4x |
| Group of selected media and entertainment companies: | | | |
| Mean | 18.7x | 15.8x | 13.8x |
| Median | 16.2x | 14.7x | 12.8x |

**STOP AND THINK** In the above portion of the merger proxy, the information was provided by investment bankers, but the document was written by lawyers. Drafting legal documents is a prized skill. For lawyers specializing in corporate transactional practice, does it matter whether they understand the content and context of the document they draft?

## 3. USING MULTIPLES TO VALUE COMPANIES

Multiples are useful because they communicate the value of a firm. Some uninformed people believe that stock price communicates the value of a firm. This is wrong. *Multiples tell us the quality of a firm's market valuation—whether the company is highly or lowly valued.* The stock price, being dependent on the number of shares outstanding, is an arbitrary number. It has one function: That is, the stock price tells us how much an investor must pay to buy one share of stock in the company. The stock price, in and of itself, communicates no other information.

EXAMPLE 9.10

### Comparing Google and McDonald's

Google and McDonald's are entirely unrelated businesses. It makes no sense to compare their financial performances (e.g., did McDonald's earn more profit than Google?). However, we can compare their valuations for the purpose of answering these questions: Does the market value Google more than McDonald's? Are innovative tech companies valued more than innovative fast-food companies? The answers may give us relevant insights. The information below is relevant to making a valuational comparison between Google and McDonald's.

| (as of or at fiscal year ended Dec. 31, 2010) | *Google* | *McDonald's* |
|---|---|---|
| Share price | $593.97 | $76.76 |
| Earnings per share (EPS) | $26.69 | $4.64 |
| Price-to-earnings ratio (P/E) | 22.3x | 16.5x |
| Net income | $8.505 billion | $4.946 billion |
| Shares outstanding | 0.321 billion | 1.053 billion |
| Market cap | $191 billion | $81 billion |

*Google share price is 7.74x more than McDonald's share price. Does this mean that Google is 7.74x more valuable?*

No. The share price, *in and of itself*, is an arbitrary number. It simply indicates how must money is required to purchase one share of stock. If Google split its stock 2-for-1 (each shareholder trades in 1 old share and gets 2 new shares) such that the shares outstanding would increase from 0.321 to 0.642 billion shares, then Google share price would decrease to $296.99 per share. Similarly, McDonald's can do a reverse stock split 1-for-7.74 (each shareholder trades in 7.74 old shares and gets 1 new share), and increase McDonald's share price from $76.76 to $593.97.

*Google earned 1.72x more net income than McDonald's. Does this mean that Google is 1.72x more valuable?*

No. Net income is simply an indication of how much profit a firm generated. The number *alone* is not a measure of value.

*How do we compare the value of Google and McDonald's?*

One comparison is the P/E multiple. The P/E multiple says that Google's equity value is 22.3x its net income, whereas McDonald's equity value is 16.5x its net income. Thus, the market is valuing Google at a higher level than McDonald's by assigning a market multiple that is higher than that of McDonald's.

EXAMPLE 9.11

## Advising In-N-Out Burger on strategic alternatives

If you are an aficionado of hamburgers and have lived in the Western states like Arizona and California, you may know that In-N-Out Burger makes wonderful fast-food. In-N-Out is a private company, and its stock is owned by the family of Harry and Esther Snyder. Suppose the family is "exploring strategic alternatives," which is a signal that the company is considering some sort of a major corporate transaction: perhaps either selling shares to the public or selling the entire company to an acquirer like McDonald's. A deal team of investment bankers, lawyers and accountants is assembled. An important consideration is the value of In-N-Out.

*Step 1: What are reasonable comparables for In-N-Out Burger?*

McDonald's and Burger King are very good comparables. McDonald's is a public company. On October 19, 2010, Burger King was acquired by an affiliate of 3G Capital, and ceased to be publicly traded company (a transaction called "going private"). However, significant data exists because it was a public company. Another comparable is Wendy's and Arby's, two smaller fast food chains operated by Wendy's Arby's Group, Inc., a public company. From this rich set of data, we can construct a comparable companies analysis.

*Step 2: Construct a comparable companies analysis for McDonald's, Burger King, and Wendy's (data as of each company's fiscal year end)*[4]

| (in $ million) | McDonald's | Burger King | Wendy's | Average |
|---|---|---|---|---|
| **Values of securities** | | | | |
| Market cap | 80,874 | 2,237 | 1,919 | Na |
| Longterm debt | 11,497 | 667 | 1,553 | Na |
| Enterprise value | 92,371 | 2,904 | 3,472 | Na |
| **Financial data** | | | | |
| Book value | 14,634 | 1,128 | 2,163 | Na |
| Net income | 4,946 | 186 | (4.3) | Na |
| EBIT | 7,431 | 332 | 132 | Na |
| EBITDA | 8,607 | 443 | 314 | Na |
| **Multiples** | | | | |
| P/B | 5.5x | 2.0x | 0.9x | 2.8x |
| P/E | 16.4x | 12.0x | -446.3x (na) | 14.2x |
| EV/EBIT | 12.4x | 8.7x | 26.3x (na) | 10.1x |
| EV/EBITDA | 10.7x | 6.6x | 11.1x (na) | 8.7x |

Note: The average P/E and EV multiples used only McDonald's and Burger King because the figures for Wendy's are unreliable due to financial problems at the company.

The accounting and financial data communicate much information about the fast food industry. It says that McDonald's is the clear market leader, judging by the combination of size and premium valuation relative to its competitors. Making a profit in the restaurant business may be hard (see the experience of Wendy's).

*Step 3: Derive valuation of In-N-Out using the company's financial data*

If we were actually advising In-N-Out, we would get private information on the firm. Because that information is not publicly available, the following analysis uses hypothetical numbers for In-N-Out's financial performance.

| (in $ million) | Book Value | Net Income | EBIT | EBITDA |
|---|---|---|---|---|
| In-N-Out's financial data | 110 | 25 | 40 | 50 |
| | x | x | x | x |
| Multiple | 2.8 | 14.2 | 10.1 | 8.7 |
| | = | = | = | = |
| Equity value | 308 | 355 | | |
| Enterprise value | | | 404 | 435 |
| In-N-Out's debt | | | 40 | 40 |
| Implied equity value of In-N-Out | 308 | 355 | 364 | 395 |

---

4. We ignore nuances of a technically correct analysis such as matching the timing of earnings and market values to account for different fiscal year ends (McDonald's December 31, Burger King June 30, Wendy's Arby's January 2). These nuances are tedious to work through in a textbook. Such adjustments are made by technically proficient financial advisers, but our purpose here is to illustrate the conceptual use of multiples, which is the important lesson. Business lawyers will not be asked to conduct a multiples analysis, but they will be expected to understand the outputs and their implications on the client and the transaction.

The valuation range for In-N-Out is from about $300 to $400 million based on this multiples analysis. Obviously, this is a broad range, but such ranges are not unusual. Valuation is part science and part art. This range also leaves much to be negotiated in a transaction with interested parties, and lawyers may be major players.

Parenthetically, note that if In-N-Out's true comparable is not the average multiples of publicly traded fast food companies, which includes McDonald's, but is instead Burger King, the multiples used would be lower and thus In-N-Out's value range would be lower as well. The multiples themselves are subject to negotiations.

This is only a hypothetical. It seems that a sale of the company is not in the immediate future: "In-N-Out remains privately owned and the Snyder family has no plans to take the company public or franchise any units." http://www.in-n-out.com/history.asp (as of June 14, 2011).

## E. THE LAW OF ONE PRICE AND ARBITRAGE

If multiples and other valuational metrics are so important to valuation, where do they come from? Why is McDonald's P/E 16.5x and Google's 22.3x? Why aren't these multiples 10.0x or 19.8x or 33.5x? Who assigns these important numbers? The capital market—a marketplace where the securities of companies are bought and sold—determines the value of companies just the way that everyday markets for foods, electronics, clothing, etc., determine the price of things. But how does the capital market determine the value of company securities? The short answer is that ultimately the values are anchored by the intrinsic, theoretical value of the companies (keeping in mind that the market of buyers and sellers—moms and pops, mutual funds, insurance companies, governments, etc.—isn't perfect). The capital markets are an aggregation of many investors seeking the maximum return for the lowest risk. Many smart investors try to figure out the value of firms by doing detailed analyses of valuation. Their activities of buying and selling set the market price and value levels just the way that the price and value of Tropicana orange juice, Polo shirts, and Titleist drivers are set in the market.

A core principle of securities pricing is the *Law of One Price*. As this section shows, risk and return can be packaged into innumerable securities. The Law of One Price is the principle that securities with the same returns and risks must be priced at the same level irrespective of how they are packaged in securities—it embodies the commonsense notion that there must be one price for the same thing. The Law of One Price is enforced by a process called arbitrage.

*Arbitrage* is the process wherein riskless profit is made by exploiting incorrectly priced securities. While the term arbitrage is fancy, Wall Street traders are not the only ones doing it. For example, not infrequently at the start of a semester, law professors are faced with the situation where a student did not do the reading, not because the student deliberately neglected the assignment but because the textbook had not arrived from the online seller. While textbooks are available at campus bookstores, students routinely shop at various places to buy the cheapest book on the market—the students are exploiting price differentials in the market and are arbitrageurs of law textbooks. Arbitrage facilitates efficient pricing. If an arbitrageur spots a mispriced asset and exploits that difference, others will soon follow. This process results in the closing of mispriced assets as quickly as they are discovered. In an efficient, liquid market, arbitrage opportunities are few and fleeting.

EXAMPLE 9.12

### The Law of One Price and arbitrage

Obviously, the price of Stock A traded in New York should be the same if it is traded in Tokyo. But securities instruments can be packaged in complex ways. Let's see how the Law of One Price and arbitrage works with some complicated securities. Suppose a bond, Bond B, can be "stripped" of its interest payments such that rights to interest payments and the principal are traded separately as Bond B(I) and Bond B(P). Other than the process of disaggregation, Bond B and its interest and principal components produce the identical cashflows. Under the Law of One Price, the following must be true: Bond B = Bond B(I) + Bond B(P).

Suppose that Bond B has a face value of $1,000 with a coupon rate of 10 percent. There are 5 years to maturity. From the time that it was issues, say 15 years ago, interest rates have increased substantially. As a result, the price of Bond B dropped significantly because it is producing only 10 percent of the face value of $1,000. Absent a discount on the market price of the bond, no investor will buy it since they have other opportunities to buy similar quality bonds that are providing greater returns consistent with the prevailing interest rates.

Assume that the current yield on Bond B is 20 percent, which means that based on the fixed interest payments ($100) relative current market price of the bond, it is producing a 20 percent rate of return. The price of Bond B is calculated as the follows.

| | Yr. 1 | Yr. 2 | Yr. 3 | Yr. 4 | Yr. 5 |
|---|---|---|---|---|---|
| Bond B interest payments | $100 | $100 | $100 | $100 | $100 |
| Bond B principal payment | 0 | 0 | 0 | 0 | $1,000 |
| Discount factor at 20% | 0.8333 | 0.6944 | 0.5787 | 0.4823 | 0.4019 |
| Present value of interest | $83.33 | $69.44 | $57.87 | $48.23 | $40.19 |
| Sum PV of interest | | | | | $299.06 |
| Present value of principal | 0 | 0 | 0 | 0 | $401.90 |
| Sum PV of bond | | | | | $700.96 |

Thus, Bond B has a market price of $700.96. With interest payments of $100 per year and a principal payment of $1,000 at the end of five years, Bond B produces a rate of return of 20%, which is the amount it should be producing based on the higher interest rate environment. We also see that Bond B(I) should trade on the market for $299.06, and Bond B(P) at $401.90. The Law of One Price states that the following must be true:

$$\text{Bond B} = \text{Bond B(I)} + \text{Bond B(P)}$$

$$\$700.96 = \$299.06 + \$401.90$$

Assume that Bond B trades at $700.96 and Bond B(P) at $401.90, but that Bond B(I) trades at $300.06 (one dollar more than its theoretical value).

*How should an investor arbitrage this price discrepancy?*

The investor should sell the overpriced security: sell Bond B(I) at $300.06 and Bond B(P) at $401.90. With the $701.96 proceeds, she should buy Bond B at $700.96.

Bond B produces the identical cash flow of the stripped components Bond B(I) and Bond B(P). Therefore, the investor makes a riskless profit of $1.00.

Note that if enough smart investors figure out this profit opportunity, the opportunity disappears because the price of Bond B(I) will decline as arbitrageurs sell this overpriced stripped bond. The price will eventually decline to its intrinsic value of $299.06, which means that the arbitrage opportunity would disappear. Thus, the Law of One Price and the process of arbitrage impose financial logic and rationality into the valuation of securities.

EXAMPLE 9.13

### Analysis of Bernie Madoff's Ponzi scheme (Part II, applying the Law of One Price)

In Example 8.3, we saw that Bernie Madoff represented that his trades consistently produced an average 12 percent yearly return, net of large hedge fund fees, for many years without any risk (see below). Without the hedge fund fees deducted, his yearly return is about 16 percent.

The average longterm returns on a market portfolio is about 11 percent. The above chart shows that Madoff found a way to make phenomenal riskless profit for many years. Moreover, an investment with Madoff supposedly had a portfolio beta of 0.06. This means that there was almost zero correlation with the market returns, as confirmed by the above graph (the market goes up and down, but Madoff's returns only go up). Are Madoff's representations about his trading in the stock market consistent with the Law of One Price and arbitrage? To earn the market return, shouldn't one have to bear the market risk such that the expectation is a portfolio beta of something in the neighborhood of 1.0?

## F. COMMENT ON VALUATION ANALYSIS

Intrinsic value is impossible to determine as a precise, single value derived from a deductive, scientific process. The typical valuation study performed for a transaction uses different methods, for example: (1) analysis of historical stock price performance, (2) comparative companies analysis using various ratios and financial inputs such as earnings, book value, revenue, EBIT and EBITDA, (3) comparative transactions analysis, which is multiples analysis for transactions, (4) theoretical value under the DCF. Such a study produces a range of reasonable values.

Lawyers will see this kind of valuation study in mergers and acquisition, leading up to a fairness opinion given by the financial adviser to the board of directors. The study is a document relied upon by the board to make its recommendation to shareholders, and as such it is disclosed in the merger proxy. Also, in the context of shareholder appraisal proceedings, the Delaware courts use different methods of valuation and assign weights to each in an effort to judicially assign the value of a going concern.

> Valuation requires technical competence and quantitative rigor in analysis. However, it also requires subjective judgment on many variables that materially affect the results. Valuations typically produce a range of values. Assumptions and subjective judgments matter. Don't be dazzled or intimidated by the seemingly scientific nature of the inquiry.

## G. CASE APPLICATION

The case below applies the Delaware block method of valuation to determine the value of shares held by shareholders who dissent in a merger that has been approved by shareholders. The Delaware block method is a combination of several generally accepted methods of valuation, including valuations based on asset value, market value, and earnings. Dissenting shareholders in a merger are forced to give up their shares, and the remedy must be based on a valuation conducted in an appraisal proceeding. In reading the case, pay particular attention to the unique aspects of a closed end investment fund and their relevance to the appraisal.

### Tri-Continental Corp. v. Battye
74 A.2d 71 (Del. 1950)

WOLCOTT, Judge, delivering the opinion of the Court:

Section 61 of the General Corporation Law Code 1935, §2093, provides that upon the merger of a corporation, stockholders who object to the merger and who fulfill the statutory requirements to register their objection shall be paid the value of their stock on the date of the merger, exclusive of any element of value arising from the expectation or accomplishment of the merger. The meaning of the word "value" under this section of the Corporation Law has never been considered by this court.

The basic concept of value under the appraisal statute is that the stockholder is entitled to be paid for that which has been taken from him, viz., his proportionate interest in a going concern. By value of the stockholder's proportionate interest in the corporate enterprise is meant the true or intrinsic value of his stock which has been taken by the merger. In determining what figure represents this true or intrinsic value, the appraiser and the courts must take into consideration all factors and elements which reasonably might enter into the fixing of value. Thus, market value, asset value, dividends, earning prospects, the nature of the enterprise and any other facts which were known or which could be ascertained as of the date of merger and which throw any light on future prospects of the merged corporation are not only pertinent to an inquiry as to the value of the dissenting stockholders' interest, but must be considered by the agency fixing the value.

The rule as stated requires that certain obvious conclusions be drawn. Thus, since intrinsic or true value is to be ascertained, the problem will not be settled by the acceptance as the sole measure of only one element entering into value without considering other elements. For example, market value may not be taken as the sole measure of the value of the stock. So, also, since value is to be fixed on a going-concern basis, the liquidating value of the stock may not be accepted as the sole measure.

General was a regulated closed-end investment company with leverage, and was engaged in the business of investing in the stock market generally seeking to acquire and hold a cross-section of the stock market. Investments were made by General primarily with the possibility of capital appreciation in view. General's portfolio held diversified investments, practically all of which fell within the class of marketable securities readily liquidated.

A regulated close-end investment company is of a peculiar nature. The common stockholder of a closed-end company has no right at any time to demand of the company his proportionate share of the company's assets.[1] A regulated investment company is required to distribute all of its income from dividends and interest to its stockholders but, in so doing, pays no tax on the amounts so distributed. It also has the option of distributing net long-term capital gains to its stockholders or retaining them and paying a flat 25% tax. As in the case of individuals, a regulated investment company has the right to deduct capital losses from its capital gains.

On September 30, 1948, the day preceding the merger, General had outstanding debentures and preferred stock equaling in value 60.8% of the total assets of the company, leaving 39.2% of the company's assets applicable to the common stock. This condition of General made applicable the principle of leverage. Simply stated, this meant that since the debentures and preferred stock of General were a fixed liability, the same amount of assets at all times was required to be set off against them. The result of this unalterable fact was that if the stock market declined, thus decreasing the value of the assets of General, all of the decrease fell upon the common stock. On the other hand, when the stock market rose, thus increasing the value of General's assets, all of the increase accrued to the benefit of the common stock.

Experience demonstrates that when the stock market declines, the market price of the common stock of closed-end investment companies with leverage declines at a more rapid rate because of the resulting shrinkage of asset value behind the common stock. Conversely, a rise in the stock market results in a rise in the market price of

---

1. In contradistinction, the stockholders of the so-called open-end company have the right at the close of business on designated days to demand from the company their proportionate share of the company's assets.

the common stock of such companies at a more rapid rate than the market is increasing generally.

The closed-end feature and leverage have a direct effect on the market value of the common stock of closed-end investment companies. When the market price of the common stock moves into a certain price range in relation to its net asset value, upward leverage disappears and the stock sells on the market at a lower price than its net asset figure. This fact, together with the inability of the common stockholder to withdraw his proportionate interest in the assets of the company, has consistently resulted in a lower market value of the common stock in comparison with its net asset value. This difference between the net asset value and the market value of the common stock of a closed-end investment company is known as discount.

The record discloses that the common stock of General, prior to the merger, was selling within the price range which brought discount into play. The appraiser found the discount rate applicable to General to be 25%. This rate of discount is accepted for the purposes of this case since the parties do not argue that this finding was error.

Discount, therefore, may be applied to net asset value to determine on any day a theoretical or constructed market value of the common stock of a closed-end investment company with leverage. On September 30, 1948, the net asset value of the common stock of General was $4.90 per share and, if the discount of 25% is applied to that figure, a market value of General's common stock on that day of $3.67 per share is constructed.

The appraiser considered various factors which all agree should be considered in valuing the common stock of General. Those factors were: The nature of the enterprise, i.e., a regulated closed-end investment company; leverage; discount; net asset value; market value; management; earnings and dividends; expenses of operation; particular stockholdings in General's portfolio; and a favorable tax situation which General had.

The appraiser found that the factors of management, earnings and dividends, expenses of operation, and the particular stockholdings of General, under the circumstances, were not entitled to be debited or credited in arriving at a value for the common stock. It is not necessary to review his reasons, for the parties are agreed that his findings in this respect were correct. Since, however, earnings and dividends of a corporation are ordinarily of prime importance in valuing common stock, we feel, in order to avoid future confusion, that we should state briefly why they are not of much importance in this case. The reason is that General was an investment company with large leverage which meant that normal income of the company necessarily went in large part to the servicing of the senior debentures and preferred stock, leaving a relatively small amount left to be paid out in dividends to the common. Actually, dividends on the common stock of General in the past were negligible, nor were the prospects for the future materially brighter.

The favorable tax situation of General was found by the appraiser to be worth 29¢ to each share of common stock. This finding is not urged as error. The favorable tax situation resulted from realized losses in 1948 and loss carryovers which would have enabled General to take profits gained before the end of 1948 equal to the realized losses incurred in 1948 and the loss carryover expiring at the end of that year, to the extent of over $1,500,000, without paying a 25% capital gains tax or distributing the proceeds to its stockholders who would then be taxed on them.

The appraiser found that, at the time of merger and prior thereto, there was no actual market of General's common stock uninfluenced by the merger and, accordingly, excluded actual market value of the stock as a factor to enter into the final determination of value. This was not error, nor would it have been error had the appraiser constructed a hypothetical uninfluenced market value by discounting the net asset value of the common stock on the day of merger and given some effect to it in his final valuation. Had there been an actual market value uninfluenced by the merger in existence, it would have been error to disregard it, but the absence of such an element does not require the construction of a hypothetical market value to be given effect in the final determination of value.

A great deal of argument in this cause has turned around the phrase "net asset value" which is simply a mathematical figure representing the total value of the assets of General less the prior claims. The net asset value of the common stock of General could be determined as of any date by computing the total market value of the securities in the portfolio, adding to that sum the cash in the company's possession, deducting the total of the outstanding liabilities, debentures and preferred stock, and dividing the final result by the number of common shares outstanding.

However, since the value of dissenting stock is to be fixed on a going-concern basis, the taking of the net asset value as the appraisal value of the stock obviously is precluded by the rule. This is so because, primarily, net asset value is a theoretical liquidating value to which the share would be entitled upon the company going out of business. Its very nature indicates that it is not the value of stock in a going concern.

Furthermore, since we are called upon to fix the value of common stock in a closed-end investment company with leverage, an additional reason exists for the refusal to fix the value of that stock at its net asset value. This reason is that the common stockholder of a closed-end company can never withdraw his proportionate interest from the company as long as it is a going concern. He can obtain his full proportionate share of the company's assets, or the net asset value of his stock, only upon liquidation of the company. He cannot obtain the net asset value of his common stock by sale of the stock because of discount which is always applicable when the stock of the closed-end investment company is selling within the necessary price range, and which prevents the sale of the common stock except at a price less than the net asset value.

Since, therefore, net asset value is, in reality, a liquidating value, it cannot be made the sole criterion of the measure of the value of the dissenting stock. The appraiser, therefore, properly concluded that net asset value as of September 30, 1948 should not be taken as the basis for arriving at the appraisal value. He preferred, and we think correctly, to construct an asset value on the basis of month-end averages of the portfolio securities over a reasonable period of time. This method resulted in an asset figure of $5.15 per share of common stock of General. The appraiser also found that, during the period over which his average was taken, the stock market was normal. This finding is not attacked as error.

The fact that the stock market was normal during the period used for the establishment of the asset value of General's common stock bears directly on the application of the principle of leverage in this case. The element of leverage, it will be recalled, operates to increase the value of the common stock of a closed-end company as the stock market rises and, conversely, operates to decrease the value of the common stock of closed-end companies as the stock market sinks. The finding that the general level of the stock market is normal means that no adjustment in the value of the common stock was required because of the element of leverage. This is important because leverage, in the valuation of the common stock of closed-end companies, must be considered and given effect to if it is an operating element at the time value is to be determined. The market being normal, leverage was not operating. Therefore, the value of the common stock of General did not have to be debited or credited because of the principle of leverage.

To the per share asset value of $5.15 so determined, the appraiser added 29¢, the value of the favorable tax situation of General, to each share of its common stock. The result of $5.44 is called by the appraiser the 'fair asset value' of a share of the common stock of General. The appraiser then arrived at the true or intrinsic value of a common share of General by applying the discount to the fair asset value of $5.44, and arrived at a value of $4.08 per share for the common stock of General.

The Vice Chancellor adopted the findings of the appraiser in every particular, but disagreed with him as to the method of arriving at the value of the common share from those findings. He differed with the method of arriving at value used by the appraiser primarily because he was of the opinion that discount "has exclusive application to the question of but one element of value, namely, market value." With this as his premise, he reached the conclusion that the appraiser, in discounting the fair asset value of $5.44, had in fact constructed a market value of the common share, and had committed error when he gave 100% weight to that constructed market value.

The Vice Chancellor was of the opinion that net asset value unaltered by the discount factor must be considered as an independent element of value because it was a value based on mere possession, an important factor when capital appreciation is the principal attraction to the investor. He, accordingly, felt that constructed market value and net asset value should be fairly weighted in order to determine the value of the shares involved. Recognizing that the weighting of different elements of value necessarily is arbitrary, he gave a weight of 40% to net asset value and a weight of 60% to constructed market value, reaching the conclusion that the value of a common share of General was $4.62.

We do not agree with the Vice Chancellor in this respect for the reason that he has treated "fair asset value" as though it were the same as "net asset value." That they are not the same is apparent when it is considered that fair asset value was arrived at from averages in a normal stock market. Furthermore, the inclusion of the value of the favorable tax position of General necessarily means that "fair asset value" includes elements of value of the common share which could not possibly be included in "net asset value" which necessarily is determined from a mathematical computation of the market values of the portfolio securities.

The 29¢ item would have accrued to the benefit of the common stockholders of General only after General's management had taken advantage of its favorable tax situation. While the possibility existed, advantage had not been taken of it at the time of the merger. The 29¢, therefore, was an entirely hidden and prospective asset. Its inclusion in the fair asset value of the common share was to give effect to the prospect of future advances in the value of the common share, and was to include an element of value which, under no circumstances, could have been reflected in a net asset value, a value fixed by the market price of General's portfolio securities.

These circumstances make it clear to us that the appraiser's fair asset value includes several elements which, in turn, affect the true value of the common shares. It includes "net asset value" and, furthermore, it includes an element of value over and above net asset value which can only represent the investment possibility of the common stock which the Vice Chancellor refers to as an important element based "on mere possession." It is, therefore, obvious that discounting of the "fair asset value" of General's common stock will not, as the Vice Chancellor held, result in a constructed market value. A constructed market value results only from the discount of net asset value. This must be the fact since discount is fixed by experience in the market, and is nothing more than the average rate of difference between the actual market prices of General's common stock and the net asset value of that stock computed from the basic fact of the market prices of General's portfolio securities.

The dissenting stockholder is entitled to receive the intrinsic value of his share in a going concern. This can mean only that he is entitled to receive that sum which represents the amount he would have received as a stockholder in one way or another as long as the company continued in business. Since we are dealing with a regulated closed-end investment company with leverage from which the stockholder cannot withdraw his proportionate interest, and since dividends on the stock of such companies are of small importance, it follows that the only way in which a common stockholder of a going closed-end company with leverage can obtain the value of his stock is by the sale of it on the market. Furthermore, whenever he seeks to do so, he, by force of circumstances, must sell at a discount, whenever this is an operating element.

The conclusion is, therefore, inescapable that the full value of the corporate assets to the corporation is not the same as the value of those assets to the common stockholder because of the factor of discount. To fail to recognize this conclusion in the valuing of common stock of a regulated closed-end company with leverage is to fail to face the economic facts and to commit error. Discount is an element of value which must be given independent effect in the valuing of common stock of regulated closed-end investment companies with leverage, and is not confined solely to the construction of a hypothetical market value.

The ultimate value of General's common stock, therefore, is the percentage of the fair asset value which could reasonably be expected, at some time, to have been realized by the common stockholder. The most critical factor to be determined in the fixing of such value is the fair asset value, itself. If it is an amount which contains within it the proportionate interest the common stock has in the assets of the company, the possibility of capital appreciation inherent in the company and the effect of leverage, then fair asset value has been properly determined. Application of the independent element of discount to that amount will give the true or intrinsic value of the common stock of the regulated closed-end investment company with leverage under consideration. The important thing to bear in mind is that value of stock in a going concern is to be measured in terms of ability to realize that value through various media. In the case of General, the only way to realize the common stock value was by the sale of the stock.

We believe that the appraiser was correct in his method of determining value and in the result reached by him. The Vice Chancellor, in weighting as he did fair asset value instead of net asset value, has in effect overbalanced the weight to be given to the element of possible capital appreciation to the extent that he has committed error.

## QUESTIONS

1. What is a closed end investment fund? What is its unique feature?
2. What is intrinsic value? How is it determined under the Delaware appraisal statute?
3. How does the market discount seen in closed-end mutual funds treated for the purpose of calculating intrinsic value?
4. What methods of valuation did the court use to determine intrinsic value?

———————————

In the case below, the defendant unlawfully acquired warrants to purchase shares in the EMS Corp. as a part of a deceptive scheme to take over the company. A warrant is a company-issued right to purchase shares in the company. The right to purchase these warrants belonged to the plaintiffs. The court held that the remedy required a determination of the hypothetical price at which the plaintiffs could have purchased the warrants. In reading the case, follow the court's use of a comparative companies analysis.

### Agranoff v. Miller
791 A.2d 880 (Del. Ch. 2001)

STRINE, Vice Chancellor.

After examining the testimony of the parties' experts, I conclude that the fair market value of the BT Warrants as of the valuation date of October 1998 was $41.02.

The parties both utilized highly qualified experts in support of their positions regarding valuation. For his part, Miller proffered the testimony of Professor Donald J. Puglisi, the MBNA America Business Professor and Professor of Finance at the University of Delaware. The plaintiffs submitted the testimony of Morton Mark Lee, a recently retired partner of KMPG LLP and now a senior managing director at Sutter Securities, a professional with thirty years of experience in valuing businesses. Both experts provided the court with helpful testimony.

As a frame for valuing EMS however, Puglisi's analysis is the preferable one. The Puglisi analysis focused on three variations of the comparable companies method of valuation, involving multiples based on EMS's revenues (the "Revenues Analysis"), earnings before interest and taxes ("EBIT"), and earnings before interest, taxes, depreciation, and amortization ("EBITDA"). The Puglisi analysis was also very user-friendly, and enabled the reader to follow the steps he used in computing his comparable companies valuation. Puglisi's report also acknowledged that a discounted cash flow ("DCF") approach would have been viable, had reliable projections of EMS's performance for the relevant time period been available. But Puglisi considered the projections that EMS had to be wildly unreliable and overly optimistic. Thus, he believed that a reliable DCF valuation was not possible.

Lee used a wider variety of valuation methods. Although Lee also believed that EMS's projections were unreliable, he purported to base a DCF analysis on a substantial negative revision of those projections that he came up with after discussions with EMS managers after the valuation date. That is, Lee discussed the projections for the years following 1998 with managers who knew what the actual results of those later years were. Based on these conversations, Lee developed revised projections that he plugged into a DCF model.

I refuse to give any weight to this technique and therefore to Lee's DCF analysis. The possibility of hindsight bias and other cognitive distortions seems untenably high. Consider this analogy. Suppose there was an interview with Sir George Martin from 1962 in which he opined as to how many number one songs he thought would be released by his new protégés, the Beatles. Could one fast-forward to 1971, interview Martin, and revise Martin's earlier projection in some reliable way, recognizing that Martin would have known the correct answer as of that date? How could Martin provide information that would not be possibly influenced in some way by his knowledge of the actual success enjoyed by the Beatles and his recollection of his earlier projection? The parties have approached this valuation exercise with the mutual understanding that they could not consider the actual results for EMS past the valuation date of October 1998. Lee's DCF analysis seems like an unreliable way to have those actual results influence the court's valuation in an indirect manner that is not susceptible to fair evaluation. Nor have the plaintiffs provided finance literature supporting the acceptance of Lee's approach to projection modification. Likewise, I also give no weight to Lee's valuations that are based solely on equity, rather than entity, valuation techniques. These techniques do not consider the different capital structures of corporations.

Instead, I choose to focus on the three variations of the comparable companies method of valuation that both Puglisi and Lee agree are appropriate tools to value EMS: analyses based on multiples of Revenues, EBIT and EBITDA. The comparable companies method of valuation determines the equity value of the company by: (1) identifying comparable publicly traded companies; (2) deriving appropriate valuation multiples from the comparable companies; (3) adjusting those multiples to account for the differences from the company being valued and the comparables; and (4) applying those multiples to the revenues, earnings, or other values for the company being valued. Comparable companies analyses are frequently calculated on a debt free basis, to derive the fair market value of the company's market value of invested capital ("MVIC"). The company's equity value is derived by subtracting the company's interest bearing debt from the company's MVIC.

[The court noted various objections and problems with the experts' analysis and methods.]

With these objections out of the way, the court can display its valuation of EMS—putting aside for a moment the question of whether a premium should be added because the BT Warrants constituted a substantial block of EMS voting power and whether a marketability discount should be subtracted because EMS shares were not traded on public markets. In coming to this intermediate step, I use Puglisi's approach of giving equal weight to the Revenues, EBIT, and EBITDA approaches and adopt his EBIT and EBITDA multiples. This analysis yields a value of $41.02 for the Warrants Shares, computed as follows:

[Note: EMS was a holding company for 62% of the stock of an operating company called Express Messenger Systems, Inc. ("Express"). EMS's value constituted 62% of Express. Thus, Express is the real subject of the valuation.]

| | With Selected Revenue Multiple | With Selected EBITDA Multiple | With Selected EBIT Multiple | Average of Three Approaches |
|---|---|---|---|---|
| Express Revenues, EBITDA, EBIT (thousands) | $50,313 | $1,520 | $960 | N/A |
| EV/Multipliers | 0.28 | 5.97 | 9.70 | N/A |
| Express Enterprise Value (thousands) | $14,088 | $9,074 | $9,312 | $10,825 |
| Less Express Net Debt (thousands) | $1,951 | $1,951 | $1,951 | $1,951 |
| Plus Value of Express NOL Carryfoward[5] (thousands) | $1,938 | $1,938 | $1,938 | $1,938 |
| Value of Common Stock of Express (thousands) | $14,075 | $9,061 | $9,299 | $10,812 |
| EMS Ownership of Express | [62%] | [62%] | [62%] | [62%] |
| Value of EMS Common Stock (thousands) | $8,727 | $5,618 | $5,765 | $6,703 |
| Number of Shares of EMS Common Stock | 163,403 | 163,403 | 163,403 | 163,403 |
| Value per Share of EMS Common Stock | $53.40 | $34.38 | $35.28 | $41.02 |

## QUESTIONS

1. The court states: "Comparable companies analyses are frequently calculated on a debt free basis, to derive the fair market value of the company's market value of invested capital ("MVIC"). The company's equity value is derived by subtracting the company's interest bearing debt from the company's MVIC." What does this mean? How does one derive equity value if enterprise value is the market value of all securities?
2. Why did the court reject a DCF analysis in this case?

---

The case below is another on the valuation of dissenting shares, and in particular the application of the DCF valuation. The litigation has a long, convoluted history. The opinion, one of several in this litigation, is itself very long and complicated. Excerpted below is only a small portion of the full opinion. The DCF valuations of two competing experts were very complicated. The Delaware court expertly analyzed the valuation models. Investment bankers, financial analysts, and economists are not the only people who are fluent in the concept of valuations. Lawyers working in corporate transactions must understand at least the basic concepts. In reading the case, pay particular attention to the details of a DCF analysis and then think about the specific reasons why the expert opinions diverged.

---

5. NOL carryfoward is net operating loss that may be carried forward as a tax deduction against future earnings. It is a tax benefit, and thus has value.

***Author's Summary of Facts***: MacAndrews & Forbes Group completed a leverage buyout of Technicolor Inc., a film processing company. Cinerama Inc. owned 4.4 percent of the common stock, and it dissented from the merger and sought an appraisal. The valuation centered on a battle of the experts. Each expert employed a DCF analysis of Technicolor, but significant methodological and input differences yielded radically different estimates of value. The plaintiff's expert, John Torkelsen, opined that the statutory fair value of Technicolor was $62.75. The defendant's expert, Professor Alfred Rappaport, opined that the statutory fair value of Technicolor was $13.14. As the court noted, "The dynamics of litigation no doubt contribute to this distressingly wide difference." The wide range of valuation well illustrates the point that valuation is part science and a large part art. Much opinion and judgment go into a valuation, which means that reasonable minds may differ quite a bit. The opinion below resolves this battle of the experts.

## *Cede & Co. v. Technicolor, Inc.*
### 1990 WL 161084 (Del. Ch. 1990)

ALLEN, Chancellor.

For the reasons set forth below I conclude, attempting to consider all pertinent factors as of the date of the merger, exclusive of elements of value arising from the expectation or accomplishment of the merger, and acting within the confines of the record created by the parties at trial, that the fair value of a share of Technicolor stock for purposes of appraisal was $21.60.

In this case the expert opinions on value cover an astonishing range. Two experts looking at the same historic data and each employing a discounted cash flow valuation technique arrive at best estimates as different as $13.14 per share and $62.75 per share.[15]

In many situations, the discounted cash flow technique is in theory the single best technique to estimate the value of an economic asset. The DCF model entails three basic components: an estimation of net cash flows that the firm will generate and when, over some period; a terminal or residual value equal to the future value, as of the end of the projection period, of the firm's cash flows beyond the projection period; and finally a cost of capital with which to discount to a present value both the projected net cash flows and the estimated terminal or residual value.

While the basic three-part structure of any two DCF models of the same firm, as of the same date, will be the same, it is probably the case (and is certainly true here) that the details of the analysis may be quite different. That is, not only will assumptions about the future differ, but different methods may be used within the model to generate inputs. This fact has a significant consequence for the way in which this matter is adjudicated. Sub-part of the DCF models used here are not interchangeable. With certain exceptions, each expert's model is a complex, interwoven whole, no part of which can be removed from that model and substituted into the alternative model.

---

15. A significant part of this difference is accounted for by the differing discount rates used in the DCF models. If one substitutes the higher discount rate used by respondent's principal expert for the lower rate used by petitioner's expert and makes no other adjustment to either DCF model the difference reduces from $49.61 a share to $20.86.

An appraisal action is a judicial, not an inquisitorial, proceeding. The statutory command to determine fair value is a command to do so in a judicial proceeding. [T]he court must decide which of the two principal experts has the greater claim overall to have correctly estimated the intrinsic value of Technicolor stock at the time of the merger. Having decided that question, it will be open to me to critically review the details of that expert's opinion in order to determine if the record will permit, and judicial judgment require, modification of any inputs in that model. What the record will not permit is either a completely independent judicially created DCF model[17] or a pastiche composed of bits of one model and pieces of the other.

The estimation of the fair value as of January 24, 1983, of Technicolor of Professor Rappaport is, in my considered opinion, a more reasonable estimation of statutory fair value than is the alternative valuation of petitioner's expert.

The following statement of the reasoning leading to this conclusion is in three principle parts reflecting the tripartite structure of the DCF model used by each witness. [Part 1] The first part treats the generation of net cash flows for the forecast period for the various Technicolor businesses and a particular legal question relating to cash flow projection upon which the parties divide. [Part 2] The second aspect of the DCF model [is] the terminal or residual value of the company at the conclusion of the forecast period. It is in connection with that aspect of the model that the methodological differences between the DCF methodology of Mr. Rappaport and that of Mr. Torkelsen will be treated. [Part 3] Finally, the selection of an appropriate cost of capital/discount rate will be discussed.

[Part 1]

A. Projection of Net Cash Flows by Line of Business

[The court meticulously analyzes various lines of Technicolor's businesses, which are valued separately, including the core business of film processing. Below is the discussion on the valuation of another business segment: One Hour Photo, a chain of stores that would provide consumers rapid "one hour" photo printing services. This was a new business for Technicolor, and the experts disagreed on its value. The court observed: "Technicolor's plan for One Hour Photo was an ambitious one. It was risky, not only because of the large capital investment it required, but also because of the nature of the One Hour Photo business."]

[A predicate legal question is whether in valuing Technicolor the court should assume the business plan for Technicolor that MacAndrews & Forbes (the acquirer)

---

17. For good reasons aside from technical competence, one might be disinclined to do so. Simply to accept one experts' view or the other would have a significant institutional or precedential advantage. The DCF model typically can generate a wide range of estimates. In the world of real transactions (capital budgeting decisions for example) the hypothetical, future-oriented, nature of the model is not thought fatal to the DCF technique because those employing it typically have an intense personal interest in having the best estimates and assumptions used as inputs. In the litigation context use of the model does not have that built-in protection. On the contrary, particularly if the court will ultimately reject both parties DCF analysis and do its own, the incentive of the contending parties is to arrive at estimates of value that are at the outer margins of plausibility-that essentially define a bargaining range. If it is understood that the court will or is likely to accept the whole of one witnesses testimony or the other, incentives will be modified. While the incentives of the real world applications of the DCF model will not be replicated, at least the parties will have incentives to make their estimate of value appear most reasonable. This would tend to narrow the range of estimates, which would unquestionably be a benefit to the process.

had for Technicolor (called the "Perelman plan"), or whether valuation should be premised upon the company as a going concern under current management (called the "Kamerman plan"), i.e., as if the company was never acquired by MacAndrews & Forbes). The plaintiff's expert, Mr. Torkelsen, valued the business based on the Perelman plan. Professor Rappaport valued it based on the Kamerman plan. The difference in assumptions led to these differences in valuation.]

| | Torkelsen's Assumed Sale Value | Rappaport's Assumed Going Concern Value | Difference |
|---|---|---|---|
| One Hour Photo | $8mm | −$7.7mm | $15.8mm |

Thus, very roughly estimated, the question of which assumption is legally appropriate with respect to sales of assets accounts for about $4.50 per share of the difference between Rappaport's $13.14 valuation and Torkelsen's $62.75 valuation.

For the following reasons I conclude, in these circumstances, that value added to the corporation by the implementation or the expectation of the implementation of Mr. Perelman's new business plan for the company is not value to which, in an appraisal action, petitioner is entitled to a pro rata share, but is value that is excluded from consideration by the statutory exclusion for value arising from the merger or its expectation.

Our statute and a long line of cases that focus our inquiry on "going concern" value recognize that the value that is relevant in an appraisal is the value of the assets in the way they are deployed in the corporation from which the shareholder will exit.

When value is created by substituting new management or by redeploying assets "in connection with the accomplishment or expectation" of a merger, that value is not, in my opinion, a part of the "going concern" in which a dissenting shareholder has a legal (or equitable) right to participate.

Thus, in my view, petitioner's entitlement in this action to fair value, exclusive of value created by or in anticipation of the merger, means he is entitled to a pro rata share of the going concern value of the enterprise and that the going concern here was the business, as of the merger date, subject to the business plan of the Kamerman management. That view is inconsistent with adoption of Mr. Torkelsen's valuation of One Hour Photo and consistent with acceptance of Professor Rappaport's valuation method and opinion. Mr. Torkelsen did not value One Hour Photo as a going concern. Rather, on the assumption that as of January 24, 1983, the controlling shareholder (MAF) intended to sell that business, he valued One Hour Photo as an $8 million ($1.75 per share) asset to be liquidated by July 1983.

Professor Rappaport valued One Hour Photo as a going concern. He concluded that it would continue to be a persistent money loser and that it was likely that the company would ultimately be forced to sell it by the end of 1984. He opined that One Hour Photo had a negative $7.7 million value (-$1.69 per share).

Professor Rappaport generated two projections of net cash flows for One Hour Photo. The first was based upon optimistic management long-term plans. These plans appear to be the only long-term plans the company generated; they are, in several respects, unlike the year-to-year plans that were used by Professor Rappaport in connection with valuing film processing. Most importantly, those planners had a record of creating good year-to-year forecasts. In addition they were only year-to-year plans and thus would be inherently more reliable.

The management plan for One Hour Photo was prepared in February 1982. It predicated a rapid annual growth rate for photofinishing (10.3%) and an emerging large share of that business (25%) going to the new on-site development processors (minilabs). Management assumed it could capture 15% to 25% of this market and generate between $882 million and $1.47 billion in revenue by 1989. This vision called for 960 Technicolor stores in place by 1986. Professor Rappaport estimated the net present value of Technicolor One Hour Photo under the management plan to be $75.1 million.

In his second, "base case" forecast, Professor Rappaport accepted management's February 1982 projections of fixed and variable cost structures, depreciation, administration, and start-up expenses. Instead, of management's revenue forecast, however, he estimated Technicolor's One Hour Photo revenue to equal the average revenue per minilab (i.e., photofinishing store) in 1982 multiplied by the number of Technicolor minilabs in operation during each year of the forecast period. Professor Rappaport assumed annual growth in revenues equal to the rate of inflation (5%). The base scenario predicted heavy operating losses for each year of the seven-year forecast period. Professor Rappaport, however, assumed that the substantial losses in the first two forecast years would convince management to cut their losses and exit the One Hour Photo business.

Professor Rappaport assumed that at the end of 1984, Technicolor would sell each minilab for $125,000. The net present value of One Hour Photo under the base forecast was negative 16.9 million.

To estimate the value of One Hour Photo at the time of the merger, Professor Rappaport used a weighted average of the two scenarios. Professor Rappaport concluded that the base forecast more reasonably estimated the value of One Hour Photo in January 1983 than did the management plan. Accordingly, he assigned only a 10% weight to the management scenario and a 90% weight to the base scenario. The result was an estimated negative 7.7 million value to One Hour Photo at the time of the merger.

Estimating the value of One Hour Photo in 1983 is a difficult task. At that time, Technicolor was a newcomer to the industry which was itself in its infancy. In comparing the competing models in their treatment of the business, two factors seemed critical. First, Mr. Torkelsen's assumption that Technicolor would sell the One Hour Photo division in 1983 is contrary to the record testimony concerning Mr. Kamerman's plan for the business. It is the value of Technicolor under that plan that is at issue in this case. Second, Professor Rappaport's weighted valuation of the business seems reasonable. For the reasons discussed below, I am convinced that management's forecast was overly optimistic and that Professor Rappaport's base scenario is the most reliable valuation of the business and therefore deserves greater weight than the management forecast.

I do not lightly criticize management's One Hour Photo forecast. As a general rule, I am of the view that management projections done for real-world purposes are deserving of substantial weight. The following reasons, however, lead me to conclude that Professor Rappaport was reasonable in heavily discounting the management plan.

1. Management had no experience in the One Hour Photo business and no track record of forecasting the businesses prospects.

2. The industry itself was in its infancy and faced uncertainty and risk.

3. Management's plan for store openings in 1982 was far off the mark. The plan, prepared in February 1982 was thus unable to include consideration of the problems

the company would face as a result of its failure to establish the strong foothold in the industry that had been anticipated. That strong, rapid accumulation of locations was viewed by Mr. Kamerman and the market as critical to success in the business. Had management prepared its report in January 1983, an entirely different estimate may have resulted.

4. Management's poor forecast of store openings in 1982 suggests that the management scenario was not accurate.

5. The stock market reaction to the announcement of Technicolor's One Hour Photo venture was strongly negative.

6. The management scenario implies a value of One Hour Photo approximately $75 million (or $16 per share). A reasonable person in 1983 would not have valued this struggling start-up business at that price.

[Part 2]

B. Methodology and Residual Values

The most basic conceptual difference in the two DCF models used is this: Professor Rappaport assumes (and Mr. Torkelsen does not) that for every company its particular set of comparative advantages establish, as of any moment, a future period of same greater or lesser length during which it will be able to earn rates of return that exceed its cost of capital. Beyond that point, the company (as of the present moment of valuation) can expect to earn no returns in excess of its cost of capital and therefore, beyond that point, no additional shareholder value will be created. Professor Rappaport calls this period during which a company's net returns can be predicted to exceed its costs of capital, the company's "value growth duration," which is a coined term. While Professor Rappaport has copyrighted some software that employs this concept, the basic idea is not unique to him. It is an application of elementary notions of neo-classical economics: profits above the cost of capital in an industry will attract competitors, who will over some time period drive returns down to the point at which returns equal the cost of capital. At that equilibrium point no new competition will be attracted into the field. The leading finance text includes a reference to this concept of a future period beyond which there is no further value created. The existence of such a point in time does not mean that there is no value attributed to the period beyond that point, but rather that there is no further value growth.

I accept as sound the methodology of Professor Rappaport. Mr. Rappaport's method is in most respects conceptually similar to that employed by Mr. Torkelsen.

In the final analysis, however, Professor Rappaport used a period to project Technicolor's most important net cash flows similar to that employed by Mr. Torkelsen (5 years). Therefore, the practical significance of this conceptual difference between the DCF model used by Rappaport and that used by Torkelsen is in connection with what each does with cash flows at the end of the projection period, that is how each creates the terminal or residual value component of his DCF analysis. To estimate residual value Rappaport capitalizes a constant (last forecasted year) cash flow; he assumes no new value creation beyond the forecast period (but nevertheless much of his total value is attributed to the residual value). In creating his estimation of residual value Torkelsen, on the other hand, increases the last forecasted year's net cash flows by 5% each year (for inflation) into infinity, before capitalizing those flows. The result—and this is the practical gist of this theoretical difference between the experts—is that Mr. Torkelsen assumes that Technicolor net profits (along with all other aspects of its cash flow) and its value will increase every year in perpetuity, while Professor Rappaport assumes there will come a time when, while it may make profits, Technicolor will not be increasing in value.

The absolute difference in the residual value of each model is large. That difference is attributable not simply to methodology but to three differences in the assumptions of the models: differing discount rates, the differing estimates of cash flows in the last year projected and the assumption by PVR of a net cash flow that is perpetually increasing at 5%, a stipulated rate of inflation. It is this last assumption that most pointedly relates to the differing DCF methodology of the witnesses. PVR's assumption of a 5% growth rate in cash flows after the projection period is striking when one recalls that PVR projects growth during the 5 year explicit forecast period in the critical film processing business at 2.3%. This 5% growth assumption adds very substantial additional value to the discounted present value of a share of Technicolor stock. That assumption alone contributes $16.56 in per share value (making all other assumptions PVR makes).

In estimating residual value, Professor Rappaport, capitalizes a constant (the last forecast year) cash flow, not a perpetually growing one. He asserts that this is consistent with an inflating (or deflating) future world because he posits that whatever the value of money and indeed whatever the size of the company's cash flows, the most reasonable assumption about the future is that there will be a future time at which the firm will not earn returns in excess of its cost of capital. That is if, after that point, one posits increases cash flows, due to inflation (or decreases due to deflation) his model stipulates off-setting increases (or decreases) in the firms overall cost of capital.

[Part 3]

## C. Discounting with the Cost of Capital

The cost of capital supplies the discount rate to reduce projected future cash flows to present value. The cost of capital is a free-standing, interchangeable component of a DCF model. It also allows room for judicial judgment to a greater extent than the record in this case permits in other areas of the DCF models.

Professor Rappaport used two cost of capital rates. For most of the cash flows (notably film processing and videocassette) he used a weighted cost of capital of 20.4%; for One Hour Photo and two small related businesses he used 17.3%.

Professor Rappaport used the Capital Asset Pricing Model (CAPM) to estimate Technicolor's costs of capital as of January 24, 1983. That model estimates the cost of company debt (on an after tax basis for a company expected to be able to utilize the tax deductibility of interest payments) by estimating the expected future cost of borrowing; it estimates the future cost of equity through a multi-factor equation and then proportionately weighs and combines the cost of equity and the cost of debt to determine a cost of capital.

The CAPM is used widely (and by all experts in this case) to estimate a firm's cost of equity capital. It does this by attempting to identify a risk-free rate for money and to identify a risk premium that would be demanded for investment in the particular enterprise in issue. In the CAPM model the riskless rate is typically derived from government treasury obligations. For a traded security the market risk premium is derived in two steps. First a market risk premium is calculated. It is the excess of the expected rate of return for a representative stock index (such as the Standard & Poor 500 or all NYSE companies) over the riskless rate. Next the individual company's "systematic risk"—that is the nondiversified risk associated with the economy as a whole as it affects this firm—is estimated. This second element of the risk premium is, in the CAPM, represented by a coefficient (beta) that measures the relative volatility of the subject firm's stock price relative to the movement of the market generally. The higher that coefficient (i.e., the higher the beta) the more volatile or risky the stock of the subject company is said to be. Of course, the riskier the investment the higher its costs of capital will be.

The CAPM is widely used in the field of financial analysis as an acceptable technique for estimating the implicit cost of capital of a firm whose securities are regularly traded. It is used in portfolio theory and in capital asset budgeting decisions. It cannot, of course, determine a uniquely correct cost of equity. Many judgments go into it. The beta coefficient can be measured in a variety of ways; the index rate of return can be determined pursuant to differing definitions, and adjustments can be made, such as the small capitalization premium, discussed below. But the CAPM methodology is certainly one of the principle "techniques or methods . . . generally considered acceptable [for estimating the cost of equity capital component of a discounted cash flow modeling] in the financial community . . .".

In accepting Professor Rappaport's method for estimating Technicolor's costs of capital, I do so mindful of the extent to which it reflects judgments. That the results of the CAPM are in all instances contestable does not mean that as a technique for estimation it is unreliable. It simply means that it may not fairly be regarded as having claims to validity independent of the judgments made in applying it.

With respect to the cost of capital aspect of the discounted cash flow methodology (in distinction to the projection of net cash flows and, in most respects, the terminal value) the record does permit the court to evaluate some of the variables, used in that model chosen as the most reasonable of the two (i.e., Professor Rappaport's) and to adjust the cost of capital accordingly. I do so with respect to two elements of Professor Rappaport's determination of costs of equity for the various Technicolor divisions. These businesses were all (excepting One Hour Photo, Consumer Photo Processing and Standard Manufacturing) assigned a cost of equity of 22.7% and a weighted average cost of capital of 20.4%. The remaining businesses were assigned a cost of equity of 20.4% and a weighted average cost of capital of 17.3%.

In fixing the 22.7% cost of equity for film processing and other businesses Professor Rappaport employed a 1.7 beta which was an estimate published by Merrill Lynch, a reputable source for December 1982. That figure seems intuitively high for a company with relatively stable cash flows. Intuition aside, however, it plainly was affected to some extent by the striking volatility in Technicolor's stock during the period surrounding the announcement of MAF proposal to acquire Technicolor for $23 per share. Technicolor stock rapidly shot up to the $23 level from a range of $9 to $12 in which it traded for all of September and the first week of October. Technicolor stock was thus a great deal more volatile than the market during this period. Applying the same measure of risk-the Merrill Lynch published beta-for September yields a significantly different beta measurement: 1.27. Looking at other evidence with respect to Technicolor betas I conclude that 1.27 is a more reasonable estimate of

Technicolor's stock beta for purposes of calculating its cost of capital on January 24, 1983, than 1.7, even though that latter figure represents a December 1982 estimation.

The second particular in which the record permits and my judgment with respect to weight of evidence requires a modification of Mr. Rappaport's cost of capital calculation relates to the so-called small capitalization effect or premium. This refers to an unexplained inability of the capital asset pricing model to replicate with complete accuracy the historic returns of stocks with the same historic betas. The empirical data show that there is a recurring premium paid by small capitalization companies. This phenomena was first noted in 1981 and has been confirmed. The greatest part of the additional return for small cap companies appears to occur in January stock prices. No theory satisfactorily explaining the phenomena has been generally accepted.

Thus, in summary, I find Professor Rappaport's calculation of a cost of capital follows an accepted technique for evaluating the cost of capital; it employs that technique in a reasonable way and, except for the two particulars noted above, in a way that is deserving of adoption by the court. Applying these adjustments they lead to a cost capital of 15.28% for the main part of Technicolor's cash flow and 14.13% for the One Hour Photo related cash flows.

## QUESTIONS

1. In this litigation, the two experts, Rappaport and Torkelsen, differed substantially on their opinions, and the court attributed this difference to the dynamics of litigation. What general lesson can you derive regarding valuation studies in both the litigation and transactional contexts?
2. What were the reasons the court found the Rappaport valuation more credible than the Torkelsen valuation?
3. Why were the residual values in the Rappaport and Torkelsen valuations so far apart?
4. There were two conceptions of value: (1) the company as a going concern, (2) the company under the Perelman plan. What are the differences? What are dissenting shareholders entitled to? Why?

## ESSENTIAL TERMS

Beta
Comparable companies
Capital Asset Pricing Model (CAPM)
Cost of capital
Cost of debt
Cost of equity
Discounted cash flow (DCF) method
EBIT and EBITDA ratios
Firm (enterprise) value
Free cash flow
Going concern
Intrinsic (theoretical) value

Liquidation value
Market risk (systematic risk)
Market multiples
Market value
P/B ratio
P/E ratio
Terminal (continuing) value
Treasury securities (Treasuries)
Unique (firm specific) risk
Weighted average cost of capital
(WAAC)

## KEY CONCEPTS

1. The concept of value can take on different meanings.
2. There are different ways of measuring market value.
3. Market value and theoretical value can and do diverge.
4. Theoretical value is calculated under the DCF methods.
5. Cost of capital is the expected return on capital provided by investors, and it is the discount rate used to discount the firm's expected return.

## REVIEW QUESTIONS

1. The theoretical value of a firm is its free cash flow discounted by the cost of capital. Why?
2. Explain in simple terms the concept of the cost of equity.
3. Why can't an investor diversify away market risk?
4. Why is the multiple of EBIT or EBITDA based on firm value and not on market cap?

# ECONOMICS OF THE FIRM

## A. EFFICIENCY

### 1. EFFICIENCY DEFINED

A course in Business Associations will most likely be the first instance that students learn the laws governing economic organizations. In laws concerning natural persons, a large segment of the first year curriculum, there may be a number of competing normative foundations: e.g., justice, fairness, and efficiency, just to name a few. In laws governing business enterprise, the primary objective is efficiency.

What is efficiency? The short, serviceable answer is that efficiency is achieved when a rule or change in state creates more benefits such that "the winners" can hypothetically compensate "the losers" and still achieve a surplus. It is a cost-benefit criterion. In first-year Torts, most students were introduced to this concept when reading *United States v. Carroll Towing Co.* and the Hand Formula found therein: Is the burden of precaution greater than the expected cost of accident? The objective of economic entities is to maximize social wealth by increasing firm value, at least in circumstances where the firm's actions do not pose significant ethical considerations (as expected, there are competing tensions between ethical actions and profit maximization).

Rules of law pertaining to economic entities can affect efficiency by allocating risk, cost, and returns among various constituencies. The next several sections discuss two prominent rules where this idea is central. These examples focus on the corporate enterprise, but they are relevant to other business entities as well.

### 2. LIMITED LIABILITY OF SHAREHOLDERS

Corporate law is founded on two important rules of limited liability. First is the rule of limited liability of shareholders. Shareholders cannot be held liable for liabilities in excess of their original investment. For example, you invest $1,000 in Enron; the company collapses; creditors of Enron cannot come to you and seek money for the company's outstanding debts.

Other economic entities provide limited liability protection for their investors. They include categories of entities that the author calls hybrid limited liability entities, "LLE" for short, including limited liability companies (LLC), limited liability partnerships (LLP), and limited partnerships (LP). These LLEs tend to be smaller, private firms.

Under the rule, a creditor's interest is only protected insofar as the firm's assets can satisfy its claim, and shareholders are protected against creditors' claims. It seems that creditors lose and shareholders win. If the rule simply facilitates a wealth transfer from creditors to shareholders as a zero sum proposition, it would be economically and morally suspect. While arguments can be made that contract creditors can bargain ex ante to protect their rights, involuntary tort creditors cannot bargain ex ante with their future tortfeasors to protect against the potential default on their claim (i.e., the problem of the judgment-proof or bankrupt defendant). Thus, if the rule of limited liability transferred wealth of $x$ from creditors to shareholders and nothing more, it would be illegitimate—why should shareholders be made wealthy at the cost of others' lives, limbs and livelihoods?

However, the rule of limited liability does more than just transfer wealth. It creates wealth such that the problem of the uncollectible credit claim is tolerated as perhaps a necessary bad outcome. First, the rule incentivizes risk-averse investors to invest in profitable but risky business endeavors. Second, it reduces a firm's cost of equity by setting a floor on an investor's potential losses. Third, it promotes diversification of investments whereas without the rule an investor would be reluctant to diversify because any one investment that blows up can wipe out the investor. Fourth, it reduces the need to monitor the business and affairs of corporations (while some monitoring is good, enhanced monitoring by all shareholders across the entire financial market would be extremely costly and thus inefficient). These combined effects tend to increase investment in economically productive enterprises and reduce the cost of diversification, monitoring, and equity. Thus, the rule of limited liability tends to create greater wealth.

## 3. BUSINESS JUDGMENT RULE

The second rule of limited liability is limited liability of officers and directors. Corporate managers are protected by the business judgment rule. This rule provides that in exercising business judgment through a business decision, a manager is presumed to have made a good faith, informed decision. Accordingly, the manager is shielded from honest mistakes, however negligent or stupid the decision may have been after the fact. Doctors are held accountable through a substantive review of their actions, but directors are protected against such review.

This strange rule of corporate law is explained by efficiency considerations. First, managers are people, and people are risk averse. We saw that risk aversion can reduce wealth enhancing incentives. Given a choice of $1,000 sum certain or a 50/50 chance at $2,200 with an expected value of $1,100, most people would choose the first option even though ex ante the second option would create more value on an expected value basis. The business judgment rule allows risk-averse managers to take more risk by freeing them of liability for bad outcomes if they are essentially acting in good faith.

Second, the business and affairs of the corporation are managed by the board of directors. Corporations need directors to serve on boards. These positions pay well for a part-time job (most directors have full-time jobs not related to the corporation), and are prestigious. However, the incentives of pay and prestige have their limits. Suppose a board seat pays $200,000 per year along with bragging rights at the local country club. After a lifetime's career, the board member also has a net worth of $5 million in the value of her home, retirement and kid's college fund, and other investments. The corporation has a market cap of $500 million, and it has liabilities on its books of $750 million. If the rule of law provided that the director would be liable for negligent actions that reduced the value of the corporation, would she worry about serving on the board? Would the corporation be able to find sufficient numbers of competent people?

Third, much of the short-term and medium-term gyrations of the economy, the stock market, and the company's share price are beyond the control of managers. For example, the financial crisis of 2008-2009 was brought about by lost confidence in financial institutions, but the stock price of Pfizer, a pharmaceutical company, suffered substantially. Can we fault Pfizer's management? In light of this reality, would we want a costly legal system to be continuously examining the propriety of corporation decisions?

---

**F.Y.I.** Regarding stupid business decisions, consider the following quote from *In re Caremark Intern. Inc. Derivative Litigation*, 698 A.2d 959, 967 (Del. Ch. 1996) (Allen, Ch.) (emphasis in original):

"What should be understood, but may not widely be understood by courts or commentators who are not often required to face such questions, is that compliance with a director's duty of care can never appropriately be judicially determined by reference to *the content of the board decision* that leads to a corporate loss, apart from consideration of the good faith *or* rationality of the process employed. That is, whether a judge or jury considering the matter after the fact, believes a decision substantively wrong, or degrees of wrong extending through 'stupid' to 'egregious' or 'irrational,' provides no ground for director liability, so long as the court determines that the process employed was either rational or employed in *a good faith* effort to advance corporate interests. To employ a different rule-one that permitted an 'objective' evaluation of the decision-would expose directors to substantive second guessing by ill-equipped judges or juries, which would, in the long-run, be injurious to investor interests."

---

## B. EFFICIENCY OF FIRM STRUCTURE

### 1. REASON WHY FIRMS EXIST

An economic enterprise can be undertaken in a number of different organizational forms. Consider the endeavor to write software. A single person can write it. But suppose she lacks the know-how to write the entire program. Independent software writers can collaborate in an "open source" environment to make software. Obviously, software can be created in a firm environment, such as Microsoft. The study of business is the study of organizations and the problems posed by them. Before undertaking a study of business organizations, one must first understand the nature of the firm.

Why do firms exist? Why do we have corporations like McDonald's or ExxonMobil or Walt Disney? Most of us will answer something like this: "They are big and the activities they engage in require a certain degree of scale that an individual proprietor or entrepreneur cannot achieve." This answer has an intuitive appeal, but it does not really answer the question. It basically says that individual persons cannot accomplish what large, complex firms can. But why not?

The lack of size is not a good answer. An entrepreneur wishing to engage in competition with McDonald's can contract for the various factors of production required to make tasty hamburgers across the United States and the world. She can lease the buildings and equipment, contract with various people for labor, obtain foods from suppliers, etc. Why engage in this activity through a firm structure? The economist Ronald Coase, famous for the Coase Theorem, provided an insight into the question.

Coase argued that firms reduce the cost of organizing and price discovery by having a set of standardized contract terms among factors of production. Rather than making a series of contracts to accomplish a complex task, an entrepreneur can enter into one contract wherein factors of productions agree "to obey the directions of an entrepreneur within certain limits." The cost of price discovery, negotiation and marketing are saved, which enhances the value of the enterprise. Thus, the firm structure, such as corporations, is efficient. Below is an excerpt from his article explaining why firms exist.

### R.H. Coase, *The Nature of the Firm*
4 Economica 386 (1937)

The main reason why it is profitable to establish a firm would seem to be that there is a cost of using the price mechanism. The most obvious cost of "organizing" production through the price mechanism is that of discovering what the relevant prices are. This cost may be reduced but it will not be eliminated by the emergence of specialists who will sell this information. The costs of negotiating and which takes place on a market must also be taken into account. Again, in certain markets, e.g., produce exchanges, a technique is devised for minimising these contract costs; but they are not eliminated. It is true that contracts are not eliminated when there is a firm but they are greatly reduced. A factor of production (or the owner thereof) does not have to make a series of contracts with the factors with whom he is co-operating within the firm, as would be necessary, of course, if this co-operation were as a direct result of the working of the price mechanism. For this series of contracts is substituted one. At this stage, it is important to note the character of the contract into which a factor enters that is employed within a firm. The contract is one whereby the factor, for a certain remuneration (which may be fixed or fluctuating), agrees to obey the directions of an entrepreneur within certain limits. The essence of the contract is that it should only state the limits to the powers of the entrepreneur. Within these limits, he can therefore direct the other factors of production.

There are, however, other disadvantages—or costs of using the price mechanism. It may be desired to make a long-term contract for the supply of some article or service. This may be due to the fact that if one contract is made for a longer period, instead of several shorter ones, then certain costs of making each contract will be avoided. Or, owing to the risk attitude of the people concerned, they may prefer to make a long rather than a short-term contract. Now, owing to the difficulty of forecasting, the longer the period of the contract is for the supply of the commodity or service, the less possible, and indeed, the less desirable it is for the person purchasing to specify what the other contracting party is expected to do. It may well be a matter of indifference to the person supplying the service or commodity which of several courses of action is taken, but not to the purchaser of that service or commodity. But the purchaser will not know which of these several courses he will want the supplier to take. Therefore, the service which is being provided is expressed in general terms, the exact details being left until a later date. All that is stated in the contract is the limits to what the persons supplying the commodity or service is expected to do. The details of what the supplier is expected to do is not stated in the contract but is decided later by the purchaser. When the direction of resources (within the limits of the contract) becomes dependent on the buyer in this way, that relationship which I term a "firm" may be obtained. A firm is likely therefore to emerge in those cases where a very short term contract would be unsatisfactory. It is obviously of more importance in the case of services labour—than it is in the case of the buying of commodities. In the case of commodities, the main items can be stated in advance and the details which will be decided later will be of minor significance.

We may sum up this section of the argument by saying that the operation of a market costs something and by forming an organisation and allowing some authority (an "entrepreneur") to direct the resources, certain marketing costs are saved. The entrepreneur has to carry out his function at less cost, taking into account the fact that he may get factors of production at a lower price than the market transactions which he supersedes, because it is always possible to revert to the open market if he fails to do this.

These, then, are the reasons why organisations such as firms exist in a specialised exchange economy in which it is generally assumed that the distribution of resources is "organised" by the price mechanism. A firm, therefore, consists of the system of relationships which comes into existence when the direction of resources is dependent on an entrepreneur.

## 2. SEPARATION OF OWNERSHIP AND CONTROL

The modern public corporation is characterized by a separation of ownership and control. The public corporation, particularly in the United States, is characterized by a diffuse shareholder base, including institutional shareholders like mutual funds, insurance companies, and pension funds, and "retail investors" who are the proverbial moms and pops. Managers have significant control of the public corporation. In this system, shareholders have limited control rights unless voting power can be aggregated into a significant voting block. They cannot force the sale of corporate assets for the purpose of distribution of monies to them; they cannot demand the payment of dividends; they cannot manage the corporation's affairs. Thus, managers, who typically have only small ownership stakes in the corporation, have significant control rights while most shareholders have little day-to-day control of the company's operations. This observation of the separation of ownership and control was noted by Adolf Berle and Gardiner Means.

In their 1932 book, they foreshadowed many of the issues that would later present themselves as the modern public corporation evolved over the course of eighty years into our current economic organization where some corporations are economically more significant than some nation states. Berle and Means raised the question of "the motive force" and "the effective distribution" of wealth when large aggregation of wealth is unified under the common direction of "the princes of industry." They identified the problem of agency cost, observing that the "separation of ownership from control produces a condition where the interests of owner and of ultimate manager may, and often do, diverge." They identified the ethical questions raised when "[s]ize alone tends to give these giant corporations a social significance," and they argued that "[n]ew responsibilities towards the owners, the workers, the consumers, and the State thus rest upon the shoulders of those in control." Below is an excerpt from their classic book.

### *Adolf Berle & Gardiner Means, The Modern Corporation and Private Property*
#### (1932)

In its new aspect the corporation is a means whereby the wealth of innumerable individuals has been concentrated into huge aggregates and whereby control over this wealth has been surrendered to a unified direction. The power attendant upon such concentration has brought forth princes of industry, whose position in the community is yet to be defined. The surrender of control over their wealth by investors has effectively broken the old property relationships and has raised the problem of defining these relationships anew. The direction of industry by persons other than those who have ventured their wealth has raised the question of the motive force back of such direction and the effective distribution of the returns from business enterprise.

Though the American law makes no distinction between the private corporation and the quasi-public, the economics of the two are essentially different. The separation of ownership from control produces a condition where the interests of owner and of ultimate manager may, and often do, diverge, and where many of the checks which formerly operated to limit the use of power disappear. Size alone tends to give these giant corporations a social significance not attached to the smaller units of private enterprise. By the use of the open market for securities, each of these corporations assumes obligations towards the investing public which transform it from a legal method clothing the rule of a few individuals into an institution at least nominally serving investors who have embarked their funds in its enterprise. New responsibilities towards the owners, the workers, the consumers, and the State thus rest upon the shoulders of those in control. In creating these new relationships, the quasi-public corporation may fairly be said to work a revolution. It has destroyed the unity that we commonly call property—has divided ownership into nominal ownership and the power formerly joined to it. Thereby the corporation has changed the nature of profit-seeking enterprise. This revolution forms the subject of the present study.

Outwardly the change is simple enough. Men are less likely to own the physical instruments of production. They are more likely to own pieces of paper, loosely known as stocks, bonds, and other securities, which have become mobile through the machinery of the public markets. Beneath this, however, lies a more fundamental shift. Physical control over the instruments of production has been surrendered in ever growing degree to centralized groups who manage property in bulk, supposedly, but by no means necessarily, for the benefit of the security holders. Power over industrial property has been cut off from the beneficial ownership of this property—or, in less technical language, from the legal right to enjoy its fruits. Control of physical assets has passed from the individual owner to those who direct the quasi-public institutions, while the owner retains an interest in their product and increase. We see, in fact, the surrender and regrouping of the incidence of ownership, which formerly bracketed full power of manual disposition with complete right to enjoy the use, the fruits, and the proceeds of physical assets. There has resulted the dissolution of the old atom of ownership into its component parts, control and beneficial ownership.

In the quasi-public corporation, such an assumption no longer holds. As we have seen, it is no longer the individual himself who uses his wealth. Those in control of that wealth, and therefore in a position to secure industrial efficiency and produce profits, are no longer, as owners, entitled to the bulk of such profits. Those who control the destinies of the typical modern corporation own so insignificant a fraction of the company's stock that the returns from running the corporation profitably accrue to them in only a very minor degree. The stockholders, on the other hand, to whom the profits of the corporation go, cannot be motivated by those profits to a more efficient use of the property, since they have surrendered all disposition of it to those in control of the enterprise. The explosion of the atom of property destroys the basis of the old assumption that the quest for profits will spur the owner of industrial property to its effective use. It consequently challenges the fundamental economic principle of individual initiative in industrial enterprise. It raises for reexamination the question of the motive force back of industry, and the ends for which the modern corporation can be or will be run.

## 3. AGENCY COST

Much of corporate law can be explained through the prism of the theory of agency cost. Berle and Means observed that managers own such an "insignificant a fraction" of the company that its profits "accrue to them in only a very small minor degree." Yet, under corporate law, the "business and affairs of every corporation . . . shall be managed by or under the direction of a board of directors." A problem exists when the interests of the economic claimants conflict with those of managers. This is the key idea of the theory of agency cost—the theory that an agency relationship always creates a cost arising from the divergence of interest between agent and principal. Much of corporate law is devoted to minimize the total deleterious effects of agency. In the excerpt below, economists Michael Jensen and William Meckling define agency cost, and they continue to argue that the capital structure of a firm should be set such that it reduces total agency cost, thus increasing firm value.

## Michael C. Jensen & William H. Meckling, Theory of the Firm: Managerial Behavior

3 J. Fin. Econ. 35 (1976)

We define an agency relationship as a contract under which one or more persons (the principal(s)) engage another person (the agent) to perform some service on their behalf which involves delegating some decision making authority to the agent. If both parties to the relationship are utility maximizers, there is good reason to believe that the agent will not always act in the best interests of the principal. The principal can limit divergences from his interest by establishing appropriate incentives for the agent and by incurring monitoring costs designed to limit the aberrant activities of the agent. In addition in some situations it will pay the agent to expend resources (bonding costs) to guarantee that he will not take certain actions which would harm the principal or to ensure that the principal will be compensated if he does take such actions. However, it is generally impossible for the principal or the agent at zero cost to ensure that the agent will make optimal decisions from the principal's viewpoint. In most agency relationships the principal and the agent will incur positive monitoring and bonding costs (non-pecuniary as well as pecuniary), and in addition there will be some divergence between the agent's decisions and those decisions which would maximize the welfare of the principal. The dollar equivalent of the reduction in welfare experienced by the principal as a result of this divergence is also a cost of the agency relationship, and we refer to this latter cost as the "residual loss." We define agency costs as the sum of:

1. the monitoring expenditures by the principal,
2. the bonding expenditures by the agent,
3. the residual loss.

Since the relationship between the stockholders and the managers of a corporation fits the definition of a pure agency relationship, it should come as no surprise to discover that the issues associated with the "separation of ownership and control" in the modern diffuse ownership corporation are intimately associated with the general problem of agency.

### EXAMPLE 10.1

---

**Gordon Gekko lashes out against agency cost in Corporate America**

There are many great speeches in Hollywood movies. One of the most memorable is Gordon Gekko's homage to greed in *Wall Street* (1987).

*The point is, ladies and gentleman, that greed, for lack of a better word, is good. Greed is right, greed works. Greed clarifies, cuts through, and captures the essence of the evolutionary spirit. Greed, in all of its forms; greed for life, for money, for love, knowledge has marked the upward surge of mankind. And greed, you mark my words, will not only save Teldar Paper, but that other malfunctioning corporation called the USA. Thank you very much.*

Immediately preceding this famous passage, Gekko talks about the problem with Teldar Paper, a company he is trying to acquire.

---

> *Today, management has no stake in the company! All together, these men sitting up here own less than three percent of the company. And where does Mr. Cromwell put his million-dollar salary? Not in Teldar stock; he owns less than one percent. You own the company. That's right, you, the stockholder. And you are all being royally screwed over by these, these bureaucrats, with their luncheons, their hunting and fishing trips, their corporate jets and golden parachutes. . . . Teldar Paper has 33 different vice presidents each earning over 200 thousand dollars a year. Now, I have spent the last two months analyzing what all these guys do, and I still can't figure it out. One thing I do know is that our paper company lost 110 million dollars last year, and I'll bet that half of that was spent in all the paperwork going back and forth between all these vice presidents. The new law of evolution in corporate America seems to be survival of the unfittest. Well, in my book you either do it right or you get eliminated. In the last seven deals that I've been involved with, there were 2.5 million stockholders who have made a pretax profit of 12 billion dollars. Thank you. I am not a destroyer of companies. I am a liberator of them!*

The film had a good script, and the scriptwriters evidently researched the business and economic issues well. Gekko's speech illustrates the problem of agency cost. He complains that Teldar Paper has a bloated cost structure arising from management's interest in keeping "their luncheons, their hunting and fishing trips, their corporate jets and golden parachutes" and their "33 different vice presidents each earning over 200 thousand dollars a year." This situation arises from the fact that "management has no stake in the company!"

If Teldar Paper is a bad company due to high agency cost, why does Gekko want to acquire it? See the movie, or better yet think about how Gekko can profit by increasing the firm value. If you answer this question correctly, you will intuit some of the reasons for mergers and acquisitions transactions and how leverage buyouts increase value. (In the movie, Gekko, the antihero who preaches that "greed is good," goes to jail for securities violations.)

## C. CAPITAL STRUCTURE

### 1. CAPITAL STRUCTURE IRRELEVANCE (AND RELEVANCE)

Given that firms need capital to engage in business, what drives the decision to borrow money from creditors or raise equity from shareholders? Why do some firms have 70 percent debt and 30 percent equity, and others are 100 percent equity financed? Are these decisions random? A good business lawyer must understand the reasons behind a client's decisions because corporate lawyers are essential to executing capital raising transactions.

We start our understanding with the wrong answer: *Capital structure is irrelevant in a world of zero taxes and bankruptcy cost.* Thus capital structure could just as well be random, and no thought need be given to it. This proposition is called the Modigliani and Miller capital structure irrelevance hypothesis, named after its authors, Nobel prize-winning economists Franco Modigliani and Merton Miller (jointly referred to as M&M).[1] Everyone, including Modigliani and Miller, knows that this hypothesis is wrong because taxes, along with death, are the only certainties in life,[2] but the M&M capital structure irrelevance hypothesis helps us to think more formally about how managers construct their firm's capital structure.

Why is capital structure irrelevant if there are no taxes and bankruptcy cost? Think about a firm that raises $1,000 to build a factory, which produces widgets. The firm must pay for the cost of production and thereafter sell the widgets on the market. Does capital structure affect the firm's operations of making and selling widgets? In other words, does the firm operate more efficiently or inefficiently because it is financed in a particular way? How a factory is financed has nothing to do with how that factory is used to make and sell things—which is the core of business.

Modigliani and Miller provided a more formal answer to this intuition. Let's see their logic. Don't be intimidated by the analysis that follows. The math used here is nothing more than addition, subtraction, and multiplication.

Assume a 100 percent equity financed firm such that the firm value (the value of all securities) equals the value of equity: $V = E$. Sally invests $x$ percent in the firm's capital such that her stake is $xV = xE$. The firm generates operating profit $P$, which belongs to all equityholders. Sally is entitled to $xP$.

Assume now a firm financed by 50 percent debt and 50 percent equity such that $V = D + E$. Sally invests $x$ percent in both debt and equity capital, such that her capital contribution remains the same: $xV = xD + xE$. The interest rate payment on debt is $R$. Without bankruptcy cost and interest expense tax shield, the firm would earn the same operating profit $P$ because the mix of capital does not affect how operating profit is made. The operating profit $P$ is divided between the claims by creditor and equityholder, where $R$ is the creditor's claim and the remaining $(P - R)$ is the equityholder's claim. Sally is entitled to: $xR + x(P - R) = xP$, which is the same as the shareholder's return in the 100 percent equity financed structure. Under these assumptions, capital structure is irrelevant.

### EXAMPLE 10.2

---

### Modigliani and Miller's capital structure irrelevance hypothesis

Let's run through a numeric example to reinforce the point. Assume that an investor takes a 10 percent ownership stake in the total capital of Firms A and B. Firm A is 100 percent equity financed. Firm B is equally financed by debt and equity. The cost of debt is 10 percent. Both firms generate operating income of 300. The firms are identical, except that they are financed with different capital structures.

---

1. Franco Modigliani & Merton H. Miller, *The Costs of Capital, Corporation Finance and the Theory of Investment*, 48 Am. Econ. Rev. 261 (1958); Franco Modigliani & Merton H. Miller, *Corporate Income Taxes and the Cost of Capital: A Correction*, 53 Am. Econ. Rev. 433 (1963).

2. "Our new Constitution is now established, and has an appearance that promises permanency; but in this world nothing can be said to be certain, except death and taxes." Benjamin Franklin letter to Jean-Baptiste Leroy, November 13, 1789.

|  | FIRM A | FIRM B |
|---|---|---|
| Capital |  |  |
|     Equity | 2,000 | 1,000 |
|     Debt at 10% | 0 | 1,000 |
| Operating income | 300 | 300 |
| Debt service |  | (100) |
| Net income | 300 | 200 |
| Investor's 10% of equity claim | 30 | 20 |
| Investor's 10% of debt claim | 0 | 10 |
| Total return to investor | 30 | 30 |

This example shows that capital structure is irrelevant to the value a firm creates. If capital structure does not affect operating income (300), how that operating income is divided through financial claims by creditors and equityholders should be irrelevant under unrealistic assumptions of no taxes and bankruptcy cost.

**EXAMPLE 10.3**

## Effect of taxes

In the real world, however, taxes and bankruptcy cost exist. Therefore, capital structure must be relevant to the value of the firm. Let's continue the above example. The same assumptions used in Example 10.2 hold, except that we assume a tax rate of 30 percent.

|  | FIRM A | FIRM B |
|---|---|---|
| Capital |  |  |
|     Equity | 2,000 | 1,000 |
|     Debt at 10% | 0 | 1,000 |
| Operating income | 300 | 300 |
| Debt service |  | (100) |
| Pretax profit | 300 | 200 |
| Taxes at 30% | 90 | 60 |
| Net income | 210 | 140 |
| 10% of equity claim | 21 | 14 |
| 10% of debt claim | 0 | 10 |
| Total return to investor | 21 | 24 |

Debt increases value because the interest expense deduction reduces tax liability, and thus capital providers pocket this surplus. The increase in value in Firm B of 30 is the tax shield: $100 \times 30\% = 30$ not paid in taxes due to the interest expense deduction.

 **STOP AND THINK** The tax effect of borrowing creates value by reducing tax liability. However, a reduction in tax liability may create bad effects. There are significant tax policy issues concerning capital structure. Consider the following article.

## John D. McKinnon, Potential Tax Change Is Red Flag for Some Firms

Wall Street Journal, April 4, 2011

Lawmakers are considering adjustments to a fundamental feature of the U.S. tax code that could have a profound effect on how companies finance their operations.

Specifically, members of Congress are focusing on code provisions that encourage companies to finance their activities through issuing debt, instead of equity. The most basic is the tax deduction typically allowed for interest payments on business debt.

The lawmakers' move, though embryonic, is raising red flags for some businesses that use lots of leverage, including financial firms and manufacturers, but offering hope of lower tax rates for many others.

The chairmen of the Senate Finance Committee and House Ways and Means Committee have asked for a study of how debt is taxed, and whether that contributes to over-leveraging by businesses and households.

From the mid-1990s to 2008, business-sector debt grew far faster than gross domestic product, hitting more than $25 trillion by one measure, before declining.

### Debt and Taxes

Removing tax breaks for business debt would affect how companies fund their activities.

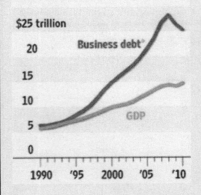

A 2010 report by a panel of outside advisers to President Barack Obama listed a change in the tax treatment of debt among the main options for a corporate tax overhaul, saying it could reduce "leverage of firms and the likelihood of future financial distress."

Favorable tax treatment makes debt-financed investments more attractive for companies than investments financed by equity, or the company's money, and is one reason for the rapid growth in debt in some sectors in the run-up to the meltdown, many experts believe. Debt has become so widely used in corporate America that some large companies now are even borrowing the money they need to pay dividends.

Tax experts have suggested that some investors can use debt deductions to make money, by borrowing to buy items that enjoy other tax breaks, such as accelerated depreciation. For certain firms and certain investments, "the effective marginal tax rate on debt-financed investment is negative," the White House study warned last year.

Lawmakers are now beginning to weigh whether they should put new limits on companies' interest deductions, as Germany has. Such a move could raise tens of billions of dollars of new tax revenue, which in turn could be used to offset the cost of cutting U.S. corporate tax rates. The top U.S. corporate rate now is 35%, among the world's highest.

Alternatively, lawmakers could choose to lower tax rates on equity-financed investments, thus balancing the tax treatment of debt and equity. For instance, Congress could make company dividends tax-deductible too, just as interest deductions are now.

Limiting debt-related deductions also could help curb the buildup of leverage by financial firms that many people believe accelerated the sector's meltdown in 2008. "We need to know whether these incentives cause businesses to become over-leveraged in a way that hurts our economy," Senate Finance Committee Chairman Max Baucus (D., Mont.) said at a recent hearing on the issue.

The benefit of tax shield increases firm value. However, it is intuitively obvious that as a firm takes on more debt (increases leverage), the risk of bankruptcy increases. Increased risk decreases firm value. The graph below illustrates these antipodal effects.

As the firm increases leverage, its value increase and reaches an apex. When its capital structure has leverage beyond the optimal ratio of $x$ between debt and equity, the firm value diminishes as the cost of bankruptcy eats into the benefit of leverage. Ultimately, a highly levered firm may be worth less than a firm capitalized by 100 percent equity.

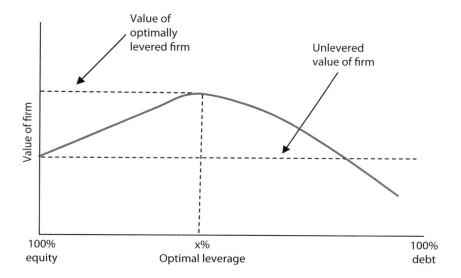

EXAMPLE 10.4

---

**The effects of leverage on investment banks**

These effects of leverage are not just theoretical ruminations of law professors or economists. They are empirical facts and can be seen in the real world. In the several years before the financial crisis of 2008, the major independent investment banks (Goldman Sachs, Morgan Stanley, Merrill Lynch, Lehman Brothers, and Bear Stearns) increased their leverage to enhance profits (see below).[3]

---

3. Robert J. Rhee, *The Decline of Investment Banking: Preliminary Thoughts on the Evolution of the Industry 1996-2008*, 5 J. Bus. L. & Tech. 75, 80-81 (2010).

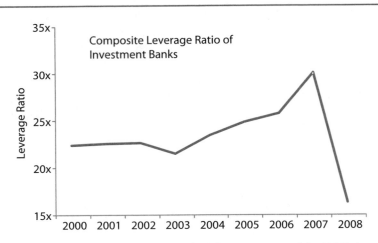

Increased leverage resulted in increase profitability as measured by ROE (see below). Note that the declining profitability of investment banks after the Dot Com technology bubble burst in 2000, and the sharp increase in profitability corresponding to a sharp increase in leverage, until the housing bubble burst in 2007 and 2008.

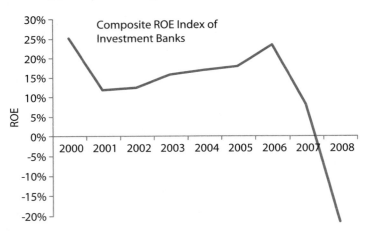

The leverage level proved to be too much. Three firms went insolvent in 2008: Bear Stearns, Merrill Lynch, and Lehman Brothers (see the negative composite ROE in 2008). The other two firms, Morgan Stanley and Goldman Sachs, barely escaped with their solvency and independence.

 In a world of taxes and bankruptcy, capital structure is an important factor in firm value. Debt tends to increase firm value until the cost of bankruptcy overtakes the benefit and begins to reduce firm value. A major consideration in decisions on corporation transactions is the optimal capital structure.

## 2. AGENCY COST AND THE ROLE OF DEBT

In addition to taxes and bankruptcy, debt also has a relation to agency cost. Michael Jensen and William Meckling argued that capital structure can be set at an optimal level that reduces total agency cost.

Imagine that a firm is 100 percent owned by an entrepreneur. The firm belongs to the entrepreneur, and he can do whatever he wishes. However, most firms are capitalized by outside capital: creditors and outside shareholders. When creditors provide capital, there is significant agency cost.

Imagine that you are a credit risk officer at JPMorgan Chase. An entrepreneur, William Conqueror, seeks a corporate loan and you must approve the loan. You are impressed with the description of the business model. You ask, "How much do you want to borrow?" Conqueror replies, "$99,900,000." You follow up, "Okay, what is the equity in the firm?" Conqueror answers, "I have put $100,000 of my own hard-earned money into this venture. There are no other equity investors." If the loan is approved, the total capital would be $100 million, and the ratio of debt to equity would be 999-to-1.

Assume that Conqueror does not have criminal intent and he really wants to advance his business plan. Are you comfortable with his proposition? From the perspective of the creditor JPMorgan Chase, what is the fundamental problem?

There is the potential for agency cost when someone else funds the entrepreneur's venture. For example, with other people's money the entrepreneur can divert some of the funds toward his own interest. Such diversion need not reach the level of illegality or fraud. Such diversion can be the purchase of a corporate jet, larger bonuses, country club membership, fresh flowers in the corporate lobby, etc.

The agency cost of debt is the highest when leverage is the highest, and it diminishes to zero as the firm is 100 percent equity financed. Similarly, with equity capital from outside shareholders, the agency cost of equity is highest when such equity is the highest, and it diminishes to zero as the firm is financed by debt and the entrepreneur's own equity.

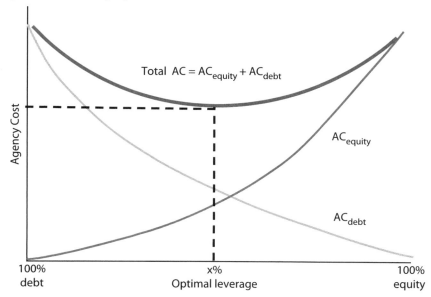

The above graph presents the effects on agency cost (AC) of different forms of capital. The total agency cost is defined as: Total AC = $AC_{equity}$ + $AC_{debt}$. The optimal capital structure is the amount of leverage that reduces the total agency cost of debt and equity.

Debt can reduce agency cost in several ways. First, to access debt, a firm must be subject to a credit check (even retail borrowers are subject to a credit check). This is done through due diligence by the creditor, who will examine the company's books and records for creditworthiness. Such monitoring by creditors tends to make managers perform at a certain level. Second, if a firm cannot meet its debt service, it can throw the firm into bankruptcy. As the author likes to say, "Debt is merciless." The prospect of losing control of the firm tends to make managers perform at a certain level.

## 3. LEVERAGE BUYOUT (LBO) AND DEBT FINANCING

A *leverage buyout* (LBO) is an acquisition of a firm using a substantial amount of debt as the acquisition financing. Since mortgages are prominent in homeownership, most homeowners engage in a leverage buyout of the home asset. Businesses also use leveraged finance. An LBO is a risky transaction because the firm is heavily levered and interest payments must be made to creditors, lest there be a default.

Why use debt to finance operations or an acquisition? As we have seen, leverage has several value enhancing properties. First, there is the interest tax shield reducing tax liability. Second, debt capital is cheaper than equity capital up to the point where the marginal (incremental) gain is outweighed by increased bankruptcy cost as reflected in an increase in the cost of equity. Third, debt can be used in the capital structure to reduce total agency cost. It incentivizes managers to perform because, unlike equityholders, creditors must be paid their interest and principal. Fourth, the process of securing credit requires the firm to undergo due diligence, a vetting process, that serves to monitor the firm and that bonds the manager's performance. Thus, debt has a number of salutary properties.

EXAMPLE 10.5

---

### LBO transaction and "juicing up" equity returns with debt

Leverage "juices up" returns on equity, meaning that the return on equity becomes more profitable. The basic intuition is that an acquirer borrows most of the money from creditors to acquire a firm and only uses a small slice of equity. As long as creditors can be paid back, there is a substantial chance that the equityholder, as the residual claimant, can earn more profit than if the acquirer used 100 percent equity. Let's see the difference in a simple stylized example.

*Acquisition Method: 100 percent equity financed*

Assume that William Conqueror seeks to acquire UK Inc. for the price of $1,000. UK is expected to generate pretax earnings of 100 for the first 5 years, and in years 6 and 7 operational efficiencies gain traction and UK is projected to generate pretax earnings of 150. The effective tax rate is 30%. At the end of year 7, Conqueror will "exit" the investment by a sale of the shares to the public (an IPO) or a sale of UK to another company. The projected exit value is $2,000, which is the projected firm value of UK at

---

the end of year 7. Firm value is the same as equity since there is debt. The cash flow and IRR are projected below.

| | Yr. 0 | Yr. 1 | Yr. 2 | Yr. 3 | Yr. 4 | Yr. 5 | Yr. 6 | Yr. 7 |
|---|---|---|---|---|---|---|---|---|
| Pretax income | | 100 | 100 | 100 | 100 | 100 | 150 | 150 |
| Taxes at 30% | | (30) | (30) | (30) | (30) | (30) | (45) | (45) |
| Net earnings | | 70 | 70 | 70 | 70 | 70 | 105 | 105 |
| Acquisition and exit | (1,000) | | | | | | | 2,000 |
| Return to equityholder | (1,000) | 70 | 70 | 70 | 70 | 70 | 105 | 2,105 |
| **Equity IRR** | **16.3%** | | | | | | | |

*Acquisition Method: 80/20 debt-to-equity financed LBO*

Assume that an IRR of 16.3 percent is insufficient return for Conqueror. His hurdle rate is 25% return. He seeks to do a LBO using 80 percent debt. The acquisition financing is thus $800 in debt and $200 of equity provided by Conqueror. Because this is a risky transaction, the interest on debt is high: 12 percent (or $96 per year). The debt matures at the end of year 7 with a principal payment due of $800. Other operating assumptions remain the same, as well as the exit valuation of UK.

| | Yr. 0 | Yr. 1 | Yr. 2 | Yr. 3 | Yr. 4 | Yr. 5 | Yr. 6 | Yr. 7 |
|---|---|---|---|---|---|---|---|---|
| Operating profit | | 100 | 100 | 100 | 100 | 100 | 150 | 150 |
| Interest expense | | (96) | (96) | (96) | (96) | (96) | (96) | (96) |
| Pretax profit | | 4 | 4 | 4 | 4 | 4 | 54 | 54 |
| Taxes at 30% | | (1) | (1) | (1) | (1) | (1) | (16) | (16) |
| Net earnings | | 3 | 3 | 3 | 3 | 3 | 38 | 38 |
| Debt repayment | | | | | | | | (800) |
| Acquisition and exit | (200) | | | | | | | 2,000 |
| Return to equityholder | (200) | 3 | 3 | 3 | 3 | 3 | 38 | 1,238 |
| **Equity IRR** | **31.1%** | | | | | | | |

Why is the IRR on equity on a debt financed acquisition so much higher? The intuition is that an equityholder uses a little of his money and a lot of creditor's money to acquire the firm; and if the firm is successful, he can pay down the debt and keep whatever remains as the residual, which can be quite a lot. In the above scenarios, Conqueror paid $1,000 in equity and received $2,105 in the 100 percent equity financing, and $200 in equity and received $1,238 in the leveraged transaction. Which do you prefer? This is the rationale for LBOs specifically and the use of leverage more generally.

We can make several observations about the differences in the acquisition funding. First, leverage "juices up" profits and equity returns. In the above Example 10.5, compare the IRRs of 16.3 percent and 31.1 percent; the use of 80 percent debt almost doubled the profitability of equity. Now we see why debt is so appealing. Examples 5.6 and 10.4 illustrate the use of leverage by investment banks during the years leading up to the financial crisis of 2008-2009, as well as the consequences of too much debt. Second, too much leverage can make a firm very risky. In the above example, the firm is barely able to service its debt ($96 in interest) from operating profit ($100). The firm is barely solvent, and there is high chance it could default if its business falters. There is little margin for error, and once there is default on debt, it triggers various contractual and legal protections for creditors.

 Debt is an important source of funding, can create value, and enhance the profitability of equity. However, it must be used correctly. The author has given two bits of wisdom to emphasize the point: (1) "creditors are merciless," and (2) "debt is great until it blows up in your face."

## 4. CONFLICT BETWEEN CREDITORS AND EQUITYHOLDERS

The interests of creditors and shareholders inherently conflict. Creditors are only interested in being paid their interest and principal. They are only interested in the firm's profit and wealth generation to the extent that their economic claim is paid. On the other hand, shareholders are residual claimants and benefit only when all other claims are paid. Therefore, they are interested in maximizing profit and wealth.

These interests conflict in the decisions on the amount of risk that the firm undertakes. Creditors tend to desire lower risk and more stable earnings. This maximizes the probability that the firm will be able to service debt. On the other hand, shareholders tend to desire to assume the level of risk that maximizes returns. Increases risk may lead to increased probability that creditors' claims cannot be satisfied. There is an inherent tension between creditors and shareholders.

## D. CASE APPLICATION

In 1989, RJR Nabisco, a maker of Nabisco brand foods and R.J. Reynolds cigarettes, was the target of a multi-billion dollar leverage buyout, the largest LBO at the time. The holders of RJR Nabisco bonds sued because the value of their bonds plummeted upon the announcement of the deal. Among the bondholders were Metropolitan Life Insurance Co. ("MetLife"), a life insurance company, which had invested over $340 million in principal amount of six separate RJR Nabisco debt issues, and Jefferson-Pilot Life Insurance Co. ("Jefferson-Pilot"), which owned $9.34 million in principal amount of three separate RJR Nabisco debt issues. The bondholders could not point to any specific restriction in the bond indenture that restricted an LBO transaction or the assumption of greater debt on RJR Nabisco's balance sheet. But they argued that the LBO transaction, which RJR Nabisco knew would reduce the value of their bonds, violated the implied covenant of good faith and fair dealing. In reading the case, think about the effect of the rule of law on the risk associated with a debt instrument and on the capital market in general.

### *Metropolitan Life Ins. Co. v. RJR Nabisco Inc.*
716 F. Supp. 1504 (S.D.N.Y. 1989)

WALKER, District Judge:

The corporate parties to this action are among the country's most sophisticated financial institutions, as familiar with the Wall Street investment community and the securities market as American consumers are with the Oreo cookies and Winston cigarettes made by defendant RJR Nabisco, Inc. The present action traces its origins to October 20, 1988, when F. Ross Johnson, then the Chief Executive Officer of RJR Nabisco, proposed a $17 billion leveraged buy-out ("LBO") of the company's shareholders, at $75 per share.[1] Within a few days, a bidding war developed among the investment group led by Johnson and the investment firm of Kohlberg Kravis Roberts & Co. ("KKR"), and others. On December 1, 1988, a special committee of RJR Nabisco directors, established by the company specifically to consider the competing proposals, recommended that the company accept the KKR proposal, a $24 billion LBO that called for the purchase of the company's outstanding stock at roughly $109 per share.

The flurry of activity late last year that accompanied the bidding war for RJR Nabisco spawned at least eight lawsuits, filed before this Court, charging the company and its former CEO with a variety of securities and common law violations. The Court agreed to hear the present action on an expedited basis, with an eye toward March 1, 1989, when RJR Nabisco was expected to merge with the KKR holding entities created to facilitate the LBO. On that date, RJR Nabisco was also scheduled to assume roughly $19 billion of new debt. After a delay unrelated to the present action, the merger was ultimately completed during the week of April 24, 1989.

Plaintiffs now allege, in short, that RJR Nabisco's actions have drastically impaired the value of bonds previously issued to plaintiffs by, in effect, misappropriating the value of those bonds to help finance the LBO and to distribute an enormous windfall to the company's shareholders. As a result, plaintiffs argue, they have unfairly suffered a multimillion dollar loss in the value of their bonds.[4]

Although the numbers involved in this case are large, and the financing necessary to complete the LBO unprecedented,[8] the legal principles nonetheless remain discrete and familiar. Yet while the instant [summary judgment] motions thus primarily require the Court to evaluate and apply traditional rules of equity and contract interpretation, plaintiffs do raise issues of first impression in the context of an LBO. At the heart of the present motions lies plaintiffs' claim that RJR Nabisco violated a restrictive covenant—*not an explicit covenant found within the four corners of the relevant bond indentures, but rather an implied covenant of good faith and fair*

---

1. A leveraged buy-out occurs when a group of investors, usually including members of a company's management team, buy the company under financial arrangements that include little equity and significant new debt. The necessary debt financing typically includes mortgages or high risk/high yield bonds, popularly known as "junk bonds." Additionally, a portion of this debt is generally secured by the company's assets. Some of the acquired company's assets are usually sold after the transaction is completed in order to reduce the debt incurred in the acquisition.

4. Agencies like Standard & Poor's and Moody's generally rate bonds in two broad categories: investment grade and speculative grade. Standard & Poor's rates investment grade bonds from "AAA" to "BBB." Moody's rates those bonds from "AAA" to "Baa3." Speculative grade bonds are rated either "BB" and lower, or "Ba1" and lower, by Standard & Poor's and Moody's, respectively. See, e.g., Standard and Poor's Debt Rating Criteria at 10-11. No one disputes that, subsequent to the announcement of the LBO, the RJR Nabisco bonds lost their "A" ratings.

8. On February 9, 1989, KKR completed its tender offer for roughly 74 percent of RJR Nabisco's common stock (of which approximately 97% of the outstanding shares were tendered) and all of its Series B Cumulative Preferred Stock (of which approximately 95% of the outstanding shares were tendered). Approximately $18 billion in cash was paid out to these stockholders. KKR acquired the remaining stock in the late April merger through the issuance of roughly $4.1 billion of pay-in-kind exchangeable preferred stock and roughly $1.8 billion in face amount of convertible debentures.

*dealing*—not to incur the debt necessary to facilitate the LBO and thereby betray what plaintiffs claim was the fundamental basis of their bargain with the company. [Emphasis added.]

RJR Nabisco defends the LBO by pointing to express provisions in the bond indentures that, *inter alia*, permit mergers and the assumption of additional debt. These provisions, as well as others that could have been included but were not, were known to the market and to plaintiffs, sophisticated investors who freely bought the bonds and were equally free to sell them at any time. Any attempt by this Court to create contractual terms post hoc, defendants contend, not only finds no basis in the controlling law and undisputed facts of this case, but also would constitute an impermissible invasion into the free and open operation of the marketplace.

For the reasons set forth below, this Court agrees with defendants. *There being no express covenant between the parties that would restrict the incurrence of new debt*, and no perceived direction to that end from covenants that are express, this Court will not imply a covenant to prevent the recent LBO and thereby create an indenture term that, while bargained for in other contexts, was not bargained for here and was not even within the mutual contemplation of the parties. [Emphasis added.]

## III. Discussion

In their first count, plaintiffs assert that

> [d]efendant RJR Nabisco owes a continuing duty of good faith and fair dealing in connection with the contract [i.e., the indentures] through which it borrowed money from MetLife, Jefferson-Pilot and other holders of its debt, including a duty not to frustrate the purpose of the contracts to the debtholders or to deprive the debtholders of the intended object of the contracts-purchase of investment-grade securities.
>
> In the "buy-out," the [c]ompany breaches the duty [or implied covenant] of good faith and fair dealing by, inter alia, destroying the investment grade quality of the debt and transferring that value to the "buy-out" proponents and to the shareholders.

In effect, plaintiffs contend that express covenants were not necessary because an implied covenant would prevent what defendants have now done.

A plaintiff always can allege a violation of an express covenant. If there has been such a violation, of course, the court need not reach the question of whether or not an *implied* covenant has been violated. That inquiry surfaces where, while the express terms may not have been technically breached, one party has nonetheless effectively deprived the other of those express, explicitly bargained-for benefits. In such a case, a court will read an implied covenant of good faith and fair dealing into a contract to ensure that neither party deprives the other of "the fruits of the agreement." In other words, the implied covenant will only aid and further the explicit terms of the agreement and will never impose an obligation "which would be inconsistent with other terms of the contractual relationship." Viewed another way, the implied covenant of good faith is breached only when one party seeks to prevent the contract's performance or to withhold its benefits. As a result, it thus ensures that parties to a contract perform the substantive, bargained-for terms of their agreement.

In contracts like bond indentures, "an implied covenant . . . derives its substance directly from the language of the Indenture, and 'cannot give the holders of Debentures any rights inconsistent with those set out in the Indenture.' *[Where] plaintiffs' contractual rights [have not been] violated, there can have been no breach of an implied covenant.*"

The appropriate analysis, then, is first to examine the indentures to determine "the fruits of the agreement" between the parties, and then to decide whether those "fruits" have been spoiled-which is to say, whether plaintiffs' contractual rights have been violated by defendants.

The American Bar Foundation's Commentaries on Indentures ("the Commentaries"), relied upon and respected by both plaintiffs and defendants, describes the rights and risks generally found in bond indentures like those at issue:

> The most obvious and important characteristic of long-term debt financing is that the holder ordinarily has not bargained for and does not expect any substantial gain in the value of the security to compensate for the risk of loss. . . . [T]he significant fact, *which accounts in part for the detailed protective provisions of the typical long-term debt financing instrument, is that the lender (the purchaser of the debt security) can expect only interest at the prescribed rate plus the eventual return of the principal.* Except for possible increases in the market value of the debt security because of changes in interest rates, the debt security will seldom be worth more than the lender paid for it. . . . It may, of course, become worth much less. Accordingly, the typical investor in a long-term debt security is primarily interested in every reasonable assurance that the principal and interest will be paid when due. . . . Short of bankruptcy, *the debt security holder can do nothing to protect himself against actions of the borrower which jeopardize its ability to pay the debt unless he . . . establishes his rights through contractual provisions set forth in the debt agreement or indenture.*

It is not necessary to decide that indentures like those at issue could never support a finding of additional benefits, under different circumstances with different parties. Rather, for present purposes, it is sufficient to conclude what obligation is *not* covered, either explicitly or implicitly, by these contracts held by these plaintiffs. Accordingly, this Court holds that the "fruits" of these indentures do not include an implied restrictive covenant that would prevent the incurrence of new debt to facilitate the recent LBO. To hold otherwise would permit these plaintiffs to straightjacket the company in order to guarantee their investment. These plaintiffs do not invoke an implied covenant of good faith to protect a legitimate, mutually contemplated benefit of the indentures; rather, they seek to have this Court create an additional benefit for which they did not bargain.

Plaintiffs argue in the most general terms that the fundamental basis of all these indentures was that an LBO along the lines of the recent RJR Nabisco transaction would never be undertaken, that indeed *no* action would be taken, intentionally or not, that would significantly deplete the company's assets. Accepting plaintiffs' theory, their fundamental bargain with defendants dictated that nothing would be done to jeopardize the extremely high probability that the company would remain able to make interest payments and repay principal over the 20 to 30 year indenture term-and perhaps by logical extension even included the right to ask a court "to make sure that plaintiffs had made a good investment." But as Judge Knapp aptly concluded in *Gardner,* "Defendants . . . were under a duty to carry out the terms of the contract, but not to make sure that plaintiffs had made a good investment. The former they have done; the latter we have no jurisdiction over." Plaintiffs' submissions and MetLife's previous undisputed internal memoranda remind the Court that a "fundamental basis" or a "fruit of an agreement" is often in the eye of the beholder, whose vision may well change along with the market, and who may, with hindsight, imagine a different bargain than the one he actually and initially accepted with open eyes.

The sort of unbounded and one-sided elasticity urged by plaintiffs would interfere with and destabilize the market. And this Court, like the parties to these contracts, cannot ignore or disavow the marketplace in which the contract is performed. Nor can it ignore the expectations of that market—expectations, for instance, that the terms of an indenture will be upheld, and that a court will not, *sua sponte*, add new substantive terms to that indenture as it sees fit.[26] The Court has no reason to believe that the market, in evaluating bonds such as those at issue here, did not discount for the possibility that any company, even one the size of RJR Nabisco, might engage in an LBO heavily financed by debt. That the bonds did not lose any of their value until the October 20, 1988 announcement of a possible RJR Nabisco LBO only suggests that the market had theretofore evaluated the risks of such a transaction as slight.

## QUESTIONS

1. This case illustrates the economic conflict between creditors and shareholders. Shareholders gained and creditors lost. How?
2. What happened to the market value of the bonds when RJR Nabisco announced the LBO? Why?
3. How did RJR Nabisco's risk profile change from the time it issued the bonds in question?
4. The court observed: "The sort of unbounded and one-sided elasticity urged by plaintiffs would interfere with and destabilize the [bond] market." Why?

---

The case below is an older Delaware case on the fiduciary duty of care. The central issue is whether the board of directors had a duty to monitor employees of the firm, and if so, the legal standard for appropriate monitoring. In reading the case, think about the problem of agency: Can the intentions and acts of the employees deviate from the best interest of the corporation? If employees must be monitored, and if monitoring is not free, who should determine the amount of cost that should be expended?

### *Graham v. Allis-Chalmers Mfg. Co.*
188 A.2d 125 (Del. 1963)

WOLCOTT, Justice.

This is a derivative action on behalf of Allis-Chalmers against its directors and four of its non-director employees. The complaint is based upon indictments of

---

26. *Cf. Broad v. Rockwell*, 642 F.2d at 943 ("Not least among the parties 'who must comply with or refer to the indenture' are the members of the investing public and their investment advisors. A large degree of uniformity in the language of debenture indentures is essential to the effective functioning of the financial markets: uniformity of the indentures that govern competing debenture issues is what makes it possible meaningfully to compare one debenture issue with another, focusing only on the business provisions of the issue . . .") (citation omitted); *Sharon Steel Corporation v. Chase Manhattan Bank, N.A.*, 691 F.2d. 1039, 1048 (2d Cir. 1982) (Winter, J.) ("[U]niformity in interpretation is important to the efficiency of capital markets. . . . [T]he creation of enduring uncertainties as to the meaning of boilerplate provisions would decrease the value of all debenture issues and greatly impair the efficient working of capital markets.").

Allis-Chalmers and the four non-director employees named as defendants herein who, with the corporation, entered pleas of guilty to the indictments. The indictments, eight in number, charged violations of the Federal anti-trust laws. The suit seeks to recover damages which Allis-Chalmers is claimed to have suffered by reason of these violations.

Allis-Chalmers is a manufacturer of a variety of electrical equipment. It employs in excess of 31,000 people, has a total of 24 plants, 145 sales offices, 5000 dealers and distributors, and its sales volume is in excess of $500,000,000 annually. The operations of the company are conducted by two groups, each of which is under the direction of a senior vice president. One of these groups is the Industries Group under the direction of Singleton, director defendant. This group is divided into five divisions. One of these, the Power Equipment Division, produced the products, the sale of which involved the anti-trust activities referred to in the indictments. The Power Equipment Division, presided over by McMullen, non-director defendant, contains ten departments, each of which is presided over by a manager or general manager.

The operating policy of Allis-Chalmers is to decentralize by the delegation of authority to the lowest possible management level capable of fulfilling the delegated responsibility. Thus, prices of products are ordinarily set by the particular department manager, except that if the product being priced is large and special, the department manager might confer with the general manager of the division. Products of a standard character involving repetitive manufacturing processes are sold out of a price list which is established by a price leader for the electrical equipment industry as a whole.

Annually, the Board of Directors reviews group and departmental profit goal budgets. On occasion, the Board considers general questions concerning price levels, but because of the complexity of the company's operations the Board does not participate in decisions fixing the prices of specific products.

The Board of Directors of fourteen members, four of whom are officers, meets once a month, October excepted, and considers a previously prepared agenda for the meeting. Supplied to the Directors at the meetings are financial and operating data relating to all phases of the company's activities. The Board meetings are customarily of several hours duration in which all the Directors participate actively. Apparently, the Board considers and decides matters concerning the general business policy of the company. By reason of the extent and complexity of the company's operations, it is not practicable for the Board to consider in detail specific problems of the various divisions.

The indictments to which Allis-Chalmers and the four non-director defendants pled guilty charge that the company and individual non-director defendants, commencing in 1956, conspired with other manufacturers and their employees to fix prices and to rig bids to private electric utilities and governmental agencies in violation of the anti-trust laws of the United States. None of the director defendants in this cause were named as defendants in the indictments. Indeed, the Federal Government acknowledged that it had uncovered no probative evidence which could lead to the conviction of the defendant directors.

The first actual knowledge the directors had of anti-trust violations by some of the company's employees was in the summer of 1959 from newspaper stories that TVA proposed an investigation of identical bids. Singleton, in charge of the Industries Group of the company, investigated but unearthed nothing. Thereafter, in November of 1959, some of the company's employees were subpoenaed before the Grand Jury. Further investigation by the company's Legal Division gave reason to suspect the illegal activity and all of the subpoenaed employees were instructed to tell the whole truth.

Thereafter, on February 8, 1960, at the direction of the Board, a policy statement relating to anti-trust problems was issued, and the Legal Division commenced a series of meetings with all employees of the company in possible areas of anti-trust activity. The purpose and effect of these steps was to eliminate any possibility of further and future violations of the antitrust laws.

As we have pointed out, there is no evidence in the record that the defendant directors had actual knowledge of the illegal anti-trust actions of the company's employees.

Plaintiffs are thus forced to rely solely upon the legal proposition advanced by them that directors of a corporation, as a matter of law, are liable for losses suffered by their corporations by reason of their gross inattention to the common law duty of actively supervising and managing the corporate affairs.

The precise charge made against these director defendants is that, even though they had no knowledge of any suspicion of wrongdoing on the part of the company's employees, they still should have put into effect a system of watchfulness which would have brought such misconduct to their attention in ample time to have brought it to an end. On the contrary, it appears that directors are entitled to rely on the honesty and integrity of their subordinates until something occurs to put them on suspicion that something is wrong. If such occurs and goes unheeded, then liability of the directors might well follow, but absent cause for suspicion there is no duty upon the directors to install and operate a corporate system of espionage to ferret out wrongdoing which they have no reason to suspect exists.

The duties of the Allis-Chalmers Directors were fixed by the nature of the enterprise which employed in excess of 30,000 persons, and extended over a large geographical area. By force of necessity, the company's Directors could not know personally all the company's employees. The very magnitude of the enterprise required them to confine their control to the broad policy decisions. That they did this is clear from the record. At the meetings of the Board in which all Directors participated, these questions were considered and decided on the basis of summaries, reports and corporate records. These they were entitled to rely on, not only, we think, under general principles of the common law, but by reason of 8 Del. C. §141(f) as well, which in terms fully protects a director who relies on such in the performance of his duties.

In the last analysis, the question of whether a corporate director has become liable for losses to the corporation through neglect of duty is determined by the circumstances. If he has recklessly reposed confidence in an obviously untrustworthy employee, has refused or neglected cavalierly to perform his duty as a director, or has ignored either willfully or through inattention obvious danger signs of employee wrongdoing, the law will cast the burden of liability upon him. This is not the case at bar, however, for as soon as it became evident that there were grounds for suspicion, the Board acted promptly to end it and prevent its recurrence.

Plaintiffs say these steps should have been taken long before, even in the absence of suspicion, but we think not, for we know of no rule of law which requires a corporate director to assume, with no justification whatsoever, that all corporate employees are incipient law violators who, but for a tight checkrein, will give free vent to their unlawful propensities.

We therefore affirm the Vice Chancellor's ruling that the individual director defendants are not liable as a matter of law merely because, unknown to them, some employees of Allis-Chalmers violated the anti-trust laws thus subjecting the corporation to loss.

The judgment of the court below is affirmed.

## QUESTIONS

1. In what way does the case illustrate the theory of agency cost?
2. In what way were the board's actions and inactions prior to the discovery of the criminal acts consistent with ex ante efficiency considerations? In other words, do we want excessive monitoring within firms? Who should determine the appropriate level of monitoring? How should that level be set?
3. Why were the directors not liable for failure to monitor? How can the different results achieved in *Graham* and *Francis* (Chapters 1 and 2) be harmonized?
4. A suit for a failure to monitor "is possibly the most difficult theory in corporation law upon which a plaintiff might hope to win a judgment." *In re Caremark Int'l Deriv. Litigation*, 698 A.2d 959 (Del. Ch. 1996) (Allen, Ch.). The case further explains:

> Obviously the level of detail that is appropriate for such an information system is a question of business judgment. And obviously too, no rationally designed information and reporting system will remove the possibility that the corporation will violate laws or regulations, or that senior officers or directors may nevertheless sometimes be misled or otherwise fail reasonably to detect acts material to the corporation's compliance with the law. But it is important that the board exercise a good faith judgment that the corporation's information and reporting system is in concept and design adequate to assure the board that appropriate information will come to its attention in a timely manner as a matter of ordinary operations, so that it may satisfy its responsibility.
>
> Thus, I am of the view that a director's obligation includes a duty to attempt in good faith to assure that a corporate information and reporting system, which the board concludes is adequate, exists, and that failure to do so under some circumstances may, in theory at least, render a director liable for losses caused by non-compliance with applicable legal standards.

Under *Caremark*, what criteria should be applied to determine the appropriate level of monitoring?

## ESSENTIAL TERMS

Agency cost
Bankruptcy cost
Business judgment rule
Capital structure
Creditor-shareholder conflict
Efficiency

Interest tax shield
Leverage buyout (LBO)
Limited liability
M&M capital structure irrelevance
Separation of ownership and control
Transaction cost

## KEY CONCEPTS

1. Organizational law is primarily concerned with efficiency.
2. The firm structure and the concept of separation of ownership and control can be explained by efficiency considerations.
3. The concept of agency cost is important. Many doctrines in organizational law, such as fiduciary duty, can be explained by the need to reduce agency cost.
4. The capital structure of a corporation is not arbitrary. Optimal capital structure must account for several factors: tax shield on interest expense, bankruptcy cost, and agency cost.
5. Creditors and shareholders have conflicting interests. Creditors want to be paid interest and principal and want a risk profile that meets this objective. Shareholders want maximum residual returns, which require greater risk-taking.

## REVIEW QUESTIONS

1. In what way do the laws of business organizations promote efficiency?
2. Is there an efficiency explanation for the phenomenon of separation of ownership and control? What issues or problems associated with the separation of ownership and control do Berle and Means identify?
3. What benefits does debt provide? How can debt be abused?

# FINANCIAL INSTRUMENTS AND CAPITAL MARKETS

## CHAPTER 11

# FINANCIAL INSTRUMENTS I (DEBT AND EQUITY)

## A. FINANCIAL INSTRUMENTS

A *financial instrument* is an intangible asset whose value is a claim to future cash. They are *securities*, which are debt and equity claims on a firm's cash flow, as well as derivatives, which are financial instruments that derive their value from some other thing. Financial instruments and tangible assets (e.g., factory buildings and commercial airplanes) are connected. Both generate future cash flow. Think about American Airlines' fleet of commercial airplanes, or Hyundai's automobile factory. The value of these capital assets is determined by how much future cash they generate. Capital assets are financed by debt or equity. Thus, financial instruments finance the purchase of capital assets and are *claims* on future cash flow generated therefrom.

**Capital assets ...... are ...... financed by**

⟸ Financial Instruments
(Debt & Equity)

Financial instruments have two principal economic functions. First, they are contractual agreements for the rent of capital between *issuers* (those who need funds to invest in capital assets) and *investors* (those who have surplus funds to rent). For a wide array of instruments, the contract is directly negotiated and memorialized in a written contract, e.g., preferred stock in a private equity transaction. Credit transactions are negotiated contracts. For equity instruments, the "contract" is found in the corporate charter, which sets forth the rights and preferences of equity instruments, and in corporate law, which provides other contract terms such as the conferral of fiduciary obligations by the managers of the firm.

Second, financial instruments disaggregate and redistribute economic risks and returns associated with a tangible asset like a factory so that investors can choose among an array of contractual arrangements providing different risk and return pro-files. Physical assets are financialized and sold in pieces to investors, a process Berle and Means described in *The Modern Corporation and Private Property* as: "Men are less likely to own the physical instruments of production. They are more likely to own pieces of paper, loosely known as stocks, bonds, and other securities, which have become mobile through the machinery of the public markets."

EXAMPLE 11.1

### Professor Kingsfield's financial dilemma

Part I (Accounting) of this book discussed Professor Kingsfield's business venture, Kingsfield Inc., which operated a successful bar and restaurant called Kingsfield Tavern. Kingsfield Inc. financed its operations through a combination of debt and equity sold to outside investors including a bank, an equipment vendor, and Professor Kingsfield's fellow law professors. Kingsfield Inc. issued financial instruments that sold claims to future cash flow to various investors.

Suppose Professor Kingsfield is rich. He has a net worth of $2 million, which could have entirely funded Kingsfield Tavern. Kingsfield Inc. need not have issued any finan-cial instruments to outside investors, and could have been a substantial corporation whose capital assets are funded by one person. Professor Kingsfield could have assumed all of the risks and returns of the business (indeed, many entrepreneurs do precisely this). Although Professor Kingsfield may be financially able to fund the venture himself, he may not want to put all eggs in one basket. He may understand that restaurants and bars fail more often than they succeed. He may be risk averse, and may want to diversify the investment of his $2 million. Thus, he'll invest some of his own money, and sell stakes in the company to creditors and outside shareholders.

Financial instruments are intangible assets whose value is a claim on future cash flow generated by tangible assets. They are contract-based claims, and they can repackage a business venture's risks and returns in ways that satisfy investor needs.

## B. DEBT

### 1. TYPES OF DEBT

An important first point about debt is that debt transactions are contracts between creditors and debtors, and as such there are many forms and terms of debt. Below are some common examples of forms of credit transactions.

- Consumer credit card
- Other consumer loans such as auto and student loans
- Residential and commercial mortgages
- Business bank loan underwritten by a single lender
- Syndicated business bank loan underwritten by a syndicate of banks

- Equipment finance and lease financing
- Publicly traded bond
- Loan secured by assets
- Unsecured loans
- Short-term credit such as commercial paper
- Repurchase agreements
- Public or private issue transaction

In corporate transactions, there are three commonly seen types of transactions. (1) Corporations can seek medium- or long-term loans in the form of a loan from financial institutions. These loans can be provided by a commercial or investment bank. If the loans are big enough, they can be underwritten by a syndicate of banks. (2) Corporations can access short-term debt for working capital purposes through the money markets. These are short-term loans provided by various financial institutions and other corporations that have excess cash to lend on a short-term basis. (3) Corporations can issue publicly traded bonds or debentures. This form of capital relies on credit extended by individual creditors, who can be the moms and pops of the world or large institutional investors like insurance companies, pension funds, hedge funds, and mutual funds.

> **F.Y.I.** Technically, a *bond* is a long-term obligation secured by a mortgage on some asset, and a *debenture* is a long-term unsecured obligation. These finer points of definition are ignored in most business conversations, and they are ignored in this book as well. This is not to suggest that the issue of security interest is unimportant; the issue is very important. Instead, an adherence to formal terminology in this limited area of the financial world is less important than the specific substantive terms of the credit.

## 2. COMMON TERMS AND ISSUES

The following are mandatory terms in all credit transactions ("mandatory" not in the sense of an externally mandated legal obligation, but in the sense that an economic transaction cannot be completed without negotiating these terms).

- *Maturity*: a fixed date upon which the debtor must repay the principal
- *Interest payment*: a rate of return that is captured by an interest payment or an implied interest payment
- *Default*: terms and conditions that define default and remedies

> **F.Y.I.** The rate of return can be set in several ways.
>
> (1) fixed rate, e.g., 8 percent
> (2) variable rate, e.g., 5 percent above some variable reference such as the prime interest rate, Treasuries, or LIBOR (London Interbank Offering Rate)
> (3) implied interest rate, e.g., zero-coupon bonds do not pay interest from the time of issuance to the repayment of principal, but there is an implied interest payment because the principal repaid is greater than the issue price

Additionally, there are many other standard terms (covenants) of credit. In a bond, the covenants are contained in a document called the *indenture*, and the bond indenture is administered by the *indenture trustee*. Commonly seen and negotiated terms are:

- *Financial restrictions*: restrictions on various financial aspects of the firm such as payment of dividends, assumption of additional debt, and maintenance of minimum financial performance relative to interest payments or principal amount
- *Restrictions on mergers and acquisitions*: restrictions on mergers and acquisitions, or conditions placed upon such transactions, such as the payment of interest and principal
- *Subordination*: bonds can be issued with express provisions on seniority, *i.e.*, where does the bondholder stand in the queue of creditors?
- *Redemption and callability*: right held by either issuer or holder for prepayment of bonds prior to maturity
- *Convertibility*: bonds can be convertible to equity instrument, and there would be a conversion term providing a precise formula for such conversion

It goes without saying that creditors want the maximum rate of return along with the maximum contractual protections, and borrowers want the opposite. From these opposing points of interest, the parties negotiate the terms of credit, which are found in the note or indenture. The terms of the credit reflect allocations of risk and return. The more contractual protections given to creditors (such as seniority or financial restrictions), creditors should expect less returns, and vice versa. Terms and conditions allocate risk, and the lawyer is a risk allocator. The lawyer should understand these principles when negotiating credit contracts.

## 3. BOND PRICING AND YIELD TO MATURITY

How is the interest rate on a credit transaction set? There are two factors: (1) the borrower's credit rating, and (2) the prevailing interest rate environment. Credit rating is intuitively understood because most adults, including law students, have an individual credit rating that determines how much one can borrow and at what rate. Corporations have credit ratings as well, and they are determined by credit rating agencies, such as Moody's, Standard & Poor's (S&P), and Fitch. The prevailing interest rate environment is a complex economic factor that no single person or institution has ultimate control over. It is important because a firm's cost of debt is calculated as a risk premium above the risk-free rate. The risk-free rate is not fixed, but instead depends on broader economic factors. For example, below is a chart indicating the yields on Treasury instruments (note that like stocks, the yields on debt instruments are subject to variance).

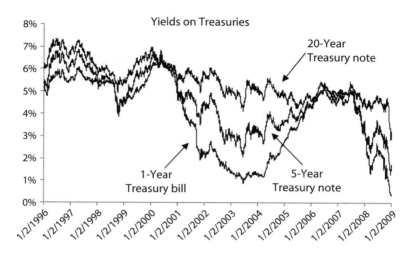

A bond will be issued with a principal amount F, sometimes called the *face value*, *par value*, or *maturity value* (all synonymous); an interest rate called the coupon C; and a maturity T. These simple factors seem to suggest that the rate of return on a bond is the stated interest payment C. For example, if the coupon on the bond is 8 percent, the bondholder is getting paid a rate of 8 percent. This is correct only at the time of issuance. As interest rates move with time and economic development, the true rate of return must adjust even if the bond is a fixed rate instrument.

How can the interest rate change when there is a contract for a fixed rate? The interest payment is contractually fixed, and cannot be changed absent renegotiation. However, the implied rate of return can change with a fixed interest payment by changing the trading price of the bond. If the bond price falls below the face value, the rate of return increases even when the coupon is fixed, and vice versa.

The *yield-to-maturity* is a formal measure of the rate of return on a bond. The bond price must reflect the yield-to-maturity, which is the appropriate rate of return based on changing credit rating and interest rates. The formula to calculate the yield is:

$$P = \frac{C}{(1+y)^1} + \frac{C}{(1+y)^2} + \ldots + \frac{C+F}{(1+y)^T}$$

Where   P   =   market price of bond
          C   =   coupon interest
          F   =   Face value (principal)
          y   =   yield to maturity

Note that the above is a present value calculation (once again we return to the concept of time value of money!). The bond represents a stream of future cash flow constituting the interest and principal payments. These payments are subject to a certain risk, which is captured in the credit rating. For an investor to buy the bond, it must be given a risk premium from the risk-free rate, which changes with time.

EXAMPLE 11.2

---

## Acme Inc.'s changing coupon rate and bond prices

At the beginning of year 2xx0 (Year 0), Acme Inc. issued a $1,000 face value Bond A with a fixed interest rate of 8 percent with a maturity at 2xx5 (Year 5). The coupon rate reflected the issuer's credit rating, and a 4 percent risk premium from the risk-free rate of 4 percent.

At the beginning of year 2xx1 (Year 1), Acme issues another $1,000 face value Bond B with a maturity at year 2xx5 (Year 5) and with the same terms as Bond A. Assume that the company's credit rating remains the same, but in the ensuing year the risk-free rate increased to 6 percent. It issues Bond B with a coupon rate of 10 percent. The coupon for Bond A has already been paid out in Year 0. The expected cash flow for both bonds for the next 5 years (Years 1 through 5) looks like this.

|  | Yr. 1 | Yr. 2 | Yr. 3 | Yr. 4 | Yr. 5 |
|---|---|---|---|---|---|
| Bond A | $80 | $80 | $80 | $80 | $1,080 |
| Bond B | $100 | $100 | $100 | $100 | $1,100 |

At the start of Year 1, Bonds A and B are economically the same. They are issued by the same company, with the same credit rating and contract terms, and maturing at the same time in Year 5. Which bond do you prefer? What must happen to the price of Bond A for you to buy it?

With all else being equal, it is obvious that Bond B is preferable. This means that the value of Bond A must adjust in a way that the yield to maturity reflects the true rate of interest. In this case, the new discount rate is 10 percent, which is the rate at which Acme issued Bond B. If so, the new price for Bond A can be calculated as this:

$$P = \frac{80}{(1+10\%)^1} + \frac{80}{(1+10\%)^2} + \frac{80}{(1+10\%)^3} + \frac{80}{(1+10\%)^4} + \frac{80+1000}{(1+10\%)^5}$$

$$P = 924.18$$

The price of Bond A must fall from $1,000, the face value, to $924.18, a difference of $75.82. This difference must equal the present value of the additional future payments given to Bond B holders under the terms of debt contract discounted at 10 percent.

$$75.82 = \frac{20}{(1+10\%)^1} + \frac{20}{(1+10\%)^2} + \frac{20}{(1+10\%)^3} + \frac{20}{(1+10\%)^4} + \frac{20}{(1+10\%)^5}$$

In other words, holders of Bond B are given $75.82 present value in additional coupon payments. Since Bond A coupon payments are contractually fixed, purchasers of Bond A must be given a $75.82 discount on the price of the bond. Thus, Bonds A and B are made equal through a repricing of Bond A in a way that yields the new interest rate.

Of course, old holders of Bond A (the original purchasers) would lose because they bought the bond at $1,000 and now the bond is worth only $924.18. But this is the risk that a bondholder takes—that interest rates would increase such that the value of their bonds decreases.

---

In Example 11.2, we saw that Bond A issued by the company provided these cash flows (80, 80, 80, 80, 1,080), and Bond B with the same terms provided these cash flows (100, 100, 100, 100, 1,100) in the same time period. The two bonds are the same, but the cash flows are different. The Law of One Price says that Bond A must equal Bond B. Therefore, Bond A must be priced at a discount that equals the discounted value of the increased cash flow from Bond B, thus making the bonds equal in price.

The Law of One Price is enforced by a process called arbitrage. *Arbitrage* is the process wherein riskless profit is made by exploiting incorrectly priced securities. For example, if Bond A did not adjust downwards in price relative to Bond B, an investor can arbitrage this mispricing in the market. She would sell Bond A and buy Bond B. By doing this, she would sell the right to these cash flows (80, 80, 80, 80, 1080) and with the proceeds buy the right to these cash flows (100, 100, 100, 100, 1100). Clearly, these risk-free opportunities to profit cannot exist for long.

EXAMPLE 11.3

---

### Zero coupon bonds

There are special forms of bonds called zero coupon bonds, in which the issuer will issue the bond at a discount to the face value. It does not pay interest. At maturity, the bond is paid at face value. For example, an investor pays $750 for Bond Z for and will get $1,000 in payment in Year 5.

| | Yr. 0 | Yr. 1 | Yr. 2 | Yr. 3 | Yr. 4 | Yr. 5 |
|---|---|---|---|---|---|---|
| Bond Z cash flow | ($750) | $0 | $0 | $0 | $0 | $1,000 |

*What is the interest rate on a zero coupon bond?* It is the yield on the bond. The yield is the implied rate of return. In other words, it is the internal rate of return (IRR) on the investment.

$$750 = \frac{1000}{(1+y)^5} \quad \Rightarrow \quad y = 5.9\%$$

In other words,

$$750 \times (1 + 5.9\%)^5 = 1000$$

Thus, we can calculate the implied interest rate of zero coupon bonds, and compare it to other bonds that pay periodic interest rates.

---

The coupon rate (or the stated interest rate in the bond instrument) is not the true rate of interest. As interest rates change, the bond price must reflect the true interest rate, which is the yield to maturity. Yield to maturity is the widely accepted measure of the rate of return, and it can provide apple-to-apple comparisons of bonds with different interest rates, prices, and maturities.

## 4. SECURITIZATION

After the financial crisis of 2008, many people might have heard about asset-backed bonds (ABS) or mortgaged-backed bonds (MBS). The causal chain in the financial crisis is easily stated. Rights to receive payment from residential mortgages were packaged into bonds and other financial instruments; when the housing market collapsed and homeowners began to default en masse on their mortgages, the value of these bonds declined; financial institutions holding these bonds discovered that the assets on their balance sheets were declining in valuation and thus equity was dissolving; this triggered a liquidity and solvency crisis among financial institutions and global financial pandemic, requiring a historic bailout of the financial sector.

ABS and MBS are bonds created through a process called securitization. Securitization is a part of a class of financial transactions called structured finance, which entail structuring cash flow and risks arising from some other transactions or events into financial instruments. Securitization is the process of converting account receivables (rights to payments) into bonds. The details of these transactions are complex, but the concept can be simplified. The transactions involve these steps: (1) the firm originating the receivables (e.g., credit card or mortgage payments) sells the rights to payment to a special purpose entity (SPE), (2) the SPE packages the receivables into bonds, (3) the proceeds from the bond sale constitute the consideration given to the originating firm, (4) the bondholders are paid principal and interest from the payment of receivables (and typically, the bonds are classified into different tranches with each having a particular place in an order of priority of payment). Below is a simple schematic of the securitization process.

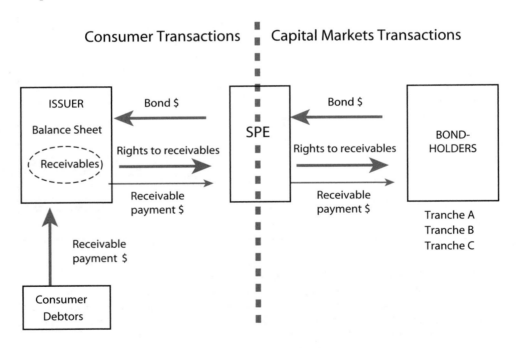

Securitization has a sound financial logic. This financing technique benefits all parties involved.

*How do issuers benefit?* Securitization benefits issuers because keeping assets on the balance sheet means that there must be corresponding capital on the liability and equity side. If the issuer does not sell its receivables, it must keep them on its balance sheet where over time the receivables are paid (and thus over time receivables decrease and cash increases). Without additional capital on its balance sheet, however, the issuer cannot engage in more business, i.e., engage in more transactions that produce the receivables. A means to sell the receivables "frees up" the issuer to engage in more transactions.

*How do the bondholders benefit?* Securitization benefits bondholders because it allows them to invest directly in the underlying activity—home ownership or credit card transactions or student loan transactions—without undertaking the firm specific risks associated with the issuer. In other words, securitization allows an investment in Bank of America's mortgage or credit card portfolio without having to invest in Bank of America's bonds or stock. It removes the risk of bad things happening to Bank of America vis-à-vis the underlying portfolio of receivables. It provides investors in the capital markets an alternative investment vehicle to invest directly in the underlying activities generating the receivables.

*How do consumers benefit?* Securitization benefits consumers because it expands the pool of capital supporting the underlying activities generating the receivables. Without securitization, the only investors in, for example, residential mortgages would be financial institutions that underwrite the mortgages, keep them on the balance sheet, and wait for payment. The amount of mortgages that could be underwritten would be limited by the capital held at these institutions. (Can a single insurance company with $10 million of equity on the balance sheet underwrite $100 billion of hurricane risk for the entire state of Florida?) Securitization allows bondholders to provide their capital in support of the underlying activities, thus dramatically increasing the amount of capital. An increase in capital means that there is a corresponding increase in amount of loans that could be made toward home purchases, education, auto purchases, credit card purchases, and other borrowing activities. (How much debt *should* be available is a policy question that is not answered or answerable by the intrinsic nature of the financing technique.)

---

What happens to the securitization process when the creditworthiness of the receivables that are packaged into bonds is consistently of poor quality?

What happens when the professionals who structure these transactions (investment bankers, attorneys and accountants) fail to understand or callously ignore the rule of "garbage in, garbage out"?

What happens when the credit rating agencies that are suppose to rate these bonds fail to appreciate the true quality of the pool of receivables constituting the source of funds to pay the principal and interest on the bonds?

---

## C. PREFERRED STOCK

*Preferred stock* is a form of equity along with common stock. The rights of preferred stock are designed in the corporation's articles of incorporation, and they are contractual in nature. The Delaware General Corporation Law section 151(a) enables a corporation to issue stock and provides:

> Every corporation may issue *one or more classes of stock* or one or more series of stock within any class thereof, any or all of which classes may be of stock with par value or stock without par value and which classes or series may have such voting

powers, full or limited, or no voting powers, and such designations, *preferences and relative, participating, operational or other special rights*, and qualifications, limitations or restrictions thereof, as shall be stated and expressed in the certificate of incorporation or of any amendment thereto, or in the resolution or resolutions providing for the issue of such stock adopted by the board of directors pursuant to authority expressly vested in it by the provisions of its certificate of incorporation. [Emphasis added.]

As the above section indicates, preferred stock, as one class of stock, can come with a variety of rights, preferences and limitations as the contract is tailored by the board of directors. The rights of preferred stockholders are contractual in nature.

Preferred stocks typically come with two preferences (priority) over common stock. First, preferred stocks typically have a *dividend preference*. They pay regular, fixed dividends, which have priority over dividend payments to common stock. Common stockholders cannot be paid dividends unless preferred stockholders are paid. Second, preferred stocks typically have a *liquidation preference*. As an equity-holder, they stand behind creditors in a liquidation, but stand ahead in priority to common stockholders, who are the residual claimants.

## 1. HYBRID NATURE OF PREFERRED STOCK

While preferred stocks are properly treated as equity, they are a hybrid instrument having features of both equity and debt.

| Equity-Like Characteristics | Debt-Like Characteristics |
| --- | --- |
| • Preferred stock is permanent capital because it has no fixed maturity date, unlike debt<br>• Dividends are subject to board discretion, unlike interest payments on debt, though dividends may cumulate into the forward year as dividends owed<br>• Preferred stockholders cannot throw the issuer into bankruptcy for dividend arrearage, though they may have contractual remedies if dividends are not paid<br>• The board of directors owes fiduciary duty to preferred stockholders<br>• Preferred stockholders may have voting rights<br>• Preferred stocks are treated as equity for accounting and tax purposes | • Preferred stock has fixed dividend payments, which resembles periodic interest payments<br>• Preferred stockholders have liquidation preference ahead of common stockholders<br>• Rights of preferred stockholders are contract based, flowing largely from the express terms of the articles of incorporation<br>• Absent a convertibility feature, preferred stockholders do not have a potential for unbounded upside economic return |

The hybrid nature of preferred stock gives the financial instrument its utility. Preferred stock can fit particular needs of the issuer. Below are some pros and cons of preferred stock.

| Pros | Cons |
|---|---|
| • Preferred stock is available when the issuer cannot raise debt due to too much leverage or too little earnings<br>• Preferred stock is equity, and so it reduces leverage or debt-to-equity ratios for the purposes of regulation of capital and credit rating<br>• Returns on preferred stock are fixed, and so it does not dilute the residual return to common stockholders as much as a new issue of common stock<br>• Dividends are subject to board discretion, and so preferred stock is more flexible than debt in terms of financial management<br>• Corporate holders of preferred stock such as insurance companies and other institutional investors have a tax advantage on income from preferred stock dividends; thus although dividends paid by issuers are not subject to a tax deduction, the dividend income for corporate holders is shielded from income tax<br>• Preferred stock can be used by venture capital funds to instill proper incentives in entrepreneurs who may hold common stock | • Because preferred stock is equity, standing behind creditors in priority, it has a higher cost of capital than debt<br>• Because preferred stock is equity, dividends are paid from net income or surplus, and thus there is not interest tax shield on distribution of dividends<br>• Preferred stock may come with special voting rights that may complicate management and control of the firm<br>• Because preferred stockholders are owed fiduciary duty along with common stockholders, fiduciary duties issues can be complicated, particularly in mergers and acquisitions where the economic pie must be shared among equityholders |

## 2. COMMON TERMS AND ISSUES

Because the rights of preferred stock are contractual in nature, there are innumerable sets of contract terms. Each set of contract terms may satisfy the particular needs of the issuer and holder at the time. However, there are some commonly used terms.

*Preferences.* Preferred stocks have dividend and liquidation preferences over common stock.

*Cumulative and noncumulative dividends.* If dividends are cumulative, any dividend not paid in the current year is carried forward as a dividend owed in the subsequent year. The accumulation of unpaid dividends is called *arrearage*. If dividends are noncumulative, any dividend not paid in the year is not carried forward. The risk of nonpayment on dividends is on the preferred stockholder.

*Redemption.* Preferred stock can be redeemed by the issuer corporation. The contract terms would specify a redemption price at which shares will be bought back, and the redemption price may include a redemption premium to the face value of the preferred stock. The right to redeem shares is an option held by the issuer, and thus the redemption premium can be thought of an option premium paid to preferred stockholders.

*Convertibility.* Preferred stock can be converted to common stock. This allows preferred stockholders to share in the residual claim instead of a fixed payment on net income. Convertible preferred stock is a common instrument in high risk venture capital investments because it allows the venture capital firm to sit in priority to the entrepreneurs, but convert to common stock if the business is successful.

*Voting.* Preferred stocks typically do not come with voting rights, but voting rights are permitted. If dividends are not paid and there is continuing arrearage, many preferred stocks allow preferred stockholders a specially designated board seat. Preferred stocks also have voting rights with respect to corporate charter amendments if they affect the rights of preferred stockholders.

## EXAMPLE 11.4

### Warren Buffett rescues Goldman Sachs by buying preferred stock

In late 2008, Warren Buffett bought a new issue of preferred stock from Goldman Sachs, which needed to shore up its equity base during the financial crisis of 2008-2009. The following is a Wall Street Journal article on the capital raise.

### *Warren Buffett Makes an Offer That Goldman Sachs Can't Refuse*
#### Wall Street Journal (Sept. 28, 2008)

Fabled investor Warren Buffett took advantage of the turmoil in the markets last week to make a shrewd $5 billion investment in the beleaguered but best-run major Wall Street securities firm, Goldman Sachs.

Mr. Buffett's Berkshire Hathaway, which owns companies in a variety of industries from insurance to candy making, is purchasing $5 billion of preferred stock with a juicy 10% dividend yield. Berkshire also is getting warrants to buy $5 billion of Goldman common stock at $115 a share, $10 below Goldman's share price when the deal was announced last Tuesday.

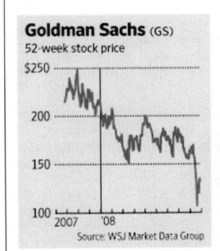

*More Stock*

Goldman issued another $5 billion in common stock on Wednesday. By week's end, Goldman rose to around $137 a share, making Mr. Buffett's deal even more attractive.

Although the deal was widely heralded as a vote of confidence in the market, it looks most like a real money-maker for Mr. Buffett.

Berkshire will get $500 million in annual dividends on the preferred shares, which is tax-advantaged for a corporation.

Preferred stock, which pays a fixed dividend but rarely fluctuates much in value, acts more like a bond than a typical common stock. Holders of preferred shares also are paid off ahead of common-stock holders if a company is liquidated.

*Plus a Premium*

Unlike most preferreds, which are callable after five years, the Goldman preferred held by Berkshire can be redeemed at any time at a 10% premium. This gives Goldman flexibility to pay off the issue if it can obtain more attractive financing later in a calmer market. If the issue is paid off, Berkshire will net a $500 million profit.

Goldman probably could have gotten a better deal by selling $5 billion of convertible preferred stock in the open market or to a group of private-equity firms.

But for Goldman, the allure of this deal is the imprimatur that comes from Mr. Buffett. With Mr. Buffett saying that a preferred investment in Goldman is safe, Goldman's lenders and those with whom it trades are apt to be reassured.

This undoubtedly will help Goldman finance its $1 trillion balance sheet, even though Mr. Buffett's purchase is expected to reduce Goldman's earnings.

Wall Street had been waiting for Mr. Buffett to make a major investment in a financial company. For months, there was speculation that he would act, but the investor bided his time and his patience appears to have been rewarded.

The five-year Goldman warrants are very valuable. Berkshire gets an opportunity to buy Goldman stock at half its 2007 peak and for a small premium to the firm's book value of around $100 per share.

## D. COMMON STOCK

### 1. COMMON TERMS

Common stock is the residual claim on the corporation's assets and earnings, and thus is the riskiest security instrument issued by the company. In a liquidation, assets remaining after liabilities and preferred stockholders are paid belong to the common stockholders. As a going concern, a corporation pays all expenses first, and the remaining income is claimed first by preferred stockholders per their dividend and net income after dividends are retained earnings belonging to the common stockholders. Common stock is permanent capital because it does not have a fixed maturity, unlike debt. Common stockholders typically do not directly negotiate with the corporation for contractual terms and protection the way that creditors can explicitly bargain. This limitation, along with their status as residual claimants, is the reason why they are said to be owed fiduciary duty by the board of directors.

One must know some basic terminology with respect to common stock. *Stock* is a generic term referencing shares of preferred or common stock of a corporation. A *share* of stock is single unit of equity security of a corporation that can be sold or transferred as an independent whole unit. The number of shares that a corporation can issue must be specified in the articles of incorporation, and that number is called the *authorized shares*. Typically this number is very big because the articles must be amended to change the authorized shares. Depending on statutory requirements, stock may state a *par value*. Among other things, par value is the legal minimum issue price. The concept of par value is a historical anachronism, and the par value is typically an arbitrarily low figure such as $0.01. At issuance, any issue price amount in excess of par value is called *additional paid in capital*. When a corporation issues shares, those shares are called *issued and outstanding*. A corporation can also buy its shares back from shareholders, a process called a *share buyback*. When stock is bought back, it is called *Treasury stock*. Treasury stock is issued but not outstanding stock.

EXAMPLE 11.5

---

### McDonald's common stock

In McDonald's 2010 annual report, the shareholder's equity of the balance sheet states the following as of fiscal year end December 31.

| | 2010 | 2009 |
|---|---|---|
| Common stock, $0.01 par value, authorized | | |
| 3.5 billion shares, issued 1,660.6 million shares | 16.6 | 16.6 |
| Additional paid-in-capital | 5,196.4 | 4,853.9 |
| Retained earnings | 33,811.7 | 31,270.8 |
| Accumulated other comprehensive income | 752.9 | 747.4 |
| Common stock in treasury, at cost; 607.0 and | | |
| 545.3 million shares | (25,143.4) | (22,854.8) |
| **Total shareholders' equity** | **14,634.2** | **14,033.9** |

McDonald's issued over 1.66 billion shares of common stock with a par value of $0.01. The "Common stock" account is the aggregated par value: Common stock = 1,660.6 million shares $\times$ $0.01 par value per share = $16.6 million. The additional paid in capital is $5,196.4 million.

1. *Approximately what percentage of authorized shares did McDonald's issue at the end of 2010?*

   McDonald's issued 1.66 billion shares. It has 3.5 billion authorized shares. It issued 47 percent of authorized shares.

2. *What are the shares issued and outstanding at fiscal year end 2010?*

   McDonald's issued 1,660.6 million shares. However, it bought back 607 million shares. Therefore, the shares outstanding are 1,053.6 million shares.

3. *At what average share price did McDonald's buy back its shares?*

   McDonald's bought back 607 million shares, and there is a debit of $25,143.4 million in the treasury stock account. Therefore, the implied average buyback price is $41.42 per share.

---

Common stocks can be designated into one or more series or classes of stock. They may have full, limited or no voting power. Typically, however, common stocks come with voting power. And, there must be at least one outstanding share of at least one class of stock constituting full voting power. The primary functions of shareholder voting are (1) to vote for directors, and (2) to vote on fundamental transactions requiring shareholder approval.

EXAMPLE 11.6

---

### Ford Motor Company's two-class stock structure

As students in Business Associations know by reading *Dodge v. Ford*, 170 N.W. 668 (Mich. 1919), Henry Ford was the founder of the Ford Motor Co. His family still controls the company today largely through a special class of common stock that has greater voting power per share. Below is the description of the two classes of common stock found in the Ford Motor Co.'s 2010 annual report.

NOTE 25. CAPITAL STOCK AND AMOUNTS PER SHARE

*Capital Stock.* All general voting power is vested in the holders of Common Stock and Class B Stock. Holders of our Common Stock have 60% of the general voting power and holders of our Class B Stock are entitled to such number of votes per share as will give them the remaining 40%. Shares of Common Stock and Class B Stock share equally in dividends when and as paid, with stock dividends payable in shares of stock of the class held. As discussed in Note 19, we are restricted in our ability to pay dividends (other than dividends payable in stock) under the terms of the amended Credit Agreement.

If liquidated, each share of Common Stock will be entitled to the first $0.50 available for distribution to holders of Common Stock and Class B Stock, each share of Class B Stock will be entitled to the next $1.00 so available, each share of Common Stock will be entitled to the next $0.50 so available and each share of Common and Class B Stock will be entitled to an equal amount thereafter.

The balance sheet provides that the company issued 3,707 million shares of Common Stock, and 71 million shares of Class B Stock. The latter constitutes 1.9 percent of total shares issued by the company, and yet the holders of Class B Stock (the Ford family) control 40 percent of the company.

---

## 2. TYPICAL TRANSACTIONS

*Dividends* are typically cash payments to shareholders. There is a controversy concerning whether dividend payments are relevant to value and the proper reasons for making dividend payments. The nature of this controversy is beyond the scope of this book. For our purposes, companies may make dividend payments for a number of reasons, including: (1) dividends give cash back to shareholders, (2) dividends reduce excess cash on the company's balance sheet, (3) dividends send a signal to the market that the management has confidence in its ability to generate future profits, and (4) shareholders expect regular dividend payments.

Common stock is issued to raise new capital, and is used as merger consideration in a share-for-share merger between two companies.

EXAMPLE 11.7

---

### McDonald's dividend payments

In McDonald's 2010 annual report, the company reported the following dividend payment information in its financial statements.

|  | 2010 | 2009 |
|---|---|---|
| *Income statement* |  |  |
| Dividends declared per common stock | $2.26 | $2.05 |
| *Cash flow statement* (under financing activities) |  |  |
| Common stock dividends | (2,408.1) | (2,235.5) |

Notice that dividends per share increased in 2010 (McDonald's did not disappoint its shareholders). In Example 11.5, we calculated that at fiscal year ended December 31, 2010, the company had outstanding issued share of 1,053.6 million. The cash flow statement says that the company paid out $2,408.1 million. This calculates to $2.28 per share. This is $0.02 per share more than the income statement's report of dividends per share, and the difference is attributable to the record date, which has a different shares outstanding figure.

---

EXAMPLE 11.8

---

### Bank of America's acquisition of Merrill Lynch

On September 15, 2008, Bank of America announced its acquisition of Merrill Lynch. On the same day, Lehman Brothers filed for bankruptcy. This was a historic day on Wall Street. Without Bank of America, Merrill Lynch would surely have collapsed during the financial crisis of 2008 because at the time it had an enormous amount of "toxic" mortgaged related securities on its balance sheet. The deal was struck as an all-stock deal in which shareholders of Merrill Lynch were given newly issued shares of Bank of America. Below is the description of the deal found in the merger proxy.

### PROPOSED MERGER—YOUR VOTE IS IMPORTANT

Dear Shareholders:

On September 15, 2008, Merrill Lynch & Co., Inc. and Bank of America Corporation announced a strategic business combination in which a subsidiary of Bank of America will merge with and into Merrill Lynch. If the merger is completed, holders of Merrill Lynch common stock will have a right to receive 0.8595 of a share of Bank of America common stock for each share of Merrill Lynch common stock held immediately prior to the merger. In connection with the merger, Bank of America expects to issue approximately 1.710 billion shares of common stock and 359,100 shares of preferred stock.

The market value of the merger consideration will fluctuate with the market price of Bank of America common stock. The following table shows the closing sale prices of Bank of America common stock and Merrill Lynch common stock as reported on the New York Stock Exchange on September 12, 2008, the last trading day before public announcement of the merger, and on October 30, 2008, the last practicable trading day before the distribution of this document. This table also shows the implied value of the merger consideration proposed for each share of Merrill Lynch common stock, which we

---

calculated by multiplying the closing price of Bank of America common stock on those dates by 0.8595, the exchange ratio.

| | Bank of America Common Stock | Merrill Lynch Common Stock | Implied Value of One Share of Merrill Lynch Common Stock |
|---|---|---|---|
| At September 12, 2008 | $33.74 | $17.05 | $29.00 |
| At October 30, 2008 | $22.78 | $17.78 | $19.58 |

\* \* \*

1. *Based on the last day of trading before the public announcement of the merger, how much premium did Merrill Lynch shareholders received?*

   Merrill Lynch stock price closed at $17.05. The merger consideration is 0.8595 shares of Bank of America stock, which closed at $33.74. Thus, each share of Merrill Lynch stock is converted under this formula: 0.8595 × $33.74 = $29.00. Merrill Lynch shareholders got an $11.95 premium, or a 70 percent premium to the closing price.

2. *From the last trading day prior to announcement to date of the proxy, October 30, 2008, Bank of America's stock declined from $33.74 to $22.78, a decline of 32 percent in a seven-week period. What could have accounted for this decline?*

   The bankruptcy filing of Lehman Brothers on September 15, 2008, was the eye of the storm for the financial crisis. However, this is only a part of the story. During the same time period, these were the stock performances of Bank of America's peers: Citigroup ($179.60 to $131.10, a decline of 27%), JPMorgan Chase ($41.17 to $37.62, a decline of 9%), Wells Fargo ($34.29 to $31.84, a decline of 7%). What else could have accounted for the relative underperformance of Bank of America's stock after the announcement of the merger with Merrill Lynch?

## E. CASE APPLICATION

The case below is a classic case in Securities Regulation. It involves real estate and service contracts. The court held that the investment arrangement was a security within the meaning of federal securities law. In reading the case, think about why the investment contracts in question should be considered a security instrument as a matter of economic reality.

### S.E.C. v. W.J. Howey Co.
#### 328 U.S. 293 (1946)

Mr. Justice MURPHY delivered the opinion of the Court.

Most of the facts are stipulated. The respondents, W.J. Howey Company and Howey-in-the-Hills Service Inc., are Florida corporations under direct common control and management. The Howey Company owns large tracts of citrus acreage in Lake County, Florida. During the past several years it has planted about 500 acres annually, keeping half of the groves itself and offering the other half to the public 'to help us finance additional development.' Howey-in-the-Hills Service, Inc., is a service company engaged in cultivating and developing many of these groves, including the harvesting and marketing of the crops.

Each prospective customer is offered both a land sales contract and a service contract, after having been told that it is not feasible to invest in a grove unless service arrangements are made. While the purchaser is free to make arrangements with other service companies, the superiority of Howey-in-the-Hills Service, Inc., is stressed. Indeed, 85% of the acreage sold during the 3-year period ending May 31, 1943, was covered by service contracts with Howey-in-the-Hills Service, Inc.

The land sales contract with the Howey Company provides for a uniform purchase price per acre or fraction thereof, varying in amount only in accordance with the number of years the particular plot has been planted with citrus trees. Upon full payment of the purchase price the land is conveyed to the purchaser by warranty deed. Purchases are usually made in narrow strips of land arranged so that an acre consists of a row of 48 trees. During the period between February 1, 1941, and May 31, 1943, 31 of the 42 persons making purchases bought less than 5 acres each. The average holding of these 31 persons was 1.33 acres and sales of as little as 0.65, 0.7 and 0.73 of an acre were made. These tracts are not separately fenced and the sole indication of several ownership is found in small land marks intelligible only through a plat book record.

The service contract, generally of a 10-year duration without option of cancellation, gives Howey-in-the-Hills Service, Inc., a leasehold interest and 'full and complete' possession of the acreage. For a specified fee plus the cost of labor and materials, the company is given full discretion and authority over the cultivation of the groves and the harvest and marketing of the crops. The company is well established in the citrus business and maintains a large force of skilled personnel and a great deal of equipment, including 75 tractors, sprayer wagons, fertilizer trucks and the like. Without the consent of the company, the land owner or purchaser has no right of entry to market the crop; thus there is ordinarily no right to specific fruit. The company is accountable only for an allocation of the net profits based upon a check made at the time of picking. All the produce is pooled by the respondent companies, which do business under their own names.

The purchasers for the most part are non-residents of Florida. They are predominantly business and professional people who lack the knowledge, skill and equipment necessary for the care and cultivation of citrus trees. They are attracted by the expectation of substantial profits. It was represented, for example, that profits during the 1943-1944 season amounted to 20% and that even greater profits might be expected during the 1944-1945 season, although only a 10% annual return was to be expected over a 10-year period. Many of these purchasers are patrons of a resort hotel owned and operated by the Howey Company in a scenic section adjacent to the groves. The hotel's advertising mentions the fine groves in the vicinity and the attention of the patrons is drawn to the groves as they are being escorted about the surrounding countryside. They are told that the groves are for sale; if they indicate an interest in the matter they are then given a sales talk.

Section 2(1) of the Act defines the term "security" to include the commonly known documents traded for speculation or investment.[3] This definition also includes "securities" of a more variable character, designated by such descriptive terms as "certificate of interest or participation in any profit-sharing agreement," "investment contract" and "in general, any interest or instrument commonly known as a 'security.' " The legal issue in this case turns upon a determination of whether, under the circumstances, the land sales contract, the warranty deed and the service contract together constitute an "investment contract" within the meaning of §2(1). An affirmative answer brings into operation the registration requirements of §5(a), unless the security is granted an exemption under §3(b). The lower courts, in reaching a negative answer to this problem, treated the contracts and deeds as separate transactions involving no more than an ordinary real estate sale and an agreement by the seller to manage the property for the buyer.

The term "investment contract" is undefined by the Securities Act or by relevant legislative reports. But the term was common in many state "blue sky" laws in existence prior to the adoption of the federal statute and, although the term was also undefined by the state laws, it had been broadly construed by state courts so as to afford the investing public a full measure of protection. Form was disregarded for substance and emphasis was placed upon economic reality. An investment contract thus came to mean a contract or scheme for "the placing of capital or laying out of money in a way intended to secure income or profit from its employment." This definition was uniformly applied by state courts to a variety of situations where individuals were led to invest money in a common enterprise with the expectation that they would earn a profit solely through the efforts of the promoter or of some one other than themselves.

By including an investment contract within the scope of §2(1) of the Securities Act, Congress was using a term the meaning of which had been crystallized by this prior judicial interpretation. It is therefore reasonable to attach that meaning to the term as used by Congress, especially since such a definition is consistent with the statutory aims. In other words, an investment contract for purposes of the Securities Act means a contract, transaction or scheme whereby a person invests his money in a common enterprise and is led to expect profits solely from the efforts of the promoter or a third party, it being immaterial whether the shares in the enterprise are evidenced by formal certificates or by nominal interests in the physical assets employed in the enterprise. . . . It permits the fulfillment of the statutory purpose of compelling full and fair disclosure relative to the issuance of "the many types of instruments that in our commercial world fall within the ordinary concept of a security." It embodies a flexible rather than a static principle, one that is capable of adaptation to meet the countless and variable schemes devised by those who seek the use of the money of others on the promise of profits.

---

3. The term "security" means any note, stock, treasury stock, bond, debenture, evidence of indebtedness, certificate of interest or participation in any profit-sharing agreement, collateral-trust certificate, preorganization certificate or subscription, transferable share, investment contract, voting-trust certificate, certificate of deposit for a security, fractional undivided interest in oil, gas, or other mineral rights, or, in general, any interest or instrument commonly known as a "security," or any certificate of interest or participation in, temporary or interim certificate for, receipt for, guarantee of, or warrant or right to subscribe to or purchase, any of the foregoing.

The transactions in this case clearly involve investment contracts as so defined. The respondent companies are offering something more than fee simple interests in land, something different from a farm or orchard coupled with management services. They are offering an opportunity to contribute money and to share in the profits of a large citrus fruit enterprise managed and partly owned by respondents. They are offering this opportunity to persons who reside in distant localities and who lack the equipment and experience requisite to the cultivation, harvesting and marketing of the citrus products. Such persons have no desire to occupy the land or to develop it themselves; they are attracted solely by the prospects of a return on their investment. Indeed, individual development of the plots of land that are offered and sold would seldom be economically feasible due to their small size. Such tracts gain utility as citrus groves only when cultivated and developed as component parts of a larger area. A common enterprise managed by respondents or third parties with adequate personnel and equipment is therefore essential if the investors are to achieve their paramount aim of a return on their investments. Their respective shares in this enterprise are evidenced by land sales contracts and warranty deeds, which serve as a convenient method of determining the investors' allocable shares of the profits. The resulting transfer of rights in land is purely incidental.

Thus all the elements of a profit-seeking business venture are present here. The investors provide the capital and share in the earnings and profits; the promoters manage, control and operate the enterprise. It follows that the arrangements whereby the investors' interests are made manifest involve investment contracts, regardless of the legal terminology in which such contracts are clothed. The investment contracts in this instance take the form of land sales contracts, warranty deeds and service contracts which respondents offer to prospective investors. And respondents' failure to abide by the statutory and administrative rules in making such offerings, even though the failure result from a bona fide mistake as to the law, cannot be sanctioned under the Act.

## QUESTIONS

1. What is the difference between these investment contracts and an ordinary real estate sale with service contract? In what way do these investment contracts resemble shares in a corporation?
2. What is an investment contract?
3. What are the essential attributes of a security?

---

The case below concerns the meaning of a "successor obligor" clause in the bond indenture. In reading the court's opinion, pay attention to the role of boilerplate contract terms in promoting an efficient capital market. In what way do the rules of contract law reduce risk? How does the rule of law promote efficiency?

**Author's Summary of Facts:** UV Industries had borrowed money in the form of an issuance of bonds. After disposing of other assets, including distribution to shareholders, UV wanted to sell the remaining assets to an acquirer, Sharon Steel Corp. The question is whether the bonds (which are liabilities of UV) can be transferred to Sharon Steel, which would then be the successor obligor of the bonds. If not, UV would have to redeem the bonds and pay the bondholders their principal and a premium. It did not want to do this, and instead wanted to sell UV along with its liabilities to Sharon Steel. The indenture containing the contract terms and rights of the UV bondholders provided:

> Nothing contained in this Indenture or in any of the Notes shall prevent any consolidation or merger of the Company with or into any other corporation . . . shall prevent *any sale, conveyance or lease of all or substantially all of the property of the Company to any other corporation* (whether or not affiliated with the Company) authorized to acquire and operate the same.

Thus, as long as "all or substantially all of the property" is sold to the acquirer, a sale of the company assets is permitted, and the obligations under the bond transfer to the successor obligor (the acquirer). If "all or substantially all of the property" is not transferred, the issuer must pay off the debt immediately. The problem was that UV was liquidated in piecemeal, and finally Sharon Steel bought off the remaining assets of the company after the other disposals were completed in the liquidation plan. UV and Sharon Steel argued that the latter acquired "all or substantially all of the property" of the UV at that time of the transfer. The indenture trustee, who administers the contract terms on behalf of the bondholders, disagreed and argued that not "all or substantiall all" properties were transferred to Sharon Steel as the successor obligor, which would mean that UV must redeem the bonds immediately.

## *Sharon Steel Corp. v. Chase Manhattan Bank, N.A.*
### 691 F.2d 1039 (2d Cir. 1982)

RALPH K. WINTER, Circuit Judge:

During 1977 and 1978, UV operated three separate lines of business. One line, electrical equipment and components, was carried on by Federal Pacific Electric Company ("Federal"). In 1978, Federal generated 60% of UV's operating revenue and 81% of its operating profits. It constituted 44% of the book value of UV's assets and 53% of operating assets. UV also owned and operated oil and gas properties, producing 2% of its operating revenue and 6% of operating profits. These were 5% of book value assets and 6% of operating assets. UV also was involved in copper and brass fabrication, through Mueller Brass, and metals mining, which together produced 13% of profits, 38% of revenue and constituted 34% of book value assets and 41% of operating assets. In addition to these operating assets, UV had cash or other liquid assets amounting to 17% of book value assets.

On December 19, 1978, UV's Board of Directors announced a plan to sell Federal. On January 19, 1979, the UV Board announced its intention to liquidate UV, subject to shareholder approval. On February 20, 1979, UV distributed proxy materials, recommending approval of (i) the sale of Federal for $345,000,000 to a subsidiary of Reliance Electric Company and (ii) a Plan of Liquidation and Dissolution to sell the remaining assets of UV over a 12-month period. The proceeds of these sales and the liquid assets were to be distributed to shareholders. The liquidation plan required "that at all times there be retained an amount of cash and other assets which the [UV Board of Directors] deems necessary to pay, or provide for the payment of, all of the liabilities, claims and other obligations . . ." of UV. The proxy statement also provided that, if the sale of Federal and the liquidation plan were approved, UV would effect an initial liquidating distribution of $18 per share to its common stockholders.

On March 26, 1979, UV's shareholders approved the sale of Federal and the liquidation plan. The following day, UV filed its Statement of Intent to Dissolve with the Secretary of State of Maine, its state of incorporation. On March 29, the sale of Federal to the Reliance Electric subsidiary for $345 million in cash was consummated. On April 9, UV announced an $18 per share initial liquidating distribution to take place on Monday, April 30.

On July 23, 1979, UV announced that it had entered into an agreement for the sale of most of its oil and gas properties to Tenneco Oil Company for $135 million cash. The deal was consummated as of October 2, 1979 and resulted in a net gain of $105 million to UV.

In November, 1979, Sharon proposed to buy UV's remaining assets. UV and Sharon entered into an "Agreement for Purchase of Assets" and an "Instrument of Assumption of Liabilities" on November 26, 1979. Under the purchase agreement, Sharon purchased all of the assets owned by UV on November 26 (i.e., Mueller Brass, UV's mining properties and $322 million in cash or the equivalent) for $518 million ($411 million of Sharon subordinated debentures due in 2000-then valued at 86% or $353,460,000-plus $107 million in cash). Under the assumption agreement, Sharon assumed all of UV's liabilities, including the public debt issued under the indentures. UV thereupon announced that it had no further obligations under the indentures or lease guaranties, based upon the successor obligor clauses.

On December 6, 1979, in an attempt to formalize its position as successor obligor, Sharon delivered to the Indenture Trustees supplemental indentures executed by UV and Sharon. The Indenture Trustees refused to sign. Similarly, Sharon delivered an assumption of the lease guaranties to both Chase and Union Planters but those Indenture Trustees also refused to sign.

## Discussion

Successor obligor clauses are "boilerplate" or contractual provisions which are standard in a certain genre of contracts. Successor obligor clauses are thus found in virtually all indentures. Such boilerplate must be distinguished from contractual provisions which are peculiar to a particular indenture and must be given a consistent, uniform interpretation. As the American Bar Foundation *Commentaries on Indentures* (1971) ("*Commentaries*") state:

> Since there is seldom any difference in the intended meaning [boilerplate] provisions are susceptible of standardized expression. The use of standardized language can result in a better and quicker understanding of those provisions and a substantial saving of time not only for the draftsman but also for the parties and all others who must comply with or refer to the indenture, including governmental bodies whose approval or authorization of the issuance of the securities is required by law.

Boilerplate provisions are thus not the consequence of the relationship of particular borrowers and lenders and do not depend upon particularized intentions of the parties to an indenture. There are no adjudicative facts relating to the parties to the litigation for a jury to find and the meaning of boilerplate provisions is, therefore, a matter of law rather than fact.

Moreover, uniformity in interpretation is important to the efficiency of capital markets. As the Fifth Circuit has stated:

> A large degree of uniformity in the language of debenture indentures is essential to the effective functioning of the financial markets: uniformity of the indentures that govern competing debenture issues is what makes it possible meaningfully to compare one debenture issue with another, focusing only on the business provisions of the issue (such as the interest rate, the maturity date, the redemption and sinking fund provisions in the conversion rate) and the economic conditions of the issuer, without being misled by peculiarities in the underlying instruments.

Whereas participants in the capital market can adjust their affairs according to a uniform interpretation, whether it be correct or not as an initial proposition, the creation of enduring uncertainties as to the meaning of boilerplate provisions would decrease the value of all debenture issues and greatly impair the efficient working of capital markets. Such uncertainties would vastly increase the risks and, therefore, the costs of borrowing with no offsetting benefits either in the capital market or in the administration of justice. Just such uncertainties would be created if interpretation of boilerplate provisions were submitted to juries sitting in every judicial district in the nation. . . .

We turn now to the meaning of the successor obligor clauses. Interpretation of indenture provisions is a matter of basic contract law. As the *Commentaries* at 2 state:

> The second fundamental characteristic of long term debt financing is that the rights of holders of the debt securities are largely a matter of contract. There is no governing body of statutory or common law that protects the holder of unsecured debt securities against harmful acts by the debtor except in the most extreme situations. . . . [T]he debt securityholder can do nothing to protect himself against actions of the borrower which jeopardize its ability to pay the debt unless he . . . establishes his rights through contractual provisions set forth in the . . . indenture.

Contract language is thus the starting point in the search for meaning and Sharon argues strenuously that the language of the successor obligor clauses clearly permits its assumption of UV's public debt. Sharon's argument is a masterpiece of simplicity: on November 26, 1979, it bought everything UV owned; therefore, the transaction was a "sale" of "all" UV's "assets." In Sharon's view, the contention of the Indenture Trustees and Debentureholders that proceeds from earlier sales in a predetermined plan of piecemeal liquidation may not be counted in determining whether a later sale involves "all assets" must be rejected because it imports a meaning not evident in the language.

Sharon's literalist approach simply proves too much. If proceeds from earlier piecemeal sales are "assets," then UV continued to own "all" its "assets" even after the Sharon transaction since the proceeds of that transaction, including the $107 million cash for cash "sale," went into the UV treasury. If the language is to be given the "literal" meaning attributed to it by Sharon, therefore, UV's "assets" were not "sold" on November 26 and the ensuing liquidation requires the redemption of the debentures by UV. Sharon's literal approach is thus self-defeating.

The words "all or substantially all" are used in a variety of statutory and contractual provisions relating to transfers of assets and have been given meaning in light of the particular context and evident purpose. Sharon argues that such decisions are distinguishable because they serve the purpose of either shareholder protection or enforcement of the substance of the Internal Revenue Code. Even if such distinctions are valid, these cases nevertheless demonstrate that a literal reading of the words "all or substantially all" is not helpful apart from reference to the underlying purpose to be served. We turn, therefore, to that purpose.

Sharon argues that the sole purpose of successor obligor clauses is to leave the borrower free to merge, liquidate or to sell its assets in order to enter a wholly new business free of public debt and that they are not intended to offer any protection to lenders. On their face, however, they seem designed to protect lenders as well by assuring a degree of continuity of assets. Thus, a borrower which sells all its assets does not have an option to continue holding the debt. It must either assign the debt or pay it off. As the *Commentaries* state at 290:

> The decision to invest in the debt obligations of a corporation is based on the repayment potential of a business enterprise possessing specific financial characteristics. The ability of the enterprise to produce earnings often depends on particular assets which it owns. Obviously, if the enterprise is changed through consolidation with or merged into another corporation or through disposition of assets, the financial characteristics and repayment potential on which the lender relied may be altered adversely.

The single reported decision construing a successor obligor clause . . . clearly held that one purpose of the clause was to insure that the principal operating assets of a borrower are available for satisfaction of the debt.

Sharon seeks to rebut such inferences by arguing that a number of transactions which seriously dilute the assets of a company are perfectly permissible under such clauses. For example, UV might merge with, or sell its assets to, a company which has a miniscule equity base and is debt heavy. They argue from these examples that the successor obligor clause was not intended to protect borrowers from the kind of transaction in which UV and Sharon engaged.

We disagree. In fact, a substantial degree of protection against diluting transactions exists for the lender. Lenders can rely, for example, on the self-interest of equityholders for protection against mergers which result in a firm with a substantially greater danger of insolvency. So far as the sale of assets to such a firm is concerned, that can occur but substantial protection exists even there since the more debt heavy the purchaser, the less likely it is that the seller's equityholders would accept anything but cash for the assets. A sale to a truly crippled firm is thus unlikely given the self-interest of the equityholders. After a sale, moreover, the lenders would continue to have the protection of the original assets. In both mergers and sales, complete protection against an increase in the borrower's risk is not available in the absence of more specific restrictions, but the self-interest of equityholders imposes a real and substantial limit to that increase in risk. The failure of successor obligor clauses to provide even more protection hardly permits an inference that they are designed solely for the benefit of borrowers.

Sharon poses hypotheticals closer to home in the hope of demonstrating that successor obligor clauses protect only borrowers: e.g., a transaction involving a sale of Federal and the oil and gas properties in the regular course of UV's business followed by an $18 per share distribution to shareholders after which the assets are sold to Sharon and Sharon assumes the indenture obligations. To the extent that a decision to sell off some properties is not part of an overall scheme to liquidate and is made in the regular course of business it is considerably different from a plan of piecemeal liquidation, whether or not followed by independent and subsequent decisions to sell off the rest. A sale in the absence of a plan to liquidate is undertaken because the directors expect the sale to strengthen the corporation as a going concern. A plan of liquidation, however, may be undertaken solely because of the financial needs and opportunities or the tax status of the major shareholders. In the latter case, relatively quick sales may be at low prices or may break up profitable asset combinations, thus drastically increasing the lender's risks if the last sale assigns the public debt. In this case, for example, tax considerations compelled completion of the liquidation within 12 months. The fact that piecemeal sales in the regular course of business are permitted thus does not demonstrate that successor obligor clauses apply to piecemeal liquidations, allowing the buyer last in time to assume the entire public debt.

We hold, therefore, that protection for borrowers as well as for lenders may be fairly inferred from the nature of successor obligor clauses. The former are enabled to sell entire businesses and liquidate, to consolidate or merge with another corporation, or to liquidate their operating assets and enter a new field free of the public debt. Lenders, on the other hand, are assured a degree of continuity of assets.

## QUESTIONS

1. What is the purpose of the successor obligor clause? In other words, why would a creditor require that "all or substantially all of the property" be transferred to the acquirer in order for the debt obligation to transfer without triggering redemption?
2. What is the purpose of boilerplate contract terms?
3. In what way is boilerplate efficiency enhancing?
4. How did the consideration of efficiency in the capital markets affect the court's decision?

## ESSENTIAL TERMS

Bank loan

Bond (and debenture)

Common stock

Convertibility

Covenants

Cumulative dividends

Debenture

Derivatives

Dividend

Dividend arrearage

Face value (maturity value)

Financial instruments

Indenture

Indenture trustee

Maturity

Par value

Preferred stock

Securities

Securitization

Security market line

Share

Stock

Stock buyback

Treasury stock

Yield to maturity

Zero coupon bond

## KEY CONCEPTS

1. There is a wide spectrum of financial instruments available for companies to use in raising capital. Financial instruments are contracts, and per freedom of contract they can be structured in innumerable ways fitting the needs of issuers and investors.
2. Debt contracts are a form of credit. They are recorded in the balance sheet of the borrower as a liability.
3. The true cost of the debt is the rate of return on the debt, which may be different from the coupon rate as the price of the debt instrument changes.
4. Preferred stock is an equity instrument that has qualities of both debt and equity.
5. Preferred stock typically has preference over common equity in terms of dividend and liquidity priority.
6. Common stock represents the residual interest in the company in liquidity priority and typically dividends as well.

## REVIEW QUESTIONS

1. In what way is preferred stock like debt? In what way is preferred stock like equity?
2. How is the coupon rate on bonds different from yield?
3. In Example 11.2, the price of Bond A fell relative to Bond B. Explain from the perspective of the Law of One Price and arbitrage why the price of Bond A must fall.

## CHAPTER 12

# FINANCIAL INSTRUMENTS II (DERIVATIVES)

*There is the anecdote of Thales the Milesian and his financial device, which involves a principle of universal application, but is attributable to him on account of his reputation for wisdom. He was reproached for his poverty, which was supposed to show that philosophy was of no use. According to the story, he knew by his skill in the stars while it was yet winter that there would be great harvest of olives in the coming year; so, having a little money, he gave deposits for the use of all the olive-presses in Chios and Miletus, which he hired at a low price because no one bid again him. When the harvest-time came, and many were wanted all at once and of a sudden, he let them out at any rate which he pleased, and made a quantity of money. Thus he showed the world that philosophers can easily be rich if they like, but that their ambition is of another sort.*
—Aristotle, *Politics*, book I, chapter 11

Aristotle's account shows that Thales used option contracts to corner the olive press market. He put "a little money" down for the right, but not the obligation, to rent the olives presses in the future for a specified rental price. When there was a great olive harvest, he exercised this right and essentially had a monopoly on the olive press market. Aristotle called this financial device "a principle of universal application." Although derivatives can be dizzyingly complex, there is nothing mysterious about the concept of a derivative. They are often as simple as Thales' option contract for olive presses. Indeed, virtually every adult, including most law students, have entered into a derivative contract and they are currently counterparties to outstanding derivatives contracts as they read this sentence (more on this point later).

A derivative is *a security instrument that derives its value from some other thing*. In simple terms, it is a financial bet on the future value of a thing. Accordingly, a derivative transaction is always a zero sum transaction, meaning that a winner's gain of $x$ is always matched by a loser's loss of $x$. The "thing" bet upon can be anything: plain vanilla derivatives can be tied to publicly traded stocks or bonds or market indices, but exotic derivatives can be tied to the weather, political developments, or other exotic securities.

 A derivative is a financial bet on the future price of an asset or a thing. Like gambling, any form of betting has winners and losers with exactly offsetting gains and losses. Thus, a derivative transaction is always a zero sum transaction.

Derivatives can be complex for two reasons. First, while simple in the form of contract, valuing a bet on the contingency of a future event is extremely complicated. Consider, for example, a fairly simple proposition: Will the Chicago Bears win next year's Super Bowl? There are only a limited number of football teams in the NFL, and there is a great quantity of information on all teams such that our opinions can be quite informed. Yet the valuation of this proposition is extremely difficult. Moreover, the valuation changes with time. At the start of the season, perhaps the Bears look formidable. The value of the proposition is high. But if the Bears are 2-6 win-loss at mid-season, the value decreases. Even the expert commentators and "talking heads" frequently make bad calls on who will win.

Second, derivatives can be complex because the value of underlying asset or thing can be complex as well. The prices of many underlying assets or things, such as the price of oil, interest rates, or financial or economic indices, can be volatile. If the value of the underlying assets cannot be easily determined because they are unique or they do not have a liquid market from which a market price is easily determined, the derivative itself may be extremely complex and difficult to value.

---

**F.Y.I.**

*Issuer* or *writer*: The person who issues the option contract to the holder, and thus is obligated to purchase or sell an asset at maturity if the holder exercises the option.

*Holder*: The person who has the right, but not the obligation, to purchase or sell an asset at maturity upon the payment of an option premium to the issuer.

*Long*: The term used to denote the purchase of a security, or the purchase of a financial option. The long position is held by the buyer.

*Short*: The term used to denote the sale of a security, or the sale of a financial option. The short position is held by the seller.

---

There are many different types of derivatives, and they can be "exotic" in structure. In the next sections, we will consider some of the "plain vanilla" derivatives.

## A. OPTIONS

### 1. CALL OPTION

A *call option* is a contract wherein an issuer sells for a premium an option giving the holder the right, but not the obligation, to buy from the issuer a specified asset at a fixed strike price on or before a maturity date.[1] Based on this definition, there are several essential contractual terms:

- Option premium $P$ is paid to the option issuer

---

1. The option to purchase the asset at any time up to the maturity is called an "American option." The option to purchase the asset only at the maturity date is called a "European option."

- Strike price $X$ is the agreed price at which the issuer will sell the underlying asset
- Maturity $T$ is the time at which the option expires

Thus, a call option transaction is a very simple contract: for a premium $P$, the option issuer agrees to sell an underlying asset at the strike price $X$ at or before the maturity $T$.

The profit and loss profile of a call option has a unique shape. Below are the profiles for the long and short positions.

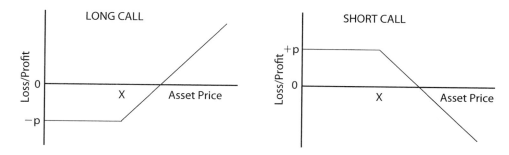

In the above diagrams, the holder of call option (the long position) has paid the issuer an option premium of $P$. The option is "in-the-money" only when the asset price $S$ exceeds the strike price $X$. When the asset price ($S = X + P$), the holder and the issuer are at breakeven (neither has made a gain . . . why?). If the asset price exceeds this breakeven point, the holder will profit. His profit is theoretically unlimited since $S$ is not capped by any artificial boundary. Notice that the issuer's profit and loss is the mirror opposite. The issuer can only earn a maximum profit of $P$, and only if the option is "out-of-the-money" such that it would irrational for the holder to exercise the option.

What is the nature of the bets in a call option transaction? The issuer is betting that the asset price will not increase past the strike price. The holder is betting that the asset price will increase and exceed the strike price. Time will tell who is right.

EXAMPLE 12.1

> **Profit and loss of call option transactions**
>
> 1. *A call option is sold with the following terms: $P = 10$ and $X = 100$. At maturity, the asset price is: $S = 120$. What is the holder's profit or loss?*
>
>    The option is in-the-money. The holder has the right to buy an asset worth 120 on the market for the contractual price of 100. She will exercise the option. The profit is 20 ($= 120 - 100$), less 10 paid in option premium. Thus, her net profit is 10 and the issuer's net loss is 10.
>
> 2. *Assume the same option terms. At maturity, the asset price is: $S = 110$. What is the holder's profit or loss?*
>
>    The option is still in-the-money. The holder's profit is 10, but the profit net of premium is 0. Neither the holder nor the issuer profits.

3. *Assume the same option terms. At maturity, the asset price is: S = 90. What is the holder's profit or loss?*

The holder will not exercise the option below it is "under water." She will not buy the asset at the contractual price of 100 from the issuer when she can get it for 90 in the market. Thus, the holder's loss is the option premium 10, which is the issuer's gain.

## 2. PUT OPTION

A *put option* gives the holder the right to sell a specified asset to the issuer. At maturity, if the market value of this asset is worth less than the strike price X, the option is in-the-money and the holder profits since she has to the right to sell the asset at a more expensive price than the current market value. If an option is out-of-the-money, the holder will not exercise the option and the loss is P.

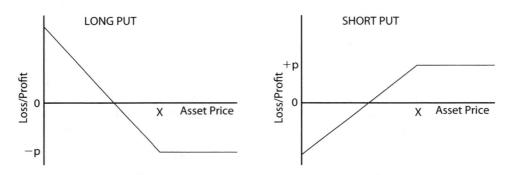

EXAMPLE 12.2

**Profit and loss of put option transactions**

1. *A put option is sold with the following terms: P = 10 and X = 100. At maturity, the asset price is: S = 80. What is the holder's profit or loss?*

The option is in-the-money. The holder has the right to sell an asset worth 80 on the market for the contractual price of 100. She will exercise the option. The profit is 20 (= 100 − 80), less 10 paid in option premium. Thus, her net profit is 10 and the issuer's net loss is 10.

2. *Assume the same option terms. At maturity, the asset price is: S = 90. What is the holder's profit or loss?*

The option is still in-the-money. The holder's profit is 10, but the profit net of premium is 0. Neither the holder nor the issuer profits.

3. *Assume the same option terms. At maturity, the asset price is: S = 110. What is the holder's profit or loss?*

The holder will not exercise the option below it is "under water." She will not sell an asset worth 110 on the market at the contractual price of 100. Thus, the holder's loss is the option premium 10, which is the issuer's gain.

Options are said to be "in-the-money," or "at-the-money," or "out-of-the money." Below are the definitions.

*In-the-money* means that if the option was exercised, it would result in a profit for the holder, which means: S > X for a call option, and S < X for a put option. Why?

*At-the-money* means that if the option was exercised, it would result in no profit for the holder or issuer, not including the option premium, that is: S = X.

*Out-of-the-money* means that if the option was exercised, it would result in a loss for the holder and thus a rational holder would choose not to exercise the option. This means: S < X for a call option, and S > X for a put option. Why?

**STOP AND THINK**

Most everyone reading this book is currently engaged in an outstanding derivative transaction. Not a Wall Street trader, you say. Consider the passage below from Peter L. Berstein, *Against the Gods: The Remarkable Story of Risk* (1998):

"Options bear a strong family resemblance to insurance policies and are often bought and sold for the same reasons. Indeed, if insurance policies were converted into marketable securities, they would be priced in the marketplace exactly as options are priced. During the time period covered by the premium payment, the buyer of an insurance policy has the right to put something to the insurance company at a prearranged price—his burned-down house, destroyed car, medical bills, even his dead body—in return for which the insurance company is obligated to pay over to him the agreed-upon value of the loss he has sustained. If the house does not burn down, if the car never has an accident, if the policyholder enjoys perfect health, and if he lives beyond his life expectancy, he will be out the premiums he has paid and collects nothing."

There is nothing mysterious or exotic about derivatives in concept. They are financial bets on the price movement of a specific asset or thing.

## 3. DERIVATIVES AS ZERO SUM TRANSACTIONS

Derivatives are zero-sum transactions. A counterparty's gain is precisely matched by the other's loss. If the long and the short option positions are transposed, we see that each counterparty's profit and loss profile is the mirror image of the other's (imagine a mirror running along the x-axis of the graph). The profit and loss lines for the long and the short are antipodes of each other.

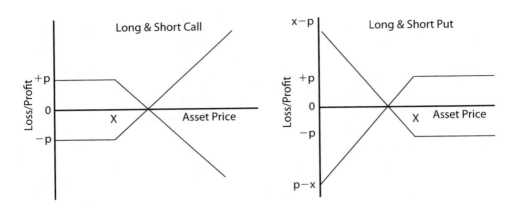

The above graphs show the zero sum nature of a derivative transaction. The long's gain is the short's loss, and vice versa.

## B. FORWARD AND FUTURES CONTRACTS

Another type of a derivative is a *forward* or *futures contract*. Both are contracts between two counterparties who agree to buy and sell an asset or a thing at a specific time in the future at a specific agreed price. Unlike an option, a forward or future contract obligated the parties to execute the contract at the agreed upon maturity date, though the parties can settle by paying the cash difference rather than actually exchange the physical asset. The profit and loss of a forward or futures contract looks like this.

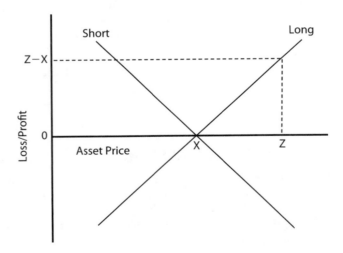

In the above diagram, the counterparties agreed to buy and sell the asset in the future at a price $x$. If the market price of the asset value falls below $x$, the party in the short position wins because he has the right to sell the asset at $x$, thus pocketing the difference between the agreed sales price and the market price. If the market price $z$ is greater than the agreed sale price $x$ (see above chart), the party in the long position earns a profit of (z–x) because she has the right to buy the asset at x which is cheaper than the market price z.

While forward and futures contracts operate under this same principle, they have important differences. A futures contract is a standardized, exchange-traded contract, meaning that contract terms and the underlying asset are standardized and set by the rules of an exchange, which is a marketplace where such contracts are publicly traded. A forward contract is specific contract between two counterparties with tailored terms meeting the needs of the parties. It is not exchange traded, and therefore these contracts typically are unique to the parties.

Another type of a derivative is a *swap*. As the name suggests, a swap is an exchange of rights to different assets. A typical swap transaction involves the exchange of a variable interest rate debt instrument with a fixed interest rate debt instrument. A fixed interest rate debt instrument pays a fixed rate, for example 8 percent. A variable interest rate debt instrument pays an interest rate that varies depending on a defined contingency such as an interest rate pegged to a variable benchmark interest rate such as the rate on US Treasuries, or the prime interest rate, or the London Interbank Borrowing Rate (LIBOR): for example, LIBOR plus 5 percent where LIBOR will vary from day to day.

## C. HEDGING

Derivatives have a Jekyll-Hyde duality about them. They can be used to increase one's exposure to risk, and thus they are instruments of financial speculation. The philosopher Thales, as described by Aristotle, was a speculator. Derivatives can also be used to hedge (reduce) risk. For example, the purchase of a special form of a put option called an automobile insurance policy, hedges the risk of the value of one's car being reduced to scrap value.

How can derivatives be used to speculate? Derivatives increase the leverage in a transaction for the purchase of the underlying assets. The same amount of money that can be used to invest in the underlying asset can be used in a derivative transaction to control far greater quantities of the underlying asset. For example, the purchase of a share of stock may cost $100, but the same amount can buy the purchase of a call option to purchase 10 shares of stock at the strike price of $110. The investors in a derivative transaction are exposing themselves to risks of the underlying assets as magnified by the greater quantity at stake.

How can derivatives be used to hedge? Derivatives can be used to sell unwanted risk to another. For example, the holder of a put option does not want downside risk in an asset, and thus she purchases a put option from the issuer who must now bear this risk.

EXAMPLE 12.3

> ### Foreign currency risk in a cross-border M&A deal
>
> This hypothetical is based on a real M&A transaction. A US real estate company is interested in acquiring a UK real estate developer for £100,000,000. At the time of signing the acquisition agreement, the exchange rate between the pound sterling (£)

and the US dollar ($) is: $1.50 = £1.00$. This means that $1.50 will buy £1.00 in London. At the time of the signing of the acquisition agreement, the consideration is expected to be $150,000,000.

At the time, the world currencies markets are volatile due to an Asian currency crisis. The U.S. company had to pay the acquisition consideration in pound sterling at closing. Closing would not take place for several months. The deal is subject to currency risk. Suppose, for example, during this time the exchange rate moved to $1.80 = £1.00$ (the dollar depreciates in value against the pound sterling). The consideration would be $180,000,000, or a $30 million (20%) increase in the budgeted cost of the acquisition. This is a real risk.

*How can the US company mitigate this risk?*

It can hedge the risk by using derivatives. For example, it can buy a put option on the U.S. dollar. If the dollar decreases in value against the pound sterling, the U.S. company "wins" and it can apply the winnings against the increased cost of the acquisition. Or, the US company can buy a call option on the pound sterling. If the pound sterling increases in value against the U.S. dollar, the U.S. company "wins." What other potential derivative transactions might work?

*Why hedge the risk at all?*

Perhaps because the U.S. company is not in the business of taking on foreign currency risk. This is what other investors may do to make money, but your client is in the business of taking risks in the real estate market. It wants insurance against a bad surprise just the way that ordinary people buy insurance against their property, health, and lives.

NOTE: In the real deal, the U.S. company chose not to hedge the currency risk because the purchase of financial insurance was considered too costly. Someone must be paid to bear the company's risk, and nothing is free in this world. The deal successfully closed anyway.

EXAMPLE 12.4

## Southwest Airlines' use of derivatives

Below is another example of how corporations routinely use derivatives to hedge risk. In this article, derivatives are a fundamental part of Southwest Airlines' business strategy.

### *Jeff Bailey, Southwest Airlines Gains Advantage by Hedging on Long-Term Oil Contracts*
N.Y. Times (Nov. 28, 2007)

Southwest Airlines, in danger for much of this year of losing its quirky dominance over the U.S. domestic airline industry, could soon be standing, once again, head-and-shoulders above its competition.

Better service? Happier and more productive workers?

Not this time. The reason for Southwest's rapidly increasing advantage over other big airlines is much simpler: It loaded up years ago on hedges against higher fuel prices. And with oil trading above $90 a barrel, most of the rest of the airline industry is facing a huge run-up in costs, and Southwest is not.

Southwest owns long-term contracts to buy most of its fuel at the equivalent of $51-a-barrel oil through 2009. The value of those hedges soared as oil raced above the $90-a-barrel mark and they are now worth more than $2 billion. Those gains would mostly be realized during the next two years.

Other major airlines passed on buying all but the shortest-term insurance against high fuel prices, giving Southwest executives a mild case of schadenfreude.

"It's true," said Scott Topping, treasurer at Southwest and keeper of the hedges. "We're not sure what to root for," in terms of oil prices. Southwest is hurt, too, by higher fuel prices, but far less than competitors, giving the carrier a distinct advantage.

Some other airlines, meanwhile, could start reporting losses as early as the current quarter, unless they are able to rapidly raise fares, said Roger King, an analyst at Credit-Sights. "Airlines were not made for $90 oil," King said in a report last week.

Just last January, it was other airlines that were enjoying the prospect of Southwest's misery. As oil dipped down to about $52 a barrel that month, it was looking like an airline with more than its share of problems.

Traditional hub-and-spoke carriers like Delta Air Lines and Northwest Airlines had deeply cut their costs by running through bankruptcy and could now profitably compete on fares with Southwest. Moreover, because they could draw more business travelers with first- and business-class seating and other perks, hub-and-spoke carriers could bring in more revenue per seat than Southwest.

Southwest also has the highest labor rates in the industry because it was the only big airline that had not demanded deep wage concessions from its workers.

Gary Kelly, chief executive at Southwest, was the architect of the fuel hedging program when he was chief financial officer. The hedges have helped keep Southwest profitable—producing gains of $455 million in 2004, $892 million in 2005 and $675 million in 2006 and $439 million for the first nine months of 2007, as oil prices nearly doubled this year. Other airlines were mostly unprotected against the increases.

## EXAMPLE 12.5

### Enron's "dirty hedges"[2]

In 2001, Enron imploded under the weight of a massive accounting scandal. At the heart of the scandal were the so called "dirty hedges" Enron used to manipulate its earnings and hide debt. The scam was operated by Andy Fastow, Enron's CFO. One of the earlier schemes was LJM1, which was so "successful" that it spawned larger schemes under LJM2 (see Example 6.2).

The scheme under LJM1 went like this. Enron had an investment in a company called Rhythms NetCommunications, a technology company that just went public. Because the stock price of Rhythms was volatile, Enron wanted to hedge the risk. The problem was that Enron could not find a counterparty to enter into a derivative trade. Enron "solved' the problem by creating its own counterparty, which was LJM1 (the first

---

2. This example is based on the descriptions in Malcolm S. Salter, *Innovation Corrupted: The Origins and Legacy of Enron's Collapse* 146-49 (2008); Malcolm S. Salters, *Innovation Corrupted: The Rise and Fall of Enron* 35-38 (Harvard Business School, April 5, 2005).

name initials of Fastow's wife and two children). Fastow set up LJM1 as a limited partnership in which he was the general partner. The LJM1 "dirty hedge" transaction constituted these steps and became a model for much larger schemes that would eventually bring down Enron.

1. Fastow capitalizes LJM1 with $1 million of his own money, and $15 million from two outside investors.
2. Enron transferred 3.4 million of its own stock valued at $276 million to LJM1 in exchange for a note from LJM1.
3. LJM1 creates a subsidiary Swap Sub. It transfers 1.6 million shares of Enron plus $3.75 million in cash.
4. Swap Sub issues Enron put options on Rhythms at the strike price of $56 per share.

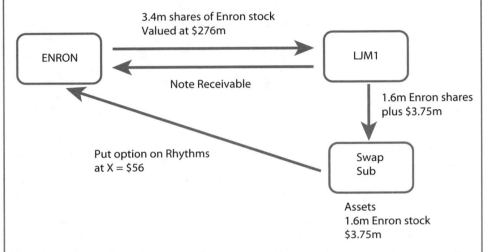

This is not a true economic hedge. Swap Sub's financial ability to pay Enron if it exercises the put option on Rhythms depends on the value of Enron's stock, which the Swap Sub would use to pay Enron. Swap Sub can execute the option only if Enron stock does not decline. If Enron's stock declines along with the stock price of Rhythms, then it may not have sufficient assets to cover Enron's loss on Rhythms under the put option, which is precisely what happened to these "dirty hedges." Bottom line, Enron was hedging exposure to risk on assets on its balance sheet with its own stock. That makes no economic sense.

NOTE: Consider the problem from a corporate governance perspective. These transactions required board approval. Consistent with its fiduciary obligations, what should the board have done? In this case, the Enron board approved (1) the Rhythms transactions without dissent, including Fastow's role in LJM1, (2) the waiver of the code of ethics allowing Fastow to serve both as Enron CFO and a general partner of LJM1, which would transact with Enron, and (3) the payment of $500,000 to Fastow in management fee for structuring the deal.

## D. PUT-CALL PARITY

In the next two sections, we delve into some technical aspects of option valuation. Lawyers will not be asked to calculate the value of options. It is not what they do. But business attorneys who work in complex transactions or sophisticated business environments should know the basic concepts of option valuation, at least enough to be conversant with the client at a basic level. The math here is not difficult, but the concepts are.

Options are subject to a law of valuation called the *put-call parity*. This means that there is a relationship between the put and the call options. There is a mathematical relationship between the call option, put option, stock price, and strike price, which is the put-call parity:

$$S + P = C + \frac{X}{(1 + R)^T}$$

The stock price $S$ plus the price of the put option $P$ must equal the call option $C$ plus strike price $X$ discounted to present value. This relationship is intuitively seen by drawing the profit and loss profiles.

If an investor owns stock (the underlying asset) and the long position on the put, the profit and loss profile of the combined position is seen below. To derive the combined position, transpose the stock and the put on top of each other and add up the gains and losses from each position. The resulting graph is seen in (S + P).

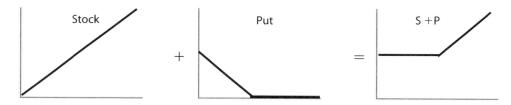

If an investor owns the discounted strike price and the long position on the call, the profit and loss profile of the combined position is seen below.

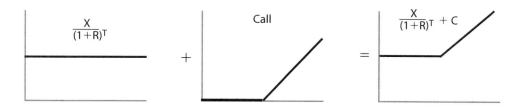

Why must the put-call parity hold? If it does not, an arbitrage opportunity occurs and an investor can make riskless profit by selling the overpriced option, and buying the underpriced option. As the above graphs show, the cash flows from the two

position, $\left( C + \dfrac{X}{(1 + R)^T} \right)$ and (S + P), are identical. Based on the Law of One

Price, financial instruments with the same cash flow must be priced the same.

EXAMPLE 12.6

## Arbitrage enforcement of the put-call parity

Assume that S = \$31, P = \$2, C = \$1, and $X/(1 + R)^T = \$32$. Assume that T = 1 year, and the risk-free rate R = 6.25%. This means that the strike price X = \$34.

$$S + P = C + \frac{X}{(1 + R)^T}$$

$$31 + 2 = 1 + \frac{34}{(1 + 6.25\%)^1}$$

The put-call parity holds true at the price of \$33 on each side of the equation. Assume now that (S + P) is overpriced, and that it is actually trading at \$35 (we don't know whether S or P or both are mispriced, but (S + P) is trading higher than the opposite side of the put-call parity).

*If an investor spots this error, can she earn a riskless profit?* Yes. She should sell (S + P), thus receiving \$35, and use the funds to buy $(C + X/(1 + R)^T)$. She would purchase a call option for \$1 and invest \$32 at the risk-free rate, which would grow to \$34 in one year at the rate of 6.25 percent. Note that there would be \$2 remaining after these purchases.

*The investor has sold the stock S and the put option P. Is the investor at risk if the stock price moves in any particular direction?* No. She is perfectly hedged. Let's see why. Assume at maturity, the stock price $S_m$ is either in-the-money or out-of-the-money as to the put option.

|  | PROFIT (LOSS) AT $S_m = 40$ | PROFIT (LOSS) AT $S_m = 20$ |
|---|---|---|
| **Short position** | | |
| S (Sold at \$31) | (9) | 11 |
| P (Sold at \$2) | 2 | (12) |
| Net profit (loss) | (7) | (1) |
| **Long position** | | |
| C (bought at \$1) | 5 | (1) |
| X/(1+R) | 2 | 2 |
| Net profit (loss) | 7 | 1 |

We see that by shorting (S + P) and going long on $(C + X/(1 + R)^T)$, the investor is perfectly hedged. If $S_m = 40$, the investor loses (7) on the short position, but gain 7 on the long position. Similarly, if $S_m = 20$, the investor loses (1) on the short position, but gains 1 on the long position.

*How does the investor achieve arbitrage if she is perfectly hedged?* Recall that she shorted (S + P) for \$35, and it only took \$33 to fund the long position $(C + X/(1 + R)^T)$. She has pocketed the \$2 difference without any risk of losing it because the long position perfected hedged the short position.

# E. VALUING OPTIONS AND THE BLACK-SCHOLES FORMULA

## 1. DETERMINANTS OF OPTION VALUE

The put-call parity states the economic relationship between the put and the call option on a common underlying asset. But it does not give us an independent means to value an option. The valuation of options and derivatives is perhaps the most difficult subject in financial economics because there is much high mathematics involved (the type of mathematics used in rocket science). We cannot cover the mathematics in this book, but we can gain an intuitive insight into the formal math using only basic arithmetic. You are warned that even the following stylized discussion using simple math can be difficult to follow, which illustrates how complex derivative valuation can be.

An option contract is legally simple. It is the right to buy (call option) or sell (put option) an asset for a fixed price by a maturity date. There are only several contract terms:

$S$ = current price of the asset
$X$ = strike price
$P$ = writer's option premium
$T$ = time

At any given point in time, the exercise value of an option is easy to calculate. The profit/loss of the holder of a call option is $V = \max [(S - X - P), - P]$. The issuer's profit/loss is $V = \min [(X - S + P), P]$. These mathematical expressions can be intimidating, but they are in fact quite simple.

EXAMPLE 12.7

---

### Exercise value of options

On January 1, Issuer writes an option for a premium of $5 giving Holder the right to purchase one share of World's Best Co. Inc. for $100 by June 30 maturity. The current stock price is $80 per share.

*What is the profit or loss for Issuer and Holder on March 31, three months before expiration of the option, for these stock prices?*

| STOCK PRICE $S_{(March\ 31)}$ | ISSUER PROFIT & LOSS $V = min [(X - S + P), P]$ | HOLDER PROFIT & LOSS $V = max [(S - X - P), -P]$ |
|---|---|---|
| $80 | min [(100 − 80 + 5), 5] = +5 | max [(80 − 100 − 5), − 5] = − 5 |
| $100 | min [(100 − 100 + 5), 5] = +5 | max [(100 − 100 − 5), − 5] = − 5 |
| $120 | min [(100 − 120 + 5), 5] = −15 | max [(120 − 100 − 5), − 5] = +15 |

Notice that the issuer can never make more money than the option premium, but the potential downside is theoretically infinite. The holder can never lose more money than the loss of the option premium paid to the issuer. The potential upside is theoretically infinite.

---

> *Assume that on March 31 the stock price is $120. Does this mean that the option has a value of $15?*
>
> No. It must be worth *more* than $15. If the option was exercise price on March 31, Holder profits by $15. But the option still has three months left until its maturity on June 30. The holders of options purchase the option precisely because it provides an option in the future. Three months of potential future upside must be compensated, meaning that it must be incorporated into the value of the option. Therefore, the value of the option on March 31 must be:
>
> $$\text{Value} = \text{Exercise Value} + \text{Time Value}$$
>
> Option value equals the exercise value only at maturity. Before maturity, there is always time value to consider. A bright elementary school graduate can calculate the exercise value. But how do we calculate the time value?

Option value depends on the interplay of six variables: the current stock price, the strike price, time to maturity, the volatility (variance) of the underlying stock price, the risk-free rate, and dividend yield. All else being equal, each factor affects option value. Because there are six variables, some of which are moving independently, the value of an option is a very challenging mathematical exercise. Option value fluctuates continuously until the maturity date at which point the exercise value equals the option value. This is why option pricing theory is so complex. Of the six variables, the most important factors affecting option value are: stock price S, strike price X, time to maturity T, and volatility $\sigma$. Let's think about this.

First, the value of the option increases as the strike price is closer to the stock price. For example, if the stock price is $100, a strike price on a call option of $150 increases the value of the option than one of $200.

Second, the value of the option increases as the maturity is further out in time. If the stock price is $100 and the strike price on a call option is $150, and if the maturity date is tomorrow, the option has little value because the stock price must increase by over 50 percent in one day to be in-the-money. But if the time to maturity was 5 years, the option has significant value because the stock need only increase in value by 8.5 percent per year for it to be in-the-money.

Third, what about volatility? When we say volatility, it means the propensity of the stock to move. Volatility and variance (i.e., riskiness of the stock) are synonymous. The simple answer here is that as stocks become more risky, the option value increases. The intuition is that stocks that move significantly up and down have a better chance of hitting the strike price than a stock whose price moves horizontally.

We can intuit several simple rules. An increase in the following variables produces these changes to the long position on call and put options.

| INCREASE IN VARIABLES | CALL | PUT |
|---|---|---|
| Stock price S | ↑ | ↓ |
| Strike price X | ↓ | ↑ |
| Time T | ↑ | ↑ |
| Volatility $\sigma$ | ↑ | ↑ |

Notice that both time T and volatility $\sigma$ affect calls and puts the same way. This is intuitively obvious. The difference between the call and the put concerns the relationship between S and X, in both the movement of S and the relative distance between S and X.

## 2. PRINCIPLE OF BLACK-SCHOLES

Although an option is a simple contract, its valuation is no simple matter. A theory of valuation was elusive because the interplay among the six variables could not be captured. In 1973, Fischer Black and Myron Scholes solved the problem.[3] Their option pricing formula, called the Black-Scholes formula, is mathematically complex, but the solution is based on the simple principle that the payoff from an option can be replicated by a synthetic portfolio of stock and borrowing (assets and liabilities that can be readily valued). Since a riskless arbitrage opportunity cannot be sustained in a competitive market, the value of the synthetic portfolio must always equal the value of the option. Thus, if can value the assets and liabilities at any given time, we can value the option.

It is helpful to see a simple option value calculation and how its determinants affect value, particularly as value relates to volatility. Assume that the current stock price S = $100, strike price X = $130, time period T = 1 year, borrowing rate R = 5 percent, and no dividends and no transaction costs. For simplicity, assume that the variance of the stock price moves ±50 percent by maturity so that the spread of possible future share prices is $[S_u, S_d] = [\$150, \$50]$. At the strike price of $130, the option would be in-the-money only if the stock goes up by 50 percent. The option payoffs are calculated as $P = \max[0, S' - X]$ where $S'$ is the share price at maturity. If the payoff is negative, meaning $X > S'$ at maturity, the option would not be exercised and so the payoff would be zero. The spread of possible option payoffs at maturity is $[(P_u = S_u - X), (P_d = S_u - X)] = [\$20, \$0]$.

Suppose the issuer wants to hedge this risk of the option being called against him. He must create a portfolio of stock and borrowing that replicates the option payoff. The hedge must be self-funding so that the purchase of the stock is funded externally by the option premium and borrowing. Based on these conditions, the issuer must purchase 1/5 share of common stock at the current price of $20 (= 1/5 of stock at price of $100 per share) to hedge the risk of an exercised option. This cost must be funded by $9.52 of borrowing, and $10.48 of option premium. Thus, the price of the option is $10.48. Why? Let's see how these figures are calculated.

These calculations assume that stock prices have a binomial distribution. Of course, stock prices typically take a distribution and the shape of this distribution is determined by the stock's volatility. The Black-Scholes option pricing formula takes this into account with complex mathematics. But the binomial assumption keeps the example simple. With this in mind, the calculation of the above values requires three steps.

---

3. Fischer Black & Myron Scholes, *The Pricing of Options and Corporate Liabilities*, 81 J. Political Econ. 637 (1973).

*Step 1: How many shares of stock must be bought to hedge the risk of the option?* This is determined by the hedge ratio $\Delta$, which is the spread of the possible option payoffs divided by the spread of the possible share prices:

$$\Delta = \frac{P_u - P_d}{S_u - S_d} = \frac{\$20 - \$0}{\$150 - \$50} = \frac{1}{5}$$

The issuer must buy 1/5 share of stock at the current price of $100. This $20 purchase must be funded by borrowing and option premium.

*Step 2: How much borrowing is required?* The borrowing amount is the present value of the difference between the option payoff and the payoff from the 1/5 share at maturity:

$$\text{Borrowing} \quad \left.\begin{aligned} &= \frac{(\Delta - S_u) - P_u}{(1 + R)} = \frac{(1/5 \times \$150) - \$20}{(1 + 5\%)} \\ &= \frac{(\Delta \times S_d) - P_d}{(1 + R)} = \frac{(1/5 \times \$50) - \$0}{(1 + 5\%)} \end{aligned}\right\} = \$9.52$$

Note that the borrowing is independent of the stock price movement. The up ($150) or down ($50) movement of the stock price does not matter.

*Step 3: What is the option premium?* The option premium is the value of the synthetic portfolio:

Option Value = Stock Value − Borrowing

Here, the option premium must be (1/5 x $100) − $9.52 = $10.48. The combined amount of borrowing ($9.52) and option premium ($10.48) exactly funds the issuer's purchase of the 1/5 share of stock ($20).

The value of the option equals the stock price minus borrowing. By replicating an option payoff from a synthetic portfolio of ordinary assets (stocks) and liabilities (borrowing), the issuer has hedged his exposure to the option risk. If this hedge is continuously maintained, the issuer has zero risk and so it is irrelevant whether the stock price goes up or down. Thus, we have a theoretical price for the option premium.

The synthetic portfolio value must equal the option value, lest there be a riskless arbitrage opportunity. Arbitrage is the simultaneous purchase and sale of securities that creates a riskless profit. Much of finance theory rests on the principle that market participants will ruthlessly exploit riskless arbitrage opportunities and so such opportunities are not sustainable. The possibility of arbitrage leads to the most fundamental principle of financial theory, the Principle of Absence of Arbitrage, which states that there is always a tradeoff between risk and reward because in the long-term there are no unbounded riskless gains. The moment such opportunities are discovered, they will be exploited until they cease to exist. Thus, this process drives the market's Law of One Price. Arbitrage keeps prices of the same assets consistent in spite of the different ways in these assets may be packaged.

In the option context, if the option price is mispriced, either higher or lower than the synthetic portfolio, an investor can always lock in a riskless profit by either selling the overpriced option or buying the underpriced option and hedging with the synthetic portfolio. We can prove this.

Assume a call option is mispriced one dollar higher than intrinsic value, i.e., $11.48. An issuer could execute an arbitrage by selling the option at $11.48, borrowing $9.52 at a rate of 5 percent and then using the $21 in hand to buy 1/5 share of stock at $20. One dollar remains, which is invested at a risk-free 5 percent. At maturity, if the stock increases to $150, the call option is in-the-money and she owes the holder $20 and the lender $10. This $30 liability is matched exactly by the 1/5 share of a $150 stock she holds. The investor's profit is $1.05.

Now, if the stock price decreases to $50, the option is out-of-the-money and she owes the holder nothing but she still owes $10 to the lender. This liability is matched by the 1/5 share of $50 stock she holds. But her profit is still $1.05. By selling the mispriced option and hedging the exposure with the purchase of the fraction of the stock, she creates a riskless profit opportunity. Thus, the option value must equal the value of the replicating portfolio.

The variance of the stock price substantially affects option value. Assume that the stock price is less risky and moves ±35 percent rather than ±50 percent. At the strike price of $130 and per the above calculations, the option premium is $2.72. If the volatility is ±75 percent, the option value is now $22.86. The change in variance from ±35 to ±50 to ±75 percent results in an increase in option value from $2.72 to $10.48 to $22.86. *Thus, increased volatility of the underlying asset increases option value.*

Variance is important, but its direction is irrelevant in maintaining the hedge. This is an ingenious, Nobel Prize winning insight by Black and Scholes: "If the hedge is maintained continuously, then the approximations mentioned above become exact, and the return on the hedged position is completely independent of the change in the value of the stock."[4] While an investor may take a position on an option because of a belief that the value of the underlying asset value will move one way or the other, that belief in the direction is not a variable in option pricing. At maturity, the option value is simply the exercise value of stock price minus the strike price. Before maturity, the variables of option value depends on the current exercise price, the time to maturity, and the variance of the underlying asset, but not any belief about where the stock price will ultimately be at maturity. The latter is simply the reason why one party will buy an option while another sells it. Without such differences of opinion, a liquid efficient market is impossible.

## F. CASE APPLICATION

Corporate officers and directors should have some familiarity with derivatives. A consistent theme in the demise of firms like Enron, Lehman Brothers, and Bear Stearns, and the problems of firms like AIG and Citigroup during the financial crisis is the failure of corporate managers to properly manage enterprise risk. In the case below, the board of directors failed to implement a proper hedging strategy and individual directors were found liable for a breach of their fiduciary duty of care.

---

4. Black & Scholes, at 641.

In reading the case, think about how derivatives can play a significant role in risk management.

*Brane v. Roth*

590 N.E.2d 587 (Ind. App. 1992)

RATLIFF, Chief Judge.

Paul H. Brane, Kenneth Richison, Ralph Dawes, and John Thompson (collectively "directors") appeal the award of $424,038.89 plus interest for Porter Roth, et al. (collectively "shareholders"), in an action against them as directors of the LaFontaine Grain Co-op ("Co-op"). We affirm.

This case involves a shareholders' action against the directors of a rural grain elevator cooperative for losses Co-op suffered in 1980 due to the directors' failure to protect its position by adequately hedging in the grain market. Paul Brane, Kenneth Richison, Ralph Dawes, and John Thompson were directors of Co-op in 1980. Eldon Richison was Co-op's manager that year who handled the buying and selling of grain. Approximately ninety percent of Co-op's business was buying and selling grain. The directors met on a monthly basis reviewing the manager's general report and financial reports prepared by Virginia Daihl, Co-op's bookkeeper. The directors also discussed maintenance and improvement matters and authorized loan transactions for Co-op. Requests for additional information on the reports were rare. The directors did not make any specific inquiry as to losses sustained in 1980.

The records show that Co-op's gross profit had fallen continually from 1977. After a substantial loss in 1979, Co-op's CPA, Michael Matchette, recommended that the directors hedge Co-op's grain position to protect itself from future losses. The directors authorized the manager to hedge for Co-op. Only a minimal amount was hedged, specifically $20,050 in hedging contracts were made, whereas Co-op had $7,300,000 in grain sales.

On February 3, 1981, Matchette presented the 1980 financial statement to the directors, indicating a net profit of only $68,684. In 1982, Matchette informed the directors of errors in his 1980 financial statement and that Co-op had actually experienced a gross loss of $227,329. The 1982 restatement was admitted over objections as Exhibit 25A. The directors consulted another accounting firm to review the financial condition of Co-op. CPA Rex E. Coulter found additional errors in Matchette's 1980 financial statement, which increased the gross loss to $424,038. Coulter's recalculation was admitted over objections as Exhibit 25B. Coulter opined that the primary cause of the gross loss was the failure to hedge.

The court entered specific findings and conclusions determining that the directors breached their duties by retaining a manager inexperienced in hedging; failing to maintain reasonable supervision over him; and failing to attain knowledge of the basic fundamentals of hedging to be able to direct the hedging activities and supervise the manager properly; and that their gross inattention and failure to protect the grain profits caused the resultant loss of $424,038.89. The court ordered prejudgment interest of 8% from December 31, 1980 to the judgment date.

The directors do argue in general that the trial court's decision is contrary to law because the shareholders failed to show proximate cause and specific damages.

[W]e find that there was probative evidence that Co-op's losses were due to a failure to hedge. Coulter testified that grain elevators should engage in hedging to protect the co-op from losses from price swings. One expert in the grain elevator business and hedging testified that co-ops should not speculate and that Co-op's losses stemmed from the failure to hedge.

Further evidence in the record supports the court's findings and its conclusions that the directors breached their duty by their failure to supervise the manager and become aware of the essentials of hedging to be able to monitor the business which was a proximate cause of Co-op's losses. Although the directors argue that they relied upon their manager and should be insulated from liability, the business judgment rule protects directors from liability only if their decisions were informed ones.

In *W & W Equipment Co. v. Mink* (1991), Ind. App., 568 N.E.2d 564, we stated that "a director cannot blindly take action and later avoid the consequences by saying he was not aware of the effect of the action he took. A director has some duty to become informed about the actions he is about to undertake." Here, the evidence shows that the directors made no meaningful attempts to be informed of the hedging activities and their effects upon Co-op's financial position. Their failure to provide adequate supervision of the manager's actions was a breach of their duty of care to protect Co-op's interests in a reasonable manner. The business judgment rule does not shield the directors from liability.

## QUESTIONS

1. What caused the losses at LaFontaine Grain?
2. What financial instrument could have been used to prevent the loss?
3. Had LaFonotaine Grain entered the proper financial transaction, what would have been the essential terms of the financial transaction?

---

The following is a complaint brought under federal securities laws and state common law. It concerns the potential acquisition of a company. The complaint avers that the defendants' attempted to influence shareholder vote to approve this transaction. At the heart of the defendants' attempt is a complex financial transaction. In reading the case, think about how the defendants used derivatives to manipulate corporate governance, and the policy implication of such tactics.

### *High River L.P. v. Mylan Labs., Inc.*
Civil Action No. 04cv02677, 2004 WL 3008276 (Dec. 10, 2004)

#### COMPLAINT

Plaintiff High River Limited Partnership ("High River"), by its undersigned counsel Boies, Schiller & Flexner LLP and Pepper Hamilton LLP, avers, upon personal knowledge of its own acts and status, and upon information and belief as to all other matters, as follows:

#### NATURE OF THE ACTION

1. This action under the federal securities laws and Pennsylvania state law arises from the unlawful vote-buying by Defendant Perry Corp. ("Perry"), together with other hedge funds and arbitrageurs, with respect to the shares of Defendant

Mylan Laboratories, Inc. ("Mylan"), and Defendants' fraudulent attempt to cause Mylan to acquire King Pharmaceuticals, Inc. ("King") at an inflated price. Defendants conduct violates federal securities laws including in that Defendants have failed to disclose their discussions and understandings, which were material to the value of the Mylan stock, and have manipulated the market for Mylan stock by buying votes and engaging in sham transactions, and further violates Pennsylvania state law by entering into transactions to purchase shareholder votes solely to disenfranchise Mylan shareholders in an intrinsically unfair result. Perry, which is owned and controlled by Defendant Richard C. Perry, has no economic interest in Mylan, but significant interests in King, and stands to profit at the expense of the Mylan shareholders if the acquisition is consummated. Defendants knew and agreed, but did not disclose to Mylan shareholders, that Perry would exercise its purchased votes to swing the Mylan shareholder vote in favor of the proposed acquisition. Perry's modus operandi has been to engage in discussions with corporate management to indicate that he will help to secure the shareholder approval of transactions, without disclosing to the investing public that he will profit from such transactions and obtain fraudulent profits through interests that are not aligned with his purported shareholder position in the corporation. By this Complaint, Plaintiff High River seeks to enjoin Defendants' attempt to manipulate the market for Mylan stock, including by rigging the Mylan shareholder vote, and to supervise Mylan's conduct to ensure that the voting process is fair. In the absence of this Court's intervention, Defendants' improper conduct will cause irreparable harm to Mylan's true shareholders.

2. Defendant Perry and other arbitrageurs have perfected a technique of purchasing significant blocks of shareholder voting rights, without at the same time acquiring economic interests in the shares, by purchasing reciprocal market positions in which the exposure to the underlying security is fully hedged. In effect, such arbitrageurs set up sham transactions, whereby a large brokerage firm sells them stock and, at the same time, through put contracts or otherwise, agrees to repurchase the stock at the same price at a later date. In this manner, while the stock is registered in Perry's name so that he can vote, he cannot lose (or gain) any money from the stock position no matter how the market moves. The brokerage firm also takes no risk because the broker has a call on the shares. The public has no way of knowing that these stock transfers are not true transfers but simply designed to manipulate the market. In substance and effect, the sole purpose of such transactions—which may involve the use of equity swaps, put and call arrangements, structured derivatives, or other arrangements that allow the buyer to go long and short on the stock at the same time—is to purchase shareholder votes. The transactions wholly separate the shareholder's voting right from any actual interest in the corporation by eliminating any ownership interest from the record owner of the stock. Because the voting right is no longer aligned with shareholder interests in the corporation, this creates an obvious incentive for the vote-buyer to cause the corporation to transfer its assets to entities in which the vote-buyer does have an economic interest.

3. Unless checked, this unlawful technique of vote-buying will compromise the integrity of the securities markets. If shareholder voting rights are divorced from shareholder ownership, legitimate expectations of corporate democracy will be undermined. The technique in fact encourages the acquisition of voting rights for

the specific purpose of dissipating corporate assets, because the vote-buyers—who have no interest in the corporation—will profit only if corporate assets are diverted from the corporation itself. In short, the practice threatens to destroy the foundations of the securities markets.

4.  Hedge funds and other arbitrageurs have profited at shareholders' expense in connection with a number of high-profile transactions, such as the merger of Hewlett-Packard Company with Compaq Computer Corporation. The Hewlett Packard deal enabled such arbitrageurs to profit from positions in Compaq stock but caused large losses to unsuspecting Hewlett Packard shareholders. Here, Defendant Perry and other hedge funds and arbitrageurs have improperly failed to disclose discussions and understandings between such arbitrageurs and Mylan, and have entered into a fraudulent scheme to purchase voting rights in order to transfer the assets of Mylan (in which they have no economic interest) to King (in which they are significant shareholders) through an overpriced acquisition. Because Perry fully hedged its investment in Mylan to ensure that its only purchase was of Mylan shareholder voting rights, it can exercise those voting rights *against* the interests of the company, without any effect on the value of its position in the Mylan shares, to profit at the expense of Mylan shareholders through its investment in King. If this scheme succeeds, Mylan shareholders will lose more than a billion dollars.

## FACTUAL BACKGROUND
### A. The King Merger

18.  On July 23, 2004, Mylan and its wholly-owned subsidiary, Summit Merger Corporation ("Summit"), entered into an Agreement and Plan of Merger (the "Merger Agreement") with King.

19.  Pursuant to the Merger Agreement, Mylan is to acquire King in a stock-for-stock transaction structured as a triangular merger pursuant to which Summit will merge into King (the "Merger"). If the Merger is completed, King shareholders will receive 0.9 shares of common stock of Mylan for each issued and outstanding share of common stock of King. Based upon the closing prices of Mylan and King stock on July 23, 2004, the date of the Merger Agreement, this offer price represented a 61% premium to King's shareholders.

20.  The total market value of Mylan shares to be issued in the Merger is estimated at approximately $4.0 billion.

### B. The Scheme or Schemes of the Perry Defendants

29.  On November 12, 2004, Perry filed a Schedule 13F with the SEC in which Perry reported that it owned 7 million shares in King and 16.9 million shares in Mylan as of September 30, 2004. Those Mylan shares represented over 6% of the outstanding shares of Mylan on September 30, 2004.

30.  On November 29, 2004, the Perry Defendants filed a joint Schedule 13D (the "Perry Schedule 13D") with the SEC in which the Perry Defendants disclosed that Perry was the indirect beneficial owner of over 26.6 million shares of common stock of Mylan, representing approximately 9.89% of the outstanding shares of Mylan.

31. The Perry Schedule 13D states that Perry supports the Merger and that Perry has hedged its position in Mylan common stock.

32. Upon information and belief, the effect of Perry's hedging its position in Mylan common stock is that Perry has purchased the votes relating to the Mylan shares identified above without acquiring any economic interest or risk in those Mylan shares. Perry has done so with the purpose of voting those shares in favor of the Merger wholly without regard to whether the Merger would be in the best interests of Mylan or its shareholders.

33. Upon information and belief, the purpose of Perry's scheme, as reported in a November 23, 2004 article in *The Daily Deal*, is to take substantial positions in both Mylan and King for the purpose of voting Mylan shares in favor of the deal in order to "capture the significant spread" between the value offered by Mylan for the King stock and the then-current market value of King stock (reported by *The Daily Deal* to be $5.35 or 47% as of Monday, November 22, 2004).

38. The exact particulars of the agreements into which the "Vote Buying Defendants" have entered to eliminate their economic risk in the Tainted Stock are not known, since they have been negotiated and executed in secrecy. Upon information and belief, the agreements involve a system of derivative contracts (such as puts, calls, options, collars, swaps and/or similar investment arrangements) pursuant to which: (a) if the value of the Tainted Stock falls, the Vote Buying Defendants will have the right to dispose of that stock for the same price they paid for it; and (b) if the value of the Tainted Stock rises, the Vote Buying Defendants will have the obligation to dispose of that stock for the same price they paid for it; or (c) the Vote Buying Defendants will pay to the derivative contract counterparty an amount equal to any increase in the value of, or will be paid by the derivative contract counterparty an amount equal to any decrease in the value of, the Tainted Stock.

39. The effect of these arrangements is to allow the Vote Buying Defendants to vote substantial blocks of Mylan shares (the Tainted Stock together with any additional shares acquired pursuant to the scheme prior to the record date for the Mylan shareholder vote on the Merger) in favor of the Merger, with a view to influencing the shareholder vote in favor of obtaining approval of the Merger, without incurring any of the economic risks attendant upon ownership of Mylan shares. In sum, the Vote Buying Defendants have in fact purchased only the voting rights of the shares divorced from all real ownership interest.

## QUESTIONS

1. How might the defendants have used a put option to accomplish their scheme?
2. How could the defendant own the acquirer's shares to vote without being exposed to economic returns of the acquirer's shares?
3. What are the policy implications when financial engineering can strip ownership of stock with voting interest?

## ESSENTIAL TERMS

At-the-money option
Black-Scholes formula
Call option
Derivative
Futures contract
Hedging
Holder
In-the-money option

Issuer (writer)
Long position
Option
Out-of-the-money option
Put option
Short position
Strike price
Swap

## KEY CONCEPTS

1. A derivative is a financial instrument that derives its value from some other thing.
2. A call option is the right but not the obligation to buy a specified asset or thing at a specific price at or before a specific date. A put option is the right but not the obligation to sell a specific asset or thing at a specific price at or before a specific date.
3. A futures or forward contract is a contract to buy an asset or a thing at a specific price at a specific date.
4. A primary use of derivatives is to hedge unwanted risk. Another use is to speculate on the markets.
5. A call option and a put option on the same asset are governed by a mathematical relationship among the two options and the asset price.
6. The core idea of option valuation is an arbitrage argument based on the premise that the cash flow of an asset can be hedged with a mixture of stock and borrowing.

## REVIEW QUESTIONS

1. What are some of the ways in which derivatives are used in corporate transactions?
2. Explain why a derivative transaction is zero sum.

# CAPITAL MARKETS

The capital market is literally a marketplace for capital. It is where entrepreneurs and firms go to rent capital from investors. There are several important aspects of the capital market. (1) In an era of globalization, many advanced economies in North America, Western Europe, and East Asia, and many rising economies elsewhere in the world need capital, and thus the capital markets are a global marketplace of finance. (2) Most neophytes in finance and economics associate the capital market with the equity capital markets and stock exchanges where stocks are public traded. This is only one aspect of the capital market. There are markets for other financial products: debt, derivatives, foreign currency, and other commodities. Of these, the credit markets are particularly important to many companies. (3) The capital market is extremely complicated and varied across products, participants, and regulatory frameworks. Many institutions and players serve vital roles therein, including lawyers.

It is beyond the scope of this book to delve deeply into the workings of the capital markets. This chapter orients one who has no prior background knowledge by broadly outlining the markets, the products, and the players in the capital markets. This chapter also discusses a key idea concerning a central function of the market: that the capital market efficiently values assets and enterprises by incorporating information into prices such that capital funds economic enterprises at prices reflecting appropriate returns to capital providers.

## A. CAPITAL MARKETS

### 1. PRIMARY AND SECONDARY MARKETS

The *primary market* is the market for newly issued securities. The *secondary market* is the trading market for already issued securities.

In the primary market, issuers receive funds from investors. Issuance of securities is regulated by federal securities laws. Unless exempted, securities must be registered with the Securities and Exchange Commission (SEC) and issuers have continuing reporting requirements, including the obligation to file financial statements in the form of 10-Qs and 10-Ks. Securities are underwritten by investment banks and sold to investors.

In the secondary market, securities are bought and sold among investors. The issuer is not involved and receives no funds from trading activities in the secondary market. An important function of the secondary market is price discovery. Trading activity in the secondary market provides information to issuers about the value of their securities. This information helps issuers assess how well they are using the funds and the appetite for more investments in the firm. While the SEC and other government agencies regulate the secondary market as well, the day-to-day mechanical aspects of trading in the secondary market are also regulated by the exchanges in which the securities trade.

## 2. EQUITY MARKETS

The markets for equity are varied. Publicly traded companies are traded in stock exchanges or in over-the-counter (OTC) market. The OTC market refers to the informal market for securities where parties trade securities on negotiated terms, as opposed to securities traded on organized exchanges.

*Stock exchanges* are formal organizations that are regulated by the SEC. Stocks traded on the exchange are called listed stocks. In the United States, there are two national stock exchanges: (1) the New York Stock Exchange (NYSE) (also called the "Big Board"), and the American Stock Exchange. Both stock exchanges are owned by NYSE Euronext, Inc., a for-profit company that owns and operates various exchanges. There are also regional stock exchanges: the Boston Stock Exchange, the Chicago Stock Exchange, the Philadelphia Stock Exchange, and the Pacific Stock Exchange. Each exchange has its own rules and procedures for trading of listed stocks.

Each exchange also sets standards and criteria for companies that seek to list their stock on the exchange. A listed company must satisfy a stock exchange's listing rules in addition to satisfying federal securities laws.

EXAMPLE 13.1

---

**NYSE listing requirements**

The following are some of listing requirements of the "Big Board." A listing company must meet at least one of several alternative financial criteria. Two such criteria under Listed Company Manual, Section 1 Listing Process, Rule 102.01C, are:

- Alternative #1 Earnings Test: aggregate pre-tax income for the last 3 years $12 million; minimum in the most recent year $5 million; minimum in the next most recent year $2 million
- Alternative #4 Assets and Equity: global market capitalization $150 million; total assets $75 million; shareholders' equity $50 million.

The rules of the exchange may also extend to matters of corporate governance. For example, the following are NYSE rules under Listed Company Manual, Section 3 Corporate Relations Responsibility:

- Rule 303A.01 Independent Directors: "Listed companies must have a majority of independent directors."
- Rule 303A.08 Shareholder Approval of Equity Compensation Plans: "Shareholders must be given the opportunity to vote on all equity-compensation plans and material revisions thereto, with limited exemptions explained below."

---

The *OTC market* is the market for stocks that are not listed on exchanges. The Nasdaq stock market is the most prominent OTC market. Nasdaq (National Association of Security Dealers Automated Quote System) is not an exchange with brick-and-mortar trading floor like the NYSE. It is a telecommunications network that links thousands of "market makers" who make markets in stocks by buying and selling. A market maker creates liquidity in the market by availing themselves as counterparties to any investor's need to buy or sell a stock. Nasdaq has an electronic price quotation system for Nasdaq-listed companies. Thus, Nasdaq is a virtual, electronic trading platform.

The public equity market is an international market. There are a number of prominent overseas stock exchanges including the London Stock Exchange, the Tokyo Stock Exchange, and the Hong Kong Stock Exchange, just to name a few. These locations are also major money centers. The capital market is a global marketplace for capital.

Publicly traded stocks are traded on exchanges or other trading platforms such as the OTC market. When we think about the equity capital markets, we must also consider the market in *private equity*. This is the domain of private equity, sometimes called venture capital, firms that provide private (non-public) capital to mostly start-up companies and other companies that cannot access the public capital markets. Start-up firms need seed money for new and developing businesses. The motivation of venture capitalists is to invest in huge potential payoff projects with potentially huge payoffs. For example, not so far in the past, companies like Amazon, eBay, and Google were mere fledging companies started by ambitious entrepreneurs, and now they are Fortune 500 companies.

Private equity firms solicit investment money from institutional investors such as insurance companies, pension funds, and banks, and rich individual investors. They invest the money in a portfolio of start-ups and other highly risky investments. For every investment in a "grand slam" like Google or eBay, there are many failed investments. The risk associated with venture capital is high. Accordingly, their benchmark (or hurdle) rates on investments are also high. These firms may have IRR requirements of 25 percent or higher.

 **STOP AND THINK** For a venture capital firm, what equity security instrument would typically be used? Why? What might some of the essential terms be?

## 3. DEBT MARKETS

The credit market is diverse. It can be classified into markets for different credit products: money markets, government securities, securitizations, and corporate debt instruments.

*Money markets* are markets for short-term debt instruments, instruments that at the time of issuance have maturity of one year or less. It is a market where issuers seek short-term funding, typically to manage working capital needs.

A major instrument in money markets is *commercial paper*, which is a short-term unsecured promissory note issued in the market by corporate borrowers and maturing within nine months. The typical maturity on commercial paper is less than 270 days, and most are less than 90 days. These maturity dates are significant because commercial paper with maturity not exceeding 270 days is exempt from registration with the SEC, thus foregoing significant registration costs, and banks can use commercial paper as collateral to borrow funds from the Federal Reserve's discount window if the maturity on the commercial paper does not exceed 90 days. Because of the short duration of the maturities, commercial paper tends to "roll over" into new issues.

There are several other short-term financing methods. A *repurchase agreement* ("repo") is a common way financial institutions, such as investment banks, fund their operations. In a "repo" the borrower sells a security with a commitment to buy the security back from the purchaser at a specified higher price at a designated future date. It is a collateralized loan where the collateral is the security sold. A *bankers acceptance* is a financing method to facilitate commercial trade transactions. It is a letter of credit issued by a bank that accepts the ultimate responsibility to repay a loan to its holder. Acceptance finance is a good method to facilitate import/export commercial transactions because a financial institution accepts the responsibility repayment of a loan.

 Let's put the importance of the money market in historic perspective. Most people remember the stock market crash associated with the financial crisis of 2008-2009, but perhaps the greatest danger posed by the crisis was a seizing up of the credit market. Most businesses are not banks and had nothing to do with the housing crisis, but they were in danger because they could not get short-term financing for working capital needs. Consider these reports from the New York Times.

- *As Stocks Rally, Credit Markets Appear Frozen*, N.Y. Times (Sept. 26, 2008): "[T]he credit market is considered the front line of the day-to-day functioning of the economy. Businesses depend on short-term loans to pay for basic costs like electric utilities and employee salaries. 'This is the engine room of the U.S. economy,' Mr. Marta said. 'It's not very sexy, it's kind of esoteric, nobody ever pays attention to it, but that's what's breaking.' [T]his was the type of critical short-term financing—including markets for commercial paper, municipal bonds and overnight bank loans—that was gumming up. Banks, apparently stocking up amid the worst financial crisis in decades, were reluctant to lend cash, sending interest rates soaring."

- *Stocks Drop Sharply and Credit Markets Seize Up*, N.Y. Times (Nov. 21, 2008): "As a new bout of fear gripped the financial markets, stocks fell sharply again on Thursday, continuing a months-long plunge that has wiped out the gains of the last decade. The credit markets seized up as confidence in the nation's financial system ebbed and people rushed to put money in Treasuries, the safest of investments. Some markets are now back to where they were before Congress approved the $700 billion financial rescue in October."

What would have been the economic impact if a wide swath of businesses could not meet payroll or ongoing expenses because the market for short-term business loans that fund day-to-day business operations stopped working?

The *Treasury market* is the market for U.S. government securities. The U.S. government is the largest single issuer of debt in the world. The U.S. Treasury issues Treasury debt instruments (Treasury bills, notes and bonds) to finance the ongoing cash needs of operating the U.S. government. Treasuries are issued in the primary market. There is an auction process in which primary dealers of Treasuries, typically large financial institutions, buy Treasuries from the U.S. government. Treasuries are then traded in the secondary market where any number of investors can buy and sell them. Because the U.S. government is the largest single debtor in the world, the Treasury market is a highly liquid market. Also, because the assumption is that the U.S. government will not default on its debts, Treasuries are also considered risk-free.

The *securitization market* is the market for asset-backed (ABS) and mortgage-backed (MBS) securities. This market converts illiquid receivables sitting on the balance sheet of originating companies like banks, mortgage originators, and credit card companies, into publicly traded bonds. This market is very large, the largest segments being credit card receivables and mortgage receivables. Of course, mortgage-related securities were at the epicenter of the housing bubble and the financial crisis of 2008-2009.

Most lawyers working with debt instruments will work in the *corporate debt market*, where corporations seek credit financing. If a corporation does not wish to issue a debt security, it can get a traditional *bank loan*. If a loan is too big or constitutes too much risk for a single lender, a loan can be syndicated by a group of banks. A bank loan can be secured or unsecured, and can be senior or junior to other creditors, depending on the negotiated transaction. Traditionally, bank loans sat on the balance sheet of lending banks, waiting to be repaid the principal. In other words, they were illiquid. Now, bank loans can be pooled into a portfolio, and be securitized into tradable financial instruments called collateralized loan obligations. The basic concept is the use of securitization process to make an illiquid loan into a liquid security instrument.

*Lease financing* is another segment of the corporate credit market. Lease financing works like this. A lessee negotiates equipment it wants to acquire. It negotiates with the manufacturer for basic terms such as price, warranty, servicing, etc. A bank or a financing company purchases the equipment, and then leases it to the lessee. Leasing financing is tax motivated. Equipment ownership may come with tax benefits such as depreciation and tax credit. If a lessee cannot take advantage of these benefits (e.g., it does not earn enough profit), lease financing can shift the tax benefits from the lessee to the financing company, and in turn secure a lower cost of borrowing.

Lastly, a major segment of the corporate debt market is the *corporate bond market*. The typical issuers of corporate bonds are public utilities, transportation companies, banks and financing companies, and industrial companies. These companies are characterized by mature, stable businesses that generate significant cash flow. The two major investors of corporate bonds are insurance companies and pension funds.

---

It would be unusual for start-up companies and firms with unstable cash flow to issue corporate bonds. Why?

Why do you think that insurance companies and pension funds are the two major investors in corporate bonds?

The corporate bond market can be broadly categorized into two types of credit rating: *investment grade* and *high yield ("junk")* bonds. Corporate bonds are rated for their default risk by credit rating agencies that assign credit ratings. There are three major credit rating agencies: Moody's, S&P, and Fitch. They use similar tiers of ratings. Below are some of their ratings.

| Moody's | S&P | Fitch | Description |
|---------|-----|-------|-------------|
| *Investment grade* | | | |
| Aaa | AAA | AAA | Prime rating |
| Aa1 | AA+ | AA+ | |
| Aa2 | AA | AA | Very high grade |
| Aa3 | AA− | AA− | |
| A1 | A+ | A+ | |
| A2 | A | A | Upper medium grade |
| A3 | A− | A− | |
| Baa1 | BBB+ | BBB+ | |
| Baa2 | BBB | BBB | Lower medium grade |
| Baa3 | BBB− | BBB− | |
| *Speculative grade* | | | |
| Ba1 | BB+ | BB+ | Start of "junk" status |
| Ba2 | BB | BB | Low grade |
| Ba3 | BB− | BB− | |
| B1 | B+ | B+ | |
| B2 | B | B | Highly speculative |
| B3 | B− | B− | |
| *Highly speculative grade* | | | |
| | CCC+ | | |
| Caa | CCC | CCC | Substantial risk |
| . . . | . . . | . . . | |
| . . . | . . . | . . . | |

Junk bonds are any bonds rated lower than Baa3 or BBB−. While the descriptive "junk" may have at one time been meant as a pejorative, business professionals do not construe it as such. It is a trade term for speculative, riskier bonds that pay higher rates than investment grade bonds. Junk bonds are simply an extension of the risk-return continuum for bonds. Junk bonds are used in leverage buyout transactions where debt is the main acquisition funding. In these transactions, they attain "junk" status because the leverage is high and therefore the default risk is also high.

## 4. DERIVATIVES, CURRENCY, AND COMMODITIES MARKETS

The capital markets also include markets for derivatives, currencies, and commodities. Like stocks and bonds, these instruments are traded on exchanges and also traded among market participants. With respect to derivatives, exchange traded derivatives are traded under standardized contract terms. On the other hand, derivatives traded in the over-the-counter market between parties can be custom-tailored contracts fitting particularized needs.

> The capital markets are vast and cover markets for the full panoply of traded financial instruments. Corporate issuers seeking capital will tap the equity and debt capital markets, which provide short-term, long-term, and permanent capital needs of corporations.

## B. MAJOR PARTICIPANTS IN THE CAPITAL MARKETS

### 1. ISSUERS AND INVESTORS

Ultimately, the capital markets connect issuers and investors. Issuers need capital, and investors have capital to rent.

Issuers are private firms that need short-term, long-term, and permanent capital to operate their business enterprises, and this is the sector where most business lawyers will be working. Issuers are also public entities such as the U.S. government, state and local governments, and foreign governments that need capital to fund government services.

Investors are people who have excess money to invest. Retail investors are the proverbial moms and pops—individual investors who buy securities and make other investments. Institutional investors are institutions that invest their monies. The range of institutions is broad. Major institutional investors in the market are insurance companies, banks, other corporations, pension fund, mutual funds, asset managers, sovereign wealth funds (investment vehicles for foreign governments), university endowments, venture capital (private equity) funds, and hedge funds.

Hedge funds have gained notoriety lately for their spectacular successes and failures. There is no single definition of a hedge fund. They are an investment vehicle like a venture capital fund. But hedge funds are distinguished by their investment strategy. Like other investors, they are constantly seeking arbitrage opportunities. They seek abnormally high returns, and so they take large risks for the potential for large gains. The hedge fund that gained the most notoriety is perhaps Long-Term Capital Management (LTCM), whose partners included several Nobel Prize winners. In the 1990s, LTCM was heavily leveraged and took massive positions in the market. The returns were abnormally good, until adverse global economic conditions in 1998 worked against the firm's trading positions. LTCM was deeply connected to Wall Street investment banks, and it was feared that a collapse of the firm would have a domino effect on the rest of Wall Street. In this respect, LTCM was a prelude to the "too big to fail" shibboleth of the financial crisis of 2008-2009. The Federal Reserve orchestrated a private bailout of LTCM to which most of the major investment banks on Wall Street provided funds.

## 2. EXCHANGES AND TRADING PLATFORMS

There are a number of exchanges that facilitate the trading of equity, debt, derivatives, and commodities. Additionally, there are non-exchange trading platforms such as the OTC market, and networks of institutional investors who trade financial instruments. Exchanges and trading platforms serve as the infrastructure necessary to facilitate the circulation of capital from investors to issuers.

## 3. INVESTMENT BANKS

Investment banks play a crucial role in the capital markets, though to many people their activities are not well known. The large multi-service investment bank provides several important services: (1) investment banking, (2) research, and (3) trading.

*Investment banking* involves helping companies to raise capital and providing corporate finance advisory services, including mergers and acquisitions. In a capital raise, investment banks serve as underwriters of stocks and bonds. The underwriting process includes valuing the securities to be issued, advising the issuer on the best method to sell the securities, gauging investor appetite for the securities, conducting due diligence on the issuer, coordinating the issuance process with accountants, lawyers, exchanges, and regulators, coordinating the sales and trading of the securities, and assuming some of the risk of the issuance by committing to purchase the securities from the issuer with the intent to sell to the ultimate investors. Basically, investment banks facilitate the entire process of securities issuance in the capital markets and assume significant risks associated with this process. This is a vital function.

Investment banking also involves providing corporate finance advisory services, including advising on mergers and acquisitions. In this capacity, the investment bank is a financial adviser, very much like a consultant. In an M&A process, the investment banker values the firm, conducts due diligence, coordinates the sale or purchase of the target company, and provides a fairness opinion to the board of directors on the acquisition consideration.

*Research* involves conducting research on companies and securities, and the investment bank disseminates this research to the investment community. This is called "sell-side" research because the investment bank is considered to be on the "sell-side" of the market, i.e., providing underwriting services to original sellers of securities (issuers) seeking to sell newly issued securities to the market. Although this research function has an inherent structural bias, it is important because it serves to disseminate information to the capital market.

*Trading* involves the trading of securities. Investment banks are also broker-dealers, two distinct roles in trading securities. As a broker, it is acting as an agent for an institutional client who seeks to buy or sell securities. As a dealer, it is using its own capital to buy or sell securities on its own account. By trading securities, investment banks provide liquidity in the market.

A brief discussion of the recent history of the investment banking industry is helpful. The Glass-Steagall Act was enacted in response to the stock market crash of 1929 and the Great Depression. It separated investment banks from commercial banks. The thought was that investment banking is inherently risky, and its activities should be separated from commercial banking, which involves the deposit of money into banks by the population at large. In the era of Glass-Steagall, investment banks were smaller firms. In 1999, the Glass-Steagall Act was repealed. As a result of industry consolidation and regulatory changes, investment banks became bigger or were acquired by larger commercial banks.

Before the financial crisis, there were only five large independent investment banks: Goldman Sachs, Morgan Stanley, Merrill Lynch, Lehman Brothers, and Bear Stearns. During the financial crisis, Bear Stearns was acquired by JPMorgan Chase, a commercial bank with major investment banking operations; Lehman Brothers filed for bankruptcy and portions of the firm were sold to Barclays, a commercial bank with major investment banking operations; and Merrill Lynch was acquired by Bank of America, a commercial bank with major investment banking operations. The two remaining investment banks, Goldman Sachs and Morgan Stanley, converted to bank holding companies. Today, investment banking is done under an umbrella of large money center banks with enormous balance sheets and international scale of operations.

## 4. CREDIT RATING AGENCIES, ACCOUNTANTS, AND LAWYERS

Credit rating agencies, lawyers, and accountants are major participants in the capital markets. As discussed, in the above section, credit rating agencies provide ratings of issuers and debt instruments. They play an essential role in the credit market.

Lawyers are important players in the capital markets. Markets are regulated and transactions require contracts. These contracts can be long and complex, reflecting the underlying complexity of the business transactions. Many contracts are based on templates of preexisting forms, for example, bond indentures and merger agreements. Managing the regulatory process, drafting contracts, and advising on legal risk are the domain of lawyers. Little more need to be said about the importance of lawyers in the capital markets.

Accounting firms are important because providing audited financial statements is the domain of accountants. The process of financial analysis and valuation begins with financial statements. Accountants provide essential information to the market. Additionally, accountants are important in transactional work. Their advice may be needed on the appropriate accounting treatment of a contemplated transaction, and they may be asked to conduct due diligence on the books and records of a transacting company.

There are many large national and international law firms that practice business law. There are also many smaller and boutique firms. Unlike law firms, there are not that many large accounting firms. In the 1980s, there was a group of eight firms called the Big Eight. But through mergers, and in the case of Arthur Andersen an implosion after the Enron scandal, the eight firms have consolidated to the Big Four:

- Deloitte Touche Tohmatsu
- Ernst & Young
- PricewaterhouseCoopers
- KPMG

The limited number of large, multinational accounting firms that can serve the auditing and accounting needs of large, multinational corporations presents an issue for regulators and policymakers.

## 5. REGULATORS

Large parts of the capital markets are regulated. With respect to non-derivative securities, the principal regulator is the SEC. Commodity futures and options markets are regulated by the Commodity Futures Trading Commission (CFTC). Also, the exchanges, while regulated by either the SEC or the CFTC, also regulate the securities and market participants. Thus, there is general division between securities and derivatives, which in the broadest sense divide the jurisdictions of the SEC and the CFTC.

### SCHEMATIC OVERVIEW OF THE CAPITAL MARKETS

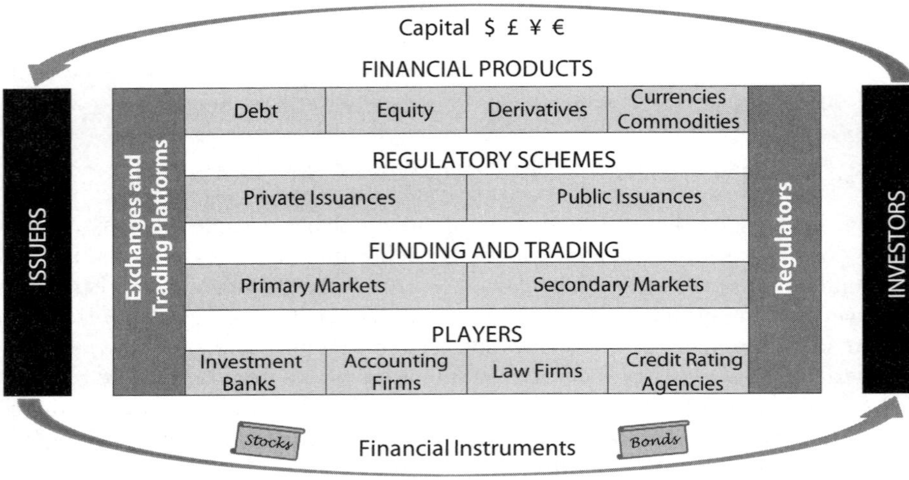

## C. EFFICIENT CAPITAL MARKET HYPOTHESIS (ECMH)

The efficient capital market hypothesis (ECMH) is the hypothesis that the capital markets incorporate information into the price of securities. As a broad thesis, this must be correct. The capital markets incorporate enormous volume of information: e.g., General Motors is short on cash; Enron is embroiled in an accounting scandal; Apple will unveil its new product in two weeks; the CEO of Google resigns; etc.

There are three forms of ECMH. The *weak form* of ECMH states that the market prices of securities incorporate past publicly disclosed information. The *semi-strong* form states that prices quickly incorporate current publicly disclosed information. The *strong form* states that prices incorporate all public and non-public information.

The weak form of ECMH must be correct.[1] We can be fairly confident that past public information is already factored into the stock price. For example, McDonald's

---

1. Frank J. Fabozzi & Franco Modigliani, Capital Markets: Institutions and Instruments 291 (4th ed. 2009) ("The preponderance of empirical evidence supports the claims that the common stock market is efficient in the weak form.").

financial performance in the past fiscal year is surely baked into its current stock price. The capital markets may not be perfect, but it is not obtuse. The validity of the weak form of ECMH means that one cannot achieve abnormal returns by studying past information such as past financial performance because that information is already baked into the stock price.

We can also be fairly confident that the strong form of ECMH is wrong.[2] As a general proposition, non-public information is not factored into stock prices. We know this empirically because upon the announcement of an acquisition with a premium, the share price of the target rises sharply to the level of the acquisition price. These observable events would not occur if the non-public information concerning the takeover has already been baked into the stock price at the time of announcement. It is true that share prices creep upwards before announcement of some positive news, suggesting that private information is leaking out and some people are engaging in illegal trading, but as a general proposition private information is not wholesale or largely baked into the share price. Indeed, studies of insider trading indicates that insiders achieve abnormal returns, suggesting that private information is not baked into the stock price.

The controversy concerns the semi-strong form of ECHM. The claim here is that prices are efficient as to all publicly disclosed information. The claim implies that price levels are rational because (1) all past and current public information is incorporated into the stock price, (2) the trades of irrational, stupid or "noisy" investors are random and so they cancel each other out, (3) any correlated trading by irrational traders would be subject to arbitrage opportunities by arbitrageurs, who would beat the noisy traders consistently until prices are brought back to a rational level. Thus, prices of securities on the market are efficient, reflecting the intrinsic value of the securities given the public information (true intrinsic value would reflect *all* public and non-public information). The implication of efficient prices is that an investor cannot consistently beat the market.

The claims of the semi-strong form of ECMH are susceptible to challenge because empirical evidence exists to contradict its claims. In the history of the stock market, there have been a number of historic stock market crashes in 1929, 1987, 2000, and most recently 2008 (see Chapter 9 discussing stock market crashes). No one can seriously claim that mortgage-backed securities or the stock of financial institutions that heavily invested in them were rationally priced in 2006. If the claim is that the prices of securities are always efficient as to public information, and thus absent trading on inside information (which is illegal), an investor has no reason to trade. But there is an enormous amount of trading in the markets. Many investors, smart and stupid, must think that they can beat the market. Moreover, the fact that stock markets have historically experienced periods of bubbles and crashes suggests that markets can be inefficient for sustained periods of time.

As a hypothesis, the semi-strong form of the ECMH will continue to be debated because it cannot be proven. Proof will require a way to confirm the intrinsic value of stocks, and then compare that value to price levels. This is a hypothetical Gordian knot because intrinsic value cannot be proven: "It is almost impossible to test

---

2. Id. ("Thus, the empirical evidence on insider trading argues against the notion that the market is efficient in the strong-form sense.").

whether stocks are *correctly valued*, because no one can measure true value with any precision. . . . It may be impossible to *prove* that market levels are, or are not, consistent with fundamentals."[3] In the end, it comes down to one's own belief about the market, and each side can point to some evidence of the correctness of their view.[4]

As a practical matter, the ECMH is not a concept that is routinely invoked in the daily practice of advising corporations or doing corporate transactions.[5] However, this economic theory figures prominently in important legal doctrines of securities laws, particularly on issues of causation and reliance in connection with securities transactions.

## D. CASE APPLICATION

Bear Stearns was one of only five large, independent investment banks left on Wall Street after a period of industry consolidation. It went insolvent during the financial crisis of 2008-2009, and in March 2008 it was rescued in a coordinated effort by JPMorgan Chase and the U.S. government wherein the former acquired Bear Stearns. The case below, brought against executives and directors of Bear Stearns, describes the events leading up to Bear Stearns' collapse. In reading it, you should think about the decisions that led to Bear Stearns' demise and the workings of a complex capital market.

### *In re Bear Stearns Cos., Securities, Derivative & ERISA Litigation*
763 F. Supp. 2d 423 (S.D.N.Y. 2011)

SWEET, District Judge.

These actions arose out of the March 2008 collapse of Bear Stearns, a well-regarded investment bank founded in 1923. This was an early and major event in the turmoil that has affected the financial markets and the national and world economies.

### 1. Bear Stearns History

Bear Stearns was the fifth largest investment bank in the world and until December 2007 had never posted a loss and was known to be conservative in its approach to risk.

Bear Stearns experienced rapid growth through the 1990s and became larger and more profitable with its business model of trading, mortgage underwriting, prime

---

3. Richard A. Brealey et al., Principles of Corporate Finance 281 (concise 2d ed., 2011).

4. Fabozzi & Franco Modigliani, supra note 1, at 291 ("Evidence on whether the stock market is price efficient in the semi-strong form is mixed."); William W. Bratton, Corporate Finance: Cases and Materials 34 (6th ed. 2008) ("The number of EMH supporters in the financial economic community appears to be dwindling rapidly.").

5. Robert J. Rhee, *The Bernie Madoff Scandal, Market Regulatory Failure, and the Business Education of Lawyers*, 35 J. Corp. L. 363, 383 n.86 (2009) ("In five years of working as an investment banker, I have never had a discussion of the ECMH with either colleagues or clients. Yet, in these five years, not a day went by without analyzing or discussing market developments, financial statements, and cost of capital with colleagues or clients. The daily tools of the trade for bankers and research analysts are accounting, financial projections, industry and strategic analysis, capital structure, betas, multiples, and DCF and EVA valuations.").

brokerage and private client services. By mid-2000, the Company increased its debt securitization, pooling and repackaging of cash flow-producing financial assets into securities that are sold to investors termed asset-backed securities ("ABS"). Bear Stearns purchased and originated mortgages to securitize and sell, and maintained billions of dollars of these assets on its own books, using them as collateral and to finance daily operations.

In 2005 and again in 2006, the SEC advised the Company of deficiencies in models it used to value mortgage-backed securities ("MBS") due to its failure to assess the risk of default or incorporate data about such risk, and further advised that its value at risk ("VaR") models did not account for key factors such as changes in housing prices.

When two hedge funds overseen by Bear Stearns collapsed in the spring of 2007, the Company's exposure to the growing housing crisis increased as it absorbed nearly two billion dollars of the hedge funds' subprime-backed assets, which were worthless within weeks.

By the late fall of 2007, the Company began to write down billions of dollars of its devalued assets. The Company's lenders became unwilling to lend it the vast sums necessary for its daily operations. In its public statements in December 2007 and January 2008, the Company offered the public misleading accounts of its earnings and asset values. Major shareholders began questioning Cayne's leadership and, on January 8, 2008, the Company announced that Cayne would step down as CEO.

On March 10, 2008, rumors began to circulate on Wall Street that Bear Stearns was facing a liquidity problem, which was denied by the Company and, on March 12, 2008, by Schwartz. The Company's liquidity fell to $2 billion on March 13, 2008 and Schwartz and JPMorgan CEO Jamie Dimon ("Dimon") began negotiations for Bear Stearns to be given access to the Federal Reserve's "window," a credit facility available to the nation's commercial banks, but not to investment banks. JPMorgan and Bear Stearns contemplated that the Company could get the facility through JPMorgan as part of a transaction in which JPMorgan bought Bear Stearns.

On March 14, 2008, it was announced that JPMorgan would provide short-term funding to Bear Stearns while the Company worked on alternative forms of financing. Bear Stearns' stock fell on the news from $57 per share to $30 per share, a 47% one-day drop.

On March 16, 2008, Dimon stated that Bear Stearns faced $40 billion in credit exposure, including mortgage liabilities, and made an offer to purchase the Company at a $2 per share, a price that Dimon claimed was necessary to protect JPMorgan.

On March 17, 2008, news of Bear Stearns' exposure led the stock to close at $4.81 per share, an 85% drop from its previous close.

JPMorgan renegotiated the price after it discovered that a mistake in the language of its guaranty agreement with Bear Stearns obligated JPMorgan to guarantee Bear Stearns' trades even if the Company's shareholders voted down the acquisition deal. Shareholders approved the sale to JPMorgan on May 29, 2008. Under the terms of the merger, shareholders received $10 of JPMorgan shares for every Bear Stearns share they held as of the date of the merger.

In June 2008 the Department of Justice, through the U.S. Attorney for the Eastern District of New York, indicted Ralph Cioffi ("Cioffi"), the originator of the hedge funds, charging that he had misled investors regarding the value of MBS and collateralized debt obligations ("CDOs") containing MBS owned by the hedge funds, and had caused $1.8 billion in losses to investors. On the same day, the SEC filed a civil complaint against Cioffi.

By July 3, 2008 the assets of Maiden Lane LLC, a holding company created to hold Bear Stearns ABS following the JPMorgan merger, had decreased in value from $30 billion to $28.9 billion. By October 22, 2008, the value of the assets had dropped another $2.1 billion, to $26.8 billion, 10.6% less than the value provided by Bear Stearns.

After Bear Stearns' March 2008 collapse, the SEC's Office of the Inspector General ("OIG") was asked to analyze the SEC's oversight of the CSE firms, with a special emphasis on Bear Stearns.

The OIG issued its conclusions in a September 25, 2008 Report, titled "SEC's Oversight of Bear Stearns and Related Entities: The Consolidated Supervised Entity Program" (the "OIG Report"), which stated that "[b]y November of 2005 the Company's ARM business was operating in excess of allocated limits, reaching new highs with respect to the net market value of its positions" and that the large concentration of business in this area left the Company exposed to declines in the riskiest part of the housing market. Certain conclusions of the OIG Report are cited throughout the Securities Complaint, constituting allegations of the Bear Stearns history and practices, including details about Bear Stearns' VaR, mortgage valuation models, and its treatment of asset values.

### 2. Bear Stearns Securitization

Mortgages packaged together for securitization are referred to as mortgage-backed securities ("MBS"), and when the mortgages are residential, those securities are referred to as residential mortgage-backed securities ("RMBS"). RMBS are, in turn, divided into layers based on the credit ratings of the underlying assets.

The "B-Pieces" of an RMBS, its riskier parts, were pooled together to form a collateralized debt obligation ("CDO") divided by the issuer into different tranches, or layers, based on gradations in credit quality. While the top tranche of a CDO may be rated "AAA," CDOs formed from RMBS are rated BBB or lower. Lower-rated tranches of CDOs, such as the "mezzanine" tranches, bear even greater risk of loss. The "equity" tranche bears the first risk of loss.

Mezzanine CDOs made up more than 75% of the total CDO market by April 2007 and contained cash flows from especially risky types of residential mortgage loans, termed "subprime" or "Alt-A" made to borrowers with a heightened risk of default, such as those who have a history of loan delinquency or default. Alt-A loans were made to borrowers with problems including lack of documentation of income and assets, high debt-to-income ratios, and troubled credit histories. Subprime and Alt-A mortgages are termed "nonprime" mortgages. Between 2003 and 2007, the total proportion of nonprime loans wrapped into the majority of all mezzanine CDOs increased dramatically market-wide.

Bear Stearns originated and purchased home loans, packaged them into RMBS, collected these RMBS to form CDOs, sold CDOs to investors and thereby acquired a large exposure to declines in the housing and credit markets.

It originated loans through two wholly-owned subsidiaries, the Bear Stearns Residential Mortgage Corporation ("BEARRES") and later through Encore Credit

Corporation ("ECC"), which the Company purchased in early 2007. ECC specialized in providing loans to borrowers with compromised credit. BEARRES made Alt-A loans to borrowers with somewhat better, but still compromised credit. The Company actively encouraged its loan originator subsidiaries to offer loans even to borrowers with poor credit scores and troubled credit histories and to originate riskier loans that "cut corners" with respect to credit scores or loan to value ("LTV") ratios. While the national rejection rate of applications was 29% in 2006, the BEARRES rejection rate was 13%.

In 2006, BEARRES and ECC originated 19,715 mortgages, worth $4.37 billion, which were securitized by Bear Stearns. Bear Stearns also purchased loans originated by other companies through its EMC Mortgage Corporation ("EMC") subsidiary, which from 1990 until 2007 purchased more than $200 billion in mortgages. In late 2006 and early 2007, because of the potential for profits from securitizing these loans, Bear Stearns managers failed to enforce basic underwriting standards and ignored due diligence findings that borrowers would be unable to pay.

Bear Stearns also funded and purchased closed-end second-lien ("CES") loans and home-equity lines of credit ("HELOCs") made to borrowers with poor credit secured by secondary liens on the home, which were to be paid after the first mortgage was satisfied and were at risk of not being paid in full if the value of the home dropped. By the end of 2006, EMC had purchased $1.2 billion of HELOC and $6.7 billion of CES loans.

Through EMC, Bear Stearns also purchased mortgages already in default, so-called "scratch and dent" loans, to securitize and sell to investors. Because of its underwriting standards, the loans that the Company purchased to package into RMBS and CDOs were especially vulnerable to declines in housing prices.

Individual nonprime home loans were wrapped into an RMBS, sold to investors, and packaged into CDOs. Especially risky tranches of RMBS were kept on the Company's books as retained interests ("RI"). The amount of RI grew throughout the Class Period, from $5.6 billion on November 30, 2006 to $9.6 billion on August 31, 2007.

Nearly all CDOs Bear Stearns structured during the Class Period were backed by a combination of RMBS and derivatives, or "synthetic securities." These synthetic securities were effectively insurance contracts in which the party buying the insurance paid a premium equivalent to the cash flow of an underlying RMBS that it was copying, and the counterparty insured against a decline or default in the underlying RMBS. Such CDOs were called "Synthetic CDOs," and a CDO backed by other CDO notes was called a "CDO squared."

To sell the largest possible CDOs, the Company retained on its books increasing amounts of the CDOs it packaged. By August 2007, this figure had reached $2.072 billion.

During the Class Period, the Company's growing accumulation of subprime-backed RMBS and CDOs, combined with its leveraging practices, left it extraordinarily vulnerable to declines in the housing market. Before the Class Period began, on multiple occasions the amount of mortgage securities held by the Company exceeded its internal concentration limits.

### 3. Leveraging

In leveraging, a company takes out a loan secured by assets in order to invest in assets with a greater rate of return than the cost of interest for the loan. The potential for loss is greater if the investment becomes worthless, because of the loan principal and all accrued interest. A 4-to-1 leverage ratio increases loss potential by about 15%, while a 35-to-1 leverage ratio increases loss potential by more than 100%.

In 2005, Bear Stearns was leveraged at a ratio of approximately 26.5-to-1. By November 2007, the Company had leveraged its net equity position of $11.8 billion to purchase $395 billion in assets, a ratio of nearly 33-to-1. Because of the interest charges required to support this leverage ratio, the amount of cash the Company needed to finance its daily operations increased dramatically during the Class Period. By the close of the Class Period, Bear Stearns' daily borrowing needs exceeded $50 billion.

### 4. The Hedge Funds

In October 2003, Cioffi started the High Grade Structured Credit Strategies Fund, LP (the "High Grade Fund") as part of Bear Stearns Asset Management ("BSAM"), which was under the supervision of Spector. The High Grade Fund consisted of a Delaware partnership to raise money from investors in the United States and a Cayman Island corporation to raise money from foreign investors.

In August 2006, Cioffi created the High Grade Structured Credit Strategies Enhanced Leverage Fund, LP ("the High Grade Enhanced Fund") (the High Grade Fund and the High Grade Enhanced Fund are collectively referred to as the "Hedge Funds"), which was structured similarly to the High Grade Fund, but with greater leverage to increase potential returns.

Bear Stearns Securities Corporation, a wholly-owned subsidiary of the Company, served as the prime broker for the Hedge Funds, and PFPC Inc., another Bear Stearns subsidiary, was the Hedge Funds' administrator. BSAM was the investment manager for the Hedge Funds. Spector was responsible for the business of both funds.

Because of BSAM's role as an asset manager, Bear Stearns was one of the few repurchase lenders willing to take the Hedge Funds' CDOs as collateral for short term lending facilities. The Hedge Funds, through BSAM, entered into repurchase agreements on favorable terms with Bear Stearns as the counterparty. By offering cash to the Hedge Funds in exchange for subprime mortgage-backed CDOs of questionable value, Bear Stearns increased it exposure to declines in the subprime market.

BSAM misrepresented the Hedge Funds' subprime exposure to hedge fund investors in "Preliminary Performance Profiles" ("PPPs") by disclosing only the Hedge Funds' direct subprime RMBS holdings. The Hedge Funds also held large amounts of subprime RMBS indirectly through purchased CDOs. Returns in the subprime CDOs, and CDOs backed by CDO-squares, diminished, resulting in diminishing yield spreads, and accelerating losses for the Hedge Funds. The High Grade Enhanced Fund experienced its first negative return in February 2007. Declines in the High Grade Fund soon followed, resulting in its first negative return in March 2007.

The Hedge Funds began to experience difficulties with margin calls and failed to disclose Bear Stearns' exposure to the declining value of the subprime-backed Hedge Fund assets it held as collateral on its own books. They continued to deteriorate throughout the spring of 2007. On April 19, 2007, Matthew M. Tannin, COO of the Hedge Funds ("Tannin"), reviewed a credit model that showed increasing losses on subprime linked assets. On May 13, 2007, Tannin stated that the High Grade Enhanced Fund had to be liquidated.

To avoid a forced "fire sale" of the thinly-traded CDOs held by the Hedge Funds, which would have required acknowledging huge declines in the value of the subprime-backed assets Bear Stearns held as collateral and would have revealed the Company's gross overvaluation of its thinly-traded assets, Spector decided to extend a line of credit to the High Grade Fund to allow it to liquidate in an orderly way by gradually selling assets into the market. This was done to avoid having other assets seized by repurchase agreement counterparties, who would mark the assets to their true value. Spector permitted the High Grade Enhanced Fund to fail, because its high leverage ratios left it virtually unsalvageable.

On June 22, 2007, Bear Stearns announced that it was entering into a $3.2 billion securitized financing agreement with the High Grade Fund in the form of a collateralized repurchase agreement. In exchange for lending the funds, Bear Stearns received as collateral CDOs backed by subprime mortgages allegedly worth between $1.7 and $2 billion. Pursuant to the agreement, Bear Stearns gave up the right to collect all of the upside in the event that the collateral saw an increase in value. Molinaro stated that the Hedge Funds' problems with their subprime-backed assets did not extend to the securities that Bear Stearns itself held, but failed to disclose that even prior to the $3.2 billion securitized financing agreement, Bear Stearns held large amounts of the Hedge Funds' toxic debt as collateral. During a June 22, 2007 conference call, Molinaro made false statements with respect to asset value and stated that the value levels attributed to the collateral it had received from the Hedge Funds "are a reflection of the market value levels that we're seeing from our street counterparties." In fact, the market for such securities had become highly illiquid, providing no basis for Molinaro's statements.

On June 26, 2007, Cayne denied any material change in the risk profile. However, because of worthless subprime-backed collateral, the risk exposure had grown substantially.

By the end of June 2007, asset sales had reduced the loan balance to $1.345 billion, but the estimated value of the collateral securing the loan had deteriorated by nearly $350 million, approximately the value of the loan Bear Stearns had given the High Grade Fund. Any further declines in the value of the assets that Bear Stearns held as collateral would be borne directly by Bear Stearns. Instead of immediately reflecting its assumption of the declining collateral in its books, the Company delayed for months, according to the OIG Report, "to delay taking a huge hit to capital."

On July 18, 2007, Bear Stearns informed investors in the Hedge Funds that they would get little money back after "unprecedented declines" in the value of AAA-rated securities used to invest in subprime mortgages. The more than $1.3 billion in collateral drawn from the Hedge Funds' subprime-backed assets, which the Company had effectively taken onto its books by assuming the assets as collateral just a month earlier, was nearly worthless as well. Bear Stearns did not make the actual book entries until the fall of 2007, months after the losses were actually incurred by the Company. The Company ultimately only wrote off a fraction of the worthless collateral it held and had originally valued at $1.3 billion.

## 5.  Valuation and Risk

The valuation of assets is governed by Statement of Financial Accounting Standards No. 157, Fair Value Measurements ("SFAS 157"). Although SFAS 157 took effect on November 15, 2007, Bear Stearns opted to comply with the standard beginning January 2007. SFAS 157 required that Bear Stearns classify its reported assets into one of three levels depending on the degree of certainty about the assets' underlying value. Assets traded in an active market were classified as Level 1 ("mark-to-market"). Level 2 ("mark-to-model") assets consisted of financial assets whose values are based on quoted prices in inactive markets, or whose values are based on models, inputs to which are observable either directly or indirectly for substantially the full term of the asset or liability. Level 3 assets, thinly traded or not traded at all, have values based on valuation techniques that require inputs that are both unobservable and significant to the overall fair value measurement. To value Level 3 assets, companies rely on models developed by management. The information supplied by valuation models is incorporated into other models used to assess risk and hedge investments, such as the models measuring VaR.

Before the Class Period began, the Company knew that declining housing prices and rising default rates were not reflected in the mortgage valuation models that were critical to the valuation of its Level 3 assets. According to the OIG Report, prior to the Company's approval as a CSE in November of 2005, "Bear Stearns used outdated models that were more than ten years old to value mortgage derivatives and had limited documentation on how the models worked."

According to the OIG Report, in November 2005, the SEC Office of Compliance Inspections and Examinations ("OCIE") found that "Bear Stearns did not periodically evaluate its VaR models, nor did it timely update inputs to its VaR models."

Bear Stearns was warned of these deficiencies in a December 2, 2005 memorandum from OCIE to Farber, the Company's Controller and Principal Accountant. According to the OIG Report, "Bear Stearns' VaR models did not capture risks associated with credit spread widening."

According to the OIG Report, in 2006, Bear Stearns' trading desks had gained ascendancy over the Company's risk managers, TM found that model review at Bear was less formalized than at other CSE firms and had devolved into a support function and Bear Stearns reported different VaR numbers to OIG regulators than its traders used for their own internal hedging purposes.

Traders were able to override risk manager marks and enter their own, more generous, marks for some assets directly into the models used for valuation and risk management by manipulating inputs into Bear Stearns' WITS system—which was the repository for raw loan data, including such crucial information as a borrower's credit score, prepayments, delinquencies, interest rates and foreclosure history—and did so to alter the value of pools of loans to enhance their profit and loss positions. [T]he risk management department was persistently understaffed, and the head of the Company's model review program "had difficulty communicating with senior managers in a productive manner."

Though Cayne and Molinaro were aware of the SEC's concerns about Bear Stearns' risk management program, the Company made no effort to revise its mortgage valuation models to reflect declines in the housing market. The head of the Company's mortgage trading desk was "vehemently opposed" to the updating of the Company's mortgage valuation models.

As the housing market declined throughout 2007 and into 2008, Bear Stearns continued to rely on its flawed valuation models. Level 3 assets, including retained interests in RMBS and the equity tranches of CDOs, made up 6-8% of the

Company's total assets at fair market value in 2005, and increased to 20-29% of total assets between the fourth quarter of 2007 and the first quarter of 2008. According to the Company's Form 10-K for the period ending November 30, 2007, the majority of the growth in the Company's Level 3 assets in 2007 came from "mortgages and mortgage-related securities," the assets that the Company was valuing using misleading models. As of August 31, 2007, the Company carried $5.8 billion in Level 3 assets backed by residential mortgages, a figure that grew close to $7.5 billion by November 30, 2007.

Risk is defined as the degree of uncertainty about future net returns, and is commonly classified into four types: (1) credit risk, relating to the potential loss due to the inability of a counterpart to meet its obligations; (2) operational risk, taking into account the errors that can be made in instructing payments or settling transactions, and including the risk of fraud and regulatory risks; (3) liquidity risk, caused by an unexpected large and stressful negative cash flow over a short period; and (4) market risk, estimating the uncertainty of future values, due to changing market conditions. The most prominent of these risks for investment bankers is market risk, since it reflects the potential economic loss caused by the decrease in the market value of a portfolio. Because of the crucial role that market losses can play in the financial health of investment banks, they are required to set aside capital to cover market risk.

VaR is a method of quantifying market risk, defined as the maximum potential loss in value of a portfolio of financial instruments with a given probability over a certain horizon. If the company's VaR is high, it must increase the amount of capital it sets aside in order to mitigate potential losses or reduce its exposure to high risk positions.

The resignation of the head of model review at the Company in March 2007 gave trading desks more power over risk managers and by the time a new risk manager arrived in the summer of 2007, the department was in a shambles and risk managers were operating in "crisis mode." By October 2007, the entire model valuation team had evaporated, except for one remaining analyst.

According to the OIG Report, it was not until "towards the end of 2007" that Bear Stearns "developed a housing led recession scenario which it could incorporate into risk management and use for hedging purposes." The mortgage-backed asset valuation inputs to the VaR models employed by the Company were never updated during the Class Period and remained a "work in progress" at the time of the Company's March 2008 collapse.

## QUESTIONS

1. Assess Bear Stearns' leverage and liquidity situation leading up to its takeover by JPMorgan Chase in March 2008.
2. Assess how Bear Stearns managed its risk. What were the specific problems, if any?
3. Why should the capital levels of financial institutions like Bear Stearns regulated?

The case below presents a classic statement of the business judgment rule. It holds for the proposition that directors cannot be held liable for honest mistakes even if the error is patently clear. In *Kamin v. American Express*, the court understood the financial and accounting issues in this case, and does not defend the correctness of the board's decision. Indeed, the board's error was clear. In reading the case, think about two issues: (1) why the board's action was so patently erroneous from the perspective of finance theory, and (2) if the board took action to enhance earnings (in this case, to not diminish earnings), how their action could have been clear business error.

## Kamin v. American Express
### 86 Misc.2d 809, 383 N.Y.S.2d 807 (N.Y. App. Div. 1976)

[Plaintiff shareholders brought a derivatives action against individual directors of the American Express Company. The defendants moved for dismissal for failure to state a cause of action.]

[T]he complaint alleges that in 1972 American Express acquired for investment 1,954,418 shares of common stock of Donaldson, Lufken and Jenrette, Inc. (hereafter DLJ), a publicly traded corporation, at a cost of $29,900,000. It is further alleged that the current market value of those shares is approximately $4,000,000. On July 28, 1975, it is alleged, the board of directors of American Express declared a special dividend to all stockholders of record pursuant to which the shares of DLJ would be distributed in kind. Plaintiffs contend further that if American Express were to sell the DLJ shares on the market, it would sustain a capital loss of $25,000,000 which could be offset against taxable capital gains on other investments. Such a sale, they allege, would result in tax savings to the company of approximately $8,000,000, which would not be available in the case of the distribution of DLJ shares to stockholders. It is alleged that on October 8, 1975 and October 16, 1975, plaintiffs demanded that the directors rescind the previously declared dividend in DLJ shares and take steps to preserve the capital loss which would result from selling the shares. This demand was rejected by the board of directors on October 17, 1975.

The crucial allegation which must be scrutinized to determine the legal sufficiency of the complaint is paragraph 19: "All of the defendant Directors engaged in or acquiesced in or negligently permitted the declaration and payment of the Dividend in violation of the fiduciary duty owed by them to Amex to care for and preserve Amex's assets in the same manner as a man of average prudence would care for his own property."

[T]here is no claim of fraud or self-dealing, and no contention that there was any bad faith or oppressive conduct.

[T]he question of whether or not a dividend is to be declared or a distribution of some kind should be made is exclusively a matter of business judgment for the board of directors. "Courts will not interfere with such discretion unless it be first made to appear that the directors have acted or are about to act in bad faith and for a dishonest purpose. It is for the directors to say, acting in good faith of course, when and to what extent dividends shall be declared. The statute confers upon the directors this power, and the minority stockholders are not in a position to question this right, so long as the directors are acting in good faith."

Thus, a complaint must be dismissed if all that is presented is a decision to pay dividends rather than pursuing some other course of conduct. A complaint which alleges merely that some course of action other than that pursued by the board of directors would have been more advantageous gives rise to no cognizable cause of action. Courts have more than enough to do in adjudicating legal rights and devising remedies for wrongs. The directors' room rather than the courtroom is the appropriate forum for thrashing out purely business questions which will have an impact on profits, market prices, competitive situations, or tax advantages.

It is not enough to allege, as plaintiffs do here, that the directors made an imprudent decision, which did not capitalize on the possibility of using a potential capital loss to offset capital gains. More than imprudence or mistaken judgment must be shown. "Questions of policy of management, expediency of contracts or action, adequacy of consideration, lawful appropriation of corporate funds to advance corporate interests, are left solely to their honest and unselfish decision, for their powers therein are without limitation and free from restraint, and the exercise of them for the common and general interests of the corporation may not be questioned, although the results show that what they did was unwise or inexpedient."

[T]he objections raised by the plaintiffs to the proposed dividend action were carefully considered and unanimously rejected by the board at a special meeting called precisely for that purpose at the plaintiffs' request. The minutes of the special meeting indicate that the defendants were fully aware that a sale rather than a distribution of the DLJ shares might result in the realization of a substantial income tax saving. Nevertheless, they concluded that there were countervailing considerations primarily with respect to the adverse effect such a sale, realizing a loss of $25,000,000, would have on the net income figures in the American Express financial statement. Such a reduction of net income would have a serious effect on the market value of the publicly traded American Express stock. This was not a situation in which the defendant directors totally overlooked facts called to their attention. They gave them consideration, and attempted to view the total picture in arriving at their decision.

All directors have an obligation, using sound business judgment, to maximize income for the benefit of all persons having a stake in the welfare of the corporate entity. What we have here as revealed both by the complaint and by the affidavits and exhibits, is that a disagreement exists between two minority stockholders and a unanimous board of directors as to the best way to handle a loss already incurred on an investment. The directors are entitled to exercise their honest business judgment on the information before them, and to act within their corporate powers. That they may be mistaken, that other courses of action might have differing consequences, or that their action might benefit some shareholders more than others present no basis for the superimposition of judicial judgment, so long as it appears that the directors have been acting in good faith. The question of to what extent a dividend shall be declared and the manner in which it shall be paid is ordinarily subject only to the qualification that the dividend be paid out of surplus. The court will not interfere unless a clear case is made out of fraud, oppression, arbitrary action, or breach of trust.

In this case it clearly appears that the plaintiffs have failed as a matter of law to make out an actionable claim. Accordingly, the motion by the defendants for summary judgment and dismissal of the complaint is GRANTED.

## QUESTIONS

1. The board of directors did not sell the company's stake in DLJ because "the adverse effect such a sale, realizing a loss of $25,000,000, would have on the net income figures in the American Express financial statement." Higher net income is good, and lower net income is bad. What was fundamentally wrong with the board's action?

2. According to finance theory, did the board destroy value in American Express? If so, by how much?

3. The court stated: "The directors' room rather than the courtroom is the appropriate forum for thrashing out purely business questions which will have an impact on profits, market prices, competitive situations, or tax advantages." Provide an efficiency justification for this statement.

---

**Author's Summary of Facts:** Basic Inc. publicly denied that it was being acquired by another company, a material misrepresentation. Plaintiffs are shareholders who sold Basic stock, and they argued that the company's misrepresentations artificially reduced the stock price. It is fair to presume that many shareholders were unaware of the misrepresentations since many shareholders do not follow company press releases or other market information in detail. A class was certified under a Rule 10b-5 action, which is a cause of action based on a material misrepresentation. The question concerns reliance: "Requiring proof of individualized reliance from each member of the proposed plaintiff class effectively would have prevented respondents from proceeding with a class action, since individual issues then would have overwhelmed the common ones."

### Basic, Inc. v. Levinson
#### 485 U.S. 224 (1988)

Justice BLACKMUN delivered the opinion of the Court.

We turn to the question of reliance and the fraud-on-the-market theory. Succinctly put:

> "The fraud on the market theory is based on the hypothesis that, in an open and developed securities market, the price of a company's stock is determined by the available material information regarding the company and its business. . . . Misleading statements will therefore defraud purchasers of stock even if the purchasers do not directly rely on the misstatements. . . . The causal connection between the defendants' fraud and the plaintiffs' purchase of stock in such a case is no less significant than in a case of direct reliance on misrepresentations."

Our task, of course, is not to assess the general validity of the theory, but to consider whether it was proper for the courts below to apply a rebuttable presumption of reliance, supported in part by the fraud-on-the-market theory.

We agree that reliance is an element of a Rule 10b-5 cause of action. Reliance provides the requisite causal connection between a defendant's misrepresentation and a plaintiff's injury. There is, however, more than one way to demonstrate the causal connection. Indeed, we previously have dispensed with a requirement of positive proof of reliance, where a duty to disclose material information had been breached, concluding that the necessary nexus between the plaintiffs' injury and the defendant's wrongful conduct had been established. Similarly, we did not require proof that material omissions or misstatements in a proxy statement decisively affected voting, because the proxy solicitation itself, rather than the defect in the solicitation materials, served as an essential link in the transaction.

The modern securities markets, literally involving millions of shares changing hands daily, differ from the face-to-face transactions contemplated by early fraud cases, and our understanding of Rule 10b-5's reliance requirement must encompass these differences.

> "In face-to-face transactions, the inquiry into an investor's reliance upon information is into the subjective pricing of that information by that investor. With the presence of a market, the market is interposed between seller and buyer and, ideally, transmits information to the investor in the processed form of a market price. Thus the market is performing a substantial part of the valuation process performed by the investor in a face-to-face transaction. The market is acting as the unpaid agent of the investor, informing him that given all the information available to it, the value of the stock is worth the market price."

Presumptions typically serve to assist courts in managing circumstances in which direct proof, for one reason or another, is rendered difficult. The courts below accepted a presumption, created by the fraud-on-the-market theory and subject to rebuttal by petitioners, that persons who had traded Basic shares had done so in reliance on the integrity of the price set by the market, but because of petitioners' material misrepresentations that price had been fraudulently depressed. Requiring a plaintiff to show a speculative state of facts, i.e., how he would have acted if omitted material information had been disclosed, or if the misrepresentation had not been made would place an unnecessarily unrealistic evidentiary burden on the Rule 10b-5 plaintiff who has traded on an impersonal market.

Arising out of considerations of fairness, public policy, and probability, as well as judicial economy, presumptions are also useful devices for allocating the burdens of proof between parties. The presumption of reliance employed in this case is consistent with, and, by facilitating Rule 10b-5 litigation, supports, the congressional policy embodied in the 1934 Act. In drafting that Act, Congress expressly relied on the premise that securities markets are affected by information, and enacted legislation to facilitate an investor's reliance on the integrity of those markets:

> "No investor, no speculator, can safely buy and sell securities upon the exchanges without having an intelligent basis for forming his judgment as to the value of the securities he buys or sells. The idea of a free and open public market is built upon the theory that competing judgments of buyers and sellers as to the fair price of a security brings [sic] about a situation where the market price reflects as nearly as possible a just price. Just as artificial manipulation tends to upset the true function of an open market, so the hiding and secreting of important information obstructs the operation of the markets as indices of real value."

The presumption is also supported by common sense and probability. Recent empirical studies have tended to confirm Congress' premise that the market price of shares traded on well-developed markets reflects all publicly available information, and, hence, any material misrepresentations. It has been noted that "it is hard to imagine that there ever is a buyer or seller who does not rely on market integrity. Who would knowingly roll the dice in a crooked crap game?" Indeed, nearly every court that has considered the proposition has concluded that where materially misleading statements have been disseminated into an impersonal, well-developed market for securities, the reliance of individual plaintiffs on the integrity of the market price may be presumed. Commentators generally have applauded the adoption of one variation or another of the fraud-on-the-market theory. An investor who buys or sells stock at the price set by the market does so in reliance on the integrity of that price. Because most publicly available information is reflected in market price, an investor's reliance on any public material misrepresentations, therefore, may be presumed for purposes of a Rule 10b-5 action.

Justice WHITE, with whom Justice O'CONNOR joins, concurring in part and dissenting in part.

I dissent from the remainder of the Court's holding because I do not agree that the "fraud-on-the-market" theory should be applied in this case.

Even when compared to the relatively youthful private cause-of-action under §10(b), the fraud-on-the-market theory is a mere babe. Yet today, the Court embraces this theory with the sweeping confidence usually reserved for more mature legal doctrines. In so doing, I fear that the Court's decision may have many adverse, unintended effects as it is applied and interpreted in the years to come.

But even as the Court attempts to limit the fraud-on-the-market theory it endorses today, the pitfalls in its approach are revealed by previous uses by the lower courts of the broader versions of the theory. Confusion and contradiction in court rulings are inevitable when traditional legal analysis is replaced with economic theorization by the federal courts.

For while the economists' theories which underpin the fraud-on-the-market presumption may have the appeal of mathematical exactitude and scientific certainty, they are-in the end-nothing more than theories which may or may not prove accurate upon further consideration. Even the most earnest advocates of economic analysis of the law recognize this. Thus, while the majority states that, for purposes of reaching its result it need only make modest assumptions about the way in which "market professionals generally" do their jobs, and how the conduct of market professionals affects stock prices, I doubt that we are in much of a position to assess which theories aptly describe the functioning of the securities industry.

Consequently, I cannot join the Court in its effort to reconfigure the securities laws, based on recent economic theories, to better fit what it perceives to be the new realities of financial markets.

## QUESTIONS

1. What is the fundamental legal and policy problem posed by this lawsuit?
2. In what way does *Basic* incorporate the ECMH into the rule of law?
3. What legal problem does the ECMH solve?

***Author's Summary of Facts:*** James Hofman, a stockbroker for Prudential Securities, told 11 customers that Jefferson Savings Bancorp was "certain" to be acquired for a big premium in the near future. It was a lie. The plaintiffs were *not* shareholders who heard the lie and acted on it. Instead, they were *all* shareholders of Jefferson Savings Bancorp who bought stock while the stockbroker was spreading his lies. The district court certified the class based on an application of the fraud-on-the-market theory.

## West v. Prudential Securities Inc.
### 282 F.3d 935 (7th Cir. 2002)

EASTERBROOK, Circuit Judge.

Causation is the shortcoming in this class certification. *Basic* describes a mechanism by which public information affects stock prices, and thus may affect traders who did not know about that information. Professional investors monitor news about many firms; good news implies higher dividends and other benefits, which induces these investors to value the stock more highly, and they continue buying until the gains are exhausted. With many professional investors alert to news, markets are efficient in the sense that they rapidly adjust to all public information; if some of this information is false, the price will reach an incorrect level, staying there until the truth emerges. This approach has the support of financial economics as well as the imprimatur of the Justices: few propositions in economics are better established than the quick adjustment of securities prices to public information.

No similar mechanism explains how prices would respond to non-public information, such as statements made by Hofman to a handful of his clients. These do not come to the attention of professional investors or money managers, so the price-adjustment mechanism just described does not operate. Sometimes full-time market watchers can infer important news from the identity of a trader (when the corporation's CEO goes on a buying spree, this implies good news) or from the sheer volume of trades (an unprecedented buying volume may suggest that a bidder is accumulating stock in anticipation of a tender offer), but neither the identity of Hofman's customers nor the volume of their trades would have conveyed information to the market in this fashion. No one these days accepts the strongest version of the efficient capital market hypothesis, under which non-public information automatically affects prices. That version is empirically false: the public announcement of news (good and bad) has big effects on stock prices, which could not happen if prices already incorporated the effect of non-public information. Thus it is hard to see how Hofman's non-public statements could have caused changes in the price of Jefferson Savings stock. *Basic* founded the fraud-on-the-market doctrine on a causal mechanism with both theoretical and empirical power; for non-public information there is nothing comparable.

Because the record here does not demonstrate that non-public information affected the price of Jefferson Savings' stock, a remand is unnecessary. What the plaintiffs have going for them is that Jefferson's stock *did* rise in price (by about $5, or 20% of its trading price) during the months when Hofman was touting an impending acquisition, plus a model of demand-pull price increases offered by their expert. Barclay started with a model devised by another economist, in which trades themselves convey information to the market and thus affect price. Hasbrouck's model assumes that some trades are by informed traders and some by uninformed traders, and that the market may be able to draw inferences about which is which. The model has not been verified empirically. Barclay approached the issue differently, assuming that *all* trades affect prices by raising demand even if no trader is well informed-as if there were an economic market in "Jefferson Savings stock" as there is in dill pickles or fluffy towels. Hofman's tips raised the demand for Jefferson Savings stock and curtailed the supply (for the tippees were less likely to sell their own shares); that combination of effects raised the stock's price. Yet investors do not want Jefferson Savings *stock* (as if they sought to paper their walls with beautiful certificates); they want monetary returns (at given risk levels), returns that are available from many financial instruments. One fundamental attribute of efficient markets is that *information*, not demand in the abstract, determines stock prices. There are so many substitutes for any one firm's stock that the effective demand curve is horizontal. It may shift up or down with new information but is not sloped like the demand curve for physical products. That is why institutional purchases (which can be large in relation to normal trading volume) do not elevate prices, while relatively small trades by insiders can have substantial effects; the latter trades convey information, and the former do not. Barclay, who took the view that the market for Jefferson Savings securities is efficient, did not explain why he departed from the normal understanding that information rather than raw demand determines securities prices.

## QUESTIONS

1. The court reasoned that the ordinary law of supply and demand does not apply to individual stocks. Why not? According to the court, in what way does an investor "want" a share of Google?
2. According to the court, what moves the price of individual stocks?
3. What fact fundamentally distinguishes *Basic* from *West*?

## ESSENTIAL TERMS

Bankers acceptance
Bank loan
Broker-dealer
CFTC
Commercial paper market
Commodities market
Corporate bond market
Credit markets
Credit rating agencies
Efficient capital markets hypothesis
Equity markets
Exchanges
Federal Reserve
High yield ("junk") bonds
Institutional investor
Investment banks
Investment grade
Issuer

Lease financing
Listing rules
Money market
Nasdaq
NYSE
Over-the-counter (OTC)
Primary market
Private equity
Publicly traded security
Repurchase agreement ("repo")
SEC
Secondary market
Securitization market
Semi-strong form of ECMH
Strong form of ECMH
Treasury market
Underwriting
Weak form of ECMH

## KEY CONCEPTS

1. The capital markets cover the entire range of financial products. They are very large, complex, and international in scope.
2. The capital markets can be categorized into the primary and secondary markets.
3. The equity and debt markets constitute the most important markets for issuers because these products provide direct financing to issuers.
4. Exchanges play an important role in regulating the standards for issuance and trading of securities.
5. The credit market has a number of credit products covering duration (short-term and long-term credit instruments), credit ratings (investment grade and non-investment grade instruments), and liquidity (illiquid instruments and publicly traded instruments).
6. The capital markets are operated by a large group of institutions and professionals including exchanges, regulators, accountants, lawyers, investment bankers, and credit rating agencies.
7. The efficient capital markets hypothesis is a hypothesis about the market's ability to incorporate information into the pricing of securities.
8. The market is weak-form efficient, and is not strong-form efficient.
9. There is some controversy with respect to whether the market is semi-strong efficient.

## REVIEW QUESTIONS

1. What are the different types of investors in the capital markets?
2. What services do investment banks provide?
3. What specific services and functions do lawyer provide in the capital markets?
4. What are the differences among the weak, semi-strong, and strong forms of ECMH?

# CORPORATE TRANSACTIONS

In business law courses such as Business Associations, Securities Regulation, and Corporate Finance, you will read many cases involving corporate transactions. As a business lawyer, you will advise business clients in such transactions. These transactions can be broadly grouped into capital raisings, mergers and acquisitions, and restructuring, the last of which typically involves a combination of different types of transactions applied with the purpose of reorganizing a firm.

## A. CAPITAL RAISING

Capital is the lifeblood of a company. It funds the capital assets necessary to engage in enterprise over the long term (see Chapter 2). As seen in Chapter 11, capital can be debt or equity. Within these two broad categories, it can take as many forms as freedom of contract allows given the unique needs of issuers and investors, which is to say that the form and terms of securities can be enormously diverse.

### 1. REASONS FOR CAPITAL RAISING

A firm may raise capital for a number of reasons. It could be a start-up company needing capital to get business started. It could be an established company needing capital to fund a new project, e.g., raise capital to expand business operations in China. It could need money for an acquisition. It could have run out of capital because of bad luck or poor management. It could restructure its capital structure, e.g., raise more equity to reduce leverage. If capital is needed for whatever reason, and the firm does not have cash on hand to fund itself, it must raise capital.

When a firm is a start-up company, it is often initially funded by the entrepreneur's own money. At some point, if this source of capital runs out or is limited, a firm will seek capital from a *venture capital* (also called *private equity*) fund.

When a firm "goes public," it seeks to sell securities to the general public and have them be traded publicly. The process of going public is called an *initial public offering* (or *IPO*).

EXAMPLE 14.1

## Goldman Sachs raises capital in the nick of time

During the financial crisis, financial institutions such as commercial banks and investment banks were caught in a liquidity crisis. The asset values on their balance sheets were declining precipitously with the collapse of the housing market, and they were heavily leveraged (see Example 5.6). This means that the small slivers of equity on their balance sheets evaporated with declining asset value. They needed to recapitalize. Some could not due to market conditions or, more likely, lack of confidence in the companies, such as Lehman Brothers and Bear Stearns. Others were more fortunate.

In September and October 2008, as Lehman Brothers filed for bankruptcy and Merrill Lynch was sold to Bank of America, Goldman Sachs completed a series of capital raisings, including sale of preferred stock to Warren Buffett's company Berkshire Hathaway and to the U.S. government under the Troubled Asset Relief Program (TARP). Below is the portion of Goldman Sachs' 2008 annual report describing its various capital raising activities during the nadir of the financial crisis of 2008-2009. The activities described below helped to prevent the firm from collapsing like some of its peers.

\* \* \*

**Stock Offerings.** In September 2008, we completed a public offering of 46.7 million shares of common stock at $123.00 per share for proceeds of $5.75 billion.

In October 2008, we issued to Berkshire Hathaway Inc. and certain affiliates 50,000 shares of 10% Cumulative Perpetual Preferred Stock, Series G (Series G Preferred Stock), and a five-year warrant to purchase up to 43.5 million shares of common stock at an exercise price of $115.00 per share, for aggregate proceeds of $5.00 billion. The allocated carrying values of the warrant and the Series G Preferred Stock on the date of issuance (based on their relative fair values) were $1.14 billion and $3.86 billion, respectively. The warrant is exercisable at any time until October 1, 2013 and the number of shares of common stock underlying the warrant and the exercise price are subject to adjustment for certain dilutive events.

In October 2008, under the U.S. Treasury's TARP Capital Purchase Program, we issued to the U.S. Treasury 10.0 million shares of Fixed Rate Cumulative Perpetual Preferred Stock, Series H (Series H Preferred Stock), and a 10-year warrant to purchase up to 12.2 million shares of common stock at an exercise price of $122.90 per share, for aggregate proceeds of $10.00 billion. The allocated carrying values of the warrant and the Series H Preferred Stock on the date of issuance (based on their relative fair values) were $490 million and $9.51 billion, respectively. Cumulative dividends on the Series H Preferred Stock are payable at 5% per annum through November 14, 2013 and at a rate of 9% per annum thereafter. The Series H Preferred Stock will be accreted to the redemption price of $10.00 billion over five years. The warrant is exercisable at any time until October 28, 2018 and the number of shares of common stock underlying the warrant and the exercise price are subject to adjustment for certain dilutive events. If, on or prior to December 31, 2009, we receive aggregate gross cash proceeds of at least $10 billion from sales of Tier 1 qualifying perpetual preferred stock or common stock, the number of shares of common stock issuable upon exercise of the warrant will be reduced by one-half of the original number of shares of common stock.

## 2. PUBLIC AND PRIVATE OFFERINGS

A capital raising can be a public offering, where securities are offered to the public. In a public offering, a regulator must be involved. A public offering undergoes a registration and disclosure process with the Securities and Exchange Commission (SEC). This process assures that the company is making disclosures to investors concerning the risks, terms, and uses of the capital. The registration process allows securities to be publicly traded in the capital markets.

A capital raising can be a private offering, which is permitted under securities laws if certain criteria are met. Such offerings need not undergo a registration and disclosure process, and thus a regulator is not involved. Privately offered security cannot be publicly traded, though they may be traded in a limited way (the intricacies of securities regulation is beyond the scope of this book). A private offering of securities is negotiated between the issuer and the capital provider(s). In this process, the lawyer's involvement may vary depending on the circumstance.

A capital raising can be negotiated directly between issuer and capital provider. This is a common process in a private offering. A typically public offering goes through an *underwriting* process. This means that a *syndicate* of investment banks acts as an intermediary in the capital market to place the issue with investors. Underwriting is done because the capital raising is complex and risky: for example, it could be a large sum or there could be many investors. Underwriting manages this process of matching the capital need of the issuer with a large group of investors. The underwriting process is negotiable, and it often entails that the underwriter share the risk of the issue by agreeing to purchase the offering with an eye toward reselling to investors or otherwise guarantying the price of an issue. A syndicate is necessary to spread the risk among underwriters.

---

From a lawyer's perspective, the most important difference between a public and private offering is the involvement of the SEC and the level of disclosure necessary for a public transaction. Regulatory scrutiny is needed for public offerings (of course), but it increases the transaction complexity and costs. Lawyers have a prominent role in this process because they draft the registration statements and manage the disclosure process.

---

## 3. CAPITAL RAISING PROCESS AND THE LAWYER'S ROLE

Lawyers are heavily involved in many capital raisings. There may be different sets of lawyers involved for the issuer and the capital providers. Lawyers are needed for the following services:

- Drafting and filing registration statement and prospectus with SEC (for a public offering)
- Drafting the terms of the security instrument
- Conducting due diligence on the issuer and the transaction
- Ensuring that the transaction is valid with respect to corporate law, corporate charter, and the rights of other capital providers
- Negotiating with creditors if the terms of existing debt do not permit the new capital raising
- Facilitating a process with other regulators, if they are involved
- Advising the board of legal and fiduciary issues

These are important services and functions in a well-functioning capital market. In performing monitoring and vetting functions, lawyers are also one of many gate-keepers of the capital market.

# B. MERGERS AND ACQUISITIONS

## 1. WHAT IS M&A?

Mergers and acquisitions (M&A) is a process in which a company may (1) sell itself to another company, in which case it is a target, (2) buy another company, in which case it is an acquirer, or (3) buy or sell certain assets.

## 2. RATIONALE FOR M&A

The rationale for M&A should not be to get bigger, though sometimes managers mistakenly (and unfortunately for shareholders) act on an unfounded assumption that bigger is better. By way of analogy, if $(1 + 1 = 2)$, why do a transaction to achieve 2 when $(1 + 1)$ is just as good? The rationale must be to enhance value. There should be a justification based on value creation through *synergy*. Continuing our math analogy, this means that $(1 + 1 > 2)$. Value is enhanced in two fundamental ways.

- *Revenue synergy*: the combination of two companies results in more revenue than the two firms acting independently. For example, two firms with different but complementary products can cross-sell these products under a common marketing strategy. One rationale for the repeal of the Glass-Steagall Act, which separated financial institutions, was to allow a financial institution to cross-sell financial products such as bank loans, securities underwriting, and insurance. Bigger may be better because it leads to more business than if the two firms were independent.
- *Cost synergy*: the combination of two companies results in less operating costs than the two firms acting independently. For example, two headquarters, two sales departments, two legal department, etc., are reduced to one. Bigger may be better because it leads to less cost than if the two firms were independent.

EXAMPLE 14.2

---

**Merger between Hewlett-Packard and Compaq**

In 2001, Hewlett-Packard and Compaq agreed to merge. Below is the press release from Hewlett-Packard announcing the merger. The typical merger announcement provides a brief justification for the merger (a more detailed justification is provided in the merger proxy).

---

---

> ## *Hewlett-Packard and Compaq Agree to Merge, Creating $87 Billion Global Technology Leader*
> ### September 3, 2001
>
> Hewlett-Packard Company (NYSE: HWP) and Compaq Computer Corporation (NYSE: CPQ) announced today a definitive merger agreement to create an $87 billion global technology leader. The new HP will offer the industry's most complete set of IT products and services for both businesses and consumers, with a commitment to serving customers with open systems and architectures. The combined company will have #1 worldwide revenue positions in servers, access devices (PCs and hand-helds) and imaging and printing, as well as leading revenue positions in IT services, storage and management software.
>
> The merger is expected to generate cost synergies reaching approximately $2.5 billion annually and drive a significantly improved cost structure. Based on both companies' last four reported fiscal quarters, the new HP would have approximate pro forma assets of $56.4 billion, annual revenues of $87.4 billion and annual operating earnings of $3.9 billion. It would also have operations in more than 160 countries and over 145,000 employees.
>
> Carly Fiorina, chairman and chief executive officer of HP, will be chairman and CEO of the new HP. Michael Capellas, chairman and chief executive officer of Compaq, will be president. Capellas and four other members of Compaq's current Board of Directors will join HP's Board upon closing.
>
> "This is a decisive move that accelerates our strategy and positions us to win by offering even greater value to our customers and partners," said Fiorina. "In addition to the clear strategic benefits of combining two highly complementary organizations and product families, we can create substantial shareowner value through significant cost structure improvements and access to new growth opportunities. At a particularly challenging time for the IT industry, this combination vaults us into a leadership role with customers and partners—together we will shape the industry for years to come."
>
> The transaction is expected to be substantially accretive to HP's pro forma earnings per share in the first full year of combined operations based on achieving planned cost synergies. Cost synergies of approximately $2.0 billion are expected in fiscal 2003, the first full year of combined operations. Fully realized synergies are expected to reach a run rate of approximately $2.5 billion by mid-fiscal 2004. These anticipated synergies result from product rationalization; efficiencies in administration, procurement, manufacturing and marketing; and savings from improved direct distribution of PCs and servers. Subject to regulatory and shareowner approvals and customary closing conditions, the transaction is expected to close in the first half of 2002. In connection with the transaction, both companies have adopted shareowner rights plans; information on these plans will be filed today with the Securities and Exchange Commission.

## 3. ACCRETION AND DILUTION

Most corporate transactions have an effect on earnings and earnings per share. Accretion means that post-transaction earnings per share increases. Dilution means that post-transaction earnings per share decreases. Accretion and dilution are important because managers want to know whether the transaction enhances or diminishes earnings. Concern over accretion and dilution is common in capital raisings and M&A deals. In the above announcement by HP, a key representation is: "The transaction is expected to be substantially accretive to HP's pro forma earnings per share in the first full year of combined operations based on achieving planned cost synergies." Much of this accretion will come from "cost synergies" valued at $2.5 billion per year.

EXAMPLE 14.3

---

### Accretion and dilution

Assume that companies Alpha and Zulu produce the results below.

|  | Alpha | Zulu |
|---|---|---|
| Net income | 100 | 100 |
| Shares outstanding | 20 | 25 |
| EPS | 5.00 | 4.00 |

The merger is modeled on different scenarios.

Scenario 1: Alpha acquires Zulu and issues 1 share of Alpha for 1 share of Zulu, and there are no synergies.

Scenario 2: Alpha acquires Zulu and issues 1 share of Alpha for 1 share of Zulu, and there are 100 in after-tax synergy gains.

Scenario 3: Alpha acquires Zulu and issues 0.8 shares of Alpha for 1 share of Zulu, and there are no synergies.

Scenario 4: Alpha acquires Zulu and issues 1.2 shares of Alpha for 1 share of Zulu, and there are 100 in after-tax synergy gains.

These transactions produce the results below.

|  | Scenario 1 | Scenario 2 | Scenario 3 | Scenario 4 |
|---|---|---|---|---|
| Combined net income | 200 | 200 | 200 | 200 |
| Synergies | 0 | 100 | 0 | 100 |
| Total net income | 200 | 300 | 200 | 300 |
| Alphas shares oustanding | 20 | 20 | 20 | 20 |
| Alpha shares issued | 25 | 25 | 20 | 30 |
| Total shares outstanding | 45 | 45 | 40 | 50 |
| EPS | 4.44 | 6.67 | 5.00 | 6.00 |
| Accretive/dilutive | Dilutive | Accretive | Neutral | Accretive |

Notice how different levels of consideration offered (shares of Alpha) change the accretion/dilution calculation. In Scenario 3, the exchange ratio of Alpha to Zulu shares of 0.8:1.0 is EPS neutral because Zulu shareholders are getting the equivalent of $4.00 EPS of Alpha shares, which earn $5.00 EPS. In Scenario 4, Zulu shareholders are getting a premium price (1.2 shares of Alpha), but the transaction is still accretive to earnings of Alpha because substantial accretive effects of the synergy gains offset the dilutive effect of the premium price given to Zulu shareholders.

## 4. M&A PROCESS AND THE LAWYER'S ROLE

The M&A process typically involves three groups of professionals: financial advisers (investment banks), lawyers, and accountants.

Financial advisers advise on the financial aspects of the deal, which can be complex. Additionally, investment bankers will typically have responsibility for managing the entire deal process. There are several reasons for this. They are the experts in the financial effects of the merger, and also coordinate additional capital raising if need. They often create the idea for a merger or acquisition to their clients. They have institutional relationships with the client and the potential M&A deal partners. Accordingly, they are in a position to coordinate the deal process.

Accountants advise on accounting issues, and are important to conduct due diligence on the company's finances. They examine the books and records.

Lawyers are also important to execute an M&A deal. There are several aspects of deal execution. Like accountants, they conduct due diligence on the legal issues. Due diligence may entail examining the company's corporate charter documents, contracts with customers and suppliers, intellectual property rights, litigation risk, environmental risk, regulatory risk, and all other matters involving the legal aspect of a company's operations.

Lawyers facilitate regulatory approval process if the merger or acquisition requires regulatory approval. For example, there may be competition or antitrust issues involved in a merger. A variety of federal agencies may have regulatory authority over the corporation, and regulatory approval may be a closing condition to the consummation of a merger. This work may include an application and review process, which may entail significant work.

Lawyers draft the merger documents, including the merger proxy, the merger agreement (contract), and employment agreements. The merger proxy and the merger agreement are the foundational documents of the transaction. They are dense, detailed documents requiring great expertise in drafting and knowledge of the transaction. This process entails a significant degree of negotiations.

Lawyers advise a corporation's board of directors on its fiduciary duty during a merger process. As any class in Business Associations demonstrates, fiduciary duty issues can be complicated.

Lastly, lawyers can be strategic advisers to the company in much the same way that financial advisers are and that typically accountants are not. Regulatory issues and deal tactics may require legal expertise at a more strategic level. Moreover, lawyers may be the best positioned or most skilled negotiator.

## Mergers and Acquisitions Process and Timeline

| Strategic Assessment | Deal Framework | Execution | Closing |
| --- | --- | --- | --- |
| • Evaluate business or strategic need<br>• Generate target or buyer list based on strategic evaluation<br>• Conduct preliminary internal assessment of acquisition or sale, including valuation<br>• Hire financial and legal advisers | • Approach target or acquirer directly or through advisers<br>• Discuss potential acquisition and gauge interest<br>• Outline broad framework for the possibility of a deal, including valuation and other important hurdle issues<br>• Sign confidentiality agreement | • Assemble internal and external deal team<br>• Conduct due diligence including financial review, document review, legal risk review, and management interviews<br>• Negotiate deal terms, including purchase price<br>• Negotiate merger contract<br>• Negotiate employment contracts<br>• Obtain fairness opinion from financial adviser<br>• Obtain lawyer's or accountant's opinion or "comfort letter", if necessary<br>• Obtain board and shareholder approval<br>• File regulatory applications and disclosures, if any | • Facilitate transition of management<br>• Prepare for integration of operations<br>• Check closing conditions or obtain waivers<br>• Obtain regulatory approval, if any |

Note: This is a generic M&A process chart. Each transaction is unique and may require a uniquely tailored process. This chart provides a broad understanding of the large steps necessary in doing an M&A transaction. One can see that these transactions are complex.

## C. RESTRUCTURING

A restructuring is when a company restructures its business, finance or both. In simple terms, the company undergoes a transformative internal change. A special form of restructuring is bankruptcy, which occurs when a creditor exercises its rights to claim the assets of the firm under the terms of the credit and the law of bankruptcy. The bankruptcy process necessarily results in a restructuring of the company's finance and, as a result, perhaps its business as well.

Many restructuring transactions take place outside of bankruptcy, though a common feature of restructuring in bankruptcy and non-bankruptcy contexts is an underperforming or distressed company. Often, an M&A transaction or a restructuring is preceded by an announcement that the company is exploring "strategic alternatives," which signals some anticipated transformative change through a restructuring, merger, or acquisition.

EXAMPLE 14.4

---

### Dynegy explores strategic alternatives

Dynegy is a publicly traded energy company. Among other things, it was involved in an aborted merger with Enron when the latter was spiraling out of control from a massive accounting scandal. Recently, Dynegy has fallen on hard times. On June 25, 2007, its stock price closed at $47.15, and on June 25, 2011, the stock closed at $5.97 (the stock has hovered around this level since late 2009). The following is an excerpt of a press release from the company.

\* \* \*

**Dynegy to Commence Open Strategic Alternatives Process to Maximize Value for Stockholders**
  **Dynegy to Engage with Seneca Capital to Immediately Appoint Independent Director to Serve on the Board and a Special Committee That Will Direct Strategic Alternatives Process Dynegy to Retain Independent Restructuring Advisor**

Houston, Nov 23, 2010 (BUSINESS WIRE)—Dynegy Inc. (NYSE: DYN) today announced that it intends to immediately commence an open strategic alternatives process to solicit proposals from potentially interested parties and carefully review its standalone restructuring alternatives, if stockholders do not vote to adopt the proposal under which an affiliate of The Blackstone Group (NYSE: BX) agreed to acquire Dynegy for $5.00 per share in cash. At this time, Dynegy anticipates that the proposal will not receive the necessary votes to be adopted. Blackstone and Dynegy therefore intend to terminate the merger agreement. The Special Meeting of Stockholders will resume today at 3:30 PM Central time.

**Open Strategic Alternatives Process**

As part of the open strategic alternatives process, Dynegy's financial advisors will contact a broad group of potential strategic and financial buyers, including Seneca Capital and Icahn Associates. Dynegy invites other interested third parties to contact Dynegy or its financial advisors. There can be no assurance that the solicitation of proposals will result in Dynegy receiving any proposal from a third party. The company does not intend to

---

disclose developments with respect to this review unless and until the Dynegy Board of Directors has approved a course of action.

**Special Committee of the Board of Directors**

A Special Committee of independent directors will oversee the open strategic alternatives process. Patricia A. Hammick, Dynegy's lead independent director, will act as the Chair of the Special Committee. In addition to Mrs. Hammick, the Special Committee will include David W. Biegler, Victor E. Grijalva, Howard B. Sheppard, and William L. Trubeck. Dynegy also intends to add an additional outside independent director to its Board and to the Special Committee immediately through discussions it will commence with Seneca Capital.

"We are committed to moving Dynegy forward and, because we believe stockholders will not approve the transaction with Blackstone, the Board will initiate an open strategic alternatives process to maximize stockholder value," said, Bruce A. Williamson, Chairman, President and Chief Executive Officer of Dynegy Inc. "We will immediately engage interested parties, including Seneca Capital and Icahn Associates, who may have an interest in making an offer to acquire Dynegy. We look forward to maintaining an open and productive dialogue with our stockholders and believe the steps being taken by the Dynegy Board make it clear that we are continuing to actively work to enhance stockholder value."

**Dynegy to Engage Independent Restructuring Advisor**

In addition to evaluating the potential sale of the company, the Special Committee will evaluate the company's forecasts and current commodity and financial market conditions as well as Dynegy's strategic alternatives. Dynegy intends to retain an independent financial restructuring advisor to conduct a review that will include strategic alternatives to create stockholder value, including management's previous analysis of individual asset sales, debt restructuring and cost cutting opportunities. The independent financial restructuring advisor will present its recommendations to the Special Committee.

**Dynegy to Engage with Seneca Capital Regarding Board Representation**

Dynegy will engage with Seneca Capital regarding the immediate appointment of a qualified, independent candidate to the Dynegy Board of Directors. The Dynegy Board currently consists of six members, five of whom are independent.

**Advisors**

Goldman, Sachs & Co. and Greenhill & Co., LLC are serving as financial advisors for the open strategic alternatives process. Sullivan & Cromwell LLP is serving as legal counsel to Dynegy.

A restructuring is driven by dissatisfaction with the status quo. A transaction may entail a combination of asset purchase or sale and capital raising. These can be some of the most complicated corporate transactions. The company may fix recurring capital needs with a recapitalization through capital raising. It may dispose of unprofitable businesses or assets. As a part of the process, the management structure may be changed. Thus, a restructuring may incorporate capital raising and M&A processes.

At last, we have come to our final Conceptual Key and the ultimate lesson of this book. Although lawyers have exclusive rights in the provision of legal services, thus necessitating their services in many corporate transactions, they provide the greatest value when they understand the business needs and circumstances of their clients. Their clients don't speak lawyerese, and they expect lawyers to solve their *business problems*. To do this effectively, lawyers must have a firm understanding of essential business concepts. Good luck in your career!

## D. CASE APPLICATION

*Author's Summary of Facts:* The court found that BarChris Construction Corp. made material misrepresentations in the registration statement filed with the SEC for a debt offering. The question is whether the various individual defendants conducted proper due diligence in the transaction to escape liability for the material representations. In reading this case, consider the significance of due diligence and the potential consequences of failing to do proper due diligence on officers, directors, accountants, investment bankers, and lawyers.

### Escott v. BarChris Construction Corp.
#### 283 F. Supp. 643 (S.D.N.Y. 1968)

McLean, District Judge.

This is an action by purchasers of 5 1/2 per cent convertible subordinated fifteen year debentures of BarChris Construction Corporation (BarChris). Plaintiffs purport to sue on their own behalf and "on behalf of all other and present and former holders" of the debentures. When the action was begun on October 25, 1962, there were nine plaintiffs. Others were subsequently permitted to intervene. At the time of the trial, there were over sixty.

The action is brought under Section 11 of the Securities Act of 1933 (15 U.S.C. §77k). Plaintiffs allege that the registration statement with respect to these debentures filed with the Securities and Exchange Commission, which became effective on May 16, 1961, contained material false statements and material omissions.

Defendants fall into three categories: (1) the persons who signed the registration statement; (2) the underwriters, consisting of eight investment banking firms, led by Drexel & Co. (Drexel); and (3) BarChris's auditors, Peat, Marwick, Mitchell & Co. (Peat, Marwick).

The signers, in addition to BarChris itself, were the nine directors of BarChris, plus its controller, defendant Trilling, who was not a director. Of the nine directors, five were officers of BarChris, i.e., defendants Vitolo, president; Russo, executive vice president; Pugliese, vice president; Kircher, treasurer; and Birnbaum, secretary. Of the remaining four, defendant Grant was a member of the firm of Perkins, Daniels, McCormack & Collins, BarChris's attorneys. He became a director in October 1960. Defendant Coleman, a partner in Drexel, became a director on April 17, 1961, as did the other two, Auslander and Rose, who were not otherwise connected with BarChris.

On the main issue of liability, the questions to be decided are (1) did the registration statement contain false statements of fact, or did it omit to state facts which should have been stated in order to prevent it from being misleading; (2) if so, were the facts which were falsely stated or omitted "material" within the meaning of the Act; (3) if so, have defendants established their affirmative defenses? [The court answered the first two questions in the affirmative.]

Before discussing these questions, some background facts should be mentioned. At the time relevant here, BarChris was engaged primarily in the construction of bowling alleys, somewhat euphemistically referred to as "bowling centers." These were rather elaborate affairs. They contained not only a number of alleys or "lanes," but also, in most cases, bar and restaurant facilities.

For some years the business had exceeded the managerial capacity of its founders. Vitolo and Pugliese are each men of limited education. Vitolo did not get beyond high school. Pugliese ended his schooling in seventh grade. Pugliese devoted his time to supervising the actual construction work. Vitolo was concerned primarily with obtaining new business. Neither was equipped to handle financial matters.

Rather early in their career they enlisted the aid of Russo, who was trained as an accountant. He first joined them in the days of the partnership, left for a time, and returned as an officer and director of B & C Bowling Alley Builders, Inc. in 1958. He eventually became executive vice president of BarChris. In that capacity he handled many of the transactions which figure in this case.

In 1959 BarChris hired Kircher, a certified public accountant who had been employed by Peat, Marwick. He started as controller and became treasurer in 1960. In October of that year, another ex-Peat, Marwick employee, Trilling, succeeded Kircher as controller. At approximately the same time Birnbaum, a young attorney, was hired as house counsel. He became secretary on April 17, 1961.

In December 1959, BarChris sold 560,000 shares of common stock to the public at $3.00 per share. This issue was underwritten by Peter Morgan & Company, one of the present defendants.

By early 1961, BarChris needed additional working capital. The proceeds of the sale of the debentures involved in this action were to be devoted, in part at least, to fill that need.

The registration statement of the debentures, in preliminary form, was filed with the Securities and Exchange Commission on March 30, 1961. A first amendment was filed on May 11 and a second on May 16. The registration statement became effective on May 16. The closing of the financing took place on May 24. On that day BarChris received the net proceeds of the financing.

By that time BarChris was experiencing difficulties in collecting amounts due from some of its customers. Some of them were in arrears in payments due to factors on their discounted notes. As time went on those difficulties increased. Although BarChris continued to build alleys in 1961 and 1962, it became increasingly apparent that the industry was overbuilt. Operators of alleys, often inadequately financed, began to fail. Precisely when the tide turned is a matter of dispute, but at any rate, it was painfully apparent in 1962.

## The Debenture Registration Statement

In preparing the registration statement for the debentures, Grant acted for BarChris. He had previously represented BarChris in preparing the registration statement for the common stock issue. In connection with the sale of common stock, BarChris had issued purchase warrants. In January 1961 a second registration statement was filed in order to update the information pertaining to these warrants. Grant had prepared that statement as well.

Some of the basic information needed for the debenture registration statement was contained in the registration statements previously filed with respect to the common stock and warrants. Grant used these old registration statements as a model in preparing the new one, making the changes which he considered necessary in order to meet the new situation.

The underwriters were represented by the Philadelphia law firm of Drinker, Biddle & Reath. John A. Ballard, a member of that firm, was in charge of that work, assisted by a young associate named Stanton.

Peat, Marwick, BarChris's auditors, who had previously audited BarChris's annual balance sheet and earnings figures for 1958 and 1959, did the same for 1960. These figures were set forth in the registration statement. In addition, Peat, Marwick undertook a so-called "S-1 review," the proper scope of which is one of the matters debated here.

The prospectus contained, among other things, a description of BarChris's business, a description of its real property, some material pertaining to certain of its subsidiaries, and remarks about various other aspects of its affairs. It also contained financial information. It included a consolidated balance sheet as of December 31, 1960, with elaborate explanatory notes. These figures had been audited by Peat, Marwick. It also contained unaudited figures as to net sales, gross profit and net earnings for the first quarter ended March 31, 1961, as compared with the similar quarter for 1960. In addition, it set forth figures as to the company's backlog of unfilled orders as of March 31, 1961, as compared with March 31, 1960, and figures as to BarChris's contingent liability, as of April 30, 1961, on customers' notes discounted and its contingent liability under the so-called alternative method of financing.

Plaintiffs challenge the accuracy of a number of these figures. They also charge that the text of the prospectus, apart from the figures, was false in a number of respects, and that material information was omitted. Each of these contentions, after eliminating duplications, will be separately considered.

[The opinion describes in great detail the misrepresentations made by the company in the registration statement and prospectus, and found them to be material.]

### The "Due Diligence" Defenses

Section 11(b) of the Act provides that:

"... no person, other than the issuer, shall be liable ... who shall sustain the burden of proof—

\* \* \*

(3) that (A) as regards any part of the registration statement not purporting to be made on the authority of an expert ... he had, after reasonable investigation, reasonable ground to believe and did believe, at the time such part of the registration statement became effective, that the statements therein were true and that there was no omission to state a material fact required to be stated therein or necessary to make the statements therein not misleading; ... and (C) as regards any part of the registration statement purporting to be made on the authority of an expert (other than

himself) . . . he had no reasonable ground to believe and did not believe, at the time such part of the registration statement became effective, that the statements therein were untrue or that there was an omission to state a material fact required to be stated therein or necessary to make the statements therein not misleading . . . ."

Section 11(c) defines "reasonable investigation" as follows:

"In determining, for the purpose of paragraph (3) of subsection (b) of this section, what constitutes reasonable investigation and reasonable ground for belief, the standard of reasonableness shall be that required of a prudent man in the management of his own property."

I turn now to the question of whether defendants have proved their due diligence defenses. The position of each defendant will be separately considered.

### Vitolo and Pugliese

They were the founders of the business who stuck with it to the end. Vitolo was president and Pugliese was vice president.

Vitolo and Pugliese are each men of limited education. It is not hard to believe that for them the prospectus was difficult reading, if indeed they read it at all.

But whether it was or not is irrelevant. The liability of a director who signs a registration statement does not depend upon whether or not he read it or, if he did, whether or not he understood what he was reading.

And in any case, Vitolo and Pugliese were not as naive as they claim to be. They were members of BarChris's executive committee. At meetings of that committee BarChris's affairs were discussed at length. They must have known what was going on. Certainly they knew of the inadequacy of cash in 1961. They knew of their own large advances to the company which remained unpaid. They knew that they had agreed not to deposit their checks until the financing proceeds were received. They knew and intended that part of the proceeds were to be used to pay their own loans.

They could not have believed that the registration statement was wholly true and that no material facts had been omitted. And in any case, there is nothing to show that they made any investigation of anything which they may not have known about or understood. They have not proved their due diligence defenses.

### Birnbaum

Birnbaum was a young lawyer, admitted to the bar in 1957, who, after brief periods of employment by two different law firms and an equally brief period of practicing in his own firm, was employed by BarChris as house counsel and assistant secretary in October 1960. Unfortunately for him, he became secretary and a director of BarChris on April 17, 1961, after the first version of the registration statement had been filed with the Securities and Exchange Commission. He signed the later amendments, thereby becoming responsible for the accuracy of the prospectus in its final form.

Although the prospectus, in its description of "management," lists Birnbaum among the "executive officers" and devotes several sentences to a recital of his career, the fact seems to be that he was not an executive officer in any real sense. He did not participate in the management of the company. As house counsel, he attended to legal matters of a routine nature. Among other things, he incorporated subsidiaries, with which BarChris was plentifully supplied. Among the subsidiaries which he incorporated were Capitol Lanes, Inc. which operated Capitol, Yonkers Lanes, Inc. which eventually operated Yonkers, and Parkway Lanes, Inc. which eventually operated Bridge. He was thus aware of that aspect of the business.

Birnbaum examined contracts. In that connection he advised BarChris that the T-Bowl contracts were not legally enforceable. He was thus aware of that fact.

One of Birnbaum's more important duties, first as assistant secretary and later as full-fledged secretary, was to keep the corporate minutes of BarChris and its subsidiaries. This necessarily informed him to a considerable extent about the company's affairs. Birnbaum was not initially a member of the executive committee, however, and did not keep its minutes at the outset. According to the minutes, the first meeting which he attended, "upon invitation of the Committee," was on March 22, 1961. He became a member shortly thereafter and kept the minutes beginning with the meeting of April 24, 1961.

It seems probable that Birnbaum did not know of many of the inaccuracies in the prospectus. He must, however, have appreciated some of them. In any case, he made no investigation and relied on the others to get it right. Unlike Trilling, he was entitled to rely upon Peat, Marwick for the 1960 figures, for as far as appears, he had no personal knowledge of the company's books of account or financial transactions. But he was not entitled to rely upon Kircher, Grant and Ballard for the other portions of the prospectus. As a lawyer, he should have known his obligations under the statute. He should have known that he was required to make a reasonable investigation of the truth of all the statements in the unexpertised portion of the document which he signed. Having failed to make such an investigation, he did not have reasonable ground to believe that all these statements were true. Birnbaum has not established his due diligence defenses except as to the audited 1960 figures.

## Auslander

Auslander was an "outside" director, i.e., one who was not an officer of BarChris. He was chairman of the board of Valley Stream National Bank in Valley Stream, Long Island. In February 1961 Vitolo asked him to become a director of BarChris. Vitolo gave him an enthusiastic account of BarChris's progress and prospects. As an inducement, Vitolo said that when BarChris received the proceeds of a forthcoming issue of securities, it would deposit $1,000,000 in Auslander's bank.

In February and early March 1961, before accepting Vitolo's invitation, Auslander made some investigation of BarChris. He obtained Dun & Bradstreet reports which contained sales and earnings figures for periods earlier than December 31, 1960. He caused inquiry to be made of certain of BarChris's banks and was advised that they regarded BarChris favorably. He was informed that inquiry of Talcott had also produced a favorable response.

On March 3, 1961, Auslander indicated his willingness to accept a place on the board. Shortly thereafter, on March 14, Kircher sent him a copy of BarChris's annual report for 1960. Auslander observed that BarChris's auditors were Peat, Marwick. They were also the auditors for the Valley Stream National Bank. He thought well of them.

Auslander was elected a director on April 17, 1961. The registration statement in its original form had already been filed, of course without his signature. On May 10, 1961, he signed a signature page for the first amendment to the registration statement which was filed on May 11, 1961. This was a separate sheet without any document attached. Auslander did not know that it was a signature page for a registration statement. He vaguley understood that it was something "for the SEC."

Auslander attended a meeting of BarChris's directors on May 15, 1961. At that meeting he, along with the other directors, signed the signature sheet for the second amendment which constituted the registration statement in its final form. Again, this was only a separate sheet without any document attached. Auslander never saw a copy of the registration statement in its final form.

At the May 15 directors' meeting, however, Auslander did realize that what he was signing was a signature sheet to a registration statement. This was the first time that he had appreciated that fact. A copy of the registration statement in its earlier form as amended on May 11, 1961 was passed around at the meeting. Auslander glanced at it briefly. He did not read it thoroughly.

At the May 15 meeting, Russo and Vitolo stated that everything was in order and that the prospectus was correct. Auslander believed this statement.

In considering Auslander's due diligence defenses, a distinction is to be drawn between the expertised and non-expertised portions of the prospectus. As to the former, Auslander knew that Peat, Marwick had audited the 1960 figures. He believed them to be correct because he had confidence in Peat, Marwick. He had no reasonable ground to believe otherwise.

As to the non-expertised portions, however, Auslander is in a different position. He seems to have been under the impression that Peat, Marwick was responsible for all the figures. This impression was not correct, as he would have realized if he had read the prospectus carefully. Auslander made no investigation of the accuracy of the prospectus. He relied on the assurance of Vitolo and Russo, and upon the information he had received in answer to his inquiries back in February and early March. These inquiries were general ones, in the nature of a credit check. The information which he received in answer to them was also general, without specific reference to the statements in the prospectus, which was not prepared until some time thereafter.

It is true that Auslander became a director on the eve of the financing. He had little opportunity to familiarize himself with the company's affairs. The question is whether, under such circumstances, Auslander did enough to establish his due diligence defense with respect to the non-expertised portions of the prospectus.

Section 11 imposes liability in the first instance upon a director, no matter how new he is. He is presumed to know his responsibility when he becomes a director. He can escape liability only by using that reasonable care to investigate the facts which a prudent man would employ in the management of his own property. In my opinion, a prudent man would not act in an important matter without any knowledge of the relevant facts, in sole reliance upon representations of persons who are comparative strangers and upon general information which does not purport to cover the particular case. To say that such minimal conduct measures up to the statutory standard would, to all intents and purposes, absolve new directors from responsibility merely because they are new. This is not a sensible construction of Section 11, when one bears in mind its fundamental purpose of requiring full and truthful disclosure for the protection of investors.

I find and conclude that Auslander has not established his due diligence defense with respect to the misstatements and omissions in those portions of the prospectus other than the audited 1960 figures.

Grant

Grant became a director of BarChris in October 1960. His law firm was counsel to BarChris in matters pertaining to the registration of securities. Grant drafted the registration statement for the stock issue in 1959 and for the warrants in January 1961. He also drafted the registration statement for the debentures. In the preliminary division of work between him and Ballard, the underwriters' counsel, Grant took initial responsibility for preparing the registration statement, while Ballard devoted his efforts in the first instance to preparing the indenture.

Grant is sued as a director and as a signer of the registration statement. This is not an action against him for malpractice in his capacity as a lawyer. Nevertheless, in considering Grant's due diligence defenses, the unique position which he occupied cannot be disregarded. As the director most directly concerned with writing the registration statement and assuring its accuracy, more was required of him in the way of reasonable investigation than could fairly be expected of a director who had no connection with this work.

There is no valid basis for plaintiffs' accusation that Grant knew that the prospectus was false in some respects and incomplete and misleading in others. Having seen him testify at length, I am satisfied as to his integrity. I find that Grant honestly believed that the registration statement was true and that no material facts had been omitted from it.

In this belief he was mistaken, and the fact is that for all his work, he never discovered any of the errors or omissions which have been recounted at length in this opinion, with the single exception of Capitol Lanes. He knew that BarChris had not sold this alley and intended to operate it, but he appears to have been under the erroneous impression that Peat, Marwick had knowingly sanctioned its inclusion in sales because of the allegedly temporary nature of the operation.

Grant contends that a finding that he did not make a reasonable investigation would be equivalent to a holding that a lawyer for an issuing company, in order to show due diligence, must make an independent audit of the figures supplied to him by his client. I do not consider this to be a realistic statement of the issue. There were errors and omissions here which could have been detected without an audit. The question is whether, despite his failure to detect them, Grant made a reasonable effort to that end.

Much of this registration statement is a scissors and paste-pot job. Grant lifted large portions from the earlier prospectuses, modifying them in some instances to the extent that he considered necessary. But BarChris's affairs had changed for the worse by May 1961. Statements that were accurate in January were no longer accurate in May. Grant never discovered this. He accepted the assurances of Kircher and Russo that any change which might have occurred had been for the better, rather than the contrary.

It is claimed that a lawyer is entitled to rely on the statements of his client and that to require him to verify their accuracy would set an unreasonably high standard. This is too broad a generalization. It is all a matter of degree. To require an audit would obviously be unreasonable. On the other hand, to require a check of matters easily verifiable is not unreasonable. Even honest clients can make mistakes. The statute imposes liability for untrue statements regardless of whether they are intentionally untrue. The way to prevent mistakes is to test oral information by examining the original written record.

Grant was entitled to rely on Peat, Marwick for the 1960 figures. He had no reasonable ground to believe them to be inaccurate. But the matters which I have mentioned were not within the expertised portion of the prospectus. As to this, Grant, was obliged to make a reasonable investigation. I am forced to find that he did not make one. After making all due allowances for the fact that Bar Chris's officers misled him, there are too many instances in which Grant failed to make an inquiry which he could easily have made which, if pursued, would have put him on his guard. In my opinion, this finding on the evidence in this case does not establish an unreasonably high standard in other cases for company counsel who are also directors. Each case must rest on its own facts. I conclude that Grant has not established his due diligence defenses except as to the audited 1960 figures.

## The Underwriters and Coleman

The underwriters other than Drexel made no investigation of the accuracy of the prospectus. One of them, Peter Morgan, had underwritten the 1959 stock issue and had been a director of BarChris. He thus had some general familiarity with its affairs, but he knew no more than the other underwriters about the debenture prospectus. They all relied upon Drexel as the "lead" underwriter.

Drexel did make an investigation. The work was in charge of Coleman, a partner of the firm, assisted by Casperson, an associate. Drexel's attorneys acted as attorneys for the entire group of underwriters. Ballard did the work, assisted by Stanton.

On April 17, 1961 Coleman became a director of BarChris. He signed the first amendment to the registration statement filed on May 11 and the second amendment, constituting the registration statement in its final form, filed on May 16. He thereby assumed a responsibility as a director and signer in addition to his responsibility as an underwriter.

The purpose of Section 11 is to protect investors. To that end the underwriters are made responsible for the truth of the prospectus. If they may escape that responsibility by taking at face value representations made to them by the company's management, then the inclusion of underwriters among those liable under Section 11 affords the investors no additional protection. To effectuate the statute's purpose, the phrase "reasonable investigation" must be construed to require more effort on the part of the underwriters than the mere accurate reporting in the prospectus of "date presented" to them by the company. It should make no difference that this data is elicited by questions addressed to the company officers by the underwriters, or that the underwriters at the time believe that the company's officers are truthful and reliable. In order to make the underwriters' participation in this enterprise of any value to the investors, the underwriters must make some reasonable attempt to verify the data submitted to them. They may not rely solely on the company's officers or on the company's counsel. A prudent man in the management of his own property would not rely on them.

It is impossible to lay down a rigid rule suitable for every case defining the extent to which such verification must go. It is a question of degree, a matter of judgment in each case. In the present case, the underwriters' counsel made almost no attempt to verify management's representations. I hold that that was insufficient.

On the evidence in this case, I find that the underwriters' counsel did not make a reasonable investigation of the truth of those portions of the prospectus which were not made on the authority of Peat, Marwick as an expert. Drexel is bound by their failure. It is not a matter of relying upon counsel for legal advice. Here the attorneys were dealing with matters of fact. Drexel delegated to them, as its agent, the business of examining the corporate minutes and contracts. It must bear the consequences of their failure to make an adequate examination.

The other underwriters, who did nothing and relied solely on Drexel and on the lawyers, are also bound by it. It follows that although Drexel and the other underwriters believed that those portions of the prospectus were true, they had no reasonable ground for that belief, within the meaning of the statute. Hence, they have not established their due diligence defence, except as to the 1960 audited figures.

The same conclusions must apply to Coleman. Although he participated quite actively in the earlier stages of the preparation of the prospectus, and contributed questions and warnings of his own, in addition to the questions of counsel, the fact is that he stopped his participation toward the end of March 1961. He made no investigation after he became a director. When it came to verification, he relied upon his counsel to do it for him. Since counsel failed to do it, Coleman is bound by that failure. Consequently, in his case also, he has not established his due diligence defense except as to the audited 1960 figures.

## QUESTIONS

1. In what way was the debenture's registration statement materially misleading?
2. Why must due diligence be performed?
3. Birnbaum, a young lawyer, is perhaps the most sympathetic defendant in this case. Why was he found liable?
4. What should Birnbaum have done to protect himself?
5. In what did Grant, another lawyer, fail to perform proper due diligence?

---

As noted in Chapter 4, *Smith v. Van Gorkom* is a classic Delaware corporate law case concerning the fiduciary duty of care. It arises from an acquisition of Trans Union by Jay Pritzker. A key accounting and finance consideration was the effect of accelerated depreciation on the company's profit, and its inability to use investment tax credits due to low profit levels. The problem motivated the company's CEO, Jerome Van Gorkom, to sell the company to Jay Pritzker. The central issue is whether the board of directors properly exercised its duty of care when it approved the sale of the company. The court ultimately held that it did not. Excerpted below is the court's factual recitation of the acquisition process, which the court ultimately found deficient. In reading this case, consider why the court found the M&A process inadequate.

### *Smith v. Van Gorkom (Part II)*
488 A.2d 858 (Del. 1985)

Horsey, Justice (for the majority):

This appeal from the Court of Chancery involves a class action brought by shareholders of the defendant Trans Union Corporation ("Trans Union" or "the Company"), originally seeking rescission of a cash-out merger of Trans Union into the defendant New T Company ("New T"), a wholly-owned subsidiary of the defendant, Marmon Group, Inc. ("Marmon"). Alternate relief in the form of damages is sought against the defendant members of the Board of Directors of Trans Union, New T, and Jay A. Pritzker and Robert A. Pritzker, owners of Marmon.

We hold: (1) that the Board's decision, reached September 20, 1980, to approve the proposed cash-out merger was not the product of an informed business judgment; (2) that the Board's subsequent efforts to amend the Merger Agreement and take other curative action were ineffectual, both legally and factually; and (3) that the Board did not deal with complete candor with the stockholders by failing to disclose all material facts, which they knew or should have known, before securing the stockholders' approval of the merger.

## I.

On August 27, 1980, Van Gorkom met with Senior Management of Trans Union. Van Gorkom reported on his lobbying efforts in Washington and his desire to find a solution to the tax credit problem more permanent than a continued program of acquisitions. Various alternatives were suggested and discussed preliminarily, including the sale of Trans Union to a company with a large amount of taxable income.

Donald Romans, Chief Financial Officer of Trans Union, stated that his department had done a "very brief bit of work on the possibility of a leveraged buy-out." This work had been prompted by a media article which Romans had seen regarding a leveraged buy-out by management. The work consisted of a "preliminary study" of the cash which could be generated by the Company if it participated in a leveraged buy-out. As Romans stated, this analysis "was very first and rough cut at seeing whether a cash flow would support what might be considered a high price for this type of transaction."

On September 5, at another Senior Management meeting which Van Gorkom attended, Romans again brought up the idea of a leveraged buy-out as a "possible strategic alternative" to the Company's acquisition program. Romans and Bruce S. Chelberg, President and Chief Operating Officer of Trans Union, had been working on the matter in preparation for the meeting. According to Romans: They did not "come up" with a price for the Company. They merely "ran the numbers" at $50 a share and at $60 a share with the "rough form" of their cash figures at the time. Their "figures indicated that $50 would be very easy to do but $60 would be very difficult to do under those figures." This work did not purport to establish a fair price for either the Company or 100% of the stock. It was intended to determine the cash flow needed to service the debt that would "probably" be incurred in a leveraged buy-out, based on "rough calculations" without "any benefit of experts to identify what the limits were to that, and so forth." These computations were not considered extensive and no conclusion was reached.

At this meeting, Van Gorkom stated that he would be willing to take $55 per share for his own 75,000 shares. He vetoed the suggestion of a leveraged buy-out by Management, however, as involving a potential conflict of interest for Management. Van Gorkom, a certified public accountant and lawyer, had been an officer of Trans Union for 24 years, its Chief Executive Officer for more than 17 years, and Chairman of its Board for 2 years. It is noteworthy in this connection that he was then approaching 65 years of age and mandatory retirement.

For several days following the September 5 meeting, Van Gorkom pondered the idea of a sale. He had participated in many acquisitions as a manager and director of Trans Union and as a director of other companies. He was familiar with acquisition procedures, valuation methods, and negotiations; and he privately considered the pros and cons of whether Trans Union should seek a privately or publicly-held purchaser.

Van Gorkom decided to meet with Jay A. Pritzker, a well-known corporate take-over specialist and a social acquaintance. However, rather than approaching Pritzker simply to determine his interest in acquiring Trans Union, Van Gorkom assembled a proposed per share price for sale of the Company and a financing structure by which to accomplish the sale. Van Gorkom did so without consulting either his Board or any members of Senior Management except one: Carl Peterson, Trans Union's Controller. Telling Peterson that he wanted no other person on his staff to know what he was doing, but without telling him why, Van Gorkom directed Peterson to calculate the feasibility of a leveraged buy-out at an assumed price per share of $55. Apart from the Company's historic stock market price,[5] and Van Gorkom's long association with Trans Union, the record is devoid of any competent evidence that $55 represented the per share intrinsic value of the Company.

Having thus chosen the $55 figure, based solely on the availability of a leveraged buy-out, Van Gorkom multiplied the price per share by the number of shares outstanding to reach a total value of the Company of $690 million. Van Gorkom told Peterson to use this $690 million figure and to assume a $200 million equity contribution by the buyer. Based on these assumptions, Van Gorkom directed Peterson to determine whether the debt portion of the purchase price could be paid off in five years or less if financed by Trans Union's cash flow as projected in the Five Year Forecast, and by the sale of certain weaker divisions identified in a study done for Trans Union by the Boston Consulting Group ("BCG study"). Peterson reported that, of the purchase price, approximately $50-80 million would remain outstanding after five years. Van Gorkom was disappointed, but decided to meet with Pritzker nevertheless.

Van Gorkom arranged a meeting with Pritzker at the latter's home on Saturday, September 13, 1980. Van Gorkom prefaced his presentation by stating to Pritzker: "Now as far as you are concerned, I can, I think, show how you can pay a substantial premium over the present stock price and pay off most of the loan in the first five years . . . . If you could pay $55 for this Company, here is a way in which I think it can be financed."

Van Gorkom then reviewed with Pritzker his calculations based upon his proposed price of $55 per share. Although Pritzker mentioned $50 as a more attractive figure, no other price was mentioned. However, Van Gorkom stated that to be sure that $55 was the best price obtainable, Trans Union should be free to accept any better offer. Pritzker demurred, stating that his organization would serve as a "stalking horse" for an "auction contest" only if Trans Union would permit Pritzker to buy 1,750,000 shares of Trans Union stock at market price which Pritzker could then sell to any higher bidder. After further discussion on this point, Pritzker told Van Gorkom that he would give him a more definite reaction soon.

---

5. The common stock of Trans Union was traded on the New York Stock Exchange. Over the five-year period from 1975 through 1979, Trans Union's stock had traded within a range of a high of $39 1/2 and a low of $24 1/4. Its high and low range for 1980 through September 19 (the last trading day before announcement of the merger) was $38 1/4-$29 1/2.

On Monday, September 15, Pritzker advised Van Gorkom that he was interested in the $55 cash-out merger proposal and requested more information on Trans Union. Van Gorkom agreed to meet privately with Pritzker, accompanied by Peterson, Chelberg, and Michael Carpenter, Trans Union's consultant from the Boston Consulting Group. The meetings took place on September 16 and 17. Van Gorkom was "astounded that events were moving with such amazing rapidity."

On Thursday, September 18, Van Gorkom met again with Pritzker. At that time, Van Gorkom knew that Pritzker intended to make a cash-out merger offer at Van Gorkom's proposed $55 per share. Pritzker instructed his attorney, a merger and acquisition specialist, to begin drafting merger documents. There was no further discussion of the $55 price. However, the number of shares of Trans Union's treasury stock to be offered to Pritzker was negotiated down to one million shares; the price was set at $38-75 cents above the per share price at the close of the market on September 19. At this point, Pritzker insisted that the Trans Union Board act on his merger proposal within the next three days, stating to Van Gorkom: "We have to have a decision by no later than Sunday [evening, September 21] before the opening of the English stock exchange on Monday morning." Pritzker's lawyer was then instructed to draft the merger documents, to be reviewed by Van Gorkom's lawyer, "sometimes with discussion and sometimes not, in the haste to get it finished."

On Friday, September 19, Van Gorkom, Chelberg, and Pritzker consulted with Trans Union's lead bank regarding the financing of Pritzker's purchase of Trans Union. The bank indicated that it could form a syndicate of banks that would finance the transaction. On the same day, Van Gorkom retained James Brennan, Esquire, to advise Trans Union on the legal aspects of the merger. Van Gorkom did not consult with William Browder, a Vice-President and director of Trans Union and former head of its legal department, or with William Moore, then the head of Trans Union's legal staff.

On Friday, September 19, Van Gorkom called a special meeting of the Trans Union Board for noon the following day. He also called a meeting of the Company's Senior Management to convene at 11:00 a.m., prior to the meeting of the Board. No one, except Chelberg and Peterson, was told the purpose of the meetings. Van Gorkom did not invite Trans Union's investment banker, Salomon Brothers or its Chicago-based partner, to attend.

Of those present at the Senior Management meeting on September 20, only Chelberg and Peterson had prior knowledge of Pritzker's offer. Van Gorkom disclosed the offer and described its terms, but he furnished no copies of the proposed Merger Agreement. Romans announced that his department had done a second study which showed that, for a leveraged buy-out, the price range for Trans Union stock was between $55 and $65 per share. Van Gorkom neither saw the study nor asked Romans to make it available for the Board meeting.

Senior Management's reaction to the Pritzker proposal was completely negative. No member of Management, except Chelberg and Peterson, supported the proposal. Romans objected to the price as being too low; he was critical of the timing and suggested that consideration should be given to the adverse tax consequences of an all-cash deal for low-basis shareholders; and he took the position that the agreement to sell Pritzker one million newly-issued shares at market price would inhibit other offers, as would the prohibitions against soliciting bids and furnishing inside information to other bidders. Romans argued that the Pritzker proposal was a "lock up" and amounted to "an agreed merger as opposed to an offer." Nevertheless, Van Gorkom proceeded to the Board meeting as scheduled without further delay.

Ten directors served on the Trans Union Board, five inside (defendants Bonser, O'Boyle, Browder, Chelberg, and Van Gorkom) and five outside (defendants Wallis, Johnson, Lanterman, Morgan and Reneker). All directors were present at the meeting, except O'Boyle who was ill. Of the outside directors, four were corporate chief executive officers and one was the former Dean of the University of Chicago Business School. None was an investment banker or trained financial analyst. All members of the Board were well informed about the Company and its operations as a going concern. They were familiar with the current financial condition of the Company, as well as operating and earnings projections reported in the recent Five Year Forecast. The Board generally received regular and detailed reports and was kept abreast of the accumulated investment tax credit and accelerated depreciation problem.

Van Gorkom began the Special Meeting of the Board with a twenty-minute oral presentation. Copies of the proposed Merger Agreement were delivered too late for study before or during the meeting. He reviewed the Company's ITC and depreciation problems and the efforts theretofore made to solve them. He discussed his initial meeting with Pritzker and his motivation in arranging that meeting. Van Gorkom did not disclose to the Board, however, the methodology by which he alone had arrived at the $55 figure, or the fact that he first proposed the $55 price in his negotiations with Pritzker.

Van Gorkom outlined the terms of the Pritzker offer as follows: Pritzker would pay $55 in cash for all outstanding shares of Trans Union stock upon completion of which Trans Union would be merged into New T Company, a subsidiary wholly-owned by Pritzker and formed to implement the merger; for a period of 90 days, Trans Union could receive, but could not actively solicit, competing offers; the offer had to be acted on by the next evening, Sunday, September 21; Trans Union could only furnish to competing bidders published information, and not proprietary information; the offer was subject to Pritzker obtaining the necessary financing by October 10, 1980; if the financing contingency were met or waived by Pritzker, Trans Union was required to sell to Pritzker one million newly-issued shares of Trans Union at $38 per share.

Van Gorkom took the position that putting Trans Union "up for auction" through a 90-day market test would validate a decision by the Board that $55 was a fair price. He told the Board that the "free market will have an opportunity to judge whether $55 is a fair price." Van Gorkom framed the decision before the Board not as whether $55 per share was the highest price that could be obtained, but as whether the $55 price was a fair price that the stockholders should be given the opportunity to accept or reject.

Attorney Brennan advised the members of the Board that they might be sued if they failed to accept the offer and that a fairness opinion was not required as a matter of law.

Romans attended the meeting as chief financial officer of the Company. He told the Board that he had not been involved in the negotiations with Pritzker and knew nothing about the merger proposal until the morning of the meeting; that his studies did not indicate either a fair price for the stock or a valuation of the Company; that he did not see his role as directly addressing the fairness issue; and that he and his people "were trying to search for ways to justify a price in connection with such a [leveraged buy-out] transaction, rather than to say what the shares are worth." Romans testified:

> I told the Board that the study ran the numbers at 50 and 60, and then the subsequent study at 55 and 65, and that was not the same thing as saying that I have a valuation of the company at X dollars. But it was a way-a first step towards reaching that conclusion.

Romans told the Board that, in his opinion, $55 was "in the range of a fair price," but "at the beginning of the range."

Chelberg, Trans Union's President, supported Van Gorkom's presentation and representations. He testified that he "participated to make sure that the Board members collectively were clear on the details of the agreement or offer from Pritzker;" that he "participated in the discussion with Mr. Brennan, inquiring of him about the necessity for valuation opinions in spite of the way in which this particular offer was couched;" and that he was otherwise actively involved in supporting the positions being taken by Van Gorkom before the Board about "the necessity to act immediately on this offer," and about "the adequacy of the $55 and the question of how that would be tested."

The Board meeting of September 20 lasted about two hours. Based solely upon Van Gorkom's oral presentation, Chelberg's supporting representations, Romans' oral statement, Brennan's legal advice, and their knowledge of the market history of the Company's stock,[9] the directors approved the proposed Merger Agreement. However, the Board later claimed to have attached two conditions to its acceptance: (1) that Trans Union reserved the right to accept any better offer that was made during the market test period; and (2) that Trans Union could share its proprietary information with any other potential bidders. While the Board now claims to have reserved the right to accept any better offer received after the announcement of the Pritzker agreement (even though the minutes of the meeting do not reflect this), it is undisputed that the Board did not reserve the right to actively solicit alternate offers.

The Merger Agreement was executed by Van Gorkom during the evening of September 20 at a formal social event that he hosted for the opening of the Chicago Lyric Opera. Neither he nor any other director read the agreement prior to its signing and delivery to Pritzker.

On Monday, September 22, the Company issued a press release announcing that Trans Union had entered into a "definitive" Merger Agreement with an affiliate of the Marmon Group, Inc., a Pritzker holding company. Within 10 days of the public announcement, dissent among Senior Management over the merger had become widespread. Faced with threatened resignations of key officers, Van Gorkom met with Pritzker who agreed to several modifications of the Agreement. Pritzker was willing to do so provided that Van Gorkom could persuade the dissidents to remain on the Company payroll for at least six months after consummation of the merger.

---

9. The Trial Court stated the premium relationship of the $55 price to the market history of the Company's stock as follows:

> . . . the merger price offered to the stockholders of Trans Union represented a premium of 62% over the average of the high and low prices at which Trans Union stock had traded in 1980, a premium of 48% over the last closing price, and a premium of 39% over the highest price at which the stock of Trans Union had traded any time during the prior six years.

Van Gorkom reconvened the Board on October 8 and secured the directors' approval of the proposed amendments-sight unseen. The Board also authorized the employment of Salomon Brothers, its investment banker, to solicit other offers for Trans Union during the proposed "market test" period.

The next day, October 9, Trans Union issued a press release announcing: (1) that Pritzker had obtained "the financing commitments necessary to consummate" the merger with Trans Union; (2) that Pritzker had acquired one million shares of Trans Union common stock at $38 per share; (3) that Trans Union was now permitted to actively seek other offers and had retained Salomon Brothers for that purpose; and (4) that if a more favorable offer were not received before February 1, 1981, Trans Union's shareholders would thereafter meet to vote on the Pritzker proposal.

It was not until the following day, October 10, that the actual amendments to the Merger Agreement were prepared by Pritzker and delivered to Van Gorkom for execution. As will be seen, the amendments were considerably at variance with Van Gorkom's representations of the amendments to the Board on October 8; and the amendments placed serious constraints on Trans Union's ability to negotiate a better deal and withdraw from the Pritzker agreement. Nevertheless, Van Gorkom proceeded to execute what became the October 10 amendments to the Merger Agreement without conferring further with the Board members and apparently without comprehending the actual implications of the amendments.

Salomon Brothers' efforts over a three-month period from October 21 to January 21 produced only one serious suitor for Trans Union-General Electric Credit Corporation ("GE Credit"), a subsidiary of the General Electric Company. However, GE Credit was unwilling to make an offer for Trans Union unless Trans Union first rescinded its Merger Agreement with Pritzker. When Pritzker refused, GE Credit terminated further discussions with Trans Union in early January.

In the meantime, in early December, the investment firm of Kohlberg, Kravis, Roberts & Co. ("KKR"), the only other concern to make a firm offer for Trans Union, withdrew its offer under circumstances hereinafter detailed.

On December 19, this litigation was commenced and, within four weeks, the plaintiffs had deposed eight of the ten directors of Trans Union, including Van Gorkom, Chelberg and Romans, its Chief Financial Officer. On January 21, Management's Proxy Statement for the February 10 shareholder meeting was mailed to Trans Union's stockholders. On January 26, Trans Union's Board met and, after a lengthy meeting, voted to proceed with the Pritzker merger. The Board also approved for mailing, "on or about January 27," a Supplement to its Proxy Statement. The Supplement purportedly set forth all information relevant to the Pritzker Merger Agreement, which had not been divulged in the first Proxy Statement.

On February 10, the stockholders of Trans Union approved the Pritzker merger proposal. Of the outstanding shares, 69.9% were voted in favor of the merger; 7.25% were voted against the merger; and 22.85% were not voted.

## QUESTIONS

1. What process was used to formulate the strategic direction of Trans Union?
2. What was the process used to determine that Jay Pritzker was the best buyer?
3. Assess Trans Union's effort to find an alternative buyer. Why might a competition among buyers have been a good thing for Trans Union?

4. How was the sales value determined?
5. If you were a board member at Trans Union, what questions would you have asked Van Gorkom and the senior management?

---

The case below involves a restructuring of a failing company. Note that it involves several different transactions, including the sale of assets, recapitalization of the firm by raising new equity capital, exchange debt for equity, and restructuring the legal terms of current debt. The case also illustrates the rights of bondholders and the inherent tension between bondholders and equityholders.

## Katz v. Oak Industries, Inc.
### 508 A.2d 873 (Del.Ch. 1986)

ALLEN, Chancellor.

Plaintiff is the owner of long-term debt securities issued by Oak Industries, Inc. ("Oak"), a Delaware corporation; in this class action he seeks to enjoin the consummation of an exchange offer and consent solicitation made by Oak to holders of various classes of its long-term debt. As detailed below that offer is an integral part of a series of transactions that together would effect a major reorganization and recapitalization of Oak. The claim asserted is in essence, that the exchange offer is a coercive device and, in the circumstances, constitutes a breach of contract.

### I.

Oak manufactures and markets component equipments used in consumer, industrial and military products (the "Components Segment"); produces communications equipment for use in cable television systems and satellite television systems (the "Communications Segment") and manufactures and markets laminates and other materials used in printed circuit board applications (the "Materials Segment"). During 1985, the Company has terminated certain other unrelated businesses. As detailed below, it has now entered into an agreement with Allied-Signal, Inc. for the sale of the Materials Segment of its business and is currently seeking a buyer for its Communications Segment.

Even a casual review of Oak's financial results over the last several years shows it unmistakably to be a company in deep trouble. During the period from January 1, 1982 through September 30, 1985, the Company has experienced unremitting losses from operations; on net sales of approximately $1.26 billion during that period it has lost over $335 million. As a result its total stockholders' equity has first shriveled (from $260 million on 12/31/81 to $85 million on 12/31/83) and then disappeared completely (as of 9/30/85 there was a $62 million deficit in its stockholders' equity accounts). Financial markets, of course, reflected this gloomy history.

Unless Oak can be made profitable within some reasonably short time it will not continue as an operating company. Oak's board of directors, comprised almost entirely of outside directors, has authorized steps to buy the company time. In February, 1985, in order to reduce a burdensome annual cash interest obligation on its $230 million of then outstanding debentures, the Company offered to exchange such debentures for a combination of notes, common stock and warrants. As a result, approximately $180 million principal amount of the then outstanding debentures were exchanged. Since interest on certain of the notes issued in that exchange offer is payable in common stock, the effect of the 1985 exchange offer was to reduce to some extent the cash drain on the Company caused by its significant debt.

About the same time that the 1985 exchange offer was made, the Company announced its intention to discontinue certain of its operations and sell certain of its properties. Taking these steps, while effective to stave off a default and to reduce to some extent the immediate cash drain, did not address Oak's longer-range problems. Therefore, also during 1985 representatives of the Company held informal discussions with several interested parties exploring the possibility of an investment from, combination with or acquisition by another company. As a result of these discussions, the Company and Allied-Signal, Inc. entered into two agreements. The first, the Acquisition Agreement, contemplates the sale to Allied-Signal of the Materials Segment for $160 million in cash. The second agreement, the Stock Purchase Agreement, provides for the purchase by Allied-Signal for $15 million cash of 10 million shares of the Company's common stock together with warrants to purchase additional common stock.

The Stock Purchase Agreement provides as a condition to Allied-Signal's obligation that at least 85% of the aggregate principal amount of all of the Company's debt securities shall have tendered and accepted the exchange offers that are the subject of this lawsuit. Oak has six classes of such long term debt. If less than 85% of the aggregate principal amount of such debt accepts the offer, Allied-Signal has an option, but no obligation, to purchase the common stock and warrants contemplated by the Stock Purchase Agreement. An additional condition for the closing of the Stock Purchase Agreement is that the sale of the Company's Materials Segment contemplated by the Acquisition Agreement shall have been concluded.

Thus, as part of the restructuring and recapitalization contemplated by the Acquisition Agreement and the Stock Purchase Agreement, the Company has extended an exchange offer to each of the holders of the six classes of its long-term debt securities. These pending exchange offers include a Common Stock Exchange Offer (available only to holders of the 9 5/8% convertible notes) and the Payment Certificate Exchange Offers (available to holders of all six classes of Oak's long-term debt securities). The Common Stock Exchange Offer currently provides for the payment to each tendering noteholder of 407 shares of the Company's common stock in exchange for each $1,000 9 5/8% note accepted. The offer is limited to $38.6 million principal amount of notes (out of approximately $83.9 million outstanding).

The Payment Certificate Exchange Offer is an any and all offer. Under its terms, a payment certificate, payable in cash five days after the closing of the sale of the Materials Segment to Allied-Signal, is offered in exchange for debt securities. The cash value of the Payment Certificate will vary depending upon the particular security tendered. In each instance, however, that payment will be less than the face amount of the obligation. The cash payments range in amount, per $1,000 of principal, from $918 to $655. These cash values however appear to represent a premium over the market prices for the Company's debentures as of the time the terms of the transaction were set.

The Payment Certificate Exchange Offer is subject to certain important conditions before Oak has an obligation to accept tenders under it. First, it is necessary that a minimum amount ($38.6 million principal amount out of $83.9 total outstanding principal amount) of the 9 5/8% notes be tendered pursuant to the Common Stock Exchange Offer. Secondly, it is necessary that certain minimum amounts of each class of debt securities be tendered, together with consents to amendments to the underlying indentures.[4] Indeed, under the offer one may not tender securities unless at the same time one consents to the proposed amendments to the relevant indentures.

The condition of the offer that tendering security holders must consent to amendments in the indentures governing the securities gives rise to plaintiff's claim of breach of contract in this case. Those amendments would, if implemented, have the effect of removing significant negotiated protections to holders of the Company's long-term debt including the deletion of all financial covenants. Such modification may have adverse consequences to debt holders who elect not to tender pursuant to either exchange offer.

Allied-Signal apparently was unwilling to commit to the $15 million cash infusion contemplated by the Stock Purchase Agreement, unless Oak's long-term debt is reduced by 85% (at least that is a condition of their obligation to close on that contract). Mathematically, such a reduction may not occur without the Company reducing the principal amount of outstanding debentures (that is the three classes outstanding notes constitute less than 85% of all long-term debt). But existing indenture covenants (See Offering Circular, pp. 38-39) prohibit the Company, so long as any of its long-term notes are outstanding, from issuing any obligation (including the Payment Certificates) in exchange for any of the debentures. Thus, in this respect, amendment to the indentures is required in order to close the Stock Purchase Agreement as presently structured.

Restrictive covenants in the indentures would appear to interfere with effectuation of the recapitalization in another way. Section 4.07 of the 13.50% Indenture provides that the Company may not "acquire" for value any of the 9 5/8% Notes or 11 5/8% Notes unless it concurrently "redeems" a proportionate amount of the 13.50% Notes. This covenant, if unamended, would prohibit the disproportionate acquisition of the 9 5/8% Notes that may well occur as a result of the Exchange Offers; in addition, it would appear to require the payment of the "redemption" price for the 13.50% Notes rather than the lower, market price offered in the exchange offer.

In sum, the failure to obtain the requisite consents to the proposed amendments would permit Allied-Signal to decline to consummate both the Acquisition Agreement and the Stock Purchase Agreement.

As to timing of the proposed transactions, the Exchange Offer requires the Company (subject to the conditions stated therein) to accept any and all tenders received by 5:00 p.m. March 11, 1986. A meeting of stockholders of the Company has been called for March 14, 1986 at which time the Company's stockholders will be asked to approve the Acquisition Agreement and the Stock Purchase Agreement as well as certain deferred compensation arrangements for key employees. Closing of

---

4. The holders of more than 50% of the principal amount of each of the 13.5% notes, the 9 5/8% notes and the 11 5/8% notes and at least 66 2/3% of the principal amount of the 13.65% debentures, 10 1/2% debentures, and 11 7/8% debentures, must validly tender such securities and consent to certain proposed amendments to the indentures governing those securities.

the Acquisition Agreement may occur on March 14, 1986, or as late as June 20, 1986 under the terms of that Agreement. Closing of the Stock Purchase Agreement must await the closing of the Acquisition Agreement and the successful completion of the Exchange Offers.

The Exchange Offers are dated February 14, 1986. This suit seeking to enjoin consummation of those offers was filed on February 27. Argument on the current application was held on March 7.

## II.

Plaintiff's claim that the Exchange Offers and Consent Solicitation constitutes a threatened wrong to him and other holders of Oak's debt securities[6] appear to be summarized in paragraph 16 of his Complaint:

The purpose and effect of the Exchange Offers is [1] to benefit Oak's common stockholders at the expense of the Holders of its debt securities, [2] to force the exchange of its debt instruments at unfair price and at less than face value of the debt instruments [3] pursuant to a rigged vote in which debt Holders who exchange, and who therefore have no interest in the vote, *must* consent to the elimination of protective covenants for debt Holders who do not wish to exchange.

[P]laintiff's claim is that no free choice is provided to bondholders by the exchange offer and consent solicitation. Under its terms, a rational bondholder is "forced" to tender and consent. Failure to do so would face a bondholder with the risk of owning a security stripped of all financial covenant protections and for which it is likely that there would be no ready market. A reasonable bondholder, it is suggested, cannot possibly accept those risks and thus such a bondholder is coerced to tender and thus to consent to the proposed indenture amendments.

## III.

I begin that analysis with two preliminary points. The first concerns what is not involved in this case. To focus briefly on this clears away much of the corporation law case law of this jurisdiction upon which plaintiff in part relies. This case does not involve the measurement of corporate or directorial conduct against that high standard of fidelity required of fiduciaries when they act with respect to the interests of the beneficiaries of their trust. Under our law—and the law generally—the relationship between a corporation and the holders of its debt securities, even convertible debt securities, is contractual in nature. Arrangements among a corporation, the underwriters of its debt, trustees under its indentures and sometimes ultimate investors are typically thoroughly negotiated and massively documented. The rights and obligations of the various parties are or should be spelled out in that documentation. The terms of the contractual relationship agreed to and not broad concepts such as fairness define the corporation's obligation to its bondholders.

---

6. It is worthy of note that a very high percentage of the principal value of Oak's debt securities are owned in substantial amounts by a handful of large financial institutions. Almost 85% of the value of the 13.50% Notes is owned by four such institutions (one investment banker owns 55% of that issue); 69.1% of the 9 5/8% Notes are owned by four financial institutions (the same investment banker owning 25% of that issue) and 85% of the 11 5/8% Notes are owned by five such institutions. Of the debentures, 89% of the 13.65% debentures are owned by four large banks; and approximately 45% of the two remaining issues is owned by two banks.

Thus, the first aspect of the pending Exchange Offers about which plaintiff complains—that "the purpose and effect of the Exchange Offers is to benefit Oak's common stockholders at the expense of the Holders of its debt"—does not itself appear to allege a cognizable legal wrong. It is the obligation of directors to attempt, within the law, to maximize the long-run interests of the corporation's stockholders; that they may sometimes do so "at the expense" of others (even assuming that a transaction which one may refuse to enter into can meaningfully be said to be at his expense) does not for that reason constitute a breach of duty. It seems likely that corporate restructurings designed to maximize shareholder values may in some instances have the effect of requiring bondholders to bear greater risk of loss and thus in effect transfer economic value from bondholders to stockholders. But if courts are to provide protection against such enhanced risk, they will require either legislative direction to do so or the negotiation of indenture provisions designed to afford such protection.

The second preliminary point concerns the limited analytical utility, at least in this context, of the word "coercive" which is central to plaintiff's own articulation of his theory of recovery. If, *pro arguendo,* we are to extend the meaning of the word coercion beyond its core meaning—dealing with the utilization of physical force to overcome the will of another—to reach instances in which the claimed coercion arises from an act designed to affect the will of another party by offering inducements to the act sought to be encouraged or by arranging unpleasant consequences for an alternative sought to be discouraged, then—in order to make the term legally meaningful at all—we must acknowledge that some further refinement is essential. Clearly some "coercion" of this kind is legally unproblematic. Parents may "coerce" a child to study with the threat of withholding an allowance; employers may "coerce" regular attendance at work by either docking wages for time absent or by rewarding with a bonus such regular attendance. Other "coercion" so defined clearly would be legally relevant (to encourage regular attendance by corporal punishment, for example). Thus, for purposes of legal analysis, the term "coercion" itself—covering a multitude of situations—is not very meaningful. For the word to have much meaning for purposes of legal analysis, it is necessary in each case that a normative judgment be attached to the concept ("inappropriately coercive" or "wrongfully coercive", etc.). But, it is then readily seen that what is legally relevant is not the conclusory term "coercion" itself but rather the norm that leads to the adverb modifying it.

In this instance, assuming that the Exchange Offers and Consent Solicitation can meaningfully be regarded as "coercive" (in the sense that Oak has structured it in a way designed-and I assume effectively so-to "force" rational bondholders to tender), the relevant legal norm that will support the judgment whether such "coercion" is wrongful or not will, for the reasons mentioned above, be derived from the law of contracts. I turn then to that subject to determine the appropriate legal test or rule.

Modern contract law has generally recognized an implied covenant to the effect that each party to a contract will act with good faith towards the other with respect to the subject matter of the contract.

It is this obligation to act in good faith and to deal fairly that plaintiff claims is breached by the structure of Oak's coercive exchange offer. Because it is an implied *contractual* obligation that is asserted as the basis for the relief sought, the appropriate legal test is not difficult to deduce. It is this: is it clear from what was expressly agreed upon that the parties who negotiated the express terms of the contract would have agreed to proscribe the act later complained of as a breach of the implied covenant of good faith had they thought to negotiate with respect to that matter. If the answer to this question is yes, then, in my opinion, a court is justified in concluding that such act constitutes a breach of the implied covenant of good faith.

IV.

Applying the foregoing standard to the exchange offer and consent solicitation, I find first that there is nothing in the indenture provisions granting bondholders power to veto proposed modifications in the relevant indenture that implies that Oak may not offer an inducement to bondholders to consent to such amendments. Such an implication, at least where, as here, the inducement is offered on the same terms to each holder of an affected security, would be wholly inconsistent with the strictly commercial nature of the relationship.

In these circumstances, while it is clear that Oak has fashioned the exchange offer and consent solicitation in a way designed to encourage consents, I cannot conclude that the offer violates the intendment of any of the express contractual provisions considered or, applying the test set out above, that its structure and timing breaches an implied obligation of good faith and fair dealing.

Accordingly, I conclude that plaintiff has failed to demonstrate a probability of ultimate success on the theory of liability asserted.

For the foregoing reasons plaintiff's application for a preliminary injunction shall be denied.

## QUESTIONS

1. Why did Allied-Signal condition its stock purchase with a successful exchange offer between Oak and its bondholders and amendments to the bond indentures?
2. In what way was the exchange offer "coercive"? The bondholders could have chosen not to tender their bonds.
3. Why doesn't the notion of fairness apply here? After all, it seems that Allied-Signal and Oak were manipulating the financial restructuring to take advantage of the bondholders. This seems unfair. Or, is this the relevant inquiry?
4. The court mentions that the typical credit transaction is "thoroughly negotiated and massively documented." What is the relevance of this comment to the court's holding?

## ESSENTIAL TERMS

Capital raising
Due diligence
Execution
Mergers and acquisitions (M&A)
Public capital offering

Private capital offering
Restructuring
Syndicate (Syndication)
Synergy
Underwriting

## KEY CONCEPTS

1. Capital raising is a process in which the company (issuer) raises capital in the capital markets.
2. A capital raising can be a public or private issue.
3. Mergers and acquisitions is a process in which entire firms are bought or sold by other companies.
4. The rationale for a M&A transaction is efficiency and wealth creation.
5. Professionals, including investment bankers, accountants, and lawyers are essential in the process of capital raising and M&A.

## REVIEW QUESTIONS

1. What are the essential functions of a lawyer in capital raisings and M&A deals?
2. What is the purpose of due diligence?
3. What are the consequences of a failure to conduct proper due diligence?
4. What skills are necessary for a transactional lawyer?

# GLOSSARY

*Italicized* terms within the definitions are terms that are defined elsewhere in this glossary.

**Accelerated depreciation** refers to several accounting methods provided by *GAAP* that permit a firm to recognize more *depreciation* expense for an asset in the earlier period of the asset's life. Accelerated depreciation has several implications. It deduces *profit* in the early periods, and thus may reduce tax liability as well. However, *cash flow* is unaffected because depreciation is a noncash expense.

**Accrual accounting** is the accounting principle that recognizes *revenue* and *expenses* at the time of the transaction irrespective of the receipt or payment of cash. As a result, cash flow may not exactly match revenue and expenses, which is the reason why the *cash flow statement* is important. For example, a company contracts to sell a machine to a buyer for $100,000; the cost of manufacturing is $80,000; the machine is delivered on December 31, 2xx0; there is 60 day term and so the buyer can pay as late as March 1, 2xx1. The company would recognize revenue and expense as of December 31. Accrual accounting is the opposite of *cash accounting*.

**Additional paid in capital (APIC)** is the amount of consideration paid to the company in a stock issuance that exceeds the *par value* of the *stock*. For example, if a company issues stock at a price of $10.00 per share, and the par value is $0.01 per share, APIC is $9.99. The par value and APIC are recorded separately in the balance sheet as "common stock" or "stock" or "capital" for aggregate par value, and commonly "additional paid in capital" for APIC.

**Agency cost** is the aggregate economic cost associated with a principal's use of an agent. Agency cost can be categorized into these component costs: monitoring, contracting, bonding, and residual loss.

**Amortization** is the expense recognizing the decline in the value of an *intangible asset*, such as intellectual property. In a more generic sense, it connotes the concept of writing off the cost of an *asset*.

**Annual report** is the annual report to shareholders that contains the audited financial statements of the company. The annual report is distinguished from a *Form 10-K* or *10-Q*, which are required *SEC* filings of financial reports and they are regulated as to form and content.

**Annuity** is a stream of fixed payments over fixed periodic intervals of time: for example, a payment of $100 for a ten-year period.

**Asset** is a probable future economic benefit obtained from a past transaction. An asset is distinguished from a *liability*.

**At-the-money option** is when the *strike price* equals the asset price such that an exercise of the *option* yields no profit or loss for the *holder* or *issuer* outside of the option premium paid: that is, S = X.

**Auditing** is the systematic process whereby an independent *auditor* vets and inspects the financial and accounting records of the audited company.

**Auditor's report (opinion letter)** is an opinion letter providing the auditor's opinion as to the fairness of the presentation of the company's financial position in accordance with *GAAP*.

**Balance sheet** is the financial statement that records a company's *assets*, *liabilities* and *equity*.

**Balance sheet formula** is the formula for the balance sheet that must always hold true: *Assets = Liabilities + Equity*.

**Bankers acceptance** is a letter of credit issued by a bank that accepts the ultimate responsibility to repay a loan to its holder. It is a financing method to facilitate commercial trade transactions.

**Bank loan** is a form of private credit transaction in which a bank provides a loan to the debtor for a defined interest payment and *maturity*.

**Bankruptcy cost** is the direct and indirect cost associated with bankruptcy. Direct costs are the transaction costs associated with processing the bankruptcy and reorganization. Indirect costs are the economic costs associated with disruptions in the firm's business, alternations of prior contracts, and opportunity costs.

**Beta** measures the covariance of the stock price to the market return. In other words, it is the sensitivity of the stock price to the market return. For example, a beta of 1.0 means that if the market return increases by 10%, the stock price increases by 10%.

**Black-Scholes formula** is the mathematical formula that calculates the theoretical value of an *option*.

**Bond** is a longterm debt that is secured by collateral, whereas a *debenture* is not secured. In common parlance, bonds and debentures are used interchangeably and this definitional distinction as to collateral is generally disregarded in common usage of the terms.

**Broker-dealer** is typically a securities firm or *investment bank* that acts as a broker and dealer in the securities market. A broker is an agent acting on behalf of a principal in a securities transaction, and a dealer is a principal that deals in securities for its own account.

**Business judgment rule** is a presumption that in making a decision or exercising judgment, directors acted on an informed basis, in good faith and in the honest belief that the action taken was in the best interests of the company. The principal purpose of the rule is to shield the board from further judicial review and liability, and one reason is that the rule promotes risk-taking by risk averse managers.

**Call option** is a derivative that grants the right but not the obligation to buy a specified asset for a specified *strike price* by a specified *maturity* or expiration date.

**Capital assets** are longterm *assets* that are used to generate *earnings* and that should be funded by longterm capital, either *debt* or *equity* or a combination of both.

**Capital Asset Pricing Model (CAPM)** The formula that provides the *cost of equity*, which is: $\beta \ (R_m - R_f) + R_f$.

**Capitalization rate** is the *discount rate* used to calculate the *perpetuity value* of an income or earnings into a single *present value*. It is used to calculate the value of some asset upon the assumption that the asset will produce a perpetual stream of income. For example, if a building produces 10 in profit from leasing and the capitalization rate is 10%, the capitalized present value of the building is 100.

**Capitalized cost** is expenditures associated with improvements in *property, plant and equipment (PP&E)* such that the expenditure is not recognized immediately as an *expense* flowing into the *income statement*, but instead is recognized as an increase in *assets* in the *balance sheet*.

**Capital raising** is the process of raising capital, which can be in the form of *debt* or *equity*, and which can be raised in the public or private capital markets.

**Capital structure** is the combination of *securities*, broadly classified into *debt* and *equity*, providing the capital needs of the firm. It is the percentage mix of debt and equity within a firm.

**Cash accounting** is the accounting system based on recognition of *revenue* and *expense* upon the receipt or payment of cash. It is not a broadly applicable principle of *GAAP* accounting, but may have use for certain limited purposes such as regulatory oversight of businesses where cash balance and solvency are important.

**Cash flow from financing** is the cash flow associated with the firm's financing activities.

**Cash flow from investing** is the cash flow associated with the firm's investing activities.

**Cash flow from operation** is the cash flow associated with the firm's operations.

**Cash flow statement** is the *financial statement* that provides the firm's cash flows from financing, investing and operations, and provides the net cash expended or generated during the fiscal year.

**CFTC** is the U.S. Commodity Futures Trading Commission, which regulates the futures and options markets.

**Commercial paper** is unsecured short-term notes issued by a company and maturing within nine months.

**Commodities market** is the market for commodities and *securities* connected to commodities. Commodities are any tangible things that are desired or are useful in the production process, including, among other things, minerals, ores, oil, gas, and farm products.

**Common stock** is the *security* in a corporation representing the *equity* interest, which is the *residual claim* in the corporation's *earnings* and *assets*.

**Comparative (peer) companies** are the group of companies that a company, which is the subject of a valuation, is compared against for the purpose of a multiples-based valuation.

**Convertibility** is the feature in a *security* that allows the holder of the security to convert it into *common stock*.

**Corporate bond market** is the market for publicly traded corporate *bonds*.

**Cost of capital** is the expected return that a firm must provide to an investor in the firm given other investment opportunities available to the investor.

**Cost of debt** is the expected return on the debt *securities* of the firm.

**Cost of equity** is the expected return on the equity *securities* of the firm. It is calculated through the *capital asset pricing model (CAPM)*.

**Cost of goods sold (COGS)** is the direct cost of the production of goods or provision of services.

**Covenants** are financial terms on *debt* instruments that protect the *creditor*. Among other things, covenants include triggers on certain rights such as early redemptions upon meeting specified financial criteria, certain negative pledges, and inspection and monitoring rights.

**Credit** has two meanings. As an accounting term, it means the right side of a *T-account* that balances a *debit* entry. As a financial term, it refers to *debt*.

**Credit markets** are the markets for *credit securities* including *bonds*.

**Creditor** is one who is owed a *debt* or obligation from the company, and thus is the person holding the claim associated with the firm's *liabilities*.

**Creditor-shareholder conflict** connotes the concept that *creditors* and *shareholders*, by nature of their different economic claims on the firm, have different interests and preferences in the way that the firm is managed. Generally, creditors are only concerned with maximizing the probability of being paid interest and principal, but shareholders are interested in maximizing the *residual return* even if the firm's actions are more risky.

**Credit rating agencies** are agencies that rate the creditworthiness of *issuers* and *debt* instruments. There are three major credit rating agencies: Moody's, S&P, and Fitch.

**Cumulative dividends** are *dividends* associated with *preferred stock* that, if not paid, are accrued as an obligation that must be paid before dividends can be paid to *common stockholders*.

**Current (short-term) assets** are cash and other *assets* that a firm expects to turn into cash within the firm's operating cycle or a year.

**Current (short-term) liabilities** are *debt* or other obligations that a firm must discharge within the firm's operating cycle or a year.

**Current ratio** is the sum of *current assets* divided by the sum of *current liabilities*.

**Debenture** is a longterm *debt* that is not secured by collateral, whereas a *bond* is secured. In common parlance, bonds and debentures are used interchangeably and this definitional distinction as to collateral is ignored (but the issue of collateral is very important).

**Debit** is the left side entry in a *T-account* used in a *double-entry bookkeeping* system.

**Debt** is a generic term referencing a liability of the obligor to a *creditor*.

**Debt-to-equity ratio** is the ratio of longterm *debt* to *equity*. It indicates the composition of the firm's *capital structure*.

**Depreciation** is the expense recognizing the decline in the value of a *tangible asset*, such as *property, plant and equipment*.

**Depreciation and amortization (D&A)** is the sum of *depreciation* and *amortization* expenses, which constitute the firm's non-cash expenses. D&A is added to *EBIT* to calculate *EBITDA*.

**Derivative** is a financial instrument whose value derives from some other thing, the most common derivatives being *futures* and *options*.

**Discounted cash flow (DCF) method** is the valuation method used to calculate the theoretical value of a firm. It is the sum of the firm's *free cash flows* in the future discounted by the firm's *cost of capital*.

**Discount factor** is the multiple applied to a *future value* to calculate its *present value,* and it is calculated as: discount factor = $1/(1+R)^T$.

**Discount rate** is rate at which a *future value* is discounted to *present value*.

**Diversification** is the process where the *unique risk* of a firm is eliminated by holding a portfolio of multiple *securities*. Under portfolio theory, *diversification* can reduce exposure to unique risk, but it cannot eliminate *market risk*.

**Dividend** is a payment, usually in cash, to *shareholders* made from *earnings* or surplus.

**Dividend arrearage** is the arrearage in dividend payments to holders of *preferred stock* that has a right to *cumulative dividends*.

**Double entry bookkeeping** is the system of accounting that maintains an equality of *debit* and *credit* entries, which balance the books.

**Due diligence** is the process of vetting a transaction by engaging in factual confirmation of vital information and representations concerning the object of the transaction. Due diligence is conducted by many parties including the principal and its lawyers, bankers and accountants.

**Earnings** is synonymous with *net income*, *profit*, and *net profit*. Unmodified, it refers to the net profit.

**Earnings before interest and tax (EBIT)** is the profit before interest and tax items are deducted.

**Earnings before interest, tax, depreciation and amortization (EBITDA)** is EBIT plus *depreciation* and *amortization* expenses, which are noncash expense and are found in the *cash flow from operations* statement. EBITDA is a figure that is commonly used because it approximates a firm's operating cash flow.

**Earnings per share (EPS) (basic and diluted)** is the *net income attributable to common stock* divided by the *shares outstanding*. Shares outstanding can be calculated as basic which includes only shares of *common stock*, or diluted which includes the share equivalent of *securities* that can be converted into common stock. For example, if net income attributable to common stock is 100, and

basic shares outstanding are 100, then EPS (basic) = $1.00/share.

**EBIT and EBITDA ratios** The ratios of *firm (enterprise) value* to *EBIT*, and *firm (enterprise) value* to *EBITDA*. For example, if enterprise value (EV) is calculated as 100, and EBIT and EBITDA are 20 and 25 respectively, EV/EBIT = 5x and EV/EBITDA = 4x.

**Efficiency** is the concept that a rule or change of state creates net wealth based on a cost-benefit analysis. For example, the *business judgment rule* is efficiency enhancing because it promotes risk-taking by managers who are otherwise *risk averse*.

**Efficient capital markets hypothesis (ECMH)** is the hypothesis that says the market incorporates various levels of information into the prices of *securities*. The hypothesis is stated in the *weak form, semi-strong form*, and *strong form*.

**Equity** is concept of a *residual claim* on the firm's *earnings* and *assets* remaining after other contractual claimants, such as employees and *creditors*, have been paid. It is considered the owner's economic interest in the firm.

**Equityholder** is the holder of the *equity*. Equityholders have various names depending on the specific business organization: for example, *shareholders*, partners, and members.

**Equity markets** refer to the market for *equity securities*, its most prominent component being the public *equity markets* associated with stock *exchanges*.

**Exchanges** are organized marketplaces where public securities are traded: for example, the *New York Stock Exchange*.

**Execution** is the process associated with completing a corporate transaction from start to closing.

**Expense** is a decrease in *equity* caused by using up *assets* in producing *revenue* or carrying out the activities of the firm.

**Face value** is the value of the *security* stated on the security certificate.

**Fair market value (FMV)** see "market value."

**Federal Reserve** is short for The Board of Governors of the Federal Reserve System, sometimes called "The Fed." It controls the central banking system in the United States, and among other things regulates the national banking system.

**Financial instruments** are *intangible assets* whose value is derived from a claim to future cash flow, and they include *securities* and *derivatives*.

**Financial statements** constitute the *balance sheet, income statement, cash flow statement,* and *statement of shareholder's equity*.

**Firm (enterprise) value** is the total *market value* of invested *securities*, and is calculated as the *market capitalization* plus longterm *debt*.

**Firm specific risk** see "unique risk."

**Form 10-K and 10-Q** are SEC mandated financial disclosures. The 10-K reports the audited fiscal year's results, and the 10-Q reports unaudited quarterly results.

**Free cash flow** is the cash flow that is free to all capital providers of the firm. It is calculated as NOPLAT plus noncash operating expenses minus investments in invested capital. NOPLAT is net operating profit less adjusted taxes. Noncash operating expenses are *depreciation* and *amortization*. Investments in invested capital are capital expenditures and investments in *working capital*. Under the *discounted cash flow* method of valuation, the sum of the free cash flow discounted by the firm's *cost of capital* is the theoretical value of the firm.

**Futures contract** is an exchange traded *derivative* where two parties agree to transact for the purchase and sale of an underlying asset in the future for a specific price.

**Future value** is the *nominal value* of an expected return in the future.

**GAAP** refers to generally accepted accounting principles, which are the principles applicable for the practice of accounting.

**GAAS** refers to generally accepted auditing standards, which are the standards applicable for the practice of auditing.

**General and administrative expense (G&A)** is overhead expense associated with a firm's operations, sometimes also called SG&A which are *sales, general and administrative expense*.

**General ledger** is the ledger that contains all financial statement accounts.

**Going concern** is a business that has an indefinite duration, which suggests that the firm is not under the threat of liquidation.

**Goodwill** is the excess of cost over the net *tangible assets* and identifiable *intangible assets* of acquired businesses. It represents the purchase of an acquired firm's good name and reputation, which have value.

**Gross profit** is *revenue* minus *cost of goods sold*.

**Gross profit margin** is the ratio of *gross profit* over *revenue*. It is one measure of a firm's profitability.

**Growth perpetuity formula** calculates the value of a perpetual, growing stream of income, and it is calculated as the annual income *capitalized* by the discount rate minus the growth rate.

**Hedging** is the process of reducing or eliminating the exposure to a particular *risk*. It is typically accomplished through the use of *derivatives*.

**High yield (junk) bonds** are noninvestment grade *bonds* based on credit ratings provided by *credit rating agencies*. They are higher risk than *investment grade* bonds.

**Historical cost** is the cost at which an *asset* is purchased.

**Holder** is the purchaser of an *option*.

**Hurdle (benchmark) rate** is the return rate that is required for an investor, and it provides the benchmark that determines whether an investor will invest in the project.

**Income statement** is the *financial statement* that provides the fiscal year's *revenue, expenses,* and *net income*, including *earnings per share* (EPS) data.

**Income statement equation** is stated as: *Revenue − Expenses = Net Income*.

**Indenture** is a contract between the issuer and bondholders, which sets forth the rights and obligations associated with the purchase of the *bond*.

**Indenture trustee** is the administrator of the rights, obligations, and procedures set forth in the *indenture*.

**Inflation** is the phenomenon where money depreciates in value over time as prices of goods and services increase over time.

**Institutional investor** is a nonretail, institutional investor, typically corporations, governments, pension funds, and other investment funds or vehicles. A retail investor is an individual investor. Institutional investors are major investors in the capital markets, and they are significant because they have much more funds to invest than the average retail investor.

**Intangible assets** are *assets* nonphysical form. Such assets include intellectual property, goodwill, leases, rights and permits. This distinguished from *tangible assets*.

**Interest tax shield** is the tax benefit provided when interest expense is deductible from taxable income. For example, if operating income is 100, interest expense is 20, and the tax rate is 25%, net profit with an interest tax shield would be 60, whereas without it net profit after taxes and interest expense would be 55. The difference of 5 is the interest tax shield.

**Internal rate of return (IRR)** is the rate of return that equates the *present value* of a stream of cash inflows and outflows to zero. For example, if an investment required a cash outflow of 100 today, and there is a single cash inflow of 201 in year 5, the IRR would be 15%. From another perspective, this means that 100 compounding at a 15% rate for 5 years will have a future value of 201.

**Interest cover ratio** measures the amount of funds available to pay interest payments due to *creditors*. It is the sum of *net income*, interest expense paid, and tax expense, divided by interest expense obligation. The higher this ratio, the more there are funds available to service the debt.

**Internal control reports** are the reports from the senior management of the company and its *auditor* certifying that the firm has adequate internal controls.

**In-the-money option** is an *option* that, if exercised, would result in a gain to the option holder and thus could be exercised at the specific point in time. For a *call option*, it means that the *strike price* is less than the asset price. For a *put option*, it means that the strike price is more than the asset price.

**Intrinsic (theoretical) value** is the theoretically correct value of the firm that is independent of the current market value of the firm, which at any given time may be equal to, greater than, or less than the intrinsic value. It is typically calculated using the *discounted cash flow* method.

**Investment bank** is a securities firm that provides a variety of services as an underwriter of *securities*, and *broker-dealer* services. Depending on the regulatory scheme and the classification of the investment bank as a depository institution or a broker-dealer, investment banks can be regulated by different agencies, including the *SEC* and the *Federal Reserve*.

**Investment grade** is a level of creditworthiness that is rated by the major *credit rating* *agencies* as generally safe, and specifically ratings of BBB or better.

**Issuer** is the seller of *securities* in the *primary market*.

**Issuer (writer)** is the seller of an *option* in a *derivative* transaction.

**Junk (high yield) bonds** see "high yield bonds."

**Lease financing** is a financial transaction that finances the purchase of equipment or property. The transactions are frequently tax motivated.

**Leverage buyout (LBO)** is the purchase of a firm in which the primary acquisition financing is in the form of *debt*.

**Leverage ratio** is the ratio of *assets* to *equity*, and it represents the degree to which the assets of the firm have been funded with *debt*.

**Listing rules** are rules published by individual *exchanges* listing the requirements in respect of *securities* and *issuers* for securities listed on the exchange.

**Liability** is a probable future sacrifice of economic benefits arising from a past transactions or events.

**Limited liability** is the rule of law providing that the *equityholder* of a firm are not liable for the *debts* and obligations of the firm. Limited liability can benefit *shareholders* in a corporation, members in a limited liability company, and partners in a limited liability partnership or limited partnership.

**Liquidation value** is the residual value left over upon a liquidation, when *assets* are sold and *liabilities* are paid off in a liquidation of the firm.

**Long position** is the position in a financial transaction representing the purchase of the *security* or *asset*.

**Long-term debt** is noncurrent debt obligation, which is a *liability* from the issuance of *debt* that is not expected to mature within a year.

**Marked-to-market** is a process of valuation and accounting where *assets*, *securities* or financial transactions are periodically revalued at market prices. This is distinguished from *historical cost*.

**Market capitalization ("market cap")** is the *market value* of equity *securities*, which is calculated as the stock price multiplied by the *shares outstanding*.

**Market multiples** are financial ratios of *comparable companies* that are used to imply the value of a peer company. For example, if the *price-to-earning* (P/E) ratio of comparable companies is 15x, and the company that is valued generates earnings of 10, the implied equity value of the company is 150.

**Market risk** is the risk associated with an investment in the market, and it cannot be eliminated through *diversification*. This is distinguished from *unique risk*.

**Market value** is the market value of an asset as determined by market prices. It is sometimes called fair market value (FMV).

**Matching principle** is the accounting principle that matches the recognition of *revenue* to *expense* recognition such that revenue and cost are recognized at the same time irrespective of cash receipt or payment.

**Maturity** refers to the expiration of a *security*. For *debt*, it is the time when the principal is due. For *derivatives*, it is the time when the option right expires, or the time when an asset must be exchanged. Equity does not have a fixed maturity.

**MD&A** is the management discussion and analysis section of the *financial statement*.

**Member's interest** is the *equity* held by members of limited liability companies.

**Mergers and acquisitions (M&A)** refers to corporate transactions where companies or substantial assets thereof are bought and sold, or combined with other companies.

**M&M capitals structure irrelevance hypothesis** is the hypothesis advanced by Modigliani and Miller stating that the *capital structure* of a firm is irrelevant to the firm's value under a special set of assumption, the most prominent being that there are no taxes or bankruptcy cost.

**Money market** is the market for short-term *debt* instruments, instruments that at the time of issuance have *maturity* of one year or less. It is a market where *issuers* seek short-term funding, typically to manage *working capital* needs.

**Nasdaq** is an *OTC* market for securities. It is a virtual, electronic trading platform for buyers and sellers of securities, and the securities traded tend to be high-tech firms.

**Negative equity (negative net worth)** is the difference between *liabilities* and *assets* when the value of liabilities exceeds the value of assets. Negative equity is possible because the *balance sheet equation* states that assets must always equal liabilities plus equity.

**Net assets** is synonymous with *equity* and *net worth*. It is assets net of liabilities.

**Net asset value (NAV)** refers to the value of *net assets*. It is sometimes states as NAV per share.

**Net cash inflow/outflow** is the net cash flow of the firm from the year's activities, and it is calculated as the net cash flow resulting from investing, financing and operations.

**Net income** is the *profit* after payment of tax expenses. It is synonymous with *net profit*, *profit*, and *earnings*.

**Net income attributable to common stock** is the *net income* available after dividends are paid on *preferred stock*.

**Net income margin** is the ratio *net income* to *revenue*. It is one measure of a firm's profitability.

**Net worth** is synonymous with *equity* and *net assets*. It is worth net of *liabilities*.

**Nominal price or value** is the price or value of a thing unadjusted for changes in price due to *inflation*. It is the stated price that has not been adjusted for *inflation* or time value.

**Noncurrent (long-term) assets** are *assets* that a firm does not expect to turn into cash within the firm's operating cycle or a year. They are assets held for the longterm.

**Noncurrent (long-term) liabilities** are *liabilities* that are *debts* or obligations whose maturities are beyond one year.

**Notes to the financial statements** are notes that clarify, augment or provide additional details concern the financial representations in the *financial statements*, including details on accounting policies.

**NYSE** is the New York Stock Exchange, colloquially called "The Big Board."

**Operating profit** is the profit from operations only, which is principally *revenue* less *cost of goods sold (COGS)* and *overhead expenses (SG&A)*. In most cases, it is synonymous with earnings before interest and tax, but there is a difference in that *EBIT* may contain special or one-off gains or losses whereas operating profit refers to the profit from continuing operations.

**Operating profit margin** is the ratio of *operating profit* to *revenue*. It is one measure of a firm's profitability.

**Option** is a derivative that grants the right but not the obligation to buy or sell a specified asset for a specified *strike price* by a specified *maturity* or expiration date. Options are fundamentally divided into *call options* and *put options*.

**Out-of-the-money option** is an *option* that, if exercised, would result in a loss to the option holder and thus would not be exercised. For a *call option*, it means that the *strike price* is greater than the asset price. For a *put option*, it means that the strike price is less than the asset price.

**Outstanding shares (basic and diluted)** see "shares outstanding."

**Over-the-counter (OTC)** refers to the informal market for *securities* where parties trade securities on negotiated terms, as opposed to securities traded on organized *exchanges*.

**Overhead expense** is any expense not directly associated with the cost of producing goods or services, and is synonymous with *sales, general and administrative expense*.

**Par value** has two definitions. For *stocks*, it is the arbitrary designation of value that must remain on the *balance sheet* as permanent capital. Par value is an anachronism from older practices in corporation that aim to protect *creditors*. For *bonds* and *preferred stock*, see "face value."

**Partner's capital** is the *equity* in a partnership.

**Partner's capital account** is the account item in a partnership that keeps track of each partner's *equity* capital in the partnership.

**Perpetuity formula** calculates the value of a perpetual stream of income, and it is calculated as the annual income *capitalized* by the *discount rate*.

**Perpetuity value** is the *present value* of a perpetual stream of cash flow or income as calculated by the *perpetuity formula* or the *growth perpetuity formula*.

**Preferred stock** is stock that stands in priority in relation to *common stock* as to *dividends* and *liquidation*. Unlike common stock, preferred stock does not have a theoretically unlimited upside. Instead, the returns on preferred stock, like those of debt, are typically set by a fixed dividend rate.

**Present value** is a *future value* discounted by an appropriate *discount rate*, which is the value equivalent in today's money of a future sum.

**Pretax profit** is the profit before deduction of tax expense.

**Price-to-book ratio (P/B)** is the ratio of *market capitalization* to *book value*.

**Price-to-earnings ratio (P/E)** is the ratio of current share price to *EPS*. Another way to calculate this ratio is to divide *market capitalization* by *net income*.

**Primary market** is the securities market where *issuers* sell *securities* to investors, and thus receive cash proceeds from the sale. This is distinguished from the *secondary market*.

**Private capital offering** is an offering of non-public *securities*.

**Private company** is a company whose securities are not publicly traded and are held privately by a group of investors.

**Private equity** is equity capital that is not publicly traded, and is typically used to finance start-up or developing companies.

**Profit** is synonymous with *net profit*, *net income*, and *earnings*. However, when "profit" is modified, it does not mean net income. For example, *pretax profit* refers to income before tax expense, and *operating profit* refers to income from operations before interest and tax expenses are deducted.

**Property, plant and equipment (PP&E)** are longterm *tangible assets* that are used in the business.

**Public company** is a company whose *securities* are publicly traded.

**Public capital offering** is an offering of *securities* to the public, and this process requires that the securities be registered with the SEC.

**Publicly-traded securities** are *securities* that are publicly traded, typically on *exchanges*, and have been registered with the SEC.

**Put option** is a *derivative* that grants the right but not the obligation to sell a specified asset for a specified *strike price* by a specified *maturity* or expiration date.

**Qualified auditor opinion** is an *audit report* stating that the *auditor* could not certify that all material aspects of the audit satisfied accounting standards or that the auditor could not verify as such. It indicates a material problem was uncovered in the audit.

**Real price or value** is the price or value of a thing adjusted for changes in price due to *inflation*.

**Repurchase agreement ("repo")** is the sale of *securities* to a buyer with an agreement that the seller will repurchase the securities at a specified higher price. It is a form of short-term collateralized financing that is typically used by *broker-dealers* and other financial institutions.

**Residual claim** is the claim of the *equity-holder*, and it includes both the *net income* (the after-tax income attributable to equity-holders) and the *net assets* (assets remaining after *liabilities* are paid).

**Restructuring** is a process in which a company substantially changes its *capital structure*, operations, or business strategy, typically in response to financial troubles.

**Retained earnings** are the *net profits* that have not been distributed to *shareholders* and thus retained by the company. It is an *equity* component in the *balance sheet*.

**Return on assets (ROA)** is calculated as the *net income* divided by the average total *assets*. It measure how much profit as a percent the assets are generating.

**Return on equity (ROE)** is calculated as the *net income* divided by the average *equity*. It measures how much profit as a percent the equity is generating.

**Revenue** is the increase in *equity* caused by the sale of services or goods, which is money gained from the sale of services or goods, and synonymous with sale.

**Risk** is the degree that an outcome may deviate from expectation.

**Risk aversion** is an aversion to variable outcomes and a preference for certain outcomes.

**Risk-free rate** is the rate associated with risk-free *securities*, which have historically been *Treasury* instruments.

**Sales** see "revenue."

**Sales, general and administrative expense (SG&A)** is the *overhead expenses* associated with the firm's operation.

**SEC** is the U.S. Securities and Exchange Commission, which regulates *securities* and *exchanges*.

**Secondary market** is the market where investors buy and sell issued *securities* from each other.

**Securitization** is the financial process whereby illiquid receivables are converted into *bonds*, and the bond principal and coupons are paid from the payment of the receivables.

**Securitization market** is the market for asset-backed (ABS) and mortgage-backed (MBS) securities.

**Securities** are intangible financial assets that whose values are tied to specific claims on a firm's *cash flow* and *assets*, and are broadly classified into *debt* and *equity securities*.

**Security market line** is the upward sloping line representing the relationship between the returns of the *security* and its *risk*.

**Semi-strong form of ECMH** is the hypothesis that all past and current public information has been incorporated into the share price.

**Separation of ownership and control** is the operating principle applicable to most public corporations and corporations that have a wide and diffuse shareholder base, and it embodies the idea that managers control the corporation even as *shareholders* and *creditors* own the economic claims.

**Shareholder** is *equityholder* in a corporation, and they hold *financial instruments* called *stock*. Stock can be in the form of *preferred* or *common stock*.

**Shareholder's equity** is the *equity* in a corporation.

**Share** is a single unit of equity security of a corporation that can be sold or transferred as an independent whole unit.

**Shares outstanding (basic and diluted),** or "outstanding shares," are the number of *shares* issued by the company and held by *shareholders*. Basic shares outstanding count the common shares only. Diluted shares outstanding count the share equivalent of *securities* that are convertible to common stock.

**Short position** is the position where an investor has sold the financial asset.

**Statement of shareholder's equity** is the *financial statement* that records changes in the *shareholder's equity* during the fiscal year, including *retained earnings*, shares issued and bought back, and *dividends*.

**Stock** is a generic term referencing shares of *preferred* or *common stock*.

**Stock buyback** occurs when a company buys back its own *stock* from *shareholders* on the market.

**Straight line method of depreciation** calculates annual *depreciation* expense as the cost of the *tangible asset* divided by the useful life of the asset. For example, if an asset costs 100 and has a useful life of 10 years, the depreciation expense under a straight line method is 10 per year.

**Strike price** is the price at which the *holder* of a *call option* can buy an asset from the issuer, or the price at which the holder of a *put option* can sell an asset to the issuer.

**Strong form of ECMH** is the hypothesis that all information, public and private, is incorporated into the price of the security.

**Swap** is a financial transaction in which one party will "swap" some asset or thing with a counterparty for some other asset or thing. Typical swaps are interest rate swaps and currency swaps. In an interest rate swap, two parties will swap a variable rate interest obligation for a fixed rate obligation. In this way, a party who is exposed to the risk of variable interest rates will obtain a fixed interest rate. In a currency swap, two parties will swap currencies. In this way, a party who does not wish to be exposed to a particular currency can eliminate the risk by swapping with the desired currency held by a counterparty.

**Syndicate (Syndication)** is a group of investors or financial institutions that co-invest in a common investment in an issue of *securities* or a loan with the purpose of spreading the risk among the syndicate.

**Synergy** is the *revenue* or *expense* benefit anticipated from efficiencies gain from a *merger and acquisition* transaction.

**Systematic risk** see "market risk."

**T-accounts** are the accounting device used to record the *debit* and the *credit* of a transaction.

**Tangible assets** are *assets* having a physical form. This is distinguished from *intangible assets*.

**Terminal (continuing) value** is the value attributed to the company from a fixed period of time in the future to infinity in a *discounted cash flow analysis*.

**Time value of money** is the idea that money changes value with different time periods. The value of money in the future is always less than the value of the same money in the present.

**Transaction cost** is the direct and indirect cost associated with transacting.

**Treasury securities (Treasuries)** are Treasury *debt* instruments, including Treasury bills, notes and bonds.

**Treasury market** is the market for *Treasury securities*.

**Treasury stock** is *stock* that was issued but has been bought back by the issuer, and thus it is stock that has been issued but is no longer outstanding.

**Underwriting** is the process of raising capital though an *investment bank* that purchase *securities* from the *issuer* with the intent to sell them on the market or that otherwise facilitates the selling of the issuer's securities.

**Unique risk** is the *risk* that is specific to the firm and can be eliminated through *diversification*. It is sometimes called firm-specific or unsystematic risk. It is distinguished from *market risk*.

**Unqualified auditor opinion** is the *auditor's opinion* that the *financial statements* comply in all material respects with *generally accepted accounting principles*. It is the report of a clean audit.

**Variance** is the statistical mean squared deviation from the expected value, which is the measure of *risk* of an expected return.

**Weak form of ECMH** states as a hypothesis that the market price of a *security* has incorporated all past publicly disclosed information. The implication is that an investor cannot earn abnormal returns based on a study of past information and history.

**Weighted average cost of capital (WACC)** is the average *cost of capital* that is based on the weight contribution of each form of capital to the total capitalization of the firm. For example, if a firm is capitalized with 100 debt, 100 preferred stock, and 100 common stock, and the cost of these securities are 8%, 10% and 15% respectively, then the WACC would be 11%.

**Working capital** is the measure of liquidity, the firm's ability to pay its current obligations. It is determined as: *Working Capital = Current Assets−Current Liabilities*.

**Yield to maturity** is the *internal rate of return* on a *bond*, which is the bond's true rate of return given that the *market price* of the bond may change even as the coupon payment remains contractually fixed.

**Zero coupon bond** is a *bond* that does not pay periodic coupons from *issuance* to *maturity*, and instead pays interest and princip